PETERSON'S

GMAT CAT®

SUCCESS

2001

*GMAT AND GMAT CAT ARE REGISTERED TRADEMARKS OF THE GRADUATE MANAGEMENT ADMISSION COUNCIL (GMAC).
THIS PUBLICATION DOES NOT INCLUDE ACTUAL GMAT® ITEMS, NOR IS IT ENDORSED OR APPROVED BY GMAC.

Peterson's
Thomson Learning

Australia • Canada • Denmark • Japan • Mexico • New Zealand • Philippines
Puerto Rico • Singapore • Spain • United Kingdom • United States

Editorial Development: American BookWorks Corporation

Editorial Review: Joan Marie Rosebush

Visit Peterson's Education Center on the Internet (World Wide Web) at
www.petersons.com

ISBN 0-7689-0524-9
ISBN 0-7689-0409-9 CD version

Printed in the United States of America

10 9 8 7 6 5 4 3 2 1

CONTENTS

CONTENTS

RED ALERT

WHAT IS THE GMAT?

The Graduate Management Admission Test (GMAT) measures verbal, quantitative, and analytical writing skills. The GMAT is used by graduate schools of business to assess the qualifications of applicants to graduate management programs. The GMAT is only one of several factors that will determine your admission to business school. Admission committees also may consider information such as undergraduate grade point average, work or internship experience, an application essay describing your career goals, and references.

The GMAT is designed to predict how well you will perform in the first year of a graduate management program. The GMAT tests neither specific knowledge of business nor achievement in a particular subject. The verbal, quantitative, and analytical writing skills that appear on the GMAT are those that you have already encountered or developed in your academic career.

Until recently, the GMAT was available throughout the world as a paper-and-pencil test. Since October 1997, however, the GMAT is available in North America and many other parts of the world *only* as a computer-adaptive test. Research has shown that scores from the paper-based test are comparable to those from the computer-based test. If you need more information about registering for the GMAT, visit **http://www.gmat.org** on the World Wide Web or contact:

GMAT
Educational Testing Service
P.O. Box 6103
Princeton, New Jersey 08541-6103
Telephone: 609-771-7330
Fax: 609-883-4349
E-mail: gmat@ets.org

WHAT IS A COMPUTER-ADAPTIVE TEST (CAT)?

A computer-adaptive test is—as the title says—adaptive. That means that each time you answer a question, the computer adjusts to your responses when determining which question to present next. For example, the first question will be of moderate difficulty. If you answer it correctly, the next question will be more difficult. If you answer it incorrectly, the next question will be easier. The computer will continue presenting questions based on your responses, with the goal of determining your ability level.

It is very important to understand that questions at the beginning of a section affect your score more than those at the end. That's because the early questions are used to determine your general ability level. Once the computer determines your general ability level, it presents questions to identify your specific ability level. As you progress farther into a section, it will be difficult to raise your score very much, even if you answer most items correctly. That's because the later questions affect your score less, as they are used to pinpoint your exact score once the computer has identified your general ability level. Therefore, take as much time as you can afford to answer the early questions correctly. Your score on each section is based on the number of questions you answer correctly, as well as the difficulty level of those questions.

You need only minimal computer skills to take the computer-based GMAT. You will have plenty of time at the test center to work through a tutorial that allows you to practice such activities as answering questions, using the mouse, using the word processor (which you will need for your essay responses), and accessing the help function.

WHAT KINDS OF QUESTIONS WILL BE ON THE GMAT CAT?

The GMAT consists of essay responses to two analytical writing questions, a verbal section, and a quantitative section, as shown in the table below. You will key in the answers to the two essay questions first, then proceed to the remaining sections. Note that questions are not grouped by type within the quantitative and verbal sections. You must be mentally prepared to switch back and forth among the different types of questions.

You will be allowed to take a 5-minute break after completing the analytical writing section and a 5-minute break between the quantitative and verbal sections. Your testing appointment, including the tutorial, will take about 4 hours.

Section	Number of Questions	Time (minutes)
Analytical Writing		
Analysis of an Issue	1 Writing Topic	30
Analysis of an Argument	1 Writing Topic	30
Quantitative	37	75
Data Sufficiency		
Problem Solving		
Verbal	41	75
Sentence Correction		
Reading Comprehension		
Critical Reading		

SCORING

One advantage of the CAT is that you can see your scores for the multiple-choice sections immediately after the test. Prior to seeing your scores, however, you have the option of canceling the results if you have reason to believe you did not perform as well as you could have. Official score reports are mailed about two weeks later and include scores for the analytical writing assessment. You will receive four separate scores:

1. *Total Score.* This score is a composite of your verbal and quantitative scores only. Analytical writing scores are not included in the total score. The range for total scores is 200 to 800.
2. *Verbal Score.* This score range is 0 to 60.
3. *Quantitative Score.* This score range is 0 to 60.
4. *Analytical Writing Assessment Score.* This score range is 0 to 6. This score is the average of four ratings of your responses to the two essay topics.

You will receive a percentile rank for each of the four GMAT scores. This percentile will indicate the percentage of examinees who scored below you.

TEST-TAKING TIPS FOR THE GMAT CAT

The purpose of *GMAT Success* is to help you prepare for the GMAT. You will increase your chances of scoring high on the GMAT by being completely familiar with the content and format you will encounter on test day. The strategies and review sections of this book, as well as the practice tests, provide lots of opportunity to review relevant content. Keep in mind the following test-taking tips, most of which are unique to the CAT format.

Understand The Directions For Each Question Type

Learn the directions for each type of question. The directions in this book are very similar to those on the actual test. Understanding the directions for each question type will save you valuable time on the day of the test.

On The Actual Exam, You Will Not See Lettered Choices That You Will Find In This Book.

You will be presented with questions that are preceded by little fill-in circles, and you merely click you mouse on the choice that you have selected as the best answer. In the essay section, there is a scrolling box into which you can type your essay using the online word processor.

Take Your Time With Questions At The Beginning Of Each Section

Remember that questions at the beginning of a section affect your score more than questions at the end. Be especially careful in choosing answers to questions in the first half of both the quantitative and verbal sections. Once the computer determines your general ability level with these initial questions, you will be unable to dramatically improve your score, even if you answer most of the questions toward the end correctly.

Be Completely Sure Of Each Answer Before Proceeding

With a CAT, you must answer each question as it is presented. You cannot skip a difficult question and return to it later as you can with a paper-and-pencil test. Nor can you review responses to questions that you have already answered. Therefore, you must be confident about your answer before you confirm it and proceed to the next question. If you are completely stumped by a question, eliminate as many answer choices as you can, select the best answer from the remaining choices, and move on.

Pace Yourself

To finish both the verbal and quantitative sections, you will need to establish a pace that allows you to spend an average of just under 2 minutes per item. You will need to work both quickly and accurately to complete each section within the 75-minute time constraint. You will still receive a score, even if you do not complete all of the questions in a section.

Be Mentally Prepared To Receive A Mix Of Different Question Types Within Each Section

On the paper-and-pencil GMAT, questions are typically grouped by type. For example, in the math section, data sufficiency questions appear together as a group, followed by problem-solving questions. On the GMAT CAT, however, the computer may select one of several question formats, depending on whether you answered the previous question right or wrong. Therefore, you must be mentally ready to switch back and forth between questions that have very different formats, both in the quantitative section and in the verbal section, to maintain focus during the test.

Use The Scratch Paper Provided At The Test Center

You will not be allowed to bring any paper or other materials into the test center, and since there is no test booklet, you will have no opportunity to underline, circle, or otherwise make notes on actual questions or problems. The test center does, however, provide as much scratch paper as you need to make notes during the test. You may want to develop a simple system for recording which answer choices you have eliminated or a way of noting key information in a reading passage. Use scratch paper to solve math problems, draw diagrams, and record any other information that helps you work accurately and quickly.

ABOUT THIS BOOK

The purpose of this book is to help you prepare for the GMAT test. As you will see below, the GMAT exam is only given on the computer, and we have provided a Web site for you to take an actual Computer Adaptive Test (CAT) on line.

There are two editions of the *GMAT CAT Success* book. One has a CD-ROM in it that provides a direct gateway to our Web site and actual GMAT CAT practice exams. Although you have purchased this book, which does not contain the CD-ROM, you can still prepare for the exam by studying the information and material provided in this edition. If, however, you still want to take an actual GMAT CAT exam, you can log on to our Web site—www.petersons.com—and you will be able to find the exam on line.

If you decide to take the online test, we suggest that you begin by taking it as a diagnostic exam. Once you have an idea of how you did and where to focus your studying, come back to the book. You can take the tests in the book, review the material throughout the book, and then go back and take the other two tests on line. Very little has been left to chance here, and you have been given a wide range of preparatory materials, both on line and in this book. Try to review as much as possible.

If you don't plan to go on line, then you should start by taking the paper-and-pencil diagnostic test. At the same time, however, it is important to be familiar with the *types* of questions that you will encounter on the exam, and the purpose of this book is to provide you with enough material so that you will be comfortable with these questions when taking the actual exam. The book is divided into several sections, the first of which is a series of brief diagnostic tests that will give you an idea of what topics you might have to review. Even though the tests in the book are paper-and-pencil tests—and not similar to the format of the CAT—you will certainly encounter the same *types* of questions on the test, and thus, these tests serve a valuable function. The second part of the book consists of in-depth review material that covers Sentence Correction, Reading Comprehension, Quantitative (math), and Critical Reasoning skills. Finally, there are additional sample tests to help you evaluate your progress.

We also suggest that you follow one of the study plans presented later in this section. These plans can be adapted to your own needs and schedule and should help you find the most effective way to study for the test, given your level of preparedness and the amount of time you have before taking the exam.

THE STUDY PLANS

It is entirely likely that, as you are preparing to take the GMAT, you are also studying for your regular college courses. As a result, your time may be limited. This section will help you prepare your own study schedule. We offer three separate study plans. The first is the **9-Week Plan**, which involves concentrated studying twice a week. The second, more leisurely, plan is the **18-Week Plan**. This is essentially the same as the former study plan but gives you more time in which to review your work, and you can study only once a week, if you wish. Finally, we offer the **Panic Plan** for those of you who only have a few weeks to prepare for the test. Of course, the more time you have to study, the easier it will be to review all of the material in this book. It will also help you feel more relaxed when you take the exam.

These plans are not set in stone. Feel free to modify them to suit your needs and your own study habits. You should also take into account your strengths and weaknesses, which can be determined from the introductory diagnostic test in this book. Focus more of your study efforts on those areas that need greater attention.

If you wish to practice taking a GMAT CAT, you can do so by logging on to our Web site at www.petersons.com and practicing with our exclusive online GMAT CAT, which mimics the look and feel of the real thing. Be sure to factor time for this into this study plan.

THE 9-WEEK PLAN—2 LESSONS PER WEEK

Week 1

Lesson 1

Diagnostic Tests

Take the Sentence Completion and Reading Comprehension Diagnostic Tests.

Lesson 2

Diagnostic Tests

Take the Quantitative (math) Diagnostic Test.

Week 2

Lesson 1

Diagnostic Test

Take the Critical Reasoning Diagnostic Test. Also check all of the answers for the entire test.

Amend this entire plan to take into account those areas in which you need to concentrate your studying.

Lesson 2

Problem Solving

Begin with the overview of this section, including the Introduction, and read from the Arithmetic section through the section on Fractions. Complete the sample problems, and check your answers.

Week 3
Lesson 1

Sentence Correction

Read the chapter on Sentence Corrections, and answer the review questions. Check your answers. Refer to the Grammar section to help clarify any points that were unclear in the Sentence Correction problems.

Lesson 2

Problem Solving

Read from the section on Decimals through the section on Powers, Exponents, and Roots. Complete the sample problems, and check your answers.

Week 4
Lesson 1

Reading Comprehension

Read and study the techniques for answering Reading Comprehension questions. Complete the sample questions, and check your answers.

Lesson 2

Problem Solving

Read through the Algebra section of the review. Complete the sample problems, and check your answers.

Week 5
Lesson 1

Critical Reasoning

Review this chapter, particularly the strategies and explanations of the different types of questions you will encounter on the GMAT. This is a section where an understanding of the directions is extremely important. Read the directions carefully, and try to memorize them to save time on the actual test.

Lesson 2

Problem Solving

Complete this chapter by reading the portion on Plane Geometry. Complete the sample problems, and check your answers.

Week 6
Lesson 1

Critical Reasoning

Answer the questions that follow the review section. Complete the sample problems, and check your answers.

Lesson 2

Data Sufficiency Review

Read and study the portion on Strategies in this chapter. Answer the solved problems, and check your answers. Like the directions for the Critical Reasoning section, these directions are also complicated and important to memorize. Take the time to learn them by heart.

Week 7
Lesson 1

Analytical Writing Assessment

There are two types of essays you will be required to write: the first asks you to analyze an issue stated in the topic, and the second asks you to critique an argument presented in the topic. Read through the explanations and strategies, and then try to outline some of the practice essays presented at the end of the chapter. You won't have time to write complete essays, but outlining them will help you develop the process of formulating an effective essay.

Lesson 2

Data Sufficiency Problems

Answer the supplementary questions that appear at the end of the review section. Check your answers carefully. If your mistakes were predominately mathematical, go back to the appropriate sections in the Problem Solving mathematics review chapter. If your errors came from not understanding how to answer the questions, reread the overview section that precedes the practice questions and, again, memorize the directions.

Week 8

Lesson 1

Sentence Correction Practice Tests

Take each of the three tests under test-taking conditions. Don't worry about time on these tests. Instead, focus on answering the questions and following directions. Give yourself an hour or so between tests. Check your answers and explanations, and review any questions that gave you trouble.

Lesson 2

Reading Comprehension Practice Tests

Under test-taking conditions, take each of the three tests. Don't worry about time on these tests. Circle those answers that you don't know so you can check them later. Give yourself an hour or so between tests. Check your answers and explanations, and review any questions that gave you trouble.

Week 9

Lesson 1

Critical Reasoning Practice Tests

Under test-taking conditions, take each of the three tests. Don't worry about time on these tests. Circle those answers that you don't know, so you can check them later. Give yourself an hour or so between tests. Check your answers and explanations, and review any questions that gave you trouble.

Lesson 2

Quantitative Practice Tests

Like the other three sections, take these tests under simulated conditions. Take each of the three tests. Don't worry about time on these tests. Circle those answers that you don't know so you can check them later. Give yourself an hour or so between tests. Check your answers and explanations, and review any questions that gave you trouble.

THE 18-WEEK PLAN—1 LESSON PER WEEK

If you are fortunate enough to have the time, the **18-Week Plan** will give you much more time to study at your leisure. This plan is ideal because you are not under any pressure and you can take more time to read through the review sections and practice as many problems as possible. You will also have more time to go back and repeat a section of the test that might have given you trouble. Because the primary focus of this book is to provide you with as much practice as possible, you will have more time to spend on this study plan.

In this plan, each lesson should be done in one week. You can surely be more relaxed about studying. In order not to lose continuity or your train of thought, there is no reason why you can't combine lessons where necessary. For example, the Problem Solving portion is spread out over several weeks in the **9-Week Plan**. The reason for this is to give you a breather so you can retain the material while spending time on other topics at the same time. In this plan, you can study all of the mathematics in one week. That week becomes "Problem Solving Week." It's the reason why we recommend altering the plan to suit your needs.

THE PANIC PLAN

Not everyone is lucky enough to have a full twenty-two weeks to study for this test—or even eleven weeks. Thus, we have provided the **Panic Plan**. Although this is not the best way to study for the GMAT—or any test—here are some pointers.

1. Read through the official test booklet or this *GMAT CAT Success*, book and memorize the directions. We've stated this several times in this chapter as well as in other chapters. If you don't have to read the directions when you take the actual exam, you will have saved yourself valuable time.

2. Read "Introduction to the GMAT," which can be found in this Red Alert section. This will help you prepare for the different types of questions that you will encounter. The introduction makes an important point about how much time you will have for each question, depending upon which test you are taking. Learn to pace yourself.

3. Take all of the tests, if you have the time. You'll learn a lot by checking your answers.

4. If you still have the time, you may want to consider going on line to practice with an actual CAT. It will help round out your studyies and give you a clear idea of how this type of computerized test works.

Diagnostic Tests
SENTENCE CORRECTION

1. Violence in the crowds at football games in small towns in Pennsylvania has gotten so out of hand that some local high schools have developed rules that aim to identify fans of the visiting team and that seat them in an area roped off for visitors.

   (A) to identify fans of the visiting team and that seat them
   (B) to identify fans of the visiting team and seat them
   (C) to identify fans of the visiting team for seating
   (D) at identifying fans of the visiting teams so as to seat them
   (E) at identifying fans of the visiting team and that seat them

2. A rise in co-ops being built next year should bring New York a few billion new dollars in construction, making the building industry's health much more vibrant than a decade ago.

   (A) making the building industry's health much more vibrant than a decade ago.
   (B) and making the building industry's health much more vibrant than a decade ago.
   (C) making the building industry's health much more vibrant than a decade ago.
   (D) to making the building industry's health much more vibrant than a decade ago.
   (E) in making the building industry's health much more vibrant than a decade ago.

3. Since the sensational book about goings-on in Roswell, New Mexico, was published, fifty-one UFOs were sighted in the South, which is more than had been sighted in any year since the end of WWII.

   (A) which is more than had been sighted
   (B) more than had been sighted
   (C) more than they had sighted
   (D) more than had reported sightings
   (E) which is more than had reported sightings

4. Despite the fact that black athletes have been raised to the level of icons in the United States, the attitude toward black people in some parts of the South is little changed from how it was at the end of the nineteenth century.

   (A) is little changed from how it was
   (B) is a little changed from how it was
   (C) has changed a little
   (D) has changed a little from how it was
   (E) is little changed from the way it was

5. In the United States today, there has been increased discussion over if a budget surplus should go toward a tax decrease or increased spending on the Medicare Program.

   (A) over if a budget surplus should go toward a tax decrease or increased spending
   (B) over whether a budget surplus should go toward a tax decrease or increased spending
   (C) about a budget surplus going toward a tax decrease or increased spending
   (D) about if a tax decrease should come from a budget surplus or increased spending
   (E) concerning a budget surplus and its going toward a tax decrease or increased spending

6. In the last fifteen years, despite the narrow nationalist vision of some countries, Kenyan marathon runners are respected throughout the running world.

   (A) are respected
   (B) are becoming better respected
   (C) which have gained respect
   (D) have gained respected
   (E) have once become respected

7. Because the Ebola virus is easily destroyed <u>and it is therefore a most exclusive virus, it is being increasingly viewed</u> as a threat to sub-Saharan life.

   (A) and it is therefore a most exclusive virus, it is being increasingly viewed
   (B) it is therefore a most exclusive virus, and it has increased viewed
   (C) and therefore a most exclusive virus, it is being increasingly viewed
   (D) and therefore it is the most exclusive virus, there is increasing view
   (E) therefore being the most exclusive virus, it is increasingly viewed

8. During the 90s, it became obvious <u>that getting corporate funding was far more efficient for social preservationists who sought financial aid</u> than to go to federal or state agencies.

   (A) that getting corporate funding was far more efficient for social preservationists who sought financial aid
   (B) that for social preservationists who sought financial aid, it was far more efficient to get corporate funding
   (C) that for social preservationists seeking financial aid, corporate organizations were far more efficient to go to
   (D) for social preservationists seeking corporate funding, going to corporate organizations was far more efficient
   (E) for social preservationists who sought financial aid, corporate organizations were far more efficient

9. Chemistry professors, <u>the Carroll Laboratories and Carroll Research Facilities were founded by Debra and Marcel Carroll in 1999 after five years of fund-raising.</u>

   (A) the Carroll Laboratories and Carroll Research Facilities were founded by Debra and Marcel Carroll in 1999 after five years of fund-raising.
   (B) Debra and Marcel Carroll founded the Carroll Laboratories and Carroll Research Facilities in 1999 after five years of fund-raising.
   (C) after five years of fund-raising, the Carroll Laboratories and Carroll Research Facilities were founded by Debra and Marcel Carroll in 1999.
   (D) the Carroll Laboratories and Carroll Research Facilities were founded in 1999 by Debra and Marcel Carroll after five years of fund-raising.
   (E) Debra and Marcel Carroll founded after five years of fund-raising the Carroll Laboratories and Carroll Research Facilities in 1999.

10. IRS provision 12Y requires that a corporation with assets greater than $500,000 send W-2 forms to their full-time employees on or before January 1.

    (A) that a corporation with assets greater than $500,000 send W-2 forms to their full-time employees on or before January 1.

    (B) a corporation with assets greater than $500,000 send W-2 forms to its full-time employees on or before January 1.

    (C) that a corporation with assets greater than $500,000 send W-2 forms to its full-time employees on or before January 1.

    (D) a corporation with assets greater than $500,000 send W-2 forms to their full-time employees on or before January 1.

    (E) a corporation with assets greater than $500,000 sends W-2 forms to its full-time employees on or before January 1.

11. The major areas of medicine in which microsurgeries are effective is in the cutting and closing of arterial and venous vessels, and in the destruction of cancers.

    (A) is in the cutting and closing of arterial and venous vessels, and in the destruction

    (B) are in the cutting and closing of arterial and venous vessels, and also the case of destroying

    (C) are the cutting, closing of arterial and venous vessels, and in the destroying

    (D) are the cutting and closing of arterial and venous vessels, and in the destruction

    (E) is in the cutting and closing of arterial and venous vessels, and the destroying

12. In 1996, a national study found that not only had many contractors licensed by a self-examining private group failed to pass qualifying exams, they in addition falsified their endorsements.

    (A) they in addition falsified their endorsements.

    (B) they had their endorsements falsified in addition.

    (C) but they had also falsified their endorsements.

    (D) they had also falsified their endorsements.

    (E) but their endorsements were falsified as well.

13. Like the government that came before it, which set new records for growth, open market capitalism is the capstone of the new government.

    (A) open market capitalism is the capstone of the new government.

    (B) the capstone of the new government is open market capitalism.

    (C) open market capitalism is the new government's capstone.

    (D) the new government has made open market capitalism its capstone.

    (E) the new government has an open market capstone of capitalism.

14. The economic forces that may affect the new public offering of stock include sharp downturns on the market, hedging and other investor strategies for preventing losses, loosening the interest rates, and fearing that the company may be underfunded.

- (A) loosening the interest rates, and fearing that the company may be underfunded.
- (B) loosening the interest rates, and a fear of the company still being underfunded.
- (C) a loosening of the interest rates, and fearing that the company may still be underfunded.
- (D) a loosening the interest rates, and a fear of the still underfunded company.
- (E) a loosening of the interest rates, and fear that the company may still be underfunded.

READING COMPREHENSION

Directions: The questions in this group are based on the content of a passage. After reading the passage, choose the best answer to each question. Answer all questions following the passage on the basis of what is *stated* or *implied* in the passage.

Reading 1

I am pleased to transmit today for immediate consideration and prompt enactment the "Cloning Prohibition Act of 1997." This legislative proposal would prohibit any attempt to create a human being using somatic cell nuclear transfer technology, the method that was used to create Dolly the sheep. This proposal will also provide for further review of the ethical and scientific issues associated with the use of somatic cell nuclear transfer in human beings.

Following the February report that a sheep had been successfully cloned using a new technique, I requested my National Bioethics Advisory Commission to examine the ethical and legal implications of applying the same cloning technology to human beings. The Commission concluded that at this time "it is morally unacceptable for anyone in the public or private sector, whether in a research or clinical setting, to attempt to create a child using somatic cell nuclear transfer cloning" and recommended that Federal legislation be enacted to prohibit such activities. I agree with the Committee's conclusion and am transmitting this legislative proposal to implement its recommendation.

Various forms of cloning technology have been used for decades, resulting in important biomedical and agricultural advances. Genes, cells, tissues, and even whole plants and animals have been cloned to develop new therapies for treating such disorders as cancer, diabetes, and cystic fibrosis. Cloning technology also holds promise for producing replacement skin, cartilage, or bone tissue for burn or accident victims and nerve tissue to treat spinal cord injury. Therefore, nothing in the "Cloning Prohibition Act of 1997" restricts activities in other areas of biomedical and agricultural research that involve: (1) the use of somatic cell nuclear transfer or other cloning technologies to clone molecules, DNA, cells, and tissues; or (2) the use of somatic cell nuclear transfer techniques to create animals.

The Commission recommended that such legislation provide for further review of the state of somatic cell nuclear transfer technology and the ethical and social issues attendant to its potential use to create human beings. My legislative proposal would implement this recommendation and assign responsibility for the review, to be completed in the fifth year after passage of the legislation, to the National Bioethics Advisory Commission.

1. We can infer from this passage that cloning

   (A) is always unethical.
   (B) is never unethical.
   (C) is only unethical when producing sheep like "Dolly."
   (D) should be totally prohibited.
   (E) is unethical is some cases.

2. Cloning has been helpful in all of the following areas EXCEPT

   (A) spinal cord injury.
   (B) cystic fibrosis.
   (C) diabetes.
   (D) cancer.
   (E) agricultural research.

3. It can be inferred that the specific audience for this passage is

   (A) a biological research organization.
   (B) a political action committee.
   (C) a legislative body.
   (D) the National Bioethics Advisory Committee.
   (E) the Supreme Court.

4. If this bit of legislation passed, when can we infer it would go into effect?

   (A) five years after passage of the legislation
   (B) in 1997
   (C) immediately
   (D) after further biological research
   (E) before a child was cloned

5. From this passage, we can assume that cloning

   (A) is a relatively new concept.
   (B) was developed to produce "Dolly."
   (C) was probably around in the nineteenth century.
   (D) has been available for decades.
   (E) occurs spontaneously in nature.

6. It can be inferred from this passage that

   (A) there may come a time when cloning a child is acceptable.
   (B) there will never be a time when cloning a child is acceptable.
   (C) there should be hard and fast rules about cloning.
   (D) cloning is an issue best left to individual states.
   (E) cloning is ethical only in clinical settings.

Reading 2

Aristotle came back to Athens in 335 B.C., and spent the next twelve years running his own version of an academy, which was called the Lyceum, named after the place in Athens where it was located, an old temple of Apollo. (French high schools are named *lycee* after Aristotle's establishment.) Aristotle's preferred mode of operation was to spend a lot of time walking around talking with his colleagues, then write down his arguments. The Aristotelians are often called the Peripatetics: people who walk around.

Aristotle wrote extensively on all subjects: politics, metaphysics, ethics, logic and science. He didn't care for Plato's rather communal Utopia, in which the women were shared by the men and the children raised by everybody, because one thing he feared was that the children would be raised by nobody. His ideal society was one run by cultured gentlemen. He saw nothing wrong with slavery, provided that slave was naturally inferior to the master, so slaves should not be Greeks. This all sounds uncomfortably similar to Jefferson's Virginia, perhaps not too surprising since Greek was a central part of a gentleman's education in Jefferson's day.

Aristotle's approach to science differed from Plato's. He agreed that the highest human faculty was reason and its supreme activity was contemplation. In addition to studying what he called "first philosophy," the metaphysics and mathematics that Plato had worked on, Aristotle thought it also very important to study "second philosophy": the world around us, from physics and mechanics to biology. Perhaps being raised in the house of a physician had given him an interest in living things.

What he achieved in those years in Athens was to begin a school of organized scientific inquiry on a scale far exceeding anything that had gone before. He first clearly defined what was scientific knowledge and why it should be sought. In other words, he single-handedly invented science as the collective, organized enterprise it is today. Plato's Academy had the equivalent of a university mathematics department, Aristotle had the first science department, truly excellent in biology but a little weak in physics. After Aristotle, there was no comparable professional science enterprise for over 2,000 years, his work was of such quality that it was accepted by all and had long been a part of the official orthodoxy of the Christian Church 2,000 years later. This was unfortunate, because Galileo questioned some of the assertions concerning simple physics and quickly found himself in serious trouble with the Church.

Aristotle's method of investigation varied from one natural science to another, depending on the problems encountered, but it usually included:

1. defining the subject
2. considering the difficulties involved by reviewing the generally accepted views on the subject and suggestions of earlier writers
3. presenting his own arguments and solutions

Again, this is the pattern that modern research papers follow. Aristotle was laying down the standard professional approach to scientific research. The arguments he used were of two types: *dialectical*, based on logical deduction; and *empirical*, based on practical considerations.

Aristotle often refitted an opposing argument by showing that it led to an absurd conclusion. This is called *reductio ad absurdum* (reducing something to absurdity). Galileo used exactly this kind of argument against Aristotle himself, to the great annoyance of Aristotelians 2,000 years after Aristotle.

Another possibility was that an argument led to a *dilemma*: an apparent contradiction. Dilemmas could sometimes be resolved by realizing that there was some ambiguity in a definition, so *precision of definitions* and usage of terms is *essential* to productive discussions in any discipline.

7. If someone is described as having a "peripatetic" nature, the word that is most closely connected to the passage's definition is

   (A) philosophical.
   (B) introspective.
   (C) Aristotelian.
   (D) changeable.
   (E) constant.

8. Which of the following can most safely be ascertained by the passage?

   (A) Aristotle was the first scientist.
   (B) Aristotle invented a version of science that is quite different from today's.
   (C) Aristotle was a philosopher first, a scientist second.
   (D) Aristotle invented science that is recognizable to today's scientists.
   (E) Aristotle was Galileo's teacher.

9. What can we infer about the concept of "Utopia" from this passage?

   (A) All Utopias have the same philosophical bases.
   (B) A Utopia should be run by cultured gentlemen.
   (C) This is one area of division between Aristotle and Plato.
   (D) This is an area of agreement between Plato and Aristotle.
   (E) Philosophy leads to Utopia.

10. From the passage, we can infer that

   (A) Aristotle's parents influenced his philosophy.
   (B) Aristotle preferred to write out his ideas before he delivered lectures at the Lyceum.
   (C) Aristotle believed in communal living.
   (D) Aristotelian and Christian thought are in agreement.
   (E) Aristotle's first scientific department excelled in physics.

Reading 3

Although most often identified as a suffragist, Elizabeth Cady Stanton (1815–1902) participated in a variety of reform initiatives during her lifetime. Setting her sights on women's emancipation and equality in all arenas—political, economic, religious, and social—Stanton viewed suffrage as an important but not paramount goal. Since childhood, Stanton had rebelled against the role assigned to women and chafed at being denied a university education because of her sex. As a young woman, she became involved in the temperance movement and antislavery movements, through which she met Henry Brewster Stanton (1805–1887), an abolitionist reformer and journalist, who she married in May 1840. While honeymooning in England, Elizabeth became outraged when she and other women were barred from a major antislavery convention. She discussed her feelings with Lucretia Mott (1793–1880), a Quaker minister from Pennsylvania and one of the American delegates to the meeting, and together they resolved to hold a women's rights convention to discuss women's secondary status when they returned to the United States.

Eight years passed before Mott and Stanton could make good on their promise, but in July 1848, more than three hundred men and women assembled in Seneca Falls, New York, for the first women's rights convention, at which Stanton's famous Declaration of Rights and Sentiments was read and adopted. Modeled after the Declaration of Independence, Stanton's document protested women's inferior legal status and put forward a list of proposals for moral, economic, and political equality of women. The most radical resolution was the demand for woman suffrage, a goal that would consume the women's movement for more than seventy years. Stanton, in close collaboration with Susan B. Anthony (1820–1906), led the suffrage fight, but along the way, she actively supported dress reform and women's health issues, greater educational and financial opportunities for women, more liberal divorce laws, and stronger women's property laws. Even more controversial than Stanton's positions on those issues, however, were her views on religion and on the Church's role in limiting women's progress, ideas that culminated in 1895 with the publication of *The Woman's Bible*.

For more than forty years before the publication of *The Woman's Bible*, Stanton had objected to religious teachings on slavery, marriage, divorce, and women's status. Two of the eighteen grievances listed in the Declaration of Rights and Sentiments concerned church affairs and the interpretation of scriptures. In reaction to church opposition to the many causes that she championed, Stanton wrote, "No reform has ever been started, but the Bible, falsely interpreted, has opposed it."

In the late 1800s, Stanton began a thorough study of the Bible and sought to establish a committee of academic and church women to contribute to the project. The names of the seven other women appeared as authors in the final published version of *The Woman's Bible, Part 1,* and several more were listed as members of the revising committee. It is believed, however, that much of the work was done by Stanton alone. Stanton concerned herself only with those parts of the Bible that mentioned women or that she believed had erroneously omitted women. The published volume, reproduced a section of the Bible text at the top of each page followed by an reinterpretation or commentary written by Stanton or another contributor.

Although *The Woman's Bible* was never accepted as a major work of Biblical scholarship, it was a best-seller, much to the horror of many suffragists. In particular, younger members of the National American Woman Suffrage Association (NAWSA), of which Stanton had once been president, felt that *The Woman's Bible* jeopardized the group's ability to gain support for suffrage amendment, and they formally denounced the publication despite Anthony's pleas not to embarrass Stanton publicly. Controversy over the book threatened to divide the suffrage movement, and although Anthony spoke in Stanton's behalf, the incident damaged their friendship and reflected the widening gap between Anthony's increasingly single-minded pursuit of suffrage and Stanton's interest in a broader agenda. Ignoring NAWSA's objections and concerned about the increased influence of conservative evangelical suffragists, Stanton published the second part of her bible in 1898. This volume, like the first, was an attempt to promote a radical liberating theology that stressed self-development and challenged the ideological basis for women's subordination. Until her death in 1902, Stanton continued to write about religious themes and to condemn cannon law for restricting women's freedom and retarding their progress.

11. It can be inferred from this passage that Elizabeth Cady Stanton

   (A) believed in the separation of church and state.
   (B) was indifferent to the power of the church.
   (C) felt that religion could be used to deny social equality.
   (D) felt that religious goals were more important than the suffrage movement.
   (E) agreed with religious teachings on marriage and divorce.

12. It can be inferred from this passage that the most difficult area that Stanton and her followers addressed was

   (A) the voting rights of women.
   (B) women's health issues.
   (C) women's property laws.
   (D) women's dress reforms.
   (E) the Church's role in regards to women's issues.

13. Stanton's *The Woman's Bible*

    (A) is regarded today as a major work of Biblical scholarship.

    (B) has taken its place alongside the Bible, according to Church scholars.

    (C) was a rallying point for the Suffragist Movement.

    (D) was equally composed by Lucretia Mott.

    (E) caused the division in NAWSA.

14. What can most positively be stated about Stanton and Anthony from this passage?

    (A) History rightfully joins their names as equals.

    (B) They started out at opposite poles and then joined.

    (C) Disagreements about religion's role drove them apart.

    (D) They were steadfast friends despite political differences.

    (E) They agreed on the role of the Church.

CRITICAL REASONING

Directions: For each question in this section, select the best of the answer choices given.

Questions 1 and 2 refer to the following passage.

A recent memorandum from the Office of Youth Services reports the statistics of crimes involving youths, defined as crimes in which the perpetrator was 18 years old or younger. For the calendar year 1998, 6 percent of all violent crimes involved youths, but in 1999, only 5 percent of all violent crimes involved youths. Based on this data, the Office Manager delivered a press release to the media to report that the social services of the Office of Youth Services has succeeded in reducing youth involvement in violent crimes.

1. Which of the following statements, if true, would demonstrate the most obvious flaw in the manager's press report?

   (A) The number of violent crimes involving adults increased from 1998 to 1999.
   (B) The procedures for reporting and tabulating violent crimes were revised in 1997.
   (C) In 1998, more than 100,000 youths were involved in violent crimes in the area that the Office of Youth Services oversees.
   (D) The number of youths who are counseled by the Office of Youth Services decreased from 1998 to 1999.
   (E) The Office Manager has only held his position since early 1999.

2. If the manager's press release about the reduction of youth involvement is true, which of the following is the most likely conclusion to draw from the information given above?

   (A) In 1997, more than 6 percent of all the violent crimes that were studied involved youths.
   (B) The number of violent crimes involving adults increased from 1998 to 1999.
   (C) The number of violent crimes involving adults decreased from 1998 to 1999.
   (D) In 2000, the number of violent crimes involving youths will decrease from 5 percent to 4 percent.
   (E) There were many more violent crimes in 1999 that involved adults than there were that involved youths.

3. The number of riders on the morning commuter train into Chicago during rush hour has remained relatively constant for the past five years, despite steady increases in the population of most of the suburbs around Chicago during the same time period. From this data, experts who study the population of large areas have concluded that most of the new people moving to the suburbs plan to work outside of the city.

Which of the following statements represents an assumption that is necessary to prove the validity of the conclusion reached in the above passage?

(A) The number of people who ride the commuter train during rush hour reached a peak five years ago.

(B) Because life in the suburbs is more pleasant and more appealing than life in the city of Chicago, more new residents of the Chicago area are likely to move to the suburbs.

(C) The statistics reporting the ridership on the rush-hour commuter trains provide a reliable way of measuring the number of people working in the city of Chicago.

(D) Systems of commuter trains are more widely used in large Midwestern cities, such as Chicago, than in Eastern cities, such as New York.

(E) The number of people who live in the city of Chicago and the surrounding suburbs is calculated by an informal census system every five years.

4. If John buys new shoes today, he will win the decathlon. If John wins the decathlon, he will receive a gold medal. If John receives a gold medal, then he will be given an advertising contract. If John receives an advertising contract, then he will earn more than a million dollars next year. If John earns more than a million dollars next year, he will become president.

Which of the following statements CANNOT logically be concluded from the fact that John will not earn more than a million dollars next year?

(A) John did not buy new shoes today.
(B) John did not win the decathlon.
(C) John did not receive a gold medal.
(D) John was not given an advertising contract.
(E) John will not become president.

5. A recent report reveals that thousands of people die each year from infections or diseases that they contracted while in the hospital for otherwise minimal operations. A health-care watchdog group, therefore, is recommending immediate national legislation to mandate periodic testing of air filtration systems in public and private hospitals.

Which of the following arguments, if true, most seriously questions the need for the proposed legislation?

(A) As a result of current health insurance limitations and regulations, most people who need medical care have very few choices of places to go to receive such care.

(B) The data that were studied to compile the report in question focuses on a few hospitals in five major urban centers across the country.

(C) Communicable diseases are currently the subject of extensive research and investigation by many doctors and researchers across the country.

(D) Most air filtration systems currently in use in major hospitals in the country are unable to limit the transmission of most germs and viruses.

(E) The report in question studied patients, covering all age ranges from infants to the elderly.

6. The worldwide population of amphibians is declining. Amphibians are the class of animals that includes frogs, lizards, and salamanders. By far, the largest single species in the class of amphibians is the frogs. Therefore, one can conclude that the number of frogs in the world is declining.

Which of the following is a necessary assumption in the above argument?

(A) Environmental factors that are causing the decline in the amphibian population affect all amphibians equally.

(B) Lizards and salamanders combine to make up the second-largest group of amphibians.

(C) The decline in the number of frogs can be more accurately measured than the decline in the numbers of other species.

(D) A decline in the number of members of any one species in a given class is generally a good indication of declines in other species.

(E) The study of the population of amphibians is important to understanding human biology and the effects of human population on other ecosystems around the world.

7. In the past three months, a record number of incidents has occurred that involve minors shooting other minors. To stop this outrageous trend, Congress must immediately pass new legislation to require stricter licensing of gun owners.

   Which of the following, if true, would most effectively weaken this argument?

   (A) The president has always been forceful in opposing strict gun licensing laws.
   (B) The children involved in the shootings are not old enough to vote for the legislators in Congress.
   (C) Most of the shootings that have occurred recently have involved licensed guns.
   (D) The shootings have occurred in a few localized areas of major cities only.
   (E) Under the proposed legislation, minors would not be allowed to own or even possess guns of any type.

Questions 8 and 9 refer to the following passage.

   In most European countries, the telephone systems are operated and controlled by numerous small, independent companies. Americans traveling through Europe uniformly express dissatisfaction with the telephone systems, reporting that calls rarely go through on the first try and then are often disconnected without warning. In the United States, the telephone service used to be operated and controlled by a single monopoly, which was broken apart by the government in favor of independent ownership. As a result, Americans can expect a decline in the quality of telephone service in this country.

8. Which of the following is an assumption being made in the above argument?

   (A) Telephones are a necessary part of conducting business in America.
   (B) More telephones are used throughout the United States than in all European countries combined.
   (C) All European countries have the same kind of telephone systems.
   (D) The primary purpose of the government in the United States is to identify and break apart monopolies.
   (E) Companies with similar forms of ownership and control will produce similar products and services.

9. Which of the following statements, if true, most effectively weakens the above argument?

    (A) Most legislators in the United States have not personally experienced the poor telephone service throughout Europe.
    (B) Managers and executives of companies in the United States typically study other companies extensively to modify methods of management.
    (C) The equipment used for most telephone service in the United States is provided by the same suppliers as for most European services.
    (D) The general standard of living is higher throughout the United States than in most areas in Europe.
    (E) Several other industries in the United States have historically been controlled by monopolies but have recently been broken apart.

10. Anthropologists have concluded that for many primitive societies, the establishment of organized systems of roads between major towns and cities was a first step toward the creation of organized forms of trade.

    Which of the following is the best statement of a likely assumption used in drawing the above conclusion?

    (A) Travel is much easier between towns after organized roads are established.
    (B) All primitive societies need organized forms of trade.
    (C) Improved transportation is likely to lead to the sharing of goods and services between living centers.
    (D) Anthropology is a science that draws on assumptions to create generalized conclusions about the history of certain cultures.
    (E) Without organized systems of roads, no travel between towns and cities would be possible.

11. A television advertisement for a luxury car claims, "More people with advanced college degrees buy our car than any other. This is proof that our car is the intelligent choice for intelligent people."

    Which of the following statements, if true, weakens the car company's claim?

    (A) Many other models of cars had significantly higher annual sales.
    (B) The television advertisement mentioned above is not broadcast in all market areas where the car is sold.
    (C) The percentage of cars sold by this company that need major mechanical repairs within two years is far less than that of any other car model.
    (D) Because of the high price of this luxury car, its typical consumer is wealthy, professionally employed, and well educated.
    (E) The luxury car market has been steadily increasing in the United States during the past ten years as the standard of living has been increasing.

12. A committee that studies national television news broadcasts has recently released a report that compiles the number of hours that major network news programs devote to reporting disasters. In 1999, twice as much time was devoted to reporting natural disasters, such as hurricanes, tornadoes, and floods, as was devoted to travel-related disasters, such as airplane and train crashes. Based on this report, one can conclude that more people die in natural disasters than in travel-related disasters.

Which of the following statements is an assumption that is being made in the above argument?

(A) The Federal Emergency Management Administration gets its financing each year from the national budget, based on the number of emergency situations that the nation experienced in the previous year.

(B) Twice as many people each year travel by air than by train.

(C) Television news producers make their decisions about what disaster stories to cover based primarily on the numbers of human lives lost.

(D) Because of unusual weather patterns experienced around the world in 1999, the United States suffered a much higher number of deaths due to natural disasters than ever before.

(E) The ratings for television news programs increase more significantly during periods of natural disasters than during periods immediately following any travel-related disasters.

13. Most of the students entering law schools in America between the years 1995 and 1999 had undergraduate degrees in either political science or English. However, reports from a study of the major undergraduate universities in America predict that for the next five years, the number of students majoring in political science or English will decrease dramatically. As a result, many law schools have concluded that a decline in enrollment is likely in the near future.

Which of the following statements, if true, would most seriously weaken the conclusion?

(A) Political science is not a required undergraduate major for students applying to law school.

(B) Many law schools have a practice of increasing the required minimum score on standardized entrance exams when application levels are high.

(C) Law schools across the country have consistently received an average of four to five applications for every available opening for incoming students.

(D) The year 2000 is an election year, and most of the candidates for president are lawyers.

(E) Political science and English majors generally have higher levels of analytical and writing skills than other students.

QUANTITATIVE

PROBLEM SOLVING

1. If $xy > 0$, which of the following CANNOT be true?

    (A) $x < 0$
    (B) $y > 0$
    (C) $x + y < 0$
    (D) $\dfrac{x}{y} > 0$
    (E) $\dfrac{x}{y} < 0$

2. If the fractions $\dfrac{1}{8}, \dfrac{2}{7}, \dfrac{3}{5}, \dfrac{4}{5}$, and $\dfrac{5}{8}$ were ordered from least to greatest, the second smallest number in the sequence would be

    (A) $\dfrac{1}{8}$
    (B) $\dfrac{2}{7}$
    (C) $\dfrac{3}{5}$
    (D) $\dfrac{4}{5}$
    (E) $\dfrac{5}{8}$

3. The price of a suit is reduced by $100 to a new price of $400. The percentage of change in the price of the suit is

   (A) 20%
   (B) 25%

   (C) $33\frac{1}{3}\%$

   (D) 40%
   (E) 50%

4. If $(0.02 \times 10^a)(1.3 \times 10^b) = 2.6 \times 10^3$, $a + b =$

   (A) 1
   (B) 2
   (C) 3
   (D) 4
   (E) 5

5. If $\dfrac{x^2 + 7x + 10}{x + 2} = 8$, what is the value of $x + 1$?

   (A) 1
   (B) 2
   (C) 3
   (D) 4
   (E) 5

6. In a certain state, a person may inherit up to $50,000 tax free, but any amount in excess of $50,000 is taxed at a rate of 8%. If Joan inherits a total of $75,000, how much tax will she have to pay?

   (A) $6,000
   (B) $5,000
   (C) $4,000
   (D) $2,000
   (E) $1,500

7. A class had 7 students. On one test, the class average was 78. One student's paper was scored incorrectly, and the resulting grade was raised 14 points. What is the corrected class average?

   (A) 80
   (B) 82
   (C) 84
   (D) 88
   (E) 92

8. The Chess Club sold raffle tickets for $1 each. One member sold 75% of his tickets and had 80 tickets left. How much money did the member collect?

 (A) $60
 (B) $75
 (C) $150
 (D) $240
 (E) $320

9. If one side of a square is increased by 5 inches and one side is decreased by 5 inches, a rectangle is formed whose area is 56 square inches. What is the perimeter of the original square, in inches?

 (A) 36
 (B) 46
 (C) 66
 (D) 78
 (E) 81

10. A pool can be filled using pipe A alone in 8 hours. Using pipe B alone, the pool can be filled in 12 hours. If both pipes are opened, how many hours will it take to fill the pool?

 (A) 20
 (B) 10
 (C) $6\frac{2}{5}$
 (D) $4\frac{4}{5}$
 (E) 4

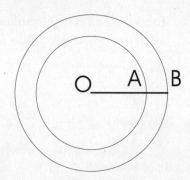

11. The figure above contains two circles with center O. If the area of the smaller circle is 25% of the area of the larger circle, and OB = 12 inches, find OA in inches.

   (A) 3
   (B) 4
   (C) 6
   (D) 8
   (E) 12

12. If $a\$\$b = 4b - a^2$, then $3\$\$2 =$

   (A) 8
   (B) 6
   (C) 2
   (D) −1
   (E) −4

13. Tile was purchased to replace flooring, at a cost of $1.20 per tile. Only $\frac{5}{8}$ of the tiles were needed, so the remaining 60 were returned for a refund. What was the cost of the tiles used for the floor?

   (A) $45
   (B) $115.20
   (C) $120
   (D) $145
   (E) $200

14. It takes 12 people 15 hours to complete a certain job. How many hours would it take 18 people, working at the same rate, to complete $\frac{2}{5}$ of the same job?

    (A) $3\frac{1}{2}$
    (B) 4
    (C) 9
    (D) $16\frac{1}{2}$
    (E) $22\frac{1}{2}$

15. Which of the following is the lowest positive integer that is divisible by each of the integers from 3 through 6 inclusive?

    (A) 30
    (B) 60
    (C) 120
    (D) 240
    (E) 360

16. How many different ways can the letters a, b, and c be arranged so that the letter a appears first and each letter must be used?

    (A) 2
    (B) 6
    (C) 9
    (D) 12
    (E) 36

17. If $x^2 + 6x + 9 = 0$, which of the following could be the value of $x - 3$?

    (A) -9
    (B) -6
    (C) -3
    (D) 3
    (E) 6

18. Ron types at an average rate of 40 words per minute. Pat types at an average rate of 60 words per minute. If Ron begins typing a manuscript at 4:20 and Pat begins typing an identical copy of the same manuscript at 5:00, at what time will they be typing the same word?

    (A) 5:10
    (B) 5:30
    (C) 5:40
    (D) 6:00
    (E) 6:20

19. A team has wins, losses, and draws in a ration of 7 to 8 to 3. If they played a total of 108 games, how many games did they win?

    (A) 6
    (B) 13
    (C) 14
    (D) 42
    (E) 48

20. Jeanine purchased two items at the grocery store for a total of $5.13. If one item cost 63 cents less than the other item, what was the cost of the more expensive item?

    (A) $2.25
    (B) $2.88
    (C) $3.20
    (D) $3.87
    (E) $4.50

21. Jeanine wants to enclose a rectangular garden adjacent to the garage. By using 10 feet along the garage as one side, she will have to purchase fencing for only three sides. If she wants to enclose 120 square feet, how many feet of fencing will she need?

    (A) 12
    (B) 22
    (C) 34
    (D) 44
    (E) 110

22. Damaged items are marked down 20% to 40%. A newspaper coupon entitles the coupon holder to an additional 15% markdown. What is the lowest price of a damaged item that was originally marked $36?

    (A) $12.60
    (B) $16.20
    (C) $18
    (D) $19.80
    (E) $23.40

DATA SUFFICIENCY

Directions: Each of the data sufficiency problems below consists of a question and two statements, labeled (1) and (2), in which certain data are given. You have to decide whether the data given in the statements are *sufficient* for answering the question. Using the data given in the statements *plus* your knowledge of mathematics and everyday facts (such as the number of days in July or the meaning of counterclockwise), you must indicate whether

- statement (1) ALONE is sufficient, but statement (2) alone is not sufficient to answer the question asked;
- statement (2) ALONE is sufficient, but statement (1) alone is not sufficient to answer the question asked;
- BOTH statements (1) and (2) TOGETHER are sufficient to answer the question asked, but NEITHER statement ALONE is sufficient;
- EACH statement ALONE is sufficient to answer the question asked;
- statements (1) and (2) TOGETHER are NOT sufficient to answer the question asked, and additional data specific to the problem are *needed*.

Numbers: All numbers are real numbers.

Figures: A figure accompanying a data sufficiency problem will conform to the information given in the question, but will not necessarily conform to the additional information given in statements (1) and (2).

Lines shown as straight can be assumed to be straight and lines that appear jagged can also be assumed to be straight.

You may assume that the position of points, angles, regions, etc., exists in the order shown and that angle measures are greater than zero.

All figures lie in a plane unless otherwise indicated.

Note: In data sufficiency problems that ask for the value of a quantity, the data given in the statements are sufficient only when it is possible to determine exactly one numerical value for the quantity.

1. If x and z are integers, how many even integers, y, are there, such that $x < y < z$?

    (1) $z - x = 6$
    (2) x is even.

2. What is the value of the odd integer n?

    (1) $\sqrt{n}$ is an integer.
    (2) $0 < n < 20$

3. What was the cost of the computer?

    (1) The computer was on sale at 30% off the regular price.
    (2) The computer was regularly priced at $1,500 but was marked down 20%.

4. Joan is 3 years older than her brother Bill. How old is Bill?

    (1) Six years from now, Joan will be 12 less than twice Bill's age.
    (2) Four years ago, Bill was 5.

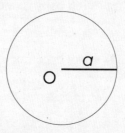

5. What is the area of the circle with the center O?

    (1) The circumference of the circle is 8π.
    (2) $a = 4$

6. Pat invests $8,000 in account A and $10,000 in account B. How much simple interest did she earn in one year?

    (1) The interest on $400 in account A and $500 in account B is $1,400.
    (2) Account A earns 5 pecent interest, and account B earns twice as much interest as account A.

7. If $2^{a+2} = 2^b$, what is $a + b$?

    (1) $2(2^a) = 2^{b-1}$
    (2) $2^{2a+1} = 128$

8. An urn contains only green and red balls. What is the ratio of green balls to red balls in the urn?

    (1) The number of green balls is 3 less than twice the number of red balls.
    (2) There are 12 red balls.

9. What is the value of the sum of a sequence of x consecutive odd integers?

   (1) $x = 3$
   (2) The smallest integer is 7.

10. If $\dfrac{x}{y} > 1$, is $x > 1$?

   (1) $y > 1$
   (2) $y < 0$

11. What is the value of x?

   (1) $x = y - (4 - x)$
   (2) $4x + y = 8$

12. The are 85 students taking psychology and/or sociology. How many students are taking both courses?

   (1) The number of students taking only psychology is 15 more than the number taking only sociology.
   (2) The number of students taking only sociology is 5 more than the number of students taking both psychology and sociology.

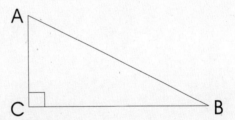

13. What is the area of triangle ABC?

   (1) AB = 25
   (2) AC = 3

14. What is the ratio of men to women enrolled in a sociology class?

   (1) The number of women enrolled in the class is 12 less than the number of men enrolled.
   (2) The number of women is $\dfrac{2}{3}$ the number of men enrolled.

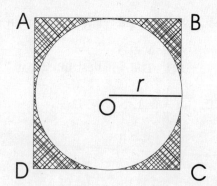

15. Circle O is inscribed in square ABCD alone. What is the area of the shaded regions?

(1) AB = 10
(2) The area of the circle is 25π

QUICK SCORE ANSWERS

Diagnostic Tests				
			Quantitative	
Sentence Correction	**Reading Comprehension**	**Critical Reasoning**	**Problem Solving**	**Data Sufficiency**
1. B	1. E	1. A	1. E 12. D	1. C
2. C	2. A	2. E	2. B 13. C	2. E
3. B	3. A	3. C	3. A 14. B	3. B
4. C	4. C	4. E	4. E 15. B	4. D
5. B	5. D	5. B	5. D 16. A	5. D
6. D	6. A	6. A	6. D 17. B	6. D
7. C	7. D	7. C	7. A 18. E	7. B
8. B	8. D	8. E	8. D 19. D	8. C
9. B	9. C	9. B	9. A 20. B	9. C
10. C	10. A	10. C	10. D 21. C	10. D
11. D	11. C	11. D	11. C 22. B	11. C
12. C	12. E	12. C		12. C
13. D	13. E	13. C		13. C
14. E	14. C			14. B
				15. D

ANSWERS AND EXPLANATIONS

SENTENCE CORRECTION

1. **The correct answer is (B).** Check the rules of parallel construction.

2. **The correct answer is (C).** Two actions are being compared; therefore, *it was* is needed after *than*. Choice (E) confuses the participant phrase *making . . .* by the inclusion of the word *in*.

3. **The correct answer is (B).** An unnecessary *which* eliminated choices (A) and (E). Choice (D) makes it sound as if the UFOs were doing the sighting.

4. **The correct answer is (C).** To what is the *it* referring? The only clear answer is choice (C).

5. **The correct answer is (B).** This questions your choice of idiom. *Over whether* is the most sound choice.

6. **The correct answer is (D).** This is a question of usage of tense. Since the sentences refer to continued action over time, choice (D) works the best.

7. **The correct answer is (C).** You are asked, once again, to understand the issue of parallel construction.

8. **The correct answer is (B).** This is another problem of parallel construction. You need to change the first part of the sentence to agree with the infinitive construction of the second part of the sentence.

9. **The correct answer is (B).** *Chemistry professors* were not founded by Debra and Marcel. This is an example of a misplaced modifier.

10. **The correct answer is (C).** This refers to proper use of the pronoun *their*, which is referring to the singular *a corporation*.

11. **The correct answer is (D).** The subject of this sentence is plural, but the verb is singular.

12. **The correct answer is (C).** When you use the idiom *not only*, *but also* must follow.

13. **The correct answer is (D).** This is a case of a misplaced modifier.

14. **The correct answer is (E).** The correct answer must have all "noun-like" things, just as the rest of the sentence does.

READING COMPREHENSION

1. **The correct answer is (E).** The passage mentions how cloning had decades of use that resulted in "important biomedical and agricultural advances." Choice (A) is an attempt to deal with issues beyond the passage, and choice (C) ignores the notion of cloning humans.

2. **The correct answer is (A).** Cloning "holds promise" in helping with this problem. All other choices have already been areas where cloning has proved helpful.

3. **The correct answer is (A).** Paragraph one states that this is a "legislative proposal." Choice (D) is mentioned as a supporting element in the proposal. Even though the topic is biological research, the audience is not limited to biologists.

4. **The correct answer is (C).** Though there would be further review fully completed, choice (A), five years after passage of this legislation, the prohibition would be immediate. Choice (E) is true but not as specific as choice (C).

5. **The correct answer is (D).** It is stated clearly at the beginning of paragraph three that cloning has been used in biomedicine and agriculture. Though cloning produced Dolly, choice (B), it was not created solely for that purpose.

6. **The correct answer is (A).** When the speaker states in paragraph two "at this time," it is implied that things may change in this area at some point in the future. Choice (B) refers to the present and is the spur for legislation, but future change is not ruled out. Though the legislation presents "hard and fast" rules, it acknowledges that new legislation may follow.

7. **The correct answer is (D).** If the Peripatetics "walk around," one can see how this could result in becoming changeable. Choice (E) is an antonym and choice (A) refers to an overall quality of the passage but not the word under question.

8. **The correct answer is (D).** Detail is provided in paragraph four. It is suggested that science existed before this time, thus choice (A) is incorrect and choice (C) is not defensible.

9. **The correct answer is (C).** Choice (C) is correct based on details provided in the second paragraph. Choice (B) refers only to Aristotle's definition. Choice (A) is not possible to defend, based on the passage.

10. **The correct answer is (A).** The passage states that Aristotle's father was a physician and, thus, gave him "an interest in living things." All the other choices are contradicted by the details in the passage.

11. **The correct answer is (C).** The goal of Stanton's *The Woman's Bible* was social equality. She may have believed choice (A), but it is not a clear inference from the passage.

12. **The correct answer is (E).** Though all other responses were important, difficult, and have taken a long time to address, nothing was more potent in Stanton's time than the relationship between the Church and women's freedom.

13. **The correct answer is (E).** Detail is provided in the last paragraph. Stanton chose not to back down from criticism and caused a rift in the NAWSA. The other choices are all contradicted in the same paragraph.

14. **The correct answer is (C).** Choice (C) is correct, based on details in the last paragraph. Choice (D) is close since Anthony spoke out on Stanton's behalf, but this was not enough, for Stanton stood for a broader agenda than Anthony.

CRITICAL REASONING

1. **The correct answer is (A).** The manager assumes because the percentage dropped from 1998 to 1999, that it is then safe to conclude that the total number of youths involved in violent crimes has also dropped. This is true only if the total number of violent crimes remains the same. If the total number of violent crimes increases, then the percentage of crimes involving youths may decrease, without the actual number of youth involvement changing at all. Choice (A) shows this flaw by suggesting that the number of violent crimes involving adults, not youths, has increased during the time period in question. Choice (B) is irrelevant to the question, because the change in reporting methods occurred before the time period. Choice (C) adds no information because it is limited to one year and provides a number of youths, but no information about the percentage. Choice (D) is insufficient because it addresses only the number of youths "who are counseled" but not the number involved in crimes. Finally, choice (E) is irrelevant because the question addresses the successes of the office as a whole, not just the performance of the manager.

2. **The correct answer is (E).** The only conclusion that makes sense from the information given is choice (E), which states that many more violent crimes involved adults than youths. This is clear because, based on the report, only 6 percent, a small fraction, involved youths. Choices (A) and (D) would each require the conclusion that a reducing trend began as early as 1997 and will continue into 2000, which cannot be concluded from the information provided. Neither choice (B) nor choice (C) can be concluded, because they address the number of adult crimes but say nothing about the youth crimes.

3. **The correct answer is (C).** The argument links ridership on the commuter train to a measurement of the people working in the city. Choice (C) restates this link and must therefore be assumed for the conclusion to be accurate. Choices (A) and (B) each present some new fact about life in and around the city, but neither one addresses the issue of the train system. Choice (D) is irrelevant by relating Chicago to New York, a fact not at issue in this problem. Choice (E) ignores the issue of the trains and provides no assistance in drawing the conclusion about the plans of the "new people" moving to the suburbs.

4. **The correct answer is (E).** This is an example of direct deductive reasoning. If the initial condition is satisfied, then any statement following will be true. If any step in this chain is NOT satisfied, then all preceding statements can be concluded NOT to have happened either. Therefore, if John does not earn a million dollars, all the statements leading up to that step, indicated by choices (A), (B), (C), and (D), must all NOT have happened. However, the final step could still occur, just through some other means. Therefore, choice (E) is the correct answer.

5. **The correct answer is (B).** The argument assumes that because the report says that some people died from diseases, national legislation is required. Choice (B) questions this reasoning by showing that the scope of the report is limited to only a few hospitals. It is possible that those hospitals, all in major cities, had something else in common that may have led to the deaths, and upgraded filtration systems may not be necessary. Choices (A), (C), and (E) all make statements about the general study of diseases but not about the actual conclusion of this argument, so they are incorrect. Choice (D) appears relevant to the argument, but it makes a statement that would actually strengthen the conclusion, not weaken it. Therefore, choice (B) is the best answer.

6. **The correct answer is (A).** The conclusion of the argument assumes that the decline in the overall class of amphibians will affect all individual species equally, so that if the frogs are the largest group, then the frogs will lose the most members. This conclusion requires the assumption in choice (A), that the cause for the decline affects all members equally. Therefore, choice (A) is the best answer. Choice (B) may be true, but it does not mention the group of frogs at all, so it is irrelevant. Choice (C) attacks the method of measurement but does not directly address the argument itself. Choice (D) is the second-best answer, suggesting that all animals would be affected equally. However, choice (A) makes this statement more directly and is a better answer. Finally, choice (E) is incorrect because it is simply irrelevant to the argument, as it says nothing about the individual members of the class.

7. **The correct answer is (C).** The argument assumes that additional licensing requirements would make a difference in the number of shootings that involve minors and would reduce the number of shootings. Choice (C) directly challenges this assumption and is the best answer because it points out that the licensing of guns did not stop "most" of the shootings in the report. Other choices do not challenge the assumption. Choices (A) and (B) are simply irrelevant to the facts of this argument. Choice (D) somewhat challenges the conclusion by suggesting that, perhaps, the study is not broad enough to justify additional legislation. However, without more information, it is not as good an answer as choice (C). Choice (E) suggests a negative effect of additional legislation, but it does not address the issue of the effect that licensing might have on limiting future shootings.

8. **The correct answer is (E).** The argument assumes that if the telephone systems in the United States are broken apart so that they have the same form of ownership as systems in Europe, then the United States systems will follow and have the same results. Choice (E) is a restatement of this assumption. Choices (A) and (D) appear to be assumptions, but only to the extent that without assuming the importance of those statements, one wouldn't be discussing this issue. But this is not sufficient to make them correct answers for this problem. Choice (B) is irrelevant as it does not address the style of ownership. It could be considered relevant if one further assumes that having more telephones in the United States might lead to even poorer service, but this requires additional assumptions that are not part of this argument. Finally, choice (C) is incorrect because the *kind* of telephone system is not relevant to the issue of ownership and performance.

9. **The correct answer is (B).** The argument makes the assumption that the American companies will invariably have the same future as the European companies. Choice (B) shows that a different result is possible as a result of the study and modifications made by managers and executives. Choice (A) is simply irrelevant to the argument. Choices (C) and (D) raise issues that are not relevant to the argument, as the argument addresses the management of the companies and the services provided. Finally, choice (E) provides a historic fact, but without additional information about the "other industries" that are mentioned, no conclusion can be drawn as to whether this statement weakens or strengthens the argument. Therefore, the best answer is choice (B).

10. **The correct answer is (C).** This argument links improved roads with increased trade; the best answer showing that connection is choice (C). Choice (A) is close but does not directly link the two ideas of transportation and trade. Choices (B) and (D) are both irrelevant by making claims that are unrelated to the argument. Choice (E) is incorrect because it is overly broad; in fact, it is possible to imagine at least *some* travel between towns even without organized roads.

11. **The correct answer is (D).** The argument suggests that because the buyers of this particular car model tend to be more educated, then the education is the reason, or cause, for their purchase of that car. To contradict, or weaken, such a claim, it is sufficient to show some other explanation for the connection. Choice (D) does this by suggesting that the cost of the car would require its buyers to be well educated, since a higher education tends to lead to a higher salary. None of the other answer choices adequately links the education level with the cost or purchase of the car.

12. **The correct answer is (C).** The conclusion of the argument directly links the amount of television coverage to the number of deaths involved in the given types of disasters. Therefore, the correct answer must make the same connection. Choice (C) directly makes the same statement, and is, therefore, the correct answer. Choices (A), (B), and (D) all present facts that, even if true, do not address the issue of the television coverage, and are, therefore, irrelevant and incorrect. Choice (E) is similar to the correct answer but does not make the logical connection as directly as choice (C) does.

13. **The correct answer is (C).** The argument assumes a direct link between the number of political science majors and English majors in undergraduate universities and the number of law school enrollments. To weaken this argument, a statement must challenge this assumption and show that the decline in the number of undergraduates in these subjects will not decrease the number of enrollments. Choice (C) does this by showing that law schools receive so many extra applications each year that the decline in those two subjects is not likely to affect overall enrollment. Choice (A), even if true, does not address the issue of the number of enrollments. Choice (B) does not link the undergraduate subjects with the number of enrollment. Choice (D) is completely irrelevant to the subject of law school applications, except if one further assumes that the election might increase interest in the law and, therefore, increase applications, but this would require too tenuous a connection. Finally, choice (E) suggests a reason for the connection between political science and English, but does not address the issue of the decline in enrollment.

QUANTITATIVE

Problem Solving

1. **The correct answer is (E).** Either x and y are greater than 0 or x and y are less than 0. In either case, the quotient $\dfrac{x}{y}$ must be greater than 0. Thus, choice (D) cannot be true.

2. **The correct answer is (B).** Convert each fraction to a decimal using long division as necessary: $\dfrac{1}{8} = 0.125$, $\dfrac{2}{7} = 0.28$, $\dfrac{3}{5} = 0.6$, $\dfrac{4}{5} = 0.8$, $\dfrac{5}{8} = 0.625$.

3. **The correct answer is (A).** The original price of the suit is $100 + $400 = $500. The problem to solve is: $100 is what percent of $500? $100 = 500x$, so $\dfrac{100}{500} = x$ or $x = \dfrac{1}{5} = 20\%$.

4. **The correct answer is (E).** $(0.02 \times 10^{a})(1.3 \times 10^{6}) = 0.026 \times 10^{a\,+\,b} = 2.6 \times 10^{a\,+\,b\,-\,2}$. Now, $2.6 \times 10^{3} = 2.6 \times 10^{a\,+\,b\,-\,2}$ means $3 = a + b - 2$ and $a + b = 5$.

5. **The correct answer is (D).** Factor and reduce the left side: $\dfrac{(x + 5)(x + 2)}{x + 2} = x + 5$. Then, $x + 5 = 8$, so $x = 3$. Therefore, $x + 1 = 3 + 1 = 4$.

6. **The correct answer is (D).** Joan must pay tax on $75,000 - $50,000 = $25,000. 8% of $25,000 = (.08)(25,000) = $2,000.

7. **The correct answer is (A).** Let $x =$ the sum of the 7 test scores. Then, $\dfrac{x}{7} = 78$, so $x = 78(7) = 546$. The corrected sum of the test scores is $546 + 14 = 560$, and the class average is $\dfrac{560}{7} = 80$.

8. **The correct answer is (D).** The remaining tickets represent 25% of the total. Thus, 80 is 25% of the total. $80 = .25x$, where x is the total number of tickets. So $x = 320$. He sold $320 - 80 = 240$, for a total of $(\$1.00)(240) = \$240.00$.

9. **The correct answer is (A).** Let x equal the length of a side of the original square. Then the area of the rectangle equals $(x + 5)(x - 5) = 56$, $x^2 - 25 = 56$, $x^2 = 81$. $x = 9$. Then, the perimeter of a square is 4 times a side length, or $4(9) = 36$ inches.

10. **The correct answer is (D).** Let $x =$ the number of hours to fill the pool with both pipes open. Pipe A alone fills $\dfrac{x}{8}$ of the pool, and pipe B fills $\dfrac{x}{12}$ of the pool. Together, $\dfrac{x}{8} + \dfrac{x}{12} = 1$, $3x + 8x = 24$, $5x = 24$, $x = \dfrac{24}{5}$, $x = 4\dfrac{4}{5}$.

11. **The correct answer is (C).** If A_L is the area of the larger circle, $A_L = \pi(12^2) = 144\pi$. If A_S is the area of the smaller circle, $A_S = \dfrac{1}{4}(144\pi) = 36\pi$. $A_S = \pi r^2 = 36\pi$, so $r^2 = 36$ and $r = 6$.

12. **The correct answer is (D).** $3\$\$2 = 4(2) - 3^2 = 8 - 9 = -1$.

13. **The correct answer is (C).** Let x equal the total number of tiles purchased. 60 tiles represent $\frac{3}{8}$ of the total, so $60 = \frac{3}{8}x$, $x = 160$. Thus, $160 - 60 = 100$ tiles were used at a cost of $\$1.20(100) = \$120.00$.

14. **The correct answer is (B).** Note that with fewer people, the job will take longer to complete, so this can be set up as an indirect proportion: $p = \frac{k}{h}$, where p is the number of people needed to complete the job and h is the number of hours needed to complete the job. Then, $12 = \frac{k}{15}$, so $k = 12(15) = 180$. For 18 people to complete the job, $18 = \frac{180}{x}$, $18x = 180$, $x = 10$ hours. To complete $\frac{2}{5}$ of the job, it would take $\frac{2}{5}(10) = 4$ hours.

15. **The correct answer is (B).** One technique you can use to solve the problem is to start dividing each number by 3, 4, 5, and 6. This quickly leads to the answer of 60. Or, find the least common multiple of 3, 2^2, 5, and $2 \cdot 3$ which is $3 \cdot 2^2 \cdot 5 = 60$.

16. **The correct answer is (A).** There is only 1 choice for the first letter, 2 choices for the second letter, and 1 choice for the third. Then, $1 \times 2 \times 1 = 2$ ways.

17. **The correct answer is (B).** Factor and solve: $(x + 3)^2 = 0$, $x + 3 = 0$, $x + -3$. Then, $-3 - 3 = -6$.

18. **The correct answer is (E).** Rate multiplied by time equals the number of words. Let x equal the number of hours Pat types. Then, $60x = 40\left(x + \frac{2}{3}\right)$. Solve for x: $60x = 40x + \frac{80}{3}$, $40x = \frac{80}{3}$, $x = \frac{4}{3} = 1\frac{1}{3}$ hours = 1 hour 20 minutes. One hour and 20 minutes past 5:00 is 6:20.

19. **The correct answer is (D).** The ratio of 7 to 8 to 3 means $7x + 8x + 3x + 108$. Solve for x: $18x = 108$, $x = 6$. The number of wins is represented by $7x = 7(6) = 42$ wins.

20. **The correct answer is (B).** Let x equal the cost of the more expensive item. Then $x - 0.63$ represents the cost of the other item. $\$5.13 = x + (x - 0.63)$, $\$5.13 = 2x - 0.63$, $2x = \$5.76$, $x = \$2.88$.

21. **The correct answer is (C).** We need $10x = 120$, where x is the length of a side adjacent to the garage. Then, $x = 12$ feet. She will need $12 + 10 + 12 = 34$ feet of fencing.

22. **The correct answer is (B).** The maximum markdown is 40%. The additional 15% markdown would make the total discount 55%. The damaged item would sell for 45% of the original price, or $(0.45)(\$36) = \$16.20$.

DATA SUFFICIENCY

1. **The correct answer is (C).** Using statement (1), you can determine that there are 5 integers between x and z, but that is not sufficient to determine how many are even. Statement (2) alone is not sufficient to answer the question. However, using trial and error and both statements will allow you to determine the answer. For example, if $x = 2$, the $z = 8$ [from statements (1) and (2)]. Then, y could be 4 or 6, which means that there are two even integers that satisfy the conditions.

2. **The correct answer is (E).** Statement (1) has many answers, such as 81 since $\sqrt{81} = 9$ or 49 since $\sqrt{49} = 7$. Statement (2) has many answers, including all the odd integers from 2 through 19. From this set, only 1, 9, and 16 have square roots that are integers; both 1 and 9 are odd integers. Thus, statements (1) and (2) together are not sufficient to answer the question asked.

3. **The correct answer is (B).** Statement (1) does not give the regular price, so the cost cannot be computed. Statement (2) provides the regular price and the mark-down percentage, so the cost could be computed.

4. **The correct answer is (D).** Let J = Joan's age now and B = Bill's age now. We have $J = B + 3$. Using statement (1), we have $J + 6 = 2(B + 6) - 12$, giving two equations in two unknowns, which is sufficient to answer the question. Statement (2) gives $B - 4 = 5$, or $B = 9$, which also is sufficient to answer the question.

5. **The correct answer is (D).** From statement (1), $C = 2\pi a = 8\pi$, so $a = 4$. Once we know a, we can find the area using $A = \pi r^2$. From statement (2), we know the length of the radius and can find the area.

6. **The correct answer is (D).** Let A equal the interest rate for account A and let B equal the interest rate for account B. The problem asks for the total = $8,000A + 10,000B$. Statement (1) translates to $400A + 500B = 1,400$. Multiply both sides of the equation by 20 to find the total. Statement (2) translates to $A = .05$ and $B = 2(.05) = .1$. Substituting these values into total = $8,000(.05) + 10,000(.1)$ will give the total.

7. **The correct answer is (B).** From the data given in the problem, we know that $a + 2 = b$ or $a - b = -2$. Using statement (1), we can simplify $2(2^a)$: $2^1(2^a) = 2^{1 + a}$. Then, $2^{1 + a} = 2^{b - 1}$. Set the exponents equal: $1 + a = b - 1$ or $a - b = -2$. Since this is the same equation formed from the problem statement, we do not have sufficient data to answer the question. Statement (2) can be written as $2^{2a + 1} = 2^7$. Then, $2a + 1 = 7$ can be solved for a. Then, b can be found using $a - b = -2$, and the question can be answered.

8. **The correct answer is (C).** The problem asks you to find $\frac{g}{r}$, where g equals the number of green balls and r equals the number of red balls. Statement (1) translates to $g = 2r - 3$, which cannot be solved for $\frac{g}{r}$. Statement (2) alone is not sufficient to answer the question since nothing is known about the number of green balls. However, using the data in statement (2) to find the number of green balls from the equation in statement (1) will allow you to answer the question.

9. **The correct answer is (C).** Statement (1) alone is not sufficient to answer the question since it only provides the number of integers in the sequence. Statement (2) alone is not sufficient to answer the question since it is not known how many integers are in the sequence. Taken together, statements (1) and (2) are sufficient to answer the question since we know the number of consecutive odd integers and the smallest integer.

10. **The correct answer is (D).** From statement (1), we can multiply both sides of the given inequality by y without reversing the inequality symbol: $y \cdot \dfrac{x}{y} > 1 \cdot y$, so $x > y$. Now, $x > y$ and $y > 1$, which implies that $x > 1$, and the question has been answered. From statement (2), if $y < 0$, $x < 0$ since the fraction $\dfrac{x}{y}$ is positive. If $x < 0$, x cannot be greater than 1, and the question has been answered.

11. **The correct answer is (C).** Statement (1) can be simplified: $x = y - 4 + x$, $0 = y - 4$, $y = 4$. Statement (2) alone is not sufficient to find the value of x, but when combined with statement (1), the value of x can be found.

12. **The correct answer is (C).** Let p equal the number of students taking only psychology, s equal the number of students taking only sociology, and b equal the number of students taking both psychology and sociology. Then, $p + s + b = 85$. Statement (1) translates to $p = 15 + s$, which combined with the given equation is not sufficient to answer the question since we have two equations with three unknowns. Statement (2) translates to $s = 5 + b$, which by itself is not sufficient to answer the question. However, using statements (1) and (2) and the given, we have three equations with three unknowns, which can be solved and, therefore, is sufficient to answer the question.

13. **The correct answer is (C).** Statement (1) alone is not sufficient to answer the question since knowing the length of the hypotenuse will not enable you to find the length of the legs of the triangle. Statement (2) alone only provides the length of one leg, which is not sufficient to answer the question. Combining statements (1) and (2) and using the Pythagorean theorem will allow you to find the length of the other leg and then the area.

14. **The correct answer is (B).** Using (1): Try some examples. If there are 20 women, there are 32 men giving a ratio of 20:32 or 5:8. If there are 24 women, there are 36 men giving a ratio of 24:36 or 2:3. Using (2): you can write $w = \dfrac{2}{3}m$, where w is the number of women and m is the number of men. This can be written as $\dfrac{w}{m} = \dfrac{2}{3}$ or $\dfrac{m}{w} = \dfrac{3}{2}$, giving the ratio of men to women as 3:2.

15. **The correct answer is (D).** Statement (1) provides data to find the area of the square ($10 \cdot 10 = 100$), the area of the circle (since AB $= 10$, $r = 5$ and the area equals 25π), and subtracting the area of the circle from the area of the square provides the area of the shaded regions. Statement (2) reverses the process. If A $= 25\pi$, $r = 5$, so that AB $= 10$.

Unit 1

SENTENCE CORRECTION STRATEGIES AND REVIEW

The sentence correction questions do not test spelling or capitalization. They do test grammar and rhetoric (usage, clarity, conciseness, and logic of expression). Although the exam will not test punctuation per se, issues of punctuation will occasionally arise in connection with a grammatical problem (run-on sentences, for example).

It is important to carefully read the underlined portion of the sentences. You will be given five choices to substitute for the underlined portion. Choice (A) will be the same as the underlined part of the sentence. Choices (B), (C), (D), and (E) will offer alternative answers. As always in a multiple-choice test, pick the best answer. Be aware that the underlined portions of the sentences can contain more than one error. Select the answer that corrects *all* the problems in the underlined part of the sentence (if there *are* any problems).

This review will start with common grammatical and rhetorical problems that are found on the test: dangling modifiers, subordination, faulty parallelism, arbitrary tense shifts, fragments, run-on sentences, noun-pronoun agreement, subject-verb agreement, illogical comparisons, wordiness, and idiomatic usage. Each of these problems will be illustrated by a sample question that is similar to those that you will encounter on the exam. That section is followed by a basic grammar overview including the parts of speech, which you may or may not need to consult, depending on how successfully you deal with the sample questions. Use the overview as a reference if you don't understand the explanations of the correct answers for the sample questions.

DANGLING MODIFIERS

SAMPLE QUESTION

To make sure his research was accurate, <u>all secondary sources were checked twice.</u>

   (A) all secondary sources were checked twice.

   (B) most of the secondary sources were checked thoroughly.

   (C) Don checked all his sources, both primary and secondary.

   (D) Don checked all his secondary sources twice.

   (E) all secondary sources were checked twice by Don.

The correct answer is (D). Choices (A), (B), and (E) contain no word that the infinitive phrase *to make sure* can effectively modify. The answer has to be either choice (C) or choice (D), and choice (C) alters the meaning of the sentence.

CLAUSES AND SUBORDINATES

Clauses are groups of words that contain a subject and predicate (verb part of the sentence). There are two main kinds of clauses. One kind is the independent clause, which makes sense when it stands alone. Independent clauses are joined by coordinating conjunctions.

I know how to clean silver, but I never learned how to clean copper.

(The two independent clauses could stand alone as complete sentences.)

I know how to clean silver. I never learned how to clean copper.

The other kind of clause is a dependent, or subordinate, clause. Although this type of clause has a subject and a predicate, it cannot stand alone.

When I learn to clean copper, I will keep my pots sparkling.

"When I learn to clean copper," by itself, does not make sense. Dependent clauses are always used as a single part of speech in a sentence. They function as nouns or adjectives or adverbs. When they function as nouns, they are called noun clauses. When they function as adjectives, they are called adjective clauses. When they are adverbs, they are called adverbial clauses. Since a dependent or subordinate clause cannot stand alone, it must be joined with an independent clause to make a sentence. A subordinate conjunction does this job. A relative pronoun (*who, that, which, what, whose,* and *whom*) may act as the subordinate conjunction. For adjective and adverbial clauses, a relative adverb (*while, when*) may act as the subordinating conjunction.

- I noticed that he was very pale.

  "That he was very pale" is a noun clause—the object of the verb "noticed." That is the subordinating conjunction.

- "Who was guilty" is not known.

  "Who was guilty" is a noun clause—the subject of the verb "is."

  "Who" is the subordinating conjunction.

- She lost the belt, which was a present.

  "Which was a present" is an adjective clause—describing the belt.

  "Which" is the subordinating conjunction.

- She lost the belt when she dropped her bag.

  "When she dropped the bag" is an adverbial clause that answers the question "when" about the predicate. "When" is the subordinating conjunction.

Clauses should clearly and logically refer to the part of the sentence they modify.

We bought the dress at Bloomingdale's that was expensive.

(Misplaced adjective clause. Did the writer mean Bloomingdale's was expensive?)

Correct: We bought a dress that was expensive at Bloomingdale's.

When finally discovered, not a sound was heard.

(Misplaced adverbial clause. Who or what is discovered?)

Correct: When finally discovered, the boys didn't make a sound.

SAMPLE QUESTION

The author won the Pulitzer Prize <u>on account his book was timely and artistic.</u>

    (A)   on account his book was timely and artistic.

    (B)   being that his book was timely and artistic.

    (C)   his book was timely and artistic.

    (D)   when his book was timely and artistic.

    (E)   because his book was timely and artistic.

The correct answer is (E). The underlined portion of the sentence is a subordinate clause—that is, a clause that cannot stand by itself as a complete thought but must be joined to the rest of the sentence with a subordinate conjunction. The only possibilities are choices (D) and (E). Choice (D) is incorrect because *when* indicates time, not cause and effect. *Being that* is improper English usage. *On account* is incorrect; it should read *on account of,* which would be much wordier than choice (E).

FAULTY PARALLELISM

Elements of equal importance within a sentence should have parallel structure or similar form.

To sing, dancing, and to laugh make life happy. (Incorrect)

To sing, to dance, and to laugh make life happy. (Correct)

He wants health, wealth, and to be happy. (Incorrect)

He wants health, wealth, and happiness. (Correct)

SAMPLE QUESTION

Sue anticipates <u>hearing from her friends and to have</u> the opportunity to see them again at her home.

- (A) hearing from her friends and to have
- (B) hearing from her friends and having
- (C) to hear from her friends and having
- (D) not only to hear from her friends but also having
- (E) not only hearing from her friends but to have

The correct answer is (B). *Hearing* and *having* are both gerunds. The other choices use a gerund phrase with an infinitive phrase, which is not parallel. Two infinitives (*to hear* and *to have*) would be correct also, but they are not among the choices listed.

WATCH ARBITRARY TENSE SHIFTS

Make sure that verb tenses indicate proper cause and effect. When two events take place simultaneously, their tenses should match.

He complained while his father listens. (Incorrect)

He complained while his father listened. (Correct)

SAMPLE QUESTION

When I saw Joanne at the class reunion, <u>I realized that I forgot how much I'd loved her.</u>

- (A) I realized that I forgot how much I'd loved her.
- (B) I realized that I had forgotten how much I'd loved her.
- (C) I had realized that I forgot how much I'd loved her.
- (D) I had realized that I had forgotten how much I loved her.
- (E) I realized that I had forgot how much I loved her.

The correct answer is (B). *Realized* and *saw* happened at the same time; they should be in the same tense. That eliminates choices (C) and (D). *Forgot* and *I'd loved* describe a similar time. The past participle of *forget* is *forgotten,* which eliminates choice (E). Choice (A) is incorrect because *forgot* and *loved* do not show the proper relationship in time. Thus, choice (B) is correct.

SENTENCES

A sentence is a group of words that expresses a complete thought. An independent clause can stand by itself and may or may not be a complete sentence.

> Beth and Terry rode the Ferris wheel; they enjoyed the ride. (Two independent clauses connected by a semicolon.)

> Beth and Terry rode the Ferris wheel. They enjoyed the ride. (Two independent clauses—each is a sentence.)

1. A simple sentence has one independent clause. A dependent clause is never a sentence by itself. Here are some simple sentences:

> John and Fred played.

> John laughed and sang.

> John and Fred ate hot dogs and drank beer.

The following is NOT an independent clause:

> Fred said. (Incorrect—*said* is a transitive verb. It needs a direct object.)

> Fred said hello. (Correct)

2. A compound sentence has at least two independent clauses.

> Darryl bought the meat, and Laverne bought the potatoes.

3. A complex sentence has one independent clause and at least one dependent clause.

> Because she left early, she missed the end.

> (*Because she left early* is the dependent clause. *She missed the end* is an independent clause.)

4. A compound-complex sentence has two independent clauses and one or more dependent clauses.

> You prefer math, and I prefer music, although I am the math major.

> (*You prefer math, and I prefer music* are the independent clauses. The dependent clause is *although I am a math major.*)

SENTENCE FRAGMENTS

These are parts of sentences that are incorrectly written with capitals and punctuation of a sentence.

Around the corner.

Because she left early.

Going to the movies.

A terrible tragedy.

Remember that sentences must have at least a subject and a verb. A dependent clause cannot stand alone as a sentence (see Clauses and Subordinates).

SAMPLE QUESTION

The enrollment for Theater 101 is noticeably down this semester. <u>All suggesting that the course is either too hard or that the instructor is incompetent.</u>

    (A) All suggesting that
    (B) Which suggests that
    (C) This statistic suggests that
    (D) Suggesting that
    (E) Suggesting the fact that

The correct answer is (C). A finite verb is missing in all the other answers. The only choice that is an independent clause is choice (C). Choices (A), (B), (D) and (E) would all be dependent clauses.

RUN-ON SENTENCES

These are sentences that are incorrectly linked.

The rain was heavy, lightning was crackling he could not row the boat. (Incorrect)

Because the rain was heavy and lightning was crackling, he could not row the boat. (Correct)

The rain was heavy. Lightning was crackling. He could not row the boat. (Correct)

SAMPLE QUESTION

Many reasons have been suggested for the decline in <u>literacy, the main</u> reason is the way students are taught history.

    (A) literacy, the main

    (B) literacy, the

    (C) literacy the main

    (D) literacy. The main

    (E) literacy The main

The correct answer is (D). The clause preceding *the main reason* is an independent clause and cannot be connected to another independent clause with a comma, which eliminates choices (A) and (B). Two independent clauses cannot be joined without punctuation or subordination, so choices (C) and (E) are also incorrect.

NOUN-PRONOUN AGREEMENT

See the sections on pronouns and nouns. Some nouns are always singular, such as everyone, someone, somebody, each, anyone, anybody, everybody, and one. They must always take a singular pronoun.

    A person may pass if they study. (Incorrect)

    A person may pass if he studies. (Correct)

SAMPLE QUESTION 1

The libertarian maintains that everyone is an individual <u>in their own right.</u>

    (A) in their own right.

    (B) in their own way.

    (C) and they are responsible for their actions.

    (D) in what they do.

    (E) in his own right.

The correct answer is (E). *Everyone* is a singular noun, and the pronoun referring to it must agree. Only choice (E) has a singular pronoun.

Review the section on case under Pronouns. If a pronoun is the object of a preposition, it must be in the objective case.

SAMPLE QUESTION 2

Everyone failed the exam <u>except Bob and her.</u>

    (A)   except Bob and her.

    (B)   excepting Bob and her.

    (C)   outside of Bob and she.

    (D)   besides Bob and she.

    (E)   except Bob and she.

The correct answer is (A). *Except* is a preposition and must take an object. *Her* is the objective case of *she,* so only choices (A) and (B) are possibilities. The correct form of the preposition is *except.* Thus, choice (A) is correct.

    If a pronoun is the subject of a clause, it must be in the nominative case.

SAMPLE QUESTION 3

The guards were ordered to shoot <u>whomever tried to escape.</u>

    (A)   whomever tried to escape.

    (B)   whoever tried to escape.

    (C)   whomever escaped.

    (D)   whomever might escape.

    (E)   whoever might try to escape.

The correct answer is (B). *Whoever* is the subject of the clause, so the answer must be in the nominative case. Only choices (B) and (E) are possible choices, and choice (E) changes verb tense without a reason.

WATCH SUBJECT/VERB AGREEMENT

Verbs must agree in number and person with their subjects. Singular verbs take singular subjects; plural verbs match plural subjects.

    The boy walks the dog.

    The boys walk the dog.

See the section on Verbs for more detailed information regarding subject-verb agreement. Be aware of collective nouns. Collective nouns are singular but denote a group. Examples are association, group, society, union, and army. When the collective noun refers to a group as a whole, it takes a singular verb; when it refers to the individuals that comprise the group, it takes a plural verb.

    The family is the most precious unit in American society.

    (*The family as a unit* is the subject; the verb is singular.)

    After years of struggle, the family begins to go their separate ways.

    (Each member is leaving separately.)

SAMPLE QUESTION

The group <u>insists that they have a right</u> to police the airwaves.

    (A) insists that they have a right

    (B) insist that they have a right

    (C) insists that it has a right

    (D) insist that is has a right

    (E) insist that it has rights itself

The answer is (C). *Group* here is used as a collective noun; it takes a singular verb, and any pronoun reference must be singular. Only choice (C) fits the criteria.

COMPARISONS

Beware of illogical comparisons. Only like things should be compared.

SAMPLE QUESTION

Your temper is <u>as bad as Bob.</u>

    (A) as bad as Bob.

    (B) worse than Bob.

    (C) as bad as Bob when you get mad.

    (D) as bad as Bob when he gets mad.

    (E) as bad as Bob's.

The correct answer is (E). The two items being compared are the *tempers* of the two individuals. Only choice (E) refers to Bob's temper. The other choices all refer just to Bob.

WATCH THESE DON'Ts

DON'T use *being that*; use *since* or *because*.

DON'T use *could of, should of, would of*; use *could have, should have, would have*.

DON'T use the preposition *of* in the following; off *of* the table, inside *of* the house.

DON'T use *this here* or *that there*; use just *this* or *that*.

DON'T misuse *then* as a coordinating conjunction; use *than* instead.

    He is better *than* he used to be. (Correct)

    He is better *then* he used to be. (Incorrect)

USE OF THE RHETORICAL

Good writing is clear and economical.

1. **Avoid Ambiguous Pronoun References**

    Tom killed Jerry. I feel sorry for him. (Who is *him*? Tom? Jerry?)

    Burt is a nice man. I don't know why they insulted him. (Who does *they* refer to?)

2. **Avoid Clichés**

    Betty is sharp as a tack.

    The math exam was easy as pie.

    It will be a cold day in August before I eat dinner with Louisa again.

3. **Avoid Redundancy**

    Harry is a man who loves to gamble. (Redundant—we know that Harry is a man.)

    Harry loves to gamble. (Correct)

    Claire is a strange one. (Redundant—*one* is not necessary)

    Claire is strange. (Correct)

    This July has been particularly hot in terms of weather. (Redundant—*in terms of weather* is not necessary.)

    This July has been particularly hot. (Correct)

4. **Avoid Wordiness**

    The phrases on the left are wordy. Use the word or phrase on the right instead.

Wordy	Preferable
the reason why is that	because
the question as to whether	whether
in a hasty manner	hastily
be aware of the fact that	know
due to the fact that	because
in light of the fact that	since
regardless of the fact that	although
for the purpose of	to

		The following are words or phrases that are commonly misused.
1.	Accept	to receive or agree to (verb) I ACCEPT your offer.
	Except	preposition that means to leave out They all left EXCEPT Dave.
2.	Adapt	to change (verb) We must ADAPT.
3.	Affect	to influence (verb) Their attitudes may well AFFECT mine.
	Effect	result (noun) What is the EFFECT of their attitudes?
4.	Allusion	a reference to something (noun) The teacher made an ALLUSION to Milton.
	Illusion	a false idea (noun) He had the ILLUSION that he was king.
5.	Among	use with more than two items (preposition) They pushed AMONG the group of soldiers.
	Between	use with two items (preposition) They pushed BETWEEN both soldiers.
6.	Amount	cannot be counted (noun) Sue has a large AMOUNT of pride.
	Number	can be counted (noun) Sue bought a NUMBER of apples.
7.	Apt	capable (adjective) She is an APT student.
	Likely	probably (adjective) We are LIKELY to receive the prize.
8.	Beside	at the side of (prepositional) He sat BESIDE me.
	Besides	in addition to (preposition) There were others there BESIDES Joe.
9.	Bring	toward the speaker (verb) BRING that to me.
	Take	away from the speaker (verb) TAKE that to him.

		The following are words or phrases that are commonly misused—*Continued.*
10.	Can	to be able to (verb) I CAN ride a bike.
	May	permission (verb) MAY I ride my bike?
11.	Famous	well-known (adjective) He is a FAMOUS movie star.
	Infamous	well-known but not for anything good (adjective) He is the INFAMOUS criminal.
12.	Fewer	can be counted (adjective) I have FEWER pennies than John.
	Less	cannot be counted (adjective) I have LESS pride than John.
13.	Imply	the speaker or writer is making a hint or suggestion (verb) He IMPLIED in his book that dogs were inferior to cats.
	Infer	to draw a conclusion from the speaker or writer (verb) The audience INFERRED that he was a dog-hater.
14.	In	something is already there (preposition) He is IN the kitchen.
	Into	something is going there (preposition) He is on his way INTO the kitchen.
15.	Irritate	to annoy (verb) His whining IRRITATED me.
	Aggravate	to make worse (verb) The soap AGGRAVATED his rash.
16.	Teach	to provide knowledge (verb) She TAUGHT him how to swim.
	Learn	to acquire knowledge (verb) He LEARNED how to swim from her.
17.	Uninterested	bored (adjective) She is UNINTERESTED in everything.
	Disinterested	impartial (adjective) He wanted a DISINTERESTED jury at his trial.

SAMPLE QUESTION 1

I am crying due to the fact that my wife left me.

   (A) due to the fact that my wife left me.

   (B) when my wife left me.

   (C) in light of the fact that my wife left me.

   (D) my wife left me.

   (E) because my wife left me.

The correct answer is (E). This is a simple cause-effect statement. Choices (A) and (C) are needlessly wordy. Choice (D) is a run-on sentence; two independent clauses need to be connected by punctuation or subordination. Choice (B) distorts the meaning—*when* does not denote cause and effect.

5. Avoid Vague Words or Phrases

   It is always preferable to use specific, concrete language rather than vague words and phrases.

   The reality of the situation necessitated action. (Vague)

   Bill shot the burglar before the burglar could shoot him. (Specific)

6. Be Articulate. Use the Appropriate Word or Phrase

SAMPLE QUESTION 2

Realizing how difficult it is to adopt to the new ways, I chose among two miserable alternatives.

   (A) adopt to the new ways, I chose among

   (B) adopt to the new ways, I chose between

   (C) adapt to the new ways, I chose among

   (D) adapt to the new ways, I chose between

   (E) adopt to the new ways, I selected

The correct answer is (D). This question tests word choice. The correct word here is *adapt*, as in *change*, rather than *adopt*, which means incorporate. *Among* is used with more than two items; *between* is used with two items.

The following unit presents a brief overview and reference section of basic grammar principles that you should also understand. Although these principles may not be directly tested on the exam, it is important to understand these basics in order to more fully understand the Sentence Correction section of the GMAT. In addition, there are numerous questions to provide additional practice. Answer the questions and carefully check your answers. This is the best way to prepare for the exam.

SENTENCE CORRECTION REVIEW

> **Directions:** In each of the following sentences, some part of the sentence or the entire sentence is underlined. Beneath each sentence you will find five ways of phrasing the underlined part. The first of these repeats the original; the other four are different. If you think the original is better than any of the alternatives, choose (A); otherwise, choose one of the others.

This is a test of correctness and effectiveness of expression. In choosing answers, follow the requirements of standard written English; that is, pay attention to grammar, choice of words, and sentence construction. Choose the answer that most effectively expresses what is presented in the original sentence; this answer should be clear and exact, without awkwardness, ambiguity, or redundancy.

1. The train rolled into the station pulled by a diesel engine.

   (A) The train rolled into the station pulled by a diesel engine.
   (B) The train, pulled by a diesel engine, rolled into the station.
   (C) The train rolled into the station by a diesel engine.
   (D) Pulled by a diesel engine into the station rolled the train.
   (E) The train rolled into the station which was pulled by a diesel engine.

   The correct answer is (B). The misplaced modifier is corrected by this form. Obviously, the *station* was not pulled by an engine.

2. My mother was delighted to learn of me doing so well at the piano.

   (A) me doing so well
   (B) my doing so well
   (C) my well doing
   (D) my doing so good
   (E) myself doing so well

   The correct answer is (B). The possessive pronoun is used with the gerund.

3. She was moved to advice him about his program for the future.

   (A) advice
   (B) council
   (C) revise
   (D) admonish
   (E) advise

   The correct amnswer is (E). This is the verb form meaning *to suggest.* The noun is *advice.*

4. Many women feel that men have been domineering, tyrannical, and <u>they humiliate their wives.</u>

    (A) they humiliate their wives.
    (B) humiliating toward there wives.
    (C) humiliating toward their wives.
    (D) humility toward their wives.
    (E) humiliate their wives.

The correct answer is (C). This choice retains the parallelism—*domineering, tyrannical,* and *humiliating.*

5. It is discouraging to read about so much crime, <u>poverty, and degradation. And war too.</u>

    (A) poverty, and degradation. And war too.
    (B) And also warfare.
    (C) And war also.
    (D) poverty, degradation, and war.
    (E) and poverty and degradation and war.

The correct answer is (D). This is an example of parallel structure. In addition, *and war too* is not a sentence.

6. I told you that a baseball team <u>is comprised of</u> nine players.

    (A) is comprised of
    (B) comprises
    (C) was comprised of
    (D) consists
    (E) is consisted of

The correct answer is (B). *Comprises* means "is made up of."

7. Their manner of speech is forthright, candid, and <u>right on.</u>

    (A) right on
    (B) with it
    (C) sharp
    (D) nitty-gritty
    (E) precise

The correct answer is (E). The original, choice (A), and choices (B) through (D) all indicate slang expressions. These are unsuitable in this sentence.

8. He awakened early in the morning, and then he showered, and then he left.

   (A) He awakened early in the morning, and then he showered, and then he left.

   (B) He awakened early in the morning. And then he showered, and then he left.

   (C) He awakened early in the morning, Then he showered and left.

   (D) He awakened early in the morning after showering, and then he left.

   (E) He awakened early in the morning, showered, and left.

The correct answer is (E). This correction avoids the awkward repetition of the original.

9. His shyness made it impossible for him to step forward <u>to except</u> the prize.

   (A) to except

   (B) to accept

   (C) accepting

   (D) expecting

   (E) to expect

The correct answer is (B). *Accept* means *to receive*; *except* means *to omit*.

10. Feeling it was shameful, their action was deplored by all.

   (A) Feeling it was shameful, their action was deplored by all.

   (B) Their action was deplored shamefully by all.

   (C) Their action, feeling it was shameful, they all deplored it.

   (D) Feeling their action was shameful, all deplored it.

   (E) Their action, feeling it was shameful, was deplored.

The correct answer is (D). This corrects the dangling participle.

SENTENCE CORRECTION PRACTICE

1. There is a possibility of him being barred from practice.

    (A) of him being barred
    (B) of he being barred
    (C) of his barring
    (D) that his being barred
    (E) of his being barred

2. When a poor woman came to them, she was always given help.

    (A) she was always given help.
    (B) she always helped.
    (C) she always gave.
    (D) they were always given help.
    (E) they were always helped.

3. In accordance to the rules, smoking is prohibited.

    (A) In accordance to
    (B) According with
    (C) In accordance with
    (D) In accord to
    (E) Accordingly

4. No one, including Steve and me, have a greater right than he to be president.

    (A) including Steve and me, have a greater right than he
    (B) including Steve and I, have a greater right than he
    (C) including Steve and me, has a greater right than he
    (D) including Steve and me, has a greater right than him
    (E) including Steve and I, has a greater right than him

5. However much we tried the motor would not start.

    (A) However much we tried the motor
    (B) However much we tried; the motor
    (C) However much we tried, The motor
    (D) However much we tried, the motor
    (E) However much we tried and the motor

6. Discretion involves the idea of choice, the exercise of will, and judging fairly.

    (A) the idea of choice, the exercise of will, and judging fairly.
    (B) the idea of choice, the exercise of will, and the practice of fair judgment.
    (C) the idea of choice; the exercise of will; and judging fairly.
    (D) choice ideas, willing exercise, and fair judgment.
    (E) the idea of choice, the exercise of will and judging fairly.

7. The climax of the play <u>occurs when the villain admitted</u> his crime.

    (A) occurs when the villain admitted
    (B) is when the villain admitted
    (C) occurred when the villain admits
    (D) occurs—when the villain admits
    (E) occurs when the villain admits

8. <u>The storm having stopped, the ship</u> regained its balance.

    (A) The storm having stopped, the ship
    (B) Having stopped, the ship
    (C) The storm having stopped, it
    (D) The storm having stopped; the ship
    (E) It having stopped, it

9. <u>David Edelson, the famous surgeon</u> is also a practicing attorney.

    (A) David Edelson, the famous surgeon
    (B) David Edelson, the famous surgeon,
    (C) David Edelson the famous surgeon
    (D) David Edelson the famous surgeon,
    (E) David Edelson is the famous surgeon

10. <u>Each of the students have</u> passed the GMAT.

    (A) Each of the students have
    (B) Each of the students has
    (C) Each, of the students, has
    (D) Each, of the students, have
    (E) Each of the passing students have

11. <u>Legal terminology is confusing, being unable</u> to memorize the necessary definitions.

    (A) Legal terminology is confusing, being unable
    (B) Legal terminology confuses me, I am unable
    (C) Legal terminology is confusing because I am unable
    (D) Being that legal terminology is confusing, I am unable
    (E) Legal terminology is confusing and being unable

12. The student was <u>bright however he</u> failed the test.

    (A) bright however he
    (B) bright, however he
    (C) bright however; he
    (D) bright; however, he
    (E) bright. however, he

13. <u>There was such a crowd that she could not find her parents.</u>

    (A) There was such a crowd that she could not find her parents.
    (B) There was such a crowd; that she could not find her parents.
    (C) There was such a crowd. That she could not find her parents.
    (D) There was such a crowd and that she could not find her parents.
    (E) There was such a crowd because she could not find her parents.

14. A serf's economic position <u>was comparable to a slave.</u>

    (A) was comparable to a slave.
    (B) was a slave.
    (C) was comparable with a slave.
    (D) was as comparable to a slave.
    (E) was comparable to a slave's.

15. The boy felt <u>he should of come.</u>

    (A) he should of come.
    (B) , he should of come.
    (C) , he should have come.
    (D) he should have come.
    (E) he should have came.

16. No sooner had the class begun <u>than Will started laughing.</u>

    (A) than Will started laughing.
    (B) when Will started laughing.
    (C) and Will started laughing.
    (D) then Will started laughing.
    (E) but Will started laughing.

17. The term expresses a formula containing three elements, consisting <u>of amount charged *a percentage*,</u> the amount loaned, and the time.

    (A) of amount charged *a percentage*,
    (B) with amount charged (a percentage),
    (C) of the amount charged (a percentage),
    (D) of charging an amount of percentage,
    (E) a percentage,

18. The court system <u>should resolve cases more rapidly and with greater economy.</u>

    (A) should resolve cases more rapidly and with greater economy.
    (B) should resolve cases more rapidly and more economically.
    (C) should resolve rapid and economic cases.
    (D) should resolve cases, more rapidly and with greater economy.
    (E) should resolve cases with speed and economically.

19. I had meant during the afternoon to call on him.

   (A) I had meant during the afternoon to call on him.
   (B) I had meant, during the afternoon, to call on him.
   (C) During the afternoon, I had meant to call on him.
   (D) I had meant to call him.
   (E) I had meant to call on him during the afternoon.

20. All the raincoats are waterproof.

   (A) All the raincoats are waterproof.
   (B) All the foregoing types of raincoats have the property of being waterproof.
   (C) All these raincoats have waterproof properties.
   (D) The properties of waterproof qualities are found in all these categories of raincoats.
   (E) Water-repellent raincoats are waterproof.

21. They gave presents to the top graduating seniors, Dave and I.

   (A) , Dave and I.
   (B) , Dave and myself.
   (C) , me and Dave.
   (D) , Dave and me.
   (E) among which were Dave and me.

22. Although she has two Ph.D.'s, her I's are illegible and her miss's look like mess's.

   (A) Ph.D.'s, her I's are illegible and her miss's look like mess's.
   (B) Ph.D.'s, her I's are illegible and her miss s look like messs.
   (C) Ph.D.es, her I'es are illegible and her misses look like messes.
   (D) Ph.D.s, her Is are illegible and her miss's look like mess's.
   (E) Ph.D.s, her Is are illegible and her miss s look like mess s.

23. She had laid the book aside because she wanted to lie in the sun.

   (A) had laid the book aside because she wanted to lie
   (B) had laid the book aside because she wanted to lay
   (C) had lain the book aside because she wanted to lie
   (D) had lain the book aside because she wanted to lay
   (E) had lied the book aside because she wanted to laid

24. <u>There were three guests, Mark, an actor, Emily, a dancer, and Dave, a musician.</u>

   (A) There were three guests, Mark, an actor, Emily, a dancer, and Dave, a musician.

   (B) There were three guests: Mark, an actor; Emily, a dancer; and Dave, a musician.

   (C) There were three guests: Mark an actor, Emily a dancer, and Dave a musician.

   (D) There were three other guests: Mark, an actor, Emily, a dancer, and Dave, a musician.

   (E) There were three guests: Mark; an actor, Emily; a dancer, and Dave; a musician.

25. <u>I told them I had been there only once or twice before.</u>

   (A) I told them I had been there only once or twice before.
   (B) I am there before once.
   (C) I was once or twice there I told them.
   (D) Once or twice I told them I was there.
   (E) I was there I told them once or twice before.

26. <u>The bridge towered above them in their car.</u>

   (A) The bridge towered above them in their car.
   (B) They could see the bridge towering above them in their car.
   (C) In their car the bridge towered above them.
   (D) From their car, they could see the bridge towering above them.
   (E) Towering above them in their car was the bridge.

27. <u>Being the girl of my dreams, I am sure she will marry me.</u>

   (A) Being the girl of my dreams, I am sure she will marry me.
   (B) She, being the girl of my dreams, will surely marry me.
   (C) I am sure she will marry me, being the girl of my dreams.
   (D) I am sure she will marry the girl of my dreams.
   (E) I, being the girl of my dreams, am sure she will marry me.

28. It is many years <u>since I see</u> such good playing.

   (A) since I see
   (B) since I will have seen
   (C) since I've seen
   (D) since I'd seen
   (E) since I will see

29. Before I left, I have told them to close the door.

    (A) I have told
    (B) I am telling
    (C) I tell
    (D) I told
    (E) I had told

30. From the very beginning, thinking as they did, are wrong.

    (A) From the very beginning, thinking as they did, are wrong.
    (B) They are wrong, thinking as they did from the very beginning.
    (C) From the very beginning, thinking as they did, is wrong.
    (D) From the very beginning, thinking as they did, they were wrong.
    (E) They, thinking from the very beginning as they did, are wrong.

31. Founded in the nineteenth century, the City University.

    (A) Founded in the nineteenth century, the City University.
    (B) The City University was founded in the nineteenth century.
    (C) The City University, found in the nineteenth century.
    (D) In the nineteenth century, founded the City University.
    (E) The City University, founded in the nineteenth century.

32. Rudyard Kipling, the famous British author, writing in the 1900s.

    (A) Rudyard Kipling, the famous author, writing in the 1900s.
    (B) Rudyard Kipling, the famous British author, written in the 1900s.
    (C) Writing in the 1900s, Rudyard Kipling, the famous British author.
    (D) In the 1900s, the famous British author, Rudyard Kipling.
    (E) Rudyard Kipling, the famous British author, wrote in the 1900s.

Quick Score Answers

1. E	7. E	13. A	18. B	23. A	28. C
2. A	8. A	14. E	19. E	24. B	29. E
3. C	9. B	15. D	20. A	25. A	30. D
4. C	10. B	16. A	21. D	26. D	31. B
5. D	11. C	17. C	22. A	27. B	32. E
6. B	12. D				

ANSWERS AND EXPLANATIONS

SENTENCE CORRECTION REVIEW

1. **The correct answer is (E).** A pronoun preceding a gerund (an *ing* verb used as a noun) must be in the possessive case. Choice (C) changes the meaning of the sentence. Choice (D) introduces the relative pronoun *that* incorrectly because there is no subordinate clause that follows.

2. **The correct answer is (A).** The meaning is clear. The poor woman was given help. In the other choices, the meaning of the sentence is changed.

3. **The correct answer is (C).** The correct idiomatic expression is *in accordance with*.

4. **The correct answer is (C).** This is the only choice that corrects the following errors: *no one* is a singular subject and must use the singular verb *has*. *Including* is a preposition and takes the objective form *me*. *He* must be used as the subject of the understood verb *has*.

5. **The correct answer is (D).** The subordinate clause, when preceding the main clause, must be separated by a comma. All the other choices use incorrect separations between the subordinate clause *however much we tried* and the main clause *the motor would not start*.

6. **The correct answer is (B).** It supplies parallel structure among the stated elements of discretion. In choice (C), the semicolon is used incorrectly. In choice (D), the meaning of the sentence is changed. In choice (E), although the punctuation is correct, the structure is not parallel.

7. **The correct answer is (E).** Since both verbs (*occurs* and *admits*) should be in the present tense. Choice (B) uses the verb *is*, which is idiomatically incorrect. Choice (D) incorrectly uses the dash in the middle of the sentence.

8. **The correct answer is (A).** *Storm* and *ship* are correctly used as subjects. The meaning is clear. In choice (B), the meaning is changed. In choice (C), the pronoun *it* does not have a logical antecedent. The use of the semicolon is incorrect in choice (D). In choice (E), the use of *it* is unclear.

9. **The correct answer is (B).** An appositive is separated from the rest of the sentence by commas. In this sentence, *the famous surgeon* is the appositive. Choices (C) and (D) use only one comma. Choice (E) has two predicates without any conjunction.

10. **The correct answer is (B).** *Each* is singular and must take a singular verb. Choice (C) and (D) use the commas incorrectly. Choice (E) changes the meaning of the sentence.

11. **The correct answer is (C).** It replaces the dangling participle *being unable* with a subordinate clause. Choice (B) is a run-on sentence. In choice (D), *being that* is an incorrect beginning. Choice (E) still contains the same dangling participle as the original sentence.

12. **The correct answer is (D).** This choice separates the two independent clauses by a semicolon and places a comma after the introductory word *however*. Choices (A) and (B) are run-on sentences. Choice (C) misplaces the semicolon. Choice (E) has a period but does not use a capital to begin the new sentence.

13. **The correct answer is (A).** Choice (B) uses the semicolon incorrectly. Choice (C) forms two sentence fragments. In choice (D), *and that* is incorrect. Choice (E) changes the meaning of the sentence.

14. **The correct answer is (E).** The elliptical *economic position* makes it necessary to use 's after *slave*. The *economic position* is being compared. In choice (B), the comparison is unclear. In choice (C), *comparable with* is idiomatically incorrect. In choice (D), the addition of *as*, which is a conjunction, is incorrect.

15. **The correct answer is (D).** The correct form is *should have*. *Of* can't be used as an auxiliary verb. In choices (B) and (C), the comma is used incorrectly. In choice (E), the incorrect past participle (came) is used.

16. **The correct answer is (A).** The only correct construction is *No sooner . . . than . . .*

17. **The correct answer is (C).** *A percentage* should be set off within parentheses. Choice (A) uses an incorrect idiom, *consisting with*. In choice (D), *charging an amount* could not be an element. Choice (E) does not give a complete description.

18. **The correct answer is (B).** It balances two adjectives (*rapidly* and *economically*). In choice (A), there is no parallel structure because an adjective, *more rapidly*, is used with a phrase, *with greater economy*. Choice (C) changes the meaning of the sentence. Choice (D) misuses the comma. Choice (E) contains the same type of error as choice (A).

19. **The correct answer is (E).** The phrase *during the afternoon* is placed so that the meaning of the sentence is clear. Choice (B) uses commas incorrectly. Choice (C) misplaces the phrases. Choice (D) omits the phrase and changes the meaning of the sentence.

20. **The correct answer is (A).** It is a simple, concise, and correct statement. Choices (B), (C), and (D) are all wordy, repetitive, and awkward sentences. Choice (E) changes the meaning of the sentence.

21. **The correct answer is (D).** The antecedent of *me* is *seniors*, which is the object of the preposition *to*. *Me* is correct because it is in the objective case. In choice (B), the reflexive pronoun *myself* is incorrect. In choice (C), the speaker incorrectly mentions himself before Dave. In choice (E), *which* is incorrectly used to refer to people.

22. **The correct answer is (A).** It is the only choice that follows this rule: Use an apostrophe (') and *s* to form the plural of abbreviations followed by periods (*Ph.D.'s*), of letter (*I's*), and of words referred to as words (*miss's* and *mess's*).

23. **The correct answer is (A).** *Laid* is the past participle of the transitive verb *to lay*. It takes an object. *To lie* is intransitive and does not take an object. All the other choices use incorrect verb forms.

24. **The correct answer is (B).** A semicolon is used to separate a series of items that contain commas. The series is introduced by a colon. The other colons do not correctly use the marks of punctuation.

25. **The correct answer is (A).** The sentence should be *past tense* and *past perfect* to indicate two actions in the past, one preceding the other.

26. **The correct answer is (D).** This is a misplaced modifier. Obviously, the bridge was not in their car.

27. **The correct answer is (B).** The dangling participle is corrected by this answer.

28. **The correct answer is (C).** The present perfect tense is needed.

29. **The correct answer is (E).** The sequence of *past tense* and *past perfect* is correct.

30. **The correct answer is (D).** Two elements are involved here—keeping the tenses consistently *in the past* and eliminating the dangling participle.

31. **The correct answer is (B).** This is the only complete sentence.

32. **The correct answer is (E).** This is the only choice that is a complete sentence.

Unit 2

BASIC GRAMMAR STRATEGIES

PARTS OF SPEECH

NOUN

A NOUN is the name of a person, place, or thing.

actor, city, lamp

There are three kinds of nouns, categorized according to the type of person, place, or thing that the noun names.

1. A *common* noun refers to a general type: *girl, park, army*.

2. A *proper* noun refers to a particular person, place, or thing, and always begins with a capital letter: *Mary, Central Park, U.S. Army*.

3. A *collective* noun signifies a number of individuals organized into one group: *team, crowd, Congress*.

Singular/Plural

Every noun has number. That means that every noun is either singular or plural. Singular means only one; plural means more than one. There are four ways to form the plurals of nouns:

1. by adding *s* to the singular (*horses, kites, rivers*)

2. by adding *es* to the singular (*buses, churches, dishes, boxes, buzzes*)

3. by changing the singular (*man* becomes *men, woman* becomes *women, child* becomes *children, baby* becomes *babies, alumnus* becomes *alumni*)

4. by leaving the singular as it is (*moose, deer,* and *sheep* are all plural as well as singular)

Note: When forming the plural of letters and numbers, add 's: A's, 150's. Otherwise, *s* denotes possession.

Case

Nouns also have case, which indicates the function of the noun in the sentence. There are three cases—the nominative case, the objective case, and the possessive case.

1. Nominative case

A noun is in the nominative case when it is the subject of a sentence: The *book* fell off the table. The *boys* and *girls* ran outside.

The subject of a sentence is the person, place, or thing that the sentence is about. Thus, "The *book* fell off the table" is about the book.

A noun is in the nominative case when it is a predicate noun. This is a noun used after a linking verb. In such cases, the predicate noun means the same as the subject.

Einstein was a *scientist*. (Einstein = scientist)

Judith was a brilliant *scholar* and gifted *teacher*. (Judith = scholar and teacher)

A noun is in the nominative case when it is used in direct address. A noun in direct address shows that someone or something is being spoken to directly. This noun is set off by commas.

Claudel, please answer the phone.

Go home, *Fido*, before you get hit by a car.

A noun is in the nominative case when it is a nominative absolute. This is a noun with a participle (see Verbs) that stands as an independent idea but is part of a sentence.

The *rain* having stopped, we went out to play.

The *bike* having crashed, the race was stopped.

A noun is in the nominative case when it is a nominative in apposition. This is one of a pair of nouns. Both nouns are equal in meaning and are next to one another. The noun in apposition is set off from the rest of the sentence by commas.

Steve, my *son*, is going to college.

That man is Syd, the *musician*.

2. Objective case

A noun is in the objective case when it is the direct object of a verb. A direct object is the receiver of the action of a verb. A verb that has a direct object is called a transitive verb.

The team elected *David*.

The team won the *game*.

A noun is in the objective case when it is the indirect object of a verb. This is a noun that shows *to* whom or *for* whom the action is taking place. The words *to* and *for* may not actually appear in the sentence, but they are understood. An indirect object must be with a direct object.

Pedro threw *Mario* the ball. (Pedro threw the ball to Mario.)

Anya bought her *mother* a gift. (Anya bought a gift for her mother.)

A noun is in the objective case when it is an objective complement. An objective complement is a noun that explains the direct object. The word *complement* indicates that this noun *completes* the meaning of the direct object.

The team elected Terry *captain*.

A noun is in the objective case when it is an objective by apposition. An objective by apposition is very much like a nominative in apposition. Again, we have a pair of nouns that are equal in meaning and are next to one another. The noun in apposition explains the other noun, but now the noun being explained is in the objective case. Therefore, the noun in apposition is called the objective by apposition. The objective by apposition is set off from the rest of the sentence by commas.

The bully pushed Steve, the little *toddler*, into the sandbox.

He gave the money to Sam, the *banker*.

A noun is in the objective case when it is an adverbial objective. This is a noun that denotes distance or time.

The storm lasted an *hour*.

The troops walked five *miles*.

A noun is in the objective case when it is an object of a preposition.

The stick fell into the *well*. (*Into* is the preposition.)

The picture fell on the *table*. (*On* is the preposition.)

See the section on prepositions.

3. Possessive case

A noun is in the possessive case when it shows ownership. The correct use of the possessive case is often tested on the exam. The following rules will help you answer such questions correctly.

(A) The possessive case of most nouns is formed by adding an apostrophe (') and *s* to the singular.

the *boy's* book

Emile's coat

(B) If the singular ends in *s,* add either just an apostrophe or an apostrophe plus a final *s.*

the *bus'* wheels; the *bus's* wheels

Charles' books; *Charles's* books

(C) The possessive case of plural nouns ending in *s* is formed by adding just an apostrophe.

the *dogs'* bones

Note: If the dog was singular, the possessive case would be *dog's.*

(D) If the plural noun does not end in *s,* then add an apostrophe and an *s.*

the *children's* toys

the *men's* boots

(E) The possessive case of compound nouns is formed by adding an apostrophe and an *s* to the last word if it is singular, or by adding an *s* and an apostrophe if the word is plural.

my *brother-in-law's* house

my *two brother's* house

(F) To show individual ownership, add an apostrophe and *s* to each owner.

Joe's and *Jim's* boats (Each owns his own boat.)

(G) To show joint ownership, add an apostrophe and *s* to the last name.

Joe and *Jim's* boat (They both own the same boat.)

PRONOUNS

A pronoun is used in place of a noun. The noun for which a pronoun is used is called the *antecedent*. The use of pronouns, particularly the relationship between a pronoun and its antecedent, is one of the most common items found on the test. Always make sure a pronoun has a clear antecedent.

> John had a candy bar and a cookie. He ate *it* quickly. (Ambiguous) (What is the antecedent of *it*—candy bar or cookie?)

> The boy rode his bike through the hedge, *which* was very large. (Ambiguous) (What was very large—the bike or the hedge?)

> The captain was very popular. *They* all like him. (Ambiguous) (Who liked him? *They* has no antecedent.)

There are ten kinds of pronouns.

1. An expletive pronoun

The words *it* and *there* followed by the subject of the sentence are expletive pronouns.

> *There* were only a few tickets left.

> *It* was a long list of chores.

When using an expletive, the verb agrees with the subject.

> There *remains* one *child* on the bus.

> There *remain* many *children* on the bus.

2. An intensive pronoun

This is a pronoun, ending in *self* or *selves*, that follows its antecedent and emphasizes it.

> He *himself* will go.

> The package was delivered to the boys *themselves*.

3. A reflexive pronoun

This is a pronoun, ending in *self* or *selves*, that is usually the object of a verb or preposition or the complement of a verb.

> I hate *myself*.

> They always laugh at *themselves*.

Myself, yourself, himself, herself, and *itself* are all singular. *Ourselves, yourselves*, and *themselves* are all plural. There is NO such pronoun as *hisself* or *theirselves*. Do NOT use *myself* instead of *I* or *me*.

4. A demonstrative pronoun

This is used in place of a noun and points out the noun. Common demonstrative pronouns are *this, that, these*, and *those*.

> I want *those*.

5. An indefinite pronoun

This pronoun refers to any number of persons or objects. Following is a list of some singular and plural indefinite pronouns.

SINGULAR

anybody, anyone, each, everybody, everyone, no one, nobody, none, somebody, someone

PLURAL

all, any, many, several, some

If the singular form is used as a subject, the verb must also be singular.

Everyone of them *sings*. (One person sings.)

If the singular form is used as an antecedent, its pronoun must be singular.

Did *anybody* on any of the teams lose *his* sneakers? (One person lost *his* sneakers.)

6. An interrogative pronoun

This pronoun is used in asking a question. Such pronouns are *who, whose, whom, what,* and *which*. *Whose* shows possession. *Whom* is in the objective case. *Whom* is used ONLY when an object pronoun is needed.

7. A reciprocal pronoun

This pronoun is used when referring to mutual relations. The reciprocal pronouns are *each other* and *one another*.

They love *one another*.

They often visit *each other's* houses.

Note that the possessive is formed by an *'s* after the word *other*.

8. A possessive pronoun

This pronoun refers to a noun that owns something. The possessive pronouns are as follows:

SINGULAR

mine (my), yours, his, hers, its

PLURAL

ours, yours, theirs

Notice that possessive pronouns do not use an *'s*. *It's* means "it is"; *its* denotes possession.

9. A relative pronoun

Nominative case—*who, that, which*

Objective case—*whom, that, which*

Possessive case—*whose*

A relative pronoun used as the *subject* of a dependent clause is in **the nominative** case.

I know *who* stole the car.

Give the prize to *whoever* won it.

A relative pronoun used as the *object* of a dependent clause is in **the objective** case.

He is the thief *whom* I know. (Object of verb *know*)

Note that the difficulty always comes between choosing *who* or *whom*. **Remem**ber that *who* is in the nominative case and is used for the appropriate **situations** discussed under Nominative Case in the section on nouns. *Whom* **is in the** objective case and is used for the appropriate situations discussed **under Objective** Case in the section on nouns.

Who is coming? (*Who* is the subject.)

Whom are you going with? (*Whom* is the object of the preposition *with*.)

The relative pronoun in the possessive case is *whose*. Notice that **there is no** apostrophe in this word. The contraction *who's* means "who is."

I know *whose* book it is. (Denotes possession)

I know *who's* on first base. (*Who's* means "who is.")

10. Personal pronouns

NOMINATIVE CASE

	Singular	Plural
First person	I	we
Second person	you	you
Third person	he, she, it	they

OBJECTIVE CASE

	Singular	Plural
First person	me	us
Second person	you	you
Third person	him, her, it	them

POSSESSIVE CASE

	Singular	Plural
First person	mine (my)	ours (our)
Second person	yours (your)	yours (your)
Third person	his, hers, its (his, her, its)	theirs (their)

Personal pronouns denote what is called *person*. First-person pronouns show the person or thing that is speaking.

> *I* am going. (First person speaking)

Second-person pronouns show the person or thing being spoken to.

> *You* are my friend. (Second person spoken to)

Third-person pronouns show the person or thing being spoken about.

> Bea did not see *her*. (Third person spoken about)

Important for the Exam

Pronouns must agree with their antecedents in person, number, and gender.

1. *Who* refers to persons only.

2. *Which* refers to animals or objects.

3. *That* refers to persons, animals, or objects.

   I don't know *who* the actor is. (Person)

   They missed their dog, *who* died. (Animal)

   I finished the book, *which* you recommended. (Object)

   They are the people *that* started the fight. (Person)

   That is the tiger *that* ran loose. (Animal)

   The light *that* failed was broken. (Object)

Singular indefinite antecedents always take a singular pronoun.

> *Everyone* of the girls lost *her* hat.

> *None* of the boys lost *his*.

> *Someone* left *his* bike outside.

Collective singular nouns take singular pronouns; collective plural nouns take plural pronouns.

> The *choir* sang *its* part beautifully.

> The *choirs* sang *their* parts beautifully.

Two or more antecedents joined by *and* take a plural pronoun.

> Dave *and* Steve lost *their* way.

Two or more singular antecedents joined by *or* or *nor* take a singular pronoun.

> Tanya *or* Charita may use *her* ball.

> Neither Tanya *nor* Charita may use *her* ball.

If two antecedents are joined by *or* or *nor* and if one is plural and the other is singular, the pronoun agrees in number with the nearer antecedent.

> Neither the *ball* nor the *rackets* were in *their* place.

Case

Remember that pronouns must also be in the correct case.

1. A pronoun must be in the nominative case when it is the subject of a sentence.

   > James and *I* went to the airport.

   > *We* freshmen helped the seniors.

   > Peter calls her more than *I* do.

   Peter calls her more than *I*. (Here, the verb *do* is understood, and *I* is the subject of the understood verb *do*.)

2. A pronoun is in objective case when it is a direct object of the verb.

   > Leaving James and *me*, they ran away.

   > John hit *them*.

   > The freshmen helped *us* seniors.

   A pronoun is the in the objective case when it is the indirect object of a verb.

   > Give *us* the ball.

3. A pronoun is in the objective case when it is an object of a preposition.

   to Ben and *me*

   with Sheila and *her*

   between you and *them*

4. A pronoun is in the possessive case when it shows ownership.

   Her car broke down.

   Theirs did also.

A pronoun is in the possessive case when it appears before a gerund (see Verbs).

   His going was a sad event.

For a more detailed analysis of the three cases, see the section on Cases of nouns.

ADJECTIVES

An adjective describes or modifies a noun or a pronoun. An adjective usually answers the question *which one?* Or *what kind?* Or *how many?* There are a number of types of adjectives you should know.

1. Articles (*a, an, the*)

   An article must agree in number with the noun or pronoun it modifies.

   a boy

   an apple

   the girls

   If the noun or pronoun begins with a consonant, use *a*. If the noun or pronoun begins with a vowel, use *an*.

   a pear

   an orange

2. Limiting adjectives point out definite nouns or tell how many there are.

   Those books belong to John.

   The *three* boys didn't see *any* birds.

3. Descriptive adjectives describe or give a quality of the noun or pronoun they modify.

   the *large* chair

   the *sad* song

4. Possessive, demonstrative, and indefinite adjectives look like the pronouns of the same name. However, the adjective does not stand alone. It describes a noun or pronoun.

   This is *mine*. (demonstrative and possessive pronouns)

   This book is *my* father's. (demonstrative and possessive adjectives)

5. Interrogative and relative adjectives look the same, but they function differently. Interrogative adjectives ask questions.

    Which way should I go?

    Whose book is this?

    What time is John coming?

    Relative adjectives join two clauses and modify some word in the dependent clause.

    I don't know *whose* book it is.

Important for the Exam

An adjective is used as a predicative adjective after a linking verb. If the modifier is describing the verb (a nonlinking verb), an adverb must be used.

The boy is *happy*. (adjective)

Joe appeared *angry*. (adjective)

The soup tasted *spicy*. (adjective)

Joe looked *angrily* at the dog. (adverb—*angrily* modifies *looked*)

Positive, Comparative, and Superlative Adjectives

1. The positive degree states the quality of an object.

2. The comparative degree compares two things. It is formed by using *less* or *more* or adding *-er* to the positive.

3. The superlative degree compares three or more things. It is formed by using *least* or *most* or adding *-est* to the positive.

Positive	Comparative	Superlative
easy	easier; more easy; less easy	easiest; most easy; least easy
pretty	prettier; more pretty; less pretty	prettiest; least pretty; most pretty

Do Not Use Two Forms Together

She is the most prettiest. (Incorrect)

She is the prettiest. (Correct)

She is the most pretty. (Correct)

VERBS

A verb denotes either action or a state of being. There are four major types of verbs: transitive, intransitive, linking, and auxiliary.

1. Transitive verbs are action words that must take a direct object. The direct object, which receives the action of the verb, is in the objective case.

   Joe *hit* the ball. (*Ball* is the direct object of *hit*.)

   Joe *kissed* Helen. (*Helen* is the direct object of *kissed*.)

2. Intransitive verbs denote action but do not take a direct object.

   The glass *broke*.

   The boy *fell*.

Important for the Exam

Set, *lay*, and *raise* are always transitive and take an object. *Sit, lie*, and *rise* are always intransitive and do NOT take a direct object.

Set the book down, *lay* the pencil down, and *raise* your hands. (*Book, pencil*, and *hands* are direct objects of *set, lay*, and *raise*.)

Sit in the chair.

She *lies* in bed all day.

The sun also *rises*.

The same verb can be transitive or intransitive, depending on the sentence.

The pitcher *threw* wildly. (Intransitive)

The pitcher *threw* the ball wildly. (Transitive)

3. Linking verbs have no action. They denote a state of being. Linking verbs mean "equal." Here are some examples: *is, are, was, were, be, been, am* (any form of the verb *to be*), *smell, taste, feel, look, seem, become, appear.*

Sometimes, these verbs are confusing because they can be linking verbs in one sentence and action verbs in another. You can tell if the verb is a linking verb if it means "equal" in the sentence.

He felt nervous. (*He* equals *nervous.*)

He felt nervously for the door bell. (*He* does not equal *door bell.*)

Linking verbs take a predicate nominative or predicate adjective. (See sections on Nouns, Pronouns, and Adjectives.)

It *is I.*

It *is she.*

4. Auxiliary verbs are sometimes called "helping" verbs. These verbs are used with an infinitive verb (*to* plus the verb) or a participle to form a verb phrase.

The common auxiliary verbs are:

all forms of *to be, to have, to do, to keep*

the verbs *can, may, must, ought to, shall, will, would, should*

He *has to go*. (auxiliary *has* plus the infinitive *to go*)

He *was going*. (auxiliary *was* plus the present participle *going*)

He *has gone*. (auxiliary *has* plus the past participle *gone*)

There is no such form as *had ought*. Use *ought to have* or *should have*.

He *ought to have gone*.

He *should have gone*.

Every verb can change its form according to five categories. Each category adds meaning to the verb. The five categories are: *tense, mood, voice, number*, and *person*.

Tense

This indicates the *time*, or *when*, the verb occurs. There are six tenses. They are:

present	past	future
present perfect	past perfect	future perfect

Three principal parts of the verb—the present, the past, and the past participle—are used to form all the tenses.

The *present tense* shows that the action is taking place in the present.

The dog *sees* the car and *jumps* out of the way.

The present tense of a regular verb looks like this:

	Singular	Plural
First person	I jump	We jump
Second person	You jump	You jump
Third person	He, she, it jumps	They jump

Notice that an *s* is added to the third-person singular.

The *past tense* shows that the action took place in the past.

The dog *saw* the car and *jumped* out of the way.

The past tense of a regular verb looks like this:

	Singular	Plural
First person	I jumped	We jumped
Second person	You jumped	You jumped
Third person	He, she, it jumped	They jumped

Notice that *-ed* is added to the verb. Sometimes just *-d* is added, as in the verb *used*, for example. In regular verbs, the past participle has the same form as the past tense, but it is used with an auxiliary verb.

The dog *had jumped*.

The *future tense* shows that the action is going to take place in the future. The future tense needs the auxiliary verbs *will* or *shall*.

The dog *will see* the car and *will jump* out of the way.

The future tense of a regular verb looks like this:

	Singular	Plural
First person	I shall jump	We shall jump
Second person	You will jump	You will jump
Third person	He, she, it will jump	They will jump

Notice that *shall* is used in the first person of the future tense.

To form the three *perfect tenses,* the verb *to have* and the past participle are used.

- The present tense of *to have* is used to form the *present perfect*.

    The dog *has seen* the car and *has jumped* out of the way.

The present perfect tense shows that the action has started in the past and is continuing or has just been implemented in the present.

- The past tense of *to have* is used to form the *past perfect*.

    The dog *had seen* the car and *had jumped* out of the way.

The past perfect tense shows that the action had been completed in the past.

- The future tense of *to have* is used to form the *future perfect*.

    The dog *will have seen* the car and *will have jumped* out of the way.

The future perfect tense shows that an action will have been completed before a definite time in the future.

The following table shows the present, past, and future tenses of *to have*.

PRESENT TENSE

	Singular	Plural
First person	I have	We have
Second person	You have	You have
Third person	He, she, it has	They have

PAST TENSE

	Singular	Plural
First person	I had	We had
Second person	You had	You had
Third person	He, she, it had	They had

FUTURE TENSE

	Singular	Plural
First person	I shall have	We shall have
Second person	You will have	You shall have
Third person	He, she, it will have	They shall have

The perfect tenses all use the past participle. Therefore, you must know the past participle of all the verbs. As we said, the past participle usually is formed by adding *-d* or *-ed* to the verb. However, there are many irregular verbs. Following is a table of the principal forms of some irregular verbs.

PRESENT	PAST	PAST PARTICIPLE
arise	arose	arisen
awake	awoke, awaked	awoke, awaked, awakened
awaken	awakened	awakened
be	was	been
bear	bore	borne
beat	beat	beaten
become	became	become
begin	began	begun
bend	bent	bent
bet	bet	bet
bid (command)	bade, bid	bidden, bid
bind	bound	bound
bite	bit	bitten
bleed	bled	bled
blow	blew	blown
break	broke	broken
bring	brought	brought
build	built	built
burn	burned, burnt	burned, burnt
burst	burst	burst
buy	bought	bought
catch	caught	caught

PRESENT	PAST	PAST PARTICIPLE
choose	chose	chosen
come	came	come
cost	cost	cost
dig	dug	dug
dive	dived, dove	dived
do	did	done
draw	drew	drawn
dream	dreamed, dreamt	dreamed, dreamt
drink	drank	drunk
drive	drove	driven
eat	ate	eaten
fall	fell	fallen
fight	fought	fought
fit	fitted	fitted
fly	flew	flown
forget	forgot	forgotten, forgot
freeze	froze	frozen
get	got	got, gotten
give	gave	given
go	went	gone
grow	grew	grown
hang (kill)	hanged	hanged
hang (suspended)	hung	hung
hide	hid	hidden
hold	held	held
know	knew	known
lay	laid	laid
lead	led	led
lend	lent	lent
lie (recline)	lay	lain
lie (untruth)	lied	lied
light	lit	lit
pay	paid	paid
raise (take up)	raised	raised
read	read	read
rid	rid	rid
ride	rode	ridden
ring	rang	rung
rise (go up)	rose	risen
run	ran	run
saw (cut)	sawed	sawed
say	said	said
see	saw	seen
set	set	set
shake	shook	shaken
shine (light)	shone	shone

PRESENT	PAST	PAST PARTICIPLE
shine (to polish)	shined	shined
show	showed	shown
shrink	shrank	shrunk, shrunken
sing	sang	sung
sit	sat	sat
slay	slew	slain
speak	spoke	spoken
spend	spent	spent
spit	spat, spit	spat, spit
spring	sprang	sprung
stand	stood	stood
steal	stole	stolen
swear	swore	sworn
swim	swam	swum
swing	swung	swung
take	took	taken
teach	taught	taught
tear	tore	torn
throw	threw	thrown
wake	waked, woke	waked, woken
wear	wore	worn
weave	wove, weaved	woven, weaved
weep	wept	wept
win	won	won
write	wrote	written

Another aspect of tense that appears on the test is the *correct sequence* or *order of tenses*. Be sure if you change tense, you know why you are doing so. Following are some rules to help you.

- When using the perfect tenses remember:

    - The present perfect tense goes with the present tense.

            present
        As Dave *steps* up to the mound, the

            present perfect
        pitcher *has thrown* the ball to first

            present perfect
        and I *have caught* it.

- The past perfect tense goes with the past tense.

    past
    Before Dave *stepped* up to the

    past perfect
    mound, the pitcher *had thrown* the

    past perfect
    ball to first and I *had caught* it.

- The future perfect goes with the future tense.

    future
    Before Dave *will step* up to the

    future perfect
    mound, the pitcher *will have thrown*

    future perfect
    the ball to first and I *shall have caught* it.

- The present participle (verb + *ing*) is used when its action occurs at the same time as the action of the main verb.

    John, *answering* the bell, *knocked* over the plant. (*Answering* and *knocked* occur at the same time.)

- The past participle is used when its action occurs before the main verb.

    The elves, *dressed* in costumes, will *march* proudly to the shoemaker. (The elves dressed *before* they will march.)

Mood

The mood or mode of a verb shows that the manner of the action. There are three moods.

1. The *indicative mood* shows that the sentence is factual. Most of what we say is in the indicative mode.

2. The *subjunctive mood* is used for conditions contrary to fact or for strong desires. The use of the subjunctive mood for the verb *to be* is a TEST ITEM.

Following is the conjugation (list of forms) of the verb *to be* in the subjunctive mood.

PRESENT

	Singular	Plural
First person	I be	We be
Second person	You be	You be
Third person	He, she, it be	They be

PAST TENSE

First person	I were	We were
Second person	You were	You were
Third person	He, she, it were	They were

If I *be* wrong, then punish me.

If he *were* king, he would pardon me.

Also, *shall* and *should* are used for the subjunctive mood.

If he *shall* fail, he will cry.

If you *should* win, don't forget us.

3. The *imperative mood* is used for commands.

Go at once!

If strong feelings are expressed, the command ends in an exclamation point. In commands, the subject "you" is not stated but is understood.

Voice

There are two voices of verbs. The active voice shows that the subject is acting upon something or doing something *to* something else. The active voice has a direct object.

    subject   object
The *car* hit the *boy*.

The passive voice shows that the subject is acted upon *by* something. Something was done *to* the subject. The direct object becomes the subject. The verb *to be* plus the past participle is used in the passive voice.

    subject
The *boy* was hit by the car.

Number

This, as before, means singular or plural. A verb must agree with its subject in number.

> The *list was* long. (Singular)

> The *lists were* long. (Plural)

Nouns appearing between subject and verb do not change subject-verb agreement.

> The *list* of chores *was* long. (Singular)

> The *lists* of chores *were* long. (Plural)

Subjects joined by *and* are singular if the subject is one person or unit.

> My *friend and colleague has* decided to leave. (Singular)

> *Five and five is* ten. (Singular)

> *Tea and milk is* my favorite drink. (Singular)

Singular subjects joined by *or, either-or,* and *neither-nor* take singular verbs.

> Either Alvin or Lynette *goes* to the movies.

If one subject is singular and one is plural, the verb agrees with the nearer subject.

> Either Alvin or the girls *go* to the movies.

The use of the expletive pronouns *there* and *it* do not change subject-verb agreement.

> There *is no one* here.

> There *are snakes in* the grass.

> Think: No one is there; snakes are in the grass.

A relative pronoun takes a verb that agrees in number with the pronoun's antecedent.

> It is the *electrician who suggests* new wiring. (Singular)

> It is the *electricians who suggest* new wiring. (Plural)

Singular indefinite pronouns take singular verbs.

> Everybody *buys* tickets.

It is hard to tell if some nouns are singular. Following is a list of tricky nouns that take singular verbs.

Collective nouns—*army, class, committee, team*

Singular nouns in plural form—*news, economics, mathematics, measles, mumps, news, politics*

Titles, although plural in form, refer to a single work—*The New York Times,* Henry James's *The Ambassadors*

The *army is* coming.

News travels fast.

Jaws is a good movie.

Don't (do not) is incorrect for third-person singular. *Doesn't (does not)* is correct.

He *doesn't* agree.

Person

Person, as before, refers to first person (speaking), second person (spoken to), third person (spoken about). A verb must agree with its subject in person.

I study. (First person)

He studies. (Third person)

Intervening nouns or pronouns do not change subject-verb agreement.

He, as well as I, *is* going. (Third person)

If there are two or more subjects joined by *or* or *nor*, the verb agrees with the nearer subject.

Either John or *we are* going. (First-person plural)

ADVERBS

An adverb describes or modifies a verb, an adjective, or another adverb. Adverbs usually answer the questions *why? where? when? how? to what degree?* Many adverbs end in *-ly*. There are two types of adverbs similar in use to the same type of adjective.

- *Interrogative adverbs* ask questions.

  - *Where* are you going?

  - *When* will you be home?

- *Relative adverbs* join two clauses and modify some word in the dependent clause.

  - No liquor is sold *where* I live.

As with adjectives, there are three degrees of comparison for adjectives and a corresponding form for each.

1. The *positive degree* is often formed by adding *-ly* to the adjective.

    She was *angry*. (adjective)

    She screamed *angrily*. (adverb)

2. The *comparative* is formed by using *more* or *less* or adding *-er* to the positive.

3. The *superlative* is formed by using *most* or *least* or adding *-est* to the positive.

Here are two typical adverbs:

POSITIVE DEGREE	COMPARATIVE DEGREE	SUPERLATIVE
easily	easier, more easily, less easily	easiest, most easily, least easily
happily	happier, more happily, less happily	happiest, most happily, least happily

CONJUNCTIONS

Conjunctions connect words, phrases, or clauses. Conjunctions can connect equal parts of speech.

and

but

for

or

Some conjunctions are used in pairs:

either . . . or

neither . . . nor

not only . . . but also

Here are some phrases and clauses using conjunctions:

John *or* Mary (Nouns are connected)

On the wall *and* in the window (Phrases are connected)

Mark had gone *but* I had not. (Clauses are connected)

Either you go *or* I will. (Clauses are connected)

Peterson's GMAT CAT Success

If the conjunction connects two long clauses, a comma is used in front of the coordinating conjunction:

Julio had gone to the game in the afternoon, but Pedro had not.

Some conjunctions are transitional:

therefore

however

moreover

finally

nevertheless

These conjunctions connect the meaning of two clauses or sentences.

Important for the Exam

Do not use *comma splices*. Comma splices occur when one connects two independent clauses with a comma, rather than with a semicolon or with a comma followed by a coordinating conjunction. An independent clause is a clause that can stand alone as a sentence.

His bike was broken; therefore, he could not ride. (Correct)

His bike was broken. Therefore he could not ride. (Correct)

His bike was broken, and, therefore, he could not ride. (Correct)

His bike was broken, therefore, he could not ride. (Incorrect)

He found his wallet, however he still left the auction. (Incorrect)

The last two sentences are comma splices and are incorrect. *Remember, two independent clauses cannot be connected by a comma.*

PREPOSITIONS

A preposition shows the relationship between a noun or pronoun and some other word in the sentence.

The following are all prepositions:

about	of
above	off
across	over
around	through
behind	to
beneath	under
during	up
for	upon
in	within
inside	without
into	

Sometimes groups of words are treated as single prepositions. Here are some examples:

> according to
>
> ahead of
>
> in front of
>
> in between

The preposition together with the noun or pronoun it introduces is called a prepositional phrase.

> *under* the table
>
> *in front of* the oil painting
>
> *behind* the glass jar
>
> *along* the waterfront
>
> *beside* the canal

Very often on the test, idiomatic expressions are given that depend upon prepositions to be correct. Following is a list of idioms that shows the correct preposition to use:

> *abhorrence of*: He showed an *abhorrence of* violence.
>
> *abound in* (or *with*): The lake *abounded with* fish.
>
> *accompanied by* (a person): He was *accompanied by* his friend.
>
> *accompanied with*: He *accompanied* his visit *with* a house gift.
>
> *accused by, of*: He was *accused by* a person *of* a crime.
>
> *adept in*: He is *adept in* jogging.
>
> *agree to* (an offer): I *agree to* the terms of the contract.
>
> *agree with* (a person): I *agree with* my son.
>
> *agree upon* (or *on*) (a plan): I *agree upon* that approach to the problem.
>
> *angry at* (a situation): I was *angry at* the delay.
>
> *available for* (a purpose): I am *available for* tutoring.
>
> *available to* (a person): Those machines are *available to* the tenants.
>
> *burden with*: I won't *burden* you *with* my problems.
>
> *centered on* (or *in*): His efforts *centered on* winning.
>
> *compare to* (shows similarity): An orange can be *compared to* a grapefruit.
>
> *compare with* (shows difference): An orange can be *compared with* a desk.

conform to (or *with*): He does not *conform to* the rules.

differ with (an opinion): I *differ with* his judgment.

differ from (a thing): The boss's car *differs from* the worker's car.

different from: His book is *different from* mine. (Use *different than* with a clause.)

employed at (salary): He is *employed at* $25 a day.

employed in (work): He is *employed in* building houses.

envious of: She is *envious of* her sister.

fearful of: She is *fearful of* thunder.

free of: She will soon be *free of* her burden.

hatred of: He has a *hatred of* violence.

hint at: They *hinted at* a surprise.

identical with: Your dress is *identical with* mine.

independent of: I am *independent of* my parents.

in search of: He went *in search of* truth.

interest in: He was not *interested in* his friends.

jealous of: He was *jealous of* them.

negligent of: He was *negligent of* his responsibilities.

object to: I *object to* waiting so long.

privilege of: He had the *privilege of* being born a millionaire.

proficient in: You will be *proficient in* grammar.

wait for: We will *wait for* them.

wait on (service): The maid *waited on* them.

Like is used as a preposition. He wanted his dog to act *like* Lassie.

Now that you have reviewed the principles of grammar, answering the Sentence Correction Questions should be easier. In the practice section that follows, answer the questions as you would on the actual examination and then check your answers. If you still don't understand the answers, go back to this section and rereview the appropriate material.

Unit 3

READING COMPREHENSION STRATEGIES AND REVIEW

As you work with GMAT practice materials and as you take the actual GMAT test, keep in mind three important principles:

1. RELAX!
2. MAINTAIN A BALANCE.
3. DO WHAT WORKS FOR *YOU*.

Relax!

You have been reading and comprehending for many years in a variety of situations. It is only reasonable to assume that on GMAT day, you will be able to perform.

Maintain a Balance

Although there will be only 8 Reading Comprehension questions on the Verbal Ability portion of the test, you cannot be leisurely about reading the material. However, it also doesn't make sense to rush through the work just to finish. Your job is to establish a rate-to-results ratio that seems best for you. That's one of the purposes of this unit—to help you maintain this balance. There are a total of 28 questions in this part of the test, and as we said earlier in this book, the better you do on the earlier questions, the better your final score will be. Therefore, move quickly, but don't rush, especially not at the risk of being inaccurate.

Do What Works for You

No one can dictate exactly what you, a unique individual, must do to achieve the best balance of efficiency and accuracy of results. Use the practice materials as a trial-and-error experiment to determine a pace and approaches that work for you. Don't try to force yourself to adopt reading approaches that cause you to think more about them (the approaches) than the real task (the test). Some approaches may simply be mismatches with your own reading styles and/or personality patterns. *There is not just one way to succeed; there are many ways.*

Read the questions carefully. No points are given for the "right answer" to a question that no one asked you.

Be calm when reading the question. If you don't understand it, read it again. Read all answer choices before selecting one. Unless you are *positive* of your choice, return to the passage to double-check.

The following suggestions have been helpful to students in multiple-choice situations.

THE 1-MINUTE OVERVIEW: LOOK OVER YOUR MAP

Let's say you are driving from New York to Los Angeles and need to arrive as soon as possible. You would not leave without taking a look at your map. Exactly what you focus your attention on on the map would be determined by the nature of your journey and the time you had available to browse. Much of the information available on the map would be irrelevant in view of your purpose. You would not, for example, spend time contemplating the size of the population of Houston and comparing it to the size of the population of Phoenix if what you really wanted was a general idea of how to get to Los Angeles.

The purpose of your first glance at the map is to determine the magnitude and general direction of your travel. As you glance, you might happen to notice a few other details that do not distract you from your general purpose.

OVERVIEWING YOUR READING TASK IS LIKE YOUR FIRST GLANCE AT THE MAP

To overview your reading task, you might

1. read the first few sentences of the passage.

2. read the first and final sentences of each paragraph (and glance through it very quickly just to see what else you might notice).

3. read the final few sentences of the passage.

4. read the question stems themselves and take a fast glance through the choices.

Although you will not be able to see all of the questions at the same time, as you can on the printed page, by taking an overview of the passage, you should now be able to

1. identify the topic of the passage, at least in general terms.

2. have a sense of what information will probably be asked in the questions.

3. evaluate your own level of comfort with this kind of material.

4. have a good idea about the overall content of each paragraph.

Remember:

- Don't be compulsive. This first run through the passage is simply a way to pick up as much as you can about the general nature of the task as rapidly as you can. If you stop to worry about any particular aspect of the passage or questions, you are defeating your purpose. You are, after all, going to read the passage carefully later.

- Some paragraphs will have topic sentences that state the main idea. However, not every paragraph has a stated topic sentence, and some stated topic sentences don't appear first or last in the paragraph. Therefore, some of the information you encounter in your overview may not seem to add a great deal to your hypothesis about what the passage entails. Don't worry, just keep going.

- Your job is to run in and "steal" information and ideas as quickly as possible. You are "casing" the reading material. Run in, get what you can, and don't be alarmed by your inability to "remove the refrigerator" at this time.

- Your overview will usually *not* enable you to *answer* any questions. Your purpose is simply to determine a general sense of direction.

- This process should take about a minute.

Now practice. The following is a practice passage. Do an overview of the passage. As each question appears on the screen, you should now have a good idea of where to find that information in the reading selection. Overviewing is now completed and you are required to zero in on the specifics that will serve to answer the questions.

Passage

For 600 years, while Western Europe groped through the Dark Ages, a magnificent culture flourished in the rain forests of Central America. The Maya were the only people in the Americas to develop an original system of writing. Their mathematics was many centuries ahead of the European system. The Mayan calendar was more accurate than the Gregorian calendar we use today. Mayan ceremonial buildings—their frescoes, sculptures, and bas-reliefs—are still admired for their grace and harmony. At its height, in the eighth century, the Mayan civilization supported 14 million people in the fragile and difficult rain forest environment. The key to it was the Mayas' sophisticated system of agriculture.

Since the time when the Lacandon Maya of Guatemala fled to the Chipas rain forest in southern Mexico after the Spanish conquest, they have been able to practice a simplified version of their ancient Mayan agriculture in peace, farming in the forest more effectively and efficiently than either modern experts or recent immigrants. In determining where to locate each plot, the Lacandon differentiate among seven types of soil, only three of which are considered appropriate for farming. Indigenous plant growth is also given careful consideration. Plots with mahogany and tropical cedar are avoided since the soils that support them are considered too wet for cultivation. In April the Lacandon clear a small plot (*milpas*) of 2 to 3 acres by setting it ablaze after clearing a firewall, generating ash that provides nutrients in which the crops can flourish.

With the forest cover gone and the danger of erosion ever-present, the Lacandon quickly plant fast-growing trees—such as banana, to provide shade—and root crops, like taro, to anchor the soil. A few weeks later they plant the staple crop, maize. Watching certain forest "indicator" plants, the Lacandon determine when to plant selected crops. Tobacco plants, for example, are planted when the wild tamarind trees flower in the forest. The entire plot, every inch, is covered with several layers of growth, representing perhaps eighty different types of vegetation. Trees shade the medium-height crops, and vines cover the ground that contains distinct subterranean layers. Each crop has unique soil, water, and light requirements as well as different responses to close associations with every other plant. To make optimum use of available nutrients and prevent the spread of plant-specific disease, each clump of one variety is separated by a minimum of 10 feet from another of the same variety.

Depending on the effectiveness of weed control, the same plot can be cultivated from three to seven years without appreciable drops in yield. Weed invasion is reduced by locating plots in the midst of mature forest, by burning debris after each harvest, and by weeding by hand, uprooting the plants. When a plot is no longer suitable for intensive cultivation, it is planted with rubber, cacao, citrus, and other trees and left fallow for five to twenty years. During this time the Lacandon harvest wild plants: useful species they have planted there for food, fiber, and construction material; and old crop plants. Although most animals require the mature forest at critical times during their life cycles, certain wild animals that the Lacandon rely upon for protein are more common in regenerating farm plots than in the pristine forest.

In the 1940s when the Lacandon lands were reclassified as national territory, eighty thousand peasant farmers migrated into the forest. The settlers learned that when they were unable to make a living by farming, the land could be cleared and sold to cattle ranchers for profit. By 1971 the Lacandon consolidation into three small reservations created circumstances that made it difficult for them to continue their traditional way of life. The Lacandon now number only about four hundred individuals, fewer than 20 percent of whom practice their traditional agriculture. Since each settlement is quite a distance from the *milpas*, daily weeding is not possible. Additionally, increased use of machetes scatters weeds widely, entrenching them rather than reducing them. The Lacandon are encouraged to depend on manufactured goods, a development that entices them to abandon their centuries-old practices to become low-paid laborers for the ranchers and loggers who now occupy former Lacandon lands.

1. Select the best statement of the main idea for paragraph 1.

   (A) Because the Gregorian calendar was generated during the Dark Ages, the Mayan calendar was more accurate.
   (B) The Maya lived in the fragile rain forest environment, supporting 14 million people.
   (C) The Maya lived in the fragile rain forest environment as Europe experienced the Dark Ages.
   (D) The Mayan civilization, which supported 14 million people, left evidence that demonstrated their remarkable skill and knowledge in several disciplines.
   (E) Older civilizations may prove to be more advanced than civilizations that coexist with them or follow them.

2. Mahogany and cedar are mentioned in paragraph 2

   (A) as evidence supporting the author's statement that the Lacandon methods are effective.
   (B) as a contrast to the reference to indigenous vegetation.
   (C) as an example of Lacandon use of indigenous vegetation as a guide to *milpas* location.
   (D) as an example of the phenomenal success of the Lacandon in preserving natural forest land.
   (E) as a transition statement.

3. It can be inferred that the Lacandon farmers

   (A) moved into the Chipas rain forest in southern Mexico in order to improve their agriculture.
   (B) were able to correct for seasonal variations such as those in temperature or rainfall by using indicator plants.
   (C) were more advanced than modern farmers, who rely upon technology.
   (D) regenerate their *milpas* in order to attract animals to provide them with protein
   (E) have successfully resisted efforts to modernize their methods.

4. Paragraph 2 focuses on

   (A) the differences between the Lacandon methods and those of the ancient Maya.
   (B) the use of native plants as indicators of when Lacandon plants should be planted.
   (C) the efficiency of Lacandon methods, which modern farmers have not been able to duplicate.
   (D) the Lacandon methods of selecting and clearing the *milpas*.
   (E) Spanish oppression of Guatemalan natives.

5. This passage suggests that the most significant factor affecting the productivity of the *milpas* is

   (A) the frequency, method, and effectiveness of weed control.
   (B) whether or not the indicator plants follow their usual cycles.
   (C) the number of years the *milpas* must lie fallow.
   (D) the proper layering and organization of crops within the *milpas*.
   (E) the degree to which those who work the *milpas* have assimilated the ancient Mayan knowledge.

6. Select the choice that contains all items that can be inferred from the passage.

   I. The presence or absence of certain indigenous plants would indicate optimum moisture for a Lacandon plot.
   II. The *milpas* remains useful to the Lacandon beyond its three- to seven-year maximum productivity cycle.
   III. The Mexican government erred in placing the Lacandon on reservations.
   IV. A Lacandon farmer might not be able to explain why certain crops should be separated from each other in the *milpas*.
   V. Peasant farmers owned the land they settled when Lacandon territory was reclassified as national territory.

   (A) I, II, III, and V
   (B) II, III, IV, and V
   (C) I, II, IV, and V
   (D) I, II, III, and IV
   (E) All of the above

7. Select the best summary statement for the article as a whole.

   (A) Using ancient methods based upon natural patterns and interactions, the Lacandon farmed the Mexican forest with remarkable success until they were placed on reservations.
   (B) The Lacandon farmers caused damage to the forest that had been their home and then sold their forest land to ranchers.
   (C) The Lacandon have been victimized over the centuries but have, until recently, been able to maintain their ancient lifestyle.
   (D) Simple, ancient methods of farming, such as those used by the Lacandon, embody a wisdom modern farmers have been unable to master.
   (E) When natives of a region are forced to live in new conditions, it is not always possible for them to continue their traditional practices.

8. Which would be the primary purpose of allowing the *milpas* to lie fallow?

   (A) Obtaining building material.
   (B) Attracting wild animals needed for protein.
   (C) Allowing the land to regenerate.
   (D) Eliminating the weeds.
   (E) Selling rubber to the loggers and cattle ranchers.

9. The Lacandon layering of crops in the *milpas* addresses which requirement of the various plants?

   (A) soil
   (B) nutrients
   (C) isolation from other plants
   (D) light
   (E) water

10. The author's purpose in stating "Although most animals require the mature forest at critical times during their life cycles" (paragraph 4) is to

   (A) establish a contrast between certain animals that are common in the *milpas* and most forest animals.
   (B) establish a cause-effect relationship.
   (C) establish the fact that the *milpas* cannot be considered a substitute for the natural forest.
   (D) embellish the information presented with interesting detail.
   (E) elaborate upon a previously stated issue.

This practice passage is longer than a typical GMAT passage (which is approximately 500 words), and it has more questions than a typical GMAT passage.

Take a look at what you found out by *overviewing*. Your overview of the passage has told you that (paragraph 1) the Maya did amazing things and the key to "it" was agriculture (paragraph 2). The Lacandon Maya fled to Mexico and farmed there using ancient methods. They clear a plot by burning (paragraph 3). They plant trees and crops, separating clumps of the same variety (paragraph 4). The plot is cultivated for three to seven years. Certain animals are more common in a regenerating plot (paragraph 5). Many peasant farmers migrated into Lacandon lands. The Lacandon are enticed to abandon their old ways.

Your overview of the questions themselves indicates that you are to gain information regarding:

   1. the main idea of paragraph 1.

   2. why the author mentions mahogany and cedar.

   3. an inference (it would take too long to determine exactly about what).

   4. the focus of the second paragraph.

   5. the most significant factor affecting *milpas* productivity.

   6. an inference (again, appearing to involve many aspects of the passage).

7. the main idea of the article as a whole.

8. the main purpose of allowing the *milpas* to lie fallow.

9. which plant requirement is accomplished by layering plants.

10. the author's purpose in making a statement about animals requiring mature forests.

Do not attempt to memorize what you overviewed. Remember, this exercise of overviewing is just to rapidly gain a general sense of direction.

BEGIN THE JOURNEY: ONE DAY AT A TIME

The next step is to return to the passage for a careful reading. You will focus upon main ideas and related details. Each paragraph is like a day's journey on your trip. Your focus is to understand the structure and intention of this material. As you read, you may make note of aspects of the passage that ring a bell as a result of your overview. Again, do not spend time deciding whether to note something or not.

The goal of your trip is to arrive as soon as possible, alive and well.

Your search for main ideas will be aided if you:

1. can identify the *subject* of each paragraph. The subject tells *who* or *what* the author is talking about.

2. can identify the *topic* of each paragraph. The topic tells what *aspect* of the subject the author has decided to focus upon. Some readers can arrive at the topic immediately, making step 1 unnecessary. Regardless, when you think you know the topic, make sure that you do not need to further narrow your choice.

3. can state in a concise sentence what (overall) the author is attempting to convey about the topic.

    This statement is the *main idea* of the paragraph. A main idea is always a statement; it will never sound like a title. A good statement of main idea is supported by at least *most*, if not all, of the details. Keep in mind that the author *may* have written a main idea sentence for you. If you can spot the author's main idea sentence, you will not have to work so hard. Questions may refer to the main idea as the central focus, the central theme, or the central idea.

4. can see in the paragraph details that support your opinion of what the main idea is.

Read the first paragraph of the practice passage and state the subject of the paragraph. If you said, "the Maya," you will need to proceed to step 2 to state a more specific topic. You would ask yourself what *aspect* of the Maya the author was discussing. If you said "accomplishments of the Maya" as the *subject*, you would be unable to be more specific in step 2, and you would simply proceed to stating in a sentence that the author wants you to understand about the accomplishments of the Maya. The step of finding a TOPIC is merely a tool to make sure that you take your thinking to a level that is as specific as possible. If you are already THERE at that appropriately specific level, be happy and continue.

Your mental flowchart would look something like this (The arrows indicate that there must be a valid relationship between items connected by the arrows):

SUBJECT → TOPIC ⟷ MAIN IDEA ⟷ DETAILS

Example

children→ learning styles of children ⟷
(Subject)   (Topic)

children have several different learning styles
(Main Idea)

Appropriate details would give specific examples of some of those styles, allowing you to see that your statement of main idea and topic were both correct.

If the passage discussed just *one* style, you would know that your *main idea* was incorrect.

Using the logic of the flowchart can help you determine if your thinking "fits" the passage. Every level of generality (subject, topic, main idea, detail) contributes something to your understanding of other levels and provides you with checks and double checks. The double arrows flow in two directions to indicate that no reader processes print in a strict general-to-specific, or specific-to-general, pattern. Although each reader may have a preferred style, the double arrows show that readers switch gears, moving back and forth from the general to the specific as they search for meaning.

When reading for topics and main ideas, do not study the details. Just read them and notice what kinds of details appear in various locations of the passage. Let your reading be driven by the purpose of gaining a sense of the main idea, organization, and purpose of the paragraph. Use the details to see if they develop, support, or refute your educated guess of what each main idea is. Just as you don't shut your eyes while driving simply because your primary goal is to arrive at your destination, and you are not particularly interested in every small detail of the day's drive, you will not shut down your mind to detail. Detail will help you judge the appropriateness of your impressions of the nature and purpose of what you are reading. On the other hand, you will not attempt to commit every detail to memory.

Now answer question 1 of the practice passage and check your thinking (and flowchart) against the one provided in the answer explanation. Read the remainder of the passage carefully. Don't try to memorize it. Remember, the passage will always be there for your reference. Then answer questions 4 and 7, checking your answers and reading the explanations. For additional practice, state the main ideas of paragraphs 3, 4, and 5.

Recall that the main idea is a sentence, not a title.

Your statements for the main idea for paragraphs 3, 4, and 7 should be similar to these:

Paragraph 3: Using the natural growth cycle of the area and effective arrangements of plants, the Lacandon pack the *milpas* with plants. (Notice that the main idea does not rattle off the details, but rather summarizes them.)

Paragraph 4: When the yield of the *milpas* begins to drop, it is allowed to lie fallow but remains useful to the Lacandon.

Paragraph 5: Political events that began in the 1940s and modernization have threatened the old ways of the Lacandon.

Congratulations! You have now arrived at your destination. Now you must return home. Your reading has enabled you to complete each day's trip, arriving safely at your destination. As you return home, the remaining GMAT questions will send you to specific "tourist attractions" for specific purposes. Remember, your only job is to make the prescribed tours and answer questions correctly.

These are questions that will require you to *use* the information in the passage to conclude, evaluate, judge, predict, and determine the author's attitude and purpose and also to tell how or why the author presented his case in a particular way. When you read for information that is *implied* in the passage, you are *making an inference* or *inferring*.

Use the information gained from your overview and initial reading to locate information rapidly. Questions that require you to read between and beyond the lines are difficult, require thought, and must be based entirely upon information that the passage has provided. Unless you are absolutely positive of your choice, you should quickly refer to the passage to be certain that your information is correct.

Your "map" and "trip to your destination" should provide you with a fairly clear idea of where to look for various pieces of information as you check.

No questions will evaluate your background knowledge. All questions are passage-dependent. Your opinions and decisions must be based entirely upon what the author has told you. If you believe you are being asked for an opinion, remember that it is the *author's* opinion, not your own, that really matters.

Your answers must be based upon ALL the information in a passage. Unless the question directs you to a specific piece of information, decisions about the reading must be based upon *everything* the passage has said. You should not base a response on anything less than a single sentence. If you are referred to a specific sentence or specific lines in the passage and asked to determine the author's intended meaning, you should read information *around* that sentence or those lines, as well, so that you are considering the information in its context.

For example, assume that the text reads as follows:

Some legislators lend overwhelming support to a flat-rate income tax, as do isolated elements of the general population. Many legislators and most citizens, finding themselves perplexed by the entire tax structure, simply don't know where to commit their support.

A question asks you to determine, according to the passage, what public opinion is regarding the flat tax. If you zip through the text, find the first reference to a flat tax located right after the words "overwhelming support," and decide that the public opinion is one of "overwhelming support," you will miss the question, as documented in the sentence following the reference to the flat tax.

As you visit tourist attractions, answering the author's questions, the following suggestions will help you notice the author's intended message.

Watch For Transition Words

Transition words are intended to guide you in following the author's thoughts and organization. They can be loosely grouped in several categories. A few examples of each type are included to give you the general idea.

More to Come Same Type of Information As Before	and, moreover, also, in addition, next, a final reason, similarly, furthermore
Change of Direction—Contrasting Information to Follow	although, however, rather, but, nevertheless, conversely, yet
Sequence Signals	next, now, first, after, later
Clarification to Follow	for example, for instance, such as, similarly, as an illustration
Please Notice This	major, vital, primary, central—any word that means *most* important

Reason-Result Relationship	since, because, as a result, cause (-s, -ed, -ing), consequently, therefore (Watch for cause-effect relationships *without* transition words.)
Comparison Signals	like, similarly, more, less, fewer
Don't Be So Sure	apparently, maybe, almost, seems, could, might, probably, was reported/alleged
Definition	is, is called, can be referred to as, is known as

Notice the organization patterns used in paragraphs. There are commonly used patterns that authors rely heavily upon in organizing information. The author must decide, before beginning to write, what the point of each paragraph is and how that point will be made in the paragraph. Commonly, authors generate paragraphs in which the main point is brought to the reader's attention by using an organizational pattern as a vehicle (illustration-example, definition, comparison-contrast, sequence, cause-effect, or description). You should be familiar with each type of paragraph, for spotting one as you read can make your task easier. However, you should also know that several patterns may appear in the same paragraph.

Spotting the paragraph type is a tool that may aid your cause, but it should not become a process that distracts you from considering what you are reading. The presence of various transition words in a paragraph may help you identify the paragraph pattern. Common patterns are described below:

Illustration-Example

The author uses either one long illustration or several shorter examples to make the point in the paragraph. Typically, the order of the examples makes very little difference, and cumulatively, they lead the reader to the main point. The first paragraph of the practice passage uses illustration-example to make the point that the Mayan accomplishments were noteworthy.

If the main point of a paragraph is that talented individuals may not do well in traditional educational settings, this point might be made by citing the educational experiences of Edison and Einstein, who were both considered unteachable by their early teachers.

Cause-Effect

Cause-effect relationships may be presented with or without transition words. They may be stated or implied. Perceiving these relationships is of the utmost importance in higher-level comprehension. Consider the following paragraph:

> Before the railroad arrived on the scene in the Great Plains, most citizens were farmers who met the needs of their families by growing their own food and who obtained what they needed within their geographical locality. With the railroad came improved ability to move goods from one location to another, making it unnecessary for each man to provide his own nourishment by farming. Citizens relocating could arrive without undergoing the rigors of stagecoach travel, and cities grew at railroad stops. Men left the farms to work in the cities. . . .

The arrival of the railroad *caused* some changes in American life that a careful reader should recognize while reading.

Definition

In a paragraph of definition, the author goes to great length to explain a special or technical term to the reader. Consider the following (bare-bones) paragraph:

> A typical tragic hero is one who falls from great height as a result of a "tragic flaw." The flaw, a character defect that may have previously lain dormant, manifests itself during the tragedy as a result of circumstances that are beyond the immediate control of the hero. Many writers of tragedy have interpreted the "fall" as one from a position of royalty or nobility. Oedipus, Macbeth, and Julius Caesar are characters who typify this view of tragedy.

Comparison-Contrast

In a paragraph of comparison and contrast, the author's point is made by presenting likenesses, differences, or both. Consider the following paragraph:

> Before World War II, the typical American woman was expected to be in her home caring for her children, cooking, and attending to family affairs. Meal preparation was an elaborate affair that was expected to occupy considerable portions of the homemaker's day. As women entered the work-force during the war, replacing the men who had vacated a variety of jobs to join the military, the expectations of society changed. Recipes appeared that featured shortened preparation time, giving acknowledgment to the fact that many women had joined the workforce. The point is that the role of women (and their approach to cooking) changed.

One might argue that this is really a *cause-effect* paragraph since the war *caused* the change in the role of women. For our purposes, either view is acceptable, since we are using the pattern as a vehicle to follow the author's thought, not as an exercise in rhetoric.

Sequence of Events

Incidents are presented in chronological, or time, order. The overall pattern of your practice passage was sequential since it began with the Spanish conquest and ended with the present time. Noting sequence is useful beyond simply listing events in time order. In noting the sequence, and then in asking yourself what this particular sequence really means, you will approach the underlying meaning.

Be Aware of the Author's Craft

Questions of craftsmanship (for example, questions 2 and 10 of your practice passage) may ask you to tell *why* the author included certain information. Noting transition words and looking for organizational patterns will help you. The same patterns occur on a sentence level, on a paragraph level, and on a passage level.

Watch the Author's Use of Language

While single-word adjectives and adverbs are most obviously helpful, verb usage gives us clues that are equally as important. While we all recognize the difference between an inquisitive child and a nosy child, we should also notice the difference between a person's walking into the room, sauntering into the room, or slithering into the room. The absence of words that carry with them certain tones of meaning is likely to mean that we are reading material of a technical or scientific nature in which the author has made a serious effort to avoid contaminating the material with any sort of emotional overlay.

Use the Same Skills You Use In Real Life To Get the Message On All Levels

Reading involves getting the message on a surface level as well as on deeper levels, understanding what is stated, what is implied, and what might be expected as a result. Reading involves reading "the lines," reading "between the lines," and reading "beyond the lines." Reflect on a time when an adult authority figure said, "No, you can't go to that movie [game, party; fill in the blank with your most vivid recollection]." Consider all the possible meanings of that single literal statement: 1. *You* can't go, but your sister can. 2. You can't go to that *movie*, but you can go to another type of activity. 3. You can go to *another* movie, but not *that* movie. 4. You can't leave the house for any purpose. In a situation like this, you probably knew *exactly* what the adult meant; it is unlikely that you had to ask questions to gain clarification. The same factors that gave you clear and certain enlightenment in that situation will give you the same enlightenment as a reader who moves smoothly from surface meaning to deep meaning.

Some of the factors that led you to understand were the general context of the comment, specific details that preceded and followed the comment, the tone of the comment, the volume of the comment, and the body language that accompanied the comment. There was no need for you to consider these factors individually; it was simply that your experience enabled you to process them simultaneously and *understand*. You were probably also able to predict that this would not be a good time to ask for an increase in your allowance.

Practicing with materials that demand the skills you will use on the GMAT will provide that helpful experience in interpretation. It will also be beneficial to you to practice judging the tone, intensity, and body language, if you will, of reading material of varied content and difficulty.

Now try your hand at the following review questions and check your answers carefully.

READING COMPREHENSION REVIEW

Passage 1

A new revolution into the understanding of the roots of the English language is under way. While acknowledging Sanskrit as the form for grammatical forms and vocabulary, scholars are now finding the same ideas in the early Greek and Latin, leading to the conclusion that all three spring from the same source. The finding of this source has intrigued philologists for centuries. The evolution of paper has saved many documents; however, what about those centuries when there was no written form of communication, no paper upon which to salvage the rudiments of language, no way of preserving traditions, folkways, and mores? How do we reconstruct those eons of time?

The focus on language as a psychological phenomenon understood by a small group of scholars has begun to reveal that language is really the product of cultural evolution. When looking into the most aged forms of language, one finds a strange uniformity. A few linguists have even begun to prognosticate that the original language can be reconstructed piece by piece into the language spoken at the dawn of human civilization.

Mankind has always sought to know about the peopling of the earth. Modern social scientists use the most modern of techniques to uncover hints into that foggy time. Because language is that form that separates man from beast, the curiosity into its evolvement has always been present. Uncovering the evolution of the language will, it is thought, lead to discoveries about how ancient peoples migrated into new lands, what they saw, what they ate, and how they came both to coexist and to collide with one another.

These findings have combined the use of anthropology, psychology, sociology, and linguistics. When combined, these disciplines have revealed that it is language that is the integral part of culture and that binds people together and signals their presence to other civilizations of both man and beast. Thus, as man has evolved, so has his language; and as he has become more intricate and involved, so has his vocabulary.

The conclusion is that new linguistic findings will neatly compare with the conclusions already drawn from a very different area of research. The human creature has produced a "family tree" whose branches closely mirror the branching of languages proposed by linguists and lead to the startling finding that both man and his language descend from a tiny population that lived more than 200,000 years ago.

1. The passage provides information to support which of the following generalizations?

   (A) Observations of the behavior of modern man reflect the culture of the original man.
   (B) Language is essential to the understanding, interpretation, and determination of the evolution of man.
   (C) Only anthropologists are capable of making the conclusions about language.
   (D) The interpretation of language demands the use of writing with paper and pen.
   (E) Seemingly, man's origin was in a number of sites yet to be discovered.

2. According to the author, which of the following is NOT true of investigating language beginnings?

   (A) Determining the survival of the fittest
   (B) Locating the cradle of civilization
   (C) Finding any artifacts possible
   (D) Using the personality indicators
   (E) Establishing migration patterns

3. The passage suggests that in seeking the origin of language, many disciplines are involved because

   (A) all of the determiners of man's beginnings are in language.
   (B) understanding motivation and habit can contribute to the discovery of language's beginning.
   (C) the entire man is involved in language, which is an important factor, but only ONE factor of man's existence.
   (D) treasures might be found, and determining worth is important.
   (E) the beginning of language has long been the concern of ONLY the linguist.

4. The author leads the reader to assume that with samples of writings

   (A) the discovery of language would be more expeditious.
   (B) the alphabet would be explained.
   (C) the language could be determined to be Greek, Roman, or Sanskrit.
   (D) the original language would be readable by modern man.
   (E) the search for language beginnings would still be incomplete.

5. The idea of Sanskrit as the ONLY beginning language is

   (A) indicated by this author.
   (B) enhanced by the findings of a group of scholars.
   (C) countermanded by findings concurrent with other languages.
   (D) definitively supported by the findings of scholars in disciplines other than linguistics.
   (E) can no longer be considered since it is not written.

6. The conclusion reached by this writer is that

(A) language is so dissident that its origins will never be known.

(B) modern science is making discoveries of linguistic origins available.

(C) language is unnecessary to determine culture.

(D) the piecing together of man's beginnings may indicate that language is not an important part of our evolution.

(E) man's beginnings have been narrowed significantly to a place in time.

Passage 2

For every piano student who loves to practice, there are probably ten who think the road to Hell is paved with ivory. So, when a teacher declared the ability to make piano lessons fun, testers became curious.

The development of software for the computer for use in teaching piano is a unique concept indeed. While self-teaching courses for piano have been around for ages, this is the first self-teaching piano course that gives students feedback the way a real teacher would give and adapts its lessons for individual students.

For a generation caught up in the Nintendo craze and its attendant "games," such an approach to teaching piano is indeed appealing. Tailoring the piano program to work with the Nintendo system is also a positive approach to appealing to the reluctant piano student. Imagine, Mom and Dad are *urging* the would-be piano student to *use* the Nintendo. Where there have been woeful wailings about too much Nintendo, imagine being *sent* to the Nintendo to play an amusing game.

The screen displays an electronic keyboard exactly like that of the piano. The student finds that it is touch-sensitive so that, like the piano, the harder the key is struck, the louder the notes sound. In addition, the electronic keyboard reproduces five other keyboard voices, a pipe organ, a vibraphone, and a harpsichord! What fun to switch from instrument to instrument!

There is also the availability of 122 other voices including flutes, drums, horns, and human choruses. The student is thus encouraged to master the lessons necessary in order to move to the instruments preferred, especially the drums.

The concept of the program is similar. The beginning lessons are like live instruction, except the explanations deal with monitor and keyboard. The early lessons are easily mastered, as the electronic keyboard displayed on the screen imitates the student's moves. When the note is played correctly, the student is prompted to move to the next note. As the program continues, the lesson plan is adjusted to provide more practice where needed.

When the student falters, an alarmed *"oops!"* flashes on the screen. The student is urged to try again. Like a real teacher, the Nintendo can sense the patterns of mistakes and suggest remedies. It can scold like a real teacher, too. If the student bangs on the keys in frustration, he is warned to "stop pounding."

The Nintendo version also tells the sloppy student: "We could write another piece using just the notes you missed!"

7. This passage provides information to support which of the following generalizations?

   (A) All children should learn to play the piano.
   (B) Playing the piano is a dull and uninteresting activity.
   (C) Using tools determined to be fun can promote learning.
   (D) Playing the piano by computer is impossible.
   (E) With a computer, all things are possible.

8. It can be inferred from the passage that computerized piano instruction provides all of the following EXCEPT

   (A) positive feedback.
   (B) negative feedback.
   (C) individualized instruction.
   (D) human presence.
   (E) rewards for learning.

9. The inclusion of a number of voices is included in the lesson to do all of the following EXCEPT

   (A) provide instruction in more instruments than the piano.
   (B) provide harmony.
   (C) encourage students to master their lessons.
   (D) increase incentives.
   (E) create interests in various instruments.

10. The teaching technique of the computer closely resembles that of the teacher in all of the following EXCEPT that it

   (A) delivers lectures as a teaching technique.
   (B) critiques performance.
   (C) rewards good work.
   (D) adjusts to the student's ability level.
   (E) shows the image of a human while the message is relayed.

11. The author indicates that most young students prefer the voice of the

   (A) teacher.
   (B) piano.
   (C) drum.
   (D) organ.
   (E) harpsichord.

12. Scolding a student for sloppy playing, the computer voice uses

   (A) irony.
   (B) caution.
   (C) criticism.
   (D) sarcasm.
   (E) satire.

Passage 3

In teaching piano via the computer, some lessons are disguised as video games. Students learn notes, for example, by shooting ducks on a staff of music. They tap out proper rhythm to keep a cartoon of "Roboman" from falling off of a bridge. There is a parachute game that teaches chords.

After every group of lessons, the student is invited to "visit" the practice room, where there is a choice of practice pieces ranging from "Chopsticks" to "Greensleeves" to "Hound Dog." Students can elect to practice with one hand or with both hands, or to allow the computer to demonstrate.

There are more than one hundred practice pieces, more than twice as many as earlier versions of teaching piano by computer. The student can also record and play back student performances and track the progress over several selections. The teacher can use the record selection to track several students simultaneously.

The course takes from six to twelve months to complete, depending upon the amount of practice the student is willing to do. A music professor testing the program thought the time estimate to be rather optimistic. The reality is that the student will *not* come out of the program as an accomplished pianist. But the student can learn to read music, play chords, and perform rhythms with optional fingering.

The program is not without its flaws. There is the presence of a metronome in the computer program. In real-life instruction, a teacher uses the metronome sparingly and only with fairly advanced students. The computer program uses it regularly to monitor student progress. This can be quite intimidating, and the incessant ticking can confuse the student as well.

The computer often asks the impossible of the student. Notes struck only slightly late caused the computer to default and require the entire selection to be redone. The constant chiding for "pounding" became annoying when the student was playing softly.

And there is the big question: Does this type of teaching make practice and learning fun? The main issue seems to be that if a student does *not* like to play the piano, that student will not like the computer version either. The price is equal to twenty private lessons, and parents can get a good sense of the student's acumen for piano. If the student succeeds here, the tendency to continue with a human teacher will be enhanced. The student who dislikes it still has the inexpensive electronic keyboard with which to experiment.

13. The passage provides information to support which of the following generalizations?

    (A) Playing the piano is a difficult feat.
    (B) Learning music is not for everyone.
    (C) Finding out what one can do through the computer can be helpful.
    (D) The computer program is not a sure way to become an accomplished pianist.
    (E) Students are excited over the computer program.

14. The length of the course can be a factor that will influence the purchaser in all of the following EXCEPT

    (A) there is no guarantee.
    (B) the possibility of completing the course in six to twelve months provides a framework for goal-setting.
    (C) the student has enough material to keep busy.
    (D) student progress is a determining factor.
    (E) the amount of practice is not specified.

15. The types of games provide

    (A) entertainment while learning.
    (B) exposure to classical elements.
    (C) nonsubliminal instruction.
    (D) disguised learning.
    (E) nonviolent competition.

16. The inclusion of so many selections of music provides

    (A) entertainment for the family.
    (B) something for everyone.
    (C) gradual increases of difficulty.
    (D) recognition of various eras of music.
    (E) holiday selections.

17. There are flaws in the system that include

    (A) necessity of consistency.
    (B) continual practicing.
    (C) a pesky voice.
    (D) a metronome.
    (E) an on-screen report.

18. The conclusion one might make is that

    (A) real pianos are not necessary anymore.
    (B) using the computer can enhance instruction.
    (C) the computer is not the best way to teach.
    (D) the computer is the best way to teach.
    (E) all great pianists learned on a computer.

Quick Score Answers

Reading Comprehension Practice Questions		Review Questions			
1. D	6. C	1. B	6. E	11. C	15. A
2. C	7. A	2. A	7. C	12. D	16. C
3. B	8. C	3. B	8. D	13. D	17. D
4. D	9. D	4. A	9. B	14. A	18. B
5. A	10. A	5. C	10. E		

ANSWERS AND EXPLANATIONS

PRACTICE QUESTIONS

1. **The correct answer is (D).** (The one that should be most similar to your thought progression.) This is a main-idea question. Your main-idea mental flowchart would be similar to this:

   > Maya→ civilization of the Maya→ civilization of the Maya seemed impressive→ details, such as calendar, buildings, frescoes, math, writing, kept 14 million people alive.

   You should reject choice (A) because it speaks only of the calendar, which is just one detail of many provided. In addition, choice (A) assumes an unjustified cause-effect relationship, suggesting that its emergence during the Dark Ages somehow made the Gregorian calendar less accurate than the Mayan calendar. Reject choice (B), which emphasizes the number of Maya, another detail. Reject choice (C), which emphasizes the concurrence of the Mayan civilization and the Dark Ages. Choice (E), which does not specifically mention the Maya but which refers to "older civilizations," is too general to fit the paragraph.

2. **The correct answer is (C).** This question asks you to understand the author's organizational scheme. The presence of mahogany or cedar (indigenous or native vegetation) indicates to the Lacandon that the land is too wet. Choice (A) should be rejected because the presence of mahogany or cedar trees does not prove that the Lacandon are successful. Choice (B) should be eliminated because mahogany and cedar trees ARE indigenous vegetation. Since the trees in question are not there as a result of the Lacandon's preservation efforts, choice (D) is not appropriate. A transition statement is one that serves as a bridge between two ideas; choice (E) should be eliminated because the trees are not mentioned as a vehicle to link ideas.

3. **The correct answer is (B).** The passage states that the Lacandon watch indicator plants to determine when to plant certain of their crops. It can be inferred that the plants bloom when natural conditions are appropriate and that this is a better gauge of planting time than an arbitrary date. Choice (A) can be eliminated since the passage states that the Lacandon FLED, indicating that their move was a necessity, not a choice. Furthermore, the reader cannot assume that they fled in order to improve agriculture. Choice (C) is tempting since the Lacandon do have certain types of agricultural knowledge that modern farmers do not have. It would be correct to say that the Lacandon are more successful in cultivating forest land than modern farmers are, but there is no basis to make a statement indicating that they are in general more advanced. Choice (D) sug-

Peterson's GMAT CAT Success

gests a cause-effect relationship that is not intended in the passage. While it is true that the animals come to the regenerating *milpas*, it is not true that the Lacandon regenerate the *milpas* simply to attract animals. Choice (E) can be eliminated because the Lacandon are now using machetes rather than pulling weeds by hand.

4. **The correct answer is (D).** This is a main-idea question. Your mental flowchart should have resembled this one: the *milpas*→ selecting and clearing the *milpas*→ selecting and clearing the *milpas* is an intricate process→ details of support (determining the type of soil, studying native plants that grow there to gain more information about what kind of land this is, clearing a fire wall, burning the area of the *milpas*). You would eliminate choice (A) because the differences between Lacandon and ancient Mayan methods are not discussed in the article. Choices (B) and (D) are details of the paragraph rather than its central idea. Neither issue is discussed at length or elaborated upon in the paragraph. Choice (E) is mentioned in the paragraph in passing but is not an idea that is further developed.

5. **The correct answer is (A).** This is an inference question, one that requires the reader to evaluate information that is provided in the passage. You would select choice (A) because the length of time that the *milpas* may be used depends on weed control (paragraph 4, sentence 1). Inability to do daily weeding is mentioned in paragraph 5, sentence 5. Weed entrenchment caused by machete use is mentioned (paragraph 5, sentence 6). Both weed-related statements are among the "circumstances that make it difficult for them to continue their traditional way of life." The reader may infer that weed control is highly important, and since no other choices receive this degree of emphasis in the passage, the reader may infer that weed control is of primary importance. Choice (B) could be eliminated because indicator plants tell the Lacandon *when* to plant. Choice (C) should be eliminated since the number of years that the *milpas* is *cultivated* is a better key to its productivity than the number of years it lies fallow. Choice (D) must be avoided because of lack of evidence. While the reader knows that crops are layered (paragraph 3), no information is implied regarding the relative importance of layering and crop placement. Choice (E) is not viable since a major point of the passage is that the Lacandon have used the ancient knowledge.

6. **The correct answer is (C).** This inference question is made more difficult because of the number of inferences that must be considered in order to find the correct answer. The best approach is to consider each possible inference separately, accepting or rejecting it. Then, make your answer choice. You would accept choice (I). If certain plants, as paragraph 2 states, indicate that the land is too wet, then there must be other plants that indicate by their presence or absence that the land is too dry or just right. Choice (II) is a correct inference. A fallow *milpas* is planted with trees and (according to paragraph 4) planted with some "useful species." Furthermore, animals that visit the fallow *milpas* are used by the Lacandon. Inference choice (III) cannot be accepted on the basis of the content of this passage. Although it is clear that the Lacandon did not benefit from the move, no information is provided to enable the reader to judge the government's action. Inference choice (IV) is correct. The Lacandon system is one that was practiced for hundreds of years. Although the planting arrangement is among the knowledge that has been handed down through the centuries, one cannot assume that a Lacandon farmer would necessarily know *why* crops should be placed as they are. Maybe the knowledge is just, "Don't plant the beans beside the corn." Inference V is correct because the peasants had to own the land in order to be able to sell it to the cattle ranchers. Correct inferences are choices (I), (II), (IV), and (V).

7. **The correct answer is (A).** You can use the same procedure for arriving at the main point of a passage that you use to determine the main idea of a single paragraph. The difference is that the main points of component paragraphs now function as details of your passage's main idea. Your map would look something like this: Lacandon→ Lacandon farming→ Lacandon people successfully farmed the rain forest of Mexico until very recently→ supporting details (paragraph 1, accomplishments of Maya; paragraph 2, locating and clearing the *milpas*; paragraph 3, plant arrangement in the *milpas*; paragraph 4, the fallow *milpas*; paragraph 5, the decline of Lacandon agriculture). You would reject choice (B) because the Lacandon neither damaged the forest nor sold their land. Reject choice (C) because the passage does not focus on the Lacandon as "victims." Reject choices (D) and (E) for the same reason: they speak of generalities (ancient methods and natives of a region). Always select the choice that, while still summarizing, is as specific to the passage as possible.

8. **The correct answer is (C).** Notice the word *primary* in the question. This is an inference question. Several choices seem possible, since paragraph 4 discusses building material, planting rubber trees, the attraction of animals to the *milpas*, and weeds. It might be tempting to select choice (D), since this passage speaks so frequently of weeds and weed-related issues; however, consider that the *milpas* will lie fallow for from five to twenty years, a considerable time if weed removal is the only issue. Choices (A) and (B) are related to the fallow *milpas* but are not the *purpose* of allowing the *milpas* to lie fallow; they are best seen as side benefits. Choice (E) is far-fetched. The key sentence supporting choice (C) is this: "When a plot is no longer suitable for intensive cultivation, it is planted with rubber, cacao, citrus, and other trees and left fallow for five to twenty years."

9. **The correct answer is (D).** The passage states that "Each crop has unique soil, water, and light requirements as well as different responses to close associations with every other plant." The requirement most closely related to layering would be light; crops located beneath other crops would require less sunlight than the plants above. Plants so layered would be in extreme proximity, making it probable that they would receive about the same amount of water, nutrients, and soil. Layered plants are not isolated.

10. **The correct answer is (A).** The word *although* signals a contrast. No cause-effect relationship is intended. The author is not considering whether the *milpas* is a substitute for the forest, choice (C). Although authors do add information for the sake of interest, this choice would be appropriate only if no others worked. Choice (E) is not an appropriate choice since the issue was not previously stated.

REVIEW QUESTIONS

1. **The correct answer is (B).** The point is carefully made that "Uncovering the evolution of the language will, it is thought, lead to discoveries about how ancient peoples migrated into new lands, what they saw, what they ate, and how they came both to coexist and to collide with one another."

2. **The correct answer is (A).** Determining the "survival of the fittest" would not necessarily help in the discovery of languages' beginnings. In fact, determining those who do not survive might create more of a discovery.

3. **The correct answer is (B).** While choice (A) is partly true, not *all* of the determiners are in language, but language evolved. But when psychologists and sociologists are able to determine habits and patterns, the beginnings of language become more clear.

Peterson's GMAT CAT Success

4. **The correct answer is (A).** The point is made that with the discovery of paper, culture can be more readily saved, leading to the assumption that without paper, this could not happen.

5. **The correct answer is (C).** The inclusion of the findings of psychologists and sociologists supports a correlation with Greek and Roman.

6. **The correct answer is (E).** The discovery of man's beginnings 200,000 years ago seems to be the positive for determining time and place.

7. **The correct answer is (C).** The Nintendo plays games, and the student in question is accustomed to having time limited there. Using the Nintendo to teach piano is a welcomed activity by the student.

8. **The correct answer is (D).** No human presence is needed.

9. **The correct answer is (B).** There is no mention that the additional 122 voices provide harmony to the piano music. The implication is that each voice represents a separate instrument and is played separately, as is the piano voice.

10. **The correct answer is (E).** There is no indicator of the image of a human delivering the lecture.

11. **The correct answer is (C).** The article states: "The student is thus encouraged to master the lessons necessary in order to move to the instruments preferred, especially the drums."

12. **The correct answer is (D).** The article states: "We could write another piece using just the notes you missed!"

13. **The correct answer is (D).** The student will not be an accomplished pianist and may hate the practicing, but still enjoy the playing.

14. **The correct answer is (A).** The lack of a guarantee can be detrimental to some purchasers of the program. However, the presence of no guarantee allows for the nonmusical student to experiment without pressure.

15. **The correct answer is (A).** The student is allowed to do all the things that regular video games do but with the requirement for performance via music rather than instinctual reaction.

16. **The correct answer is (C).** The student chooses the selections according to individual preference.

17. **The correct answer is (D).** The metronome: "In real-life instruction, a teacher uses the metronome sparingly and only with fairly advanced students."

18. **The correct answer is (B).** The computer program takes one to twelve months, and then the human instructor is needed.

Unit 4

CRITICAL REASONING STRATEGIES AND REVIEW

The Critical Reasoning problems on the GMAT CAT may be interspersed with the Sentence Correction and Reading Comprehension questions in the Verbal section. This section contains 41 questions, and of those, 12 to 13 will be Critical Reasoning questions. These problems may be characterized as arguments that you must analyze and evaluate. Each argument consists of three components: a *conclusion* and *facts* to support the conclusion as well as *assumptions* that relate facts to the conclusion.

Consider the following sample argument:

United Artists' most recent film is based on a best-selling novel and stars Brad Heartthrob. Therefore, the film is expected to do well at the box office.

The first step in tackling a problem such as this is to identify the three components.

Fact 1: film based on a popular novel

Fact 2: star is Brad H.

Conclusion: film should be successful

The assumptions are unstated (hereafter, *hidden assumptions* or HA's); they are additional pieces of information about each fact in the argument. For example:

HA for fact 1: Fans of book are expected to help sales of tickets.

HA for fact 2: Brad H.'s presence should contribute to the success of the film.

These HA's help you see how the facts lead to the given conclusion.

You can often, though not always, distinguish fact from conclusion by spotting "signal words" that introduce each component. Conclusions may be signaled by words like *as, therefore* (as in the example above), *so, thus,* and *in conclusion.* Detailed facts, which are more specific than conclusions, may be flagged by such words as *due to, because, a study shows,* and *in addition.*

Once you *identify* the components, you must answer questions that ask you to *evaluate* these components.

The GMAT offers three basic question types in the Critical Reasoning section, each focusing on one of the three components. They are, in descending order of frequency: the Additional Fact question, the Conclusion question, and the Hidden Assumption question. Following is a discussion of each type.

CRITICAL REASONING STRATEGIES AND REVIEW

ADDITIONAL FACT QUESTIONS

Additional Fact questions focus on the supporting details of the argument. You are presented with a complete argument and are asked to *either* weaken or strengthen the argument by considering five multiple-choice statements. These statements are new facts about the argument, which you must accept as true. Some Additional Fact questions ask for a weakening of an argument; others ask you to strengthen what you read.

For example, in the preceding argument regarding United Artists' new movie, an Additional Fact question might offer the following five choices:

   (A)   The film will play only in urban areas.

   (B)   The producers of the film have cast their next movie without Brad H.

   (C)   The film is not likely to win an Academy Award.

   (D)   The book upon which the film is based is a worldwide hit.

   (E)   Brad H.'s popularity ratings are at an all time low.

The correct answer is (D). If the question asks you to weaken the argument, you will choose a statement that either weakens a given fact or disputes an HA and, in consequence, makes the conclusion illogical. Choice (E) best weakens this argument by disputing the HA that Brad H. will attract moviegoers. The conclusion no longer logically follows.

For a strengthening choice, you would choose a statement to bolster a given fact or HA to support the conclusion. The correct strengthening choice here would be choice (D), for it elaborates on the fact about the book's popularity, thus supporting the conclusion.

Wrong choices, called distracters, usually follow a pattern. They may touch upon the argument only marginally, such as choices (A), (B), and (C); they may accomplish the opposite task (strengthen when you want to weaken); or they may not be the best strengthening or weakening statement [e.g., choice (A) is not the best weakening statement when compared to (E)].

CONCLUSION QUESTIONS

At times, arguments will be missing the conclusion. A series of facts, along with unstated HA's, will lead to the final statement that you then must supply. Sound arguments are linear, in that you can usually predict in what general direction the facts are headed. You may also consider the conclusion an inference: you are inferring the conclusion from the specific statements and associated HA's.

Consider the following argument:

The newest book by England's favorite political satirist has received warm praise from critics. In addition, there is a strong market in the UK for political satire.

You are now asked to choose the statement that best completes this series of facts.

- (A) Political satire transfers well to other countries.
- (B) The author of this book is a member of Parliament.
- (C) People read book reviews before making purchases.
- (D) Such a book will be banned by the current Tory government.
- (E) The book will do well in British bookstores.

The correct answer is (E). Although a series of facts does not usually have just one possible conclusion, there is only one *best* conclusion in the given choices. The best answer here would be one that follows the path that the facts are taking but goes one step beyond the facts by making a more general statement.

Distracters may read too much into the facts. In the preceding example, choice (D) is a statement that steps too far from the given facts; you cannot reach the conclusion from the facts alone. Another sort of distracter introduces more detail instead of making the leap to a conclusion; examples of this would be choices (A), (B), and (C).

HIDDEN ASSUMPTION QUESTIONS

To tackle the Hidden Assumption question, you must directly face the hidden statements that underlie the argument. Each HA statement meets the following two criteria: it gives you extra information about the existing facts instead of supplying new facts, *and* it must be true for the argument to be valid.

For example:

The Republican candidate for governor of State X will get the education vote. More than $200,000 was donated to her campaign fund by the state teachers' union. The same union donated only half that amount to the Democratic candidate's campaign.

You would then be asked to choose the statement that best reveals an assumption underlying the preceding argument.

- (A) The Republican candidate is a former teacher.
- (B) The Democratic candidate will lose the election.
- (C) A donation usually indicates approval of a candidate.
- (D) Most teachers have joined the union.
- (E) Unions endorse candidates in each election.

The correct answer is (C). An excellent test of an HA is the negation test: If you think a choice is an HA, negate it and see if it seriously affects the validity of the conclusion—the right answer should.

For example, suppose you are struggling between choices (C) and (D). If choice (D) were falsified, you would now have the statement "Most teachers have not joined the union." Does that mean that the Republican candidate is now likely not to win the education vote? She may still. Negation of choice (C) gives you, "Donations usually don't indicate approval of a candidate." This negative statement does the most direct harm to the conclusion that the Republican candidate will get teachers' votes; it makes the connection between the facts and conclusion illogical. Choice (C) is correct.

Distracters associated with this question type include statements such as choice (D), which doesn't support the conclusion enough, as well as irrelevant statements such as choices (A), (B), and (E), besides being marginal to the problem, these statements also introduce new facts, whereas choice (C) elaborates on the facts given.

SUMMARY

The best possible suggestion for doing well on the Critical Reasoning section of the GMAT is to understand how the problems are constructed, what the test is asking you to do, and then to practice. Keep in mind the following steps when tackling this section of the exam:

1. Read each paragraph carefully.

2. Distinguish conclusion from fact, and consider the HA's based on given facts.

3. Read the question carefully.

4. For Additional Fact questions, make sure of your task (strengthen or weaken) before proceeding. Choose the statement that directly addresses a given fact, HA, or conclusion.

5. For conclusion questions, think in a linear fashion: Where are the facts headed? Choose a statement that goes one logical step further from the given facts.

6. For HA questions, remember to choose a statement that supports the argument with more information about given issues. Try the negation test.

7. Complete as many practice problems as you can. Note which question types you have the most difficulty with and which distracters trip you up most often. Being aware of your own strengths and weaknesses on this section should help you to be more successful at it.

CRITICAL REASONING REVIEW

ADDITIONAL FACT QUESTIONS

1. The trend in the United States banking industry of several small community banks merging into fewer large, interstate banks has consumers worried about service. Many consumers worry that, as banks become larger and fewer in number, the competition in the banking industry will decrease, and consumers will lose services and will pay higher fees. As a result, many consumers are urging their legislators to enact legislation to limit the size of any individual banking company.

    The fears of the consumers discussed in the preceding argument would most be allayed by which of the following facts?

    (A) The federal government recently enacted legislation to increase the maximum amounts of deposits that will be insured.
    (B) A limitation on mergers between interstate banks could be construed as a violation of the Commerce Clause of the United States Constitution.
    (C) Larger banks are able to generate higher profits for their investors with lower levels of risk.
    (D) As a bank increases in size, its overhead costs for operation will decrease, and it will be able to improve the services to its consumers.
    (E) Large governmentally operated banks have functioned successfully in other countries for many years without any decrease in services to their consumers and with service fees that are less than many private banks.

2. Of the graduating students from Governor Smith Academy, a private high school, 93 percent go on to attend college. From Eastern High, the public high school in the same city, only 74 percent go on to attend college. As a result, many parents with children about to enter high school believe that Governor Smith Academy gives students a better education than they can get at Eastern High School.

    Which of the following statements, if true, would cast the most doubt on the conclusion about Governor Smith Academy?

    (A) Until 1992, Governor Smith Academy was exclusively a girls' school, but Eastern High School has always been coeducational.
    (B) Governor Smith Academy requires students to pass an admissions examination before entering, but Eastern High School admits all applicants who live in the city.
    (C) Eastern High School has problems with severe student violence during school hours.
    (D) Governor Smith Academy has a higher percentage of students attending Ivy League colleges than any other high school in the state.
    (E) Eastern High School receives its funding from local property taxes, while Governor Smith Academy receives funding from tuition costs and from alumni donations.

3. *Television Advertisement:* "Leonardo da Vinci was a genius, and everyone recognizes his art as the greatest in the world. At Acme Art Supply Company, you can get modern, improved art supplies so you will be able to create works of art even better than Leonardo da Vinci's."

Which of the following statements, if true, most effectively shows the flaws in the claims made in this advertisement?

(A) Leonardo da Vinci, at the time he was painting in the fifteenth century, was sponsored by patrons who provided him with the opportunity to use the best materials then available in the world.

(B) Most of the customers of Acme Art Supply Company are hobbyists who are not professionally trained and who do not realize the value of using professional-quality art supplies.

(C) The art supplies at Acme Art Supply Company are more expensive than similar supplies that are available at any other supply store in the area.

(D) An art professor from the local community college supplies all of his students with materials from the Acme Art Supply Company.

(E) Even when using supplies from Acme Art Supply Company, many amateur artists create projects that art critics call inferior and childish.

4. While some job loss is inevitable in a changing American economy, the current phase of corporate downsizing has reached the level of becoming an epidemic. Many employees are being fired simply to enhance profits for top management and company shareholders. Even so, some economists see improvement in the fact that the total number of new jobs being created is increasing at a steady rate.

Which of the following facts, if true, would show that the economists' view of improvement is incorrect?

(A) The new jobs that are being created come as a result of governmental tax incentives to large corporations.

(B) Corporate downsizing is not actually resulting in higher profits for shareholders, as was expected.

(C) Many of the new jobs are low-paying entry-level positions that do not provide healthcare or pension benefits.

(D) A separate study of corporate shareholders reveals that many of them would be willing to forgo higher profits in order to increase hiring levels.

(E) Other countries are experiencing similar increases in job creation.

5. High doses of niacin in a person's diet have been shown to raise HDL levels, which doctors call the "good" cholesterol, and to lower levels of triglycerides and LDL, the so-called "bad" cholesterol. As a result of this study, some nutritionists are now recommending diets that are extremely high in niacin.

Which of the following facts, if true, would most effectively question the recommendations of the nutritionists?

(A) The original study was conducted on a sample of hospital patients who initially had dangerously high cholesterol levels.

(B) High doses of niacin have been shown to reduce the clotting factors in blood, thereby reducing a person's ability to heal after receiving minor injuries.

(C) When levels of triglycerides decrease, patients report higher levels of stamina and improved physical endurance.

(D) The doctors who reported the results of the study had once been discredited for falsifying the results of their research.

(E) Other studies have shown that the body eventually reaches a maximum plateau with regard to its LDL level.

CONCLUSION QUESTIONS

1. A consumer watchdog group recently reported the results of a study surrounding the deregulation of the U.S. banking industry, which has allowed for more mergers between banks and has allowed banks more freedom in setting their interest rates for their customers. The report shows that customers now have access to higher savings interest rates and lower borrowing interest rates. At the same time, banks are reporting record profits.

From the results of this study, what can be concluded about the effect of deregulation of the American banking industry?

(A) Deregulation has hurt the banking industry by limiting the number of options allowed to the customers of small local banks.

(B) Deregulation has been a success because it has given the banks the ability to raise their interest rates and force their customers to pay the highest rates possible.

(C) As a result of the deregulation of the banking industry, investments in other industries will increase, resulting in a stronger economy nationwide.

(D) Deregulation has been a success because it allows both the banks and their customers to realize savings and profits at the same time.

(E) Because deregulation has lowered the interest rates that customers will have to pay, many banks will be driven out of business in the near future.

2. A report from the head of the city's school department reveals that the school department had a large surplus in its health insurance account at the end of 1994.

The same report showed that at the end of 1995, the school department suffered a deficit of $300,000 in the same account. Despite this decline, the school department reported no significant changes in costs over the two-year period that was studied.

What can be concluded from the results of this report?

(A) The school department's budget for health costs is excessively high.

(B) More teachers were provided with health insurance payments during 1995 than in 1994.

(C) The costs that are related to operating the school department's health insurance program must have increased dramatically from 1994 to 1995.

(D) The health insurance account received less funding in 1995 than it did in 1994.

(E) The health insurance budget will show an even greater deficit in 1996 than it did in 1995.

3. In a game of Monopoly, if a player owns a hotel on Boardwalk, he must own both Boardwalk and Park Place. If he owns a hotel in Marvin Gardens, he must own Marvin Gardens and either Boardwalk or Park Place. If he owns Park Place, he also owns Marvin Gardens.

If the player described above does not own Park Place, which of the following conclusions may be drawn?

(A) The player owns a hotel on Boardwalk.

(B) The player owns a hotel in Marvin Gardens but does not own a hotel on Boardwalk.

(C) The player owns Marvin Gardens and Boardwalk but does not own a hotel on either property.

(D) The player does not own a hotel on Marvin Gardens.

(E) The player does not own a hotel on Boardwalk.

4. As the temperature of a solution of water and chemical X increases, the reactivity of chemical X also increases. As the temperature of a mixture of chemical X and chemical Y increases, the reactivity of chemical Y increases but the reactivity of chemical X remains constant. As the temperature of a solution of water and chemical Y increases, the reactivity of chemical Y remains constant.

From the above information, what conclusion may be drawn?

(A) A change in temperature has no effect on the reactivity of chemical Y.

(B) A change in temperature has no effect on the reactivity of chemical X.

(C) When combined, chemical X and chemical Y display different reaction levels than when studied separately.

(D) When combined with chemical X, chemical Y demonstrates the same reactive properties as it does when it is studied alone.

(E) A change in temperature produces a greater effect on chemical Y than it does on chemical X.

5. *Advertisement:* Seven out of ten municipal employees choose Green Arrow Underwriters as their health insurance provider.

From the information provided in this advertisement, what further conclusion may be drawn?

(A) Green Arrow Underwriters has the cheapest premium rates of any other insurance company available.

(B) All other health insurance providers, excluding Green Arrow Underwriters, provide services to less than 50 percent of the municipal employees.

(C) Municipal employees need less health insurance coverage than employees in other industries.

(D) Green Arrow Underwriters provides more valuable services and better customer assistance than any of its competitors.

(E) Except for Green Arrow Underwriters, the health insurance industry is suffering a decline in the rate of obtaining new customers.

HIDDEN ASSUMPTION QUESTIONS

1. In order to ensure a successful vote on the issue of abortion rights, the governor is pressuring the leaders of the state political party to replace several delegates to the national convention. The governor is insisting that certain individuals with a history of voting in favor of abortion rights be replaced with new delegates who have voted against abortion rights in the past.

The governor's actions demonstrate that he is making which of the following assumptions?

(A) Voting on abortion issues is an important part of the national political agenda.

(B) The current delegates will probably not share the governor's views on such issues as the national budget or federal spending limits.

(C) The proposed new delegates will continue to vote on abortion issues in the same way that they have voted in the past.

(D) The national delegation will not have an opportunity to vote on any issues other than abortion rights.

(E) Governors of other states will be making similar changes to their states' delegations, so that the issue of abortion rights will be guaranteed to be decided as this governor desires.

2. To travel on public transportation from City Hall to the convention center, the most direct route requires passengers to ride the Blue Bus line to Center Street, collect a token at Center Street station, then ride the subway to Middle Street. This weekend, there will be a big political rally, so the city should hire extra token vendors for the Center Street station.

The conclusion for the preceding argument depends upon which of the following assumptions?

(A) The mayor will be working at City Hall this weekend and will need to use public transportation to go to the convention center.

(B) There is no way to get from City Hall to the convention center without going through the Center Street station.

(C) The political rally will draw thousands of people to the city from all parts of the state.

(D) Because of the political rally, traffic at the Center Street station will increase.

(E) The city's public transportation system does not allow passengers to buy tokens in advance.

3. The newspaper just reported that a man won this year's national baking contest for the first time in its history. The contest has used both male and female judges for many years. This must have been the first year that the contest was open to male participants.

Which of the following is an assumption upon which the speaker's conclusion is based?

(A) The newspaper has never before reported the results of the national baking contest.
(B) Male judges are more likely to vote for a male contestant than a female contestant.
(C) Men have tried to enter the national baking contest for several years but have been denied.
(D) Men are generally superior to women and would be able to beat them in any kind of competition.
(E) Men are better bakers than women and could win this contest every year.

4. Today is Tuesday, and yesterday was Monday. Therefore, tomorrow will be Wednesday.

This speaker's conclusion depends on which of the following assumptions?

(A) Wednesday is the day that precedes Thursday.
(B) Tuesday always follows Monday.
(C) If, in any given week, Tuesday follows Monday, then Wednesday will follow Tuesday.
(D) Every week consists of seven days that are arranged in a particular order.
(E) The speaker always schedules a certain meeting to occur on Wednesday.

5. In the animal world, when any species becomes overpopulated, naturalists observe that the animals begin fighting among themselves and become cannibalistic. Sociologists have been reporting for years that the human population of the world is growing at an uncontrollable rate, and the world's cities will be overpopulated in about ten years. As a result, human societies will begin experiencing a global breakdown, and we can expect an international war within the next ten years.

Which of the following statements represents a hidden assumption upon which the preceding argument depends?

(A) Human social behaviors follow the same patterns as the behaviors of animals.

(B) Major cities do not always have adequate budgets to provide resources for all their residents.

(C) Naturalists and sociologists use the same research methods in studying their subjects and reporting results.

(D) The study that showed cannibalistic patterns in animals studied only carnivorous animals.

(E) The population of the world has doubled in the past five years, and its rate of growth will increase even faster in the future.

Quick Score Answers		
Additional Fact Questions	**Conclusion Questions**	**Hidden Assumption Questions**
1. D	1. D	1. C
2. B	2. D	2. D
3. E	3. E	3. E
4. C	4. C	4. C
5. B	5. B	5. A

ANSWERS AND EXPLANATIONS

ADDITIONAL FACT QUESTIONS

1. **The correct answer is (D).** The consumers assume that bank mergers will result in higher fees and fewer services. Choice (D) contradicts this assumption and would be the best response for weakening the conclusion. Choice (A) is irrelevant, as nothing in the argument addresses insurance of deposits or federal involvement. Choice (B) is irrelevant because the argument is not concerned with whether or not such mergers are allowable but whether they are a good move for consumers. Choice (C) focuses on investors and not customers. Choice (E) is somewhat informative, but is not as directly addressed to this argument as choice (D).

2. **The correct answer is (B).** This argument assumes that the percentage of students moving on to college reflects on the quality of the education at the two high schools. Choice (B) contradicts this assumption by suggesting that the students at Governor Smith Academy may have entered school with better academic abilities than the public school students. Choice (A) is incorrect because nothing in the argument suggests any difference between male and female students. Although student violence might reflect on students' abilities to learn, choice (C) is irrelevant to this particular argument without more information. Choice (D) addresses the end results of the students attending college, but too many other factors could be part of this result. Choice (E) is insufficient without more information in the argument that taxes or funding have anything to do with the quality of the education.

3. **The correct answer is (E).** This argument depends on the assumption that the quality of an artist's materials leads directly to the quality of the finished product and that no other factors are involved. Choice (E) shows that even with the best materials, some artists do not create excellent art. Choice (A) is incorrect in that it does not recognize the individual quality of the artist. Choice (B) does not address the quality of the finished product, so it is insufficient. Choice (C) is irrelevant because nothing in the argument suggests that the cost of the materials is a factor. Choice (D) is insufficient without additional information about the finished works of art produced by the students involved.

4. **The correct answer is (C).** The economists assume that creation of any new jobs is a positive sign. Choice (C) questions this assumption by showing that the new jobs may be inadequate to support individuals or families and, thereby, may not improve the general economy. Choice (A) provides irrelevant information, because the conclusion does not depend on the reason for the creation of the new jobs. Choices (B) and (D) are incorrect because the argument does not seem to be concerned with the motivation for downsizing. Choice (E) provides irrelevant information, because nothing in the argument suggests that the economies in other countries are related to this issue.

5. **The correct answer is (B).** The nutritionists assume that people should take in high levels of niacin because high niacin shows a positive result in this one study. Choice (B) suggests that high doses of niacin may have a negative effect, despite the positive results of this study. Choice (A) might have an effect, but without further information linking the effect of this information on the result, the information provided is insufficient to weaken the argument. Choice (C) would strengthen, not weaken, the argument. Choice (D) illustrates an "ad homonym" attack by questioning the researchers and not the quality or results of the research. Choice (E) is irrelevant to the argument.

CONCLUSION QUESTIONS

1. **The correct answer is (D).** The information given in the argument shows that banks have benefited from deregulation by collecting higher profits, and customers have benefited by receiving better interest rates for both saving and borrowing. The best answer, then, is choice (D), which reports both of these results. Choice (B) has the correct result, that deregulation has been a success, but it gives reasons that contradict the premises provided in the argument. Choices (A), (C), and (E) all go too far beyond the scope of the provided information and, therefore, do not make acceptable conclusions.

2. **The correct answer is (D).** The premises of this argument show that while costs remained constant for this two-year period, the final budget decreased. From this, a logical conclusion would be choice (D), that the budget received less funding to start with in 1995 than in 1994.

   Choice (A) may or may not be true, but there is not enough information in the argument to make this decision. Choices (B) and (C) contradict the premise that costs remained constant. Choice (E) may be a reasonable inference for the future, but without additional information about the 1996 budget, it stretches too far beyond the information provided and is not as good a response as choice (D).

3. **The correct answer is (E).** This is a direct "if-then" type argument. Choice (A) is incorrect because the first sentence of the argument required Park Place in order to own a hotel on Boardwalk. This same reasoning explains why choice (E) must be correct. In fact, notice that choices (A) and (E) are direct opposites of one another— one of them must be true! Choices (B) and (C) could both be true but cannot be concluded from the information given. Choice (D) is incorrect because the player could still own a hotel in Marvin Gardens by owning Boardwalk instead of Park Place.

4. **The correct answer is (C).** Choices (A), (B), and (D) are all incorrect because the premises show that both chemical X and chemical Y display changes in reactivity when combined. Choice (C) is the best answer because it reflects this change. Choice (E) is incorrect because nothing in the argument addresses the degree of the changes on either chemical.

5. **The correct answer is (B).** This is a very short statement, so there is not much that can be concluded. Choices (A), (C), (D), and (E) all state conclusions that require information outside the scope of the information provided. Only choice (B) remains limited to the known material. If Green Arrow provides coverage to "seven out of ten"—i.e., 70 percent—the rest of the industry can only cover the remaining 30 percent. Therefore, choice (B) is a reasonable conclusion.

HIDDEN ASSUMPTION QUESTIONS

1. **The correct answer is (C).** The governor is choosing new delegates based upon their past voting records. This shows the assumption that they will continue to vote the same way, so choice (C) is the best answer. Choices (A) and (D) are incorrect because the importance of the issue is not made part of this argument; this argument is based upon the fact that the governor is making these decisions for whatever reason he chooses. Choice (B) is irrelevant to this particular argument because nothing in this argument mentions the budget issues. Choice (E) is incorrect because there is nothing in the argument to suggest that activities in other states have anything to do with this governor's actions.

2. **The correct answer is (D).** This argument concludes that additional token vendors are necessary as a result of the rally. Choice (D) shows the best assumption, that the rally will increase use of the Center Street station, where token vendors will be required. Choice (A) is incorrect because there is no reason to believe that the mayor has anything to do with this particular rally. Choice (B) is incorrect because the argument merely says that the route discussed is the *best* route, not the *only* one. Choice (C) is probably the second-best choice, because it suggests that the traffic on public transportation will increase, but choice (D) is better by directly making this statement. Choice (E) is not directly related to the argument without making the connection directly to the Center Street station.

3. **The correct answer is (E).** The speaker considers that since a man won in the first year that men were allowed to enter and assumes that men could win this contest anytime they enter. Choice (E), therefore, is the best answer. Choice (D) is similar, but it goes too far beyond the argument. Choices (A), (B), and (C) do not address the results of this contest and are, therefore, irrelevant.

4. **The correct answer is (C).** This appears to be a simple argument because it presents a relatively common issue, the days of the week, but analysis may be complicated. Choices (A), (B), and (D) are all true statements, using the standard calendar, but they do not directly address this as a logical argument. Only choice (C) provides information that could be a hidden assumption for this argument, linking the information in the premise with the conclusion. Choice (E) is irrelevant because nothing in the argument suggests any connection to the speaker's meeting schedule.

5. **The correct answer is (A).** This argument begins with information about animal behavior and then makes a conclusion about human behavior. Thus, the best assumption is one that connects human behavior to the observed animal behavior. Choice (B) is incorrect because nothing in the argument considers cities' budgets. Choice (C) is close but is not as good an answer as choice (A) because it does not address the conclusion reached. Choice (D) might question the validity of the result of the animal study, but it does not make any connection to the human behavior. Choice (E) is incorrect because it makes no connection between the animal study and human behavior.

Unit 5

ANALYTICAL WRITING ASSESSMENT STRATEGIES

Although scored separately from the rest of the GMAT, the 1-hour Analytical Writing Assessment will be the first of the tests you will be taking. It consists of writing two 30-minute essays on two topics that you will not know ahead of time and for which you will not be given any choice. One of the topics will ask for an analysis of an issue, and the second will call for an analysis of an argument. If you are already computer literate, you should have very little problem using the online word processor on this section of the test. If not, don't worry. There will be enough time to learn how to use the mouse, the keyboard, and the word processor, so that you will be able to write the two essays.

WHY ESSAYS?

You may be wondering why a student in business management is required to demonstrate his or her writing skills. However, when you stop to consider what good management entails, it becomes clear that one of the most important qualities of a good manager is effective communication, which includes both written and verbal skills. Hence, this is the reason for the essay component of the GMAT.

SCORING

Each essay will be scored on a scale of 0 to 6 and an NR for a blank paper or a nonverbal response.

The general qualities that are taken into consideration for the essays are

(A) thoughtful, perceptive analysis of the issue or a critique of the argument presented.

(B) development of ideas clearly, persuasively, or logically, using insightful reasons and/or relevant examples.

(C) coherent organization.

(D) language fluency.

(E) grammar, usage, and mechanics.

Based on the level of skill demonstrated in the above-mentioned areas, following is a summary score guide.

6   An outstanding essay
5   A strong essay
4   An adequate essay
3   A limited essay
2   A seriously flawed essay
1   A fundamentally deficient essay
0   An essay that is completely unreadable or not written on the assigned topic

The essays are scored using the holistic method, which means the score will be based on the overall impression your essay makes rather than on attention to minor details. Each essay will be read by two readers, and if their scores fall within a point of each other's, which is usually the case, the two scores are averaged. If the scores differ by a wider spread, then the essay will be read by a third reader.

Since the holistic method is used, minor infractions of grammar and usage are supposed to be set aside in arriving at a score. Also, since you, the writer, have only 30 minutes to write each essay, all you will probably have time for is one draft. So it is important that you compose as much of the essay in your head as possible before you start to write. This unit will help you develop some basic techniques for doing so.

As mentioned earlier, the Analytical Writing Assessment requires that you write two 30-minute essays, one analyzing an issue stated in the topic and the other critiquing an argument that is presented in the topic. The "issue" topic generally presents you with two positions on a subject, and you are expected to state and defend the position of your choice by using reasons and persuasive examples. The "argument" topic presents you with one strong position on a subject, and you are expected to critique or find fault with the line of reasoning and the evidence employed to support it. Each essay should consist of 4 to 5 paragraphs.

However, before discussing the differences in how to approach the two types of essay, it might be worthwhile to focus on the common elements of a good essay.

WHAT IS AN ESSAY?

An essay is basically an attempt in writing to express a personal opinion on a subject as convincingly and persuasively as possible.

The fundamental *fives* of a good essay are:

1. Content
2. Cogency
3. Clarity
4. Coherency
5. Correctness

Let's discuss each one separately.

CONTENT

People read an article to the end only if they find it interesting, surprising, or informative. However, in the context in which you are writing these essays, and the fact that the readers must read each essay to the end, use your common sense. Don't try too hard to be unique in your perspective or reasoning, but, on the other hand, avoid clichés and well-worn expressions. Try to avoid melodrama and understatement. In other words, take the subject seriously, respond honestly, and use examples from your own experience or the experience of people you know of personally or through your reading, and that will take care of ensuring both the individuality of your essay and the reader's interest.

COGENCY

If you express your thoughts and point of view about the subject in the context of what you know and believe at the time of writing, you will have no difficulty in being convincing. Remember, no one expects you to be an expert on the subject of the topic since you will have no prior knowledge of what the topic will be. If you use a voice that is not yours, not only will the reader find it difficult to understand you, but the quality of your writing will suffer.

CLARITY

Time is of the essence here, both for you and the readers. Avoid vague, general words and try to use concrete, specific examples and language to avoid wordiness.

Example

Scenes depicting violence on many TV entertainment shows have a bad influence on viewers, particularly the young.

Better

Scenes depicting violence on TV, such as the beating of a youth by a gang of teens in an episode of "In The Heat of the Night," encourage violence in young people, because they rarely show the result of violence, such as broken limbs or the bloodied face of the victim.

COHERENCY

Even though you explore several ideas about a subject in your essay, they should all be related or connected. Therefore, it is important that as you move from one idea to another that you make clear the connecting link between them. These connecting links can express opposition or contrast, addition or amplification, result or effect, relations in time or place, and time sequence, to mention a few. This is where transitional words or phrases become very important, particularly when you move from exploring an idea in one paragraph to exploring another in the next paragraph. Some of the more frequently used transitions signal the following:

Opposition

but, however, contrary to, although, nevertheless, in opposition to, on the other hand

Example

Many people believe that marijuana is extremely harmful under any circumstance, and therefore should remain illegal. *However,* people with pain-wracked bodies cannot live without its soothing effect and believe it should be legalized.

Addition

furthermore, in addition, moreover, further, also

Example

Many teenage couples cannot handle financial pressure. *Furthermore,* they find it difficult to cope with the responsibility of raising a child.

Result

consequently, thus, as a result, therefore

Example

Ralph worked overtime all summer. *As a result,* he was able to pay his tuition fees for the fall.

Time

sometimes, often, never, seldom, after, now, before, frequently, at the same time

Example

Edward is determined to make a success of himself. He *often* tries to work on several different projects *at the same time.*

Place

here, there, above, elsewhere, farther on, below

Example

There are several dilapidated houses at the intersection of the roads. *Farther on* down Lake Road, however, several beautiful mansions dot the lakefront.

Time Sequence

first, second, last or lastly, then, before, next, finally

Example

Pamela worked on her term paper into the early hours of the morning. *Finally,* at 7 a.m., she went to bed exhausted.

CORRECTNESS

If you have reached this stage in your formal education, chances are that you have more than a basic command of the English language. However, when you must write under the pressure of time, it is likely that you will make some mistakes in your essay. Sometimes, as you read over the essay, you will discover that you can more succinctly express the same idea or information. In other instances, you will find that you have inadvertently made an error in grammar or punctuation. As this may occur in both essays, this may be the appropriate time to point out some of the more common errors.

SENTENCE ERRORS

FRAGMENTS

The collie tried to run away from the rampaging elephant. Although it was useless.

The collie tried to run away from the rampaging elephant, although he knew it was useless.

RUN-ONS

John and Mary wanted to leave, but their hostess asked them to stay, so they sat down again with the Johnsons to have another cup of coffee, and John even had another piece of the apple pie that Rita Johnson had made.

John and Mary wanted to leave, but their hostess asked them to stay. So they sat down again with the Johnsons to have another cup of coffee. John even had another piece of the apple pie that Rita Johnson had made.

VERB ERRORS

The sergeant was ask to report to the colonel immediately.

The sergeant was ask*ed* to report to the colonel immediately.

PREPOSITION ERRORS

Parents often do not trust their children. As a result, they create avoidable problems.

(Who does the "they" refer to—the children or the parents?)

Watch out for those places where you have repeated a word or omitted a word in the rush to finish the essay on time.

PROCESS

There are four basic steps to writing an essay:

1. Read (about 2 minutes).
2. Plan (about 3 minutes).
3. Write (about 20 minutes).
4. Proofread and edit (about 5 minutes).

STEP 1—READING THE TOPIC

Read the topic to determine the issue to which you are asked to respond. This may sound like unnecessary advice, but bear in mind that if you don't read the topic at least twice, you are in danger of misunderstanding what the issue is or going off on a tangent. If that happens, you may wind up with a score of 0, no matter how well you write.

STEP 2—PLANNING THE ESSAY

Unlike the essays or papers you write at home or in the library, where there is no time limit and that you can write, revise, or even start over, this GMAT essay must be as near perfect as you can make it the first time you write it. The fact that you have a limited amount of time makes it imperative that you know ahead of time what your position is, what your main supporting points are, and what examples or information you will use to explain your points.

STEP 3—WRITING THE ESSAY

Once you have a basic plan, you are ready to begin.

Introduction

Many people find it difficult to begin at the beginning, partly from anxiety and partly because the introduction or the first paragraph must be clear, strong, and effective. In fact, isn't it logical that you can introduce a subject better if you know what it is and how it is developed? Ask any author of a textbook, and you will discover that the introduction to the book was the last section written.

Body

It is a good idea to begin by writing the second paragraph. We will discuss in the following section what the second and following paragraphs of the essay should cover for both kinds of analysis.

Conclusion

If the body paragraphs of your essay have done their jobs well, the concluding paragraph needs only to restate briefly your position and summarize the supporting ideas. If you have time, a sentence (or two) that suggests new areas of action or a solution can be included.

STEP 4—PROOFREADING AND EDITING

Next to planning, this is the most crucial part of your essay. You must spend the last 4 to 5 minutes checking for errors that you made in your haste to finish on time. Some of these were discussed in the previous section under Correctness. Also, look out for words you may have omitted or repeated in haste, a punctuation mark that is either unclear or left out, letters in a word that have been transposed, and wordiness; then make the necessary corrections. Finally, only if you have time, change any words or phrases that you don't think express your idea clearly.

WRITING THE ESSAYS

ANALYSIS OF AN ISSUE

The analysis topic presents you with two positions on a subject. You are required to choose one position and explain the reasons for your choice.

Topic

There is a growing body of people who feel that affirmative action should be ended because it encourages reverse discrimination, exacerbates racial tensions, and throws doubt on the worth of any achievement by a member of a minority. However, there is also a large body of people who believe that the best way for white America to make reparations for slavery and other forms of discrimination against minorities is not only to continue, but to expand affirmative action programs.

Which position do you find more compelling? Explain your position using reasons and/or examples drawn from your personal experiences, observations, or readings.

Step 1. Read the topic to determine the issue and choose your position.

Position A—End affirmative action

Reasons
- (A) reverse discrimination
- (B) racial tensions
- (C) devalues minority achievement

Position B—Continue and expand affirmative action

Reasons
- (A) reparation for slavery
- (B) other forms of discrimination

Notice that once you have read and analyzed the topic, you practically have an outline for your essay, particularly since the reasons to defend the position are also stated in the essay. All you have to plan beyond this is to think of examples to illustrate each of the supporting reasons. If you do not like all or some of the reasons presented, or if there are no reasons stated in the topic, spend a couple of minutes brainstorming for more and add them to the lists.

Let's see if we can come up with additional reasons:

Position A—End Affirmative Action

Reasons
- (D) fails to challenge some recipients to do their best
- (E) can actually inhibit sense of self-worth

Position B—Continue and expand affirmative action

Reasons
- (C) helps to break down social segregation
- (D) diminishes suspicions and prejudices between the groups through familiarity

Step 2. Plan—Now you can create a brief outline for either position that will look somewhat like this:

Position A

Paragraph 1—Introduction: End affirmative action

Paragraph 2—Reason A: Encourages reverse discrimination

Paragraph 3—Reason B: Throws doubt on the worth of a minority person's achievement

Paragraph 4—Reason C: Does not build self-esteem in a recipient

Paragraph 5—Conclusion: Restate your position and summarize the reasons once again

Position B

The same format applies, except that you state the opposing position in the introductory paragraph and present your reasons in paragraphs 2, 3, and 4. Again, the concluding paragraph will restate your position and summarize the reasons.

Step 3. **Now, you're on your own. Write the essay!**

Step 4. **Proofread and edit (remember to save a few minutes for this step)**

ANALYSIS OF AN ARGUMENT

The argument topic presents you with one strong, clear position on a controversial topic. What you are required to do is to find fault with the reasoning expressed in the argument and the evidence on which the argument is based. You are also expected to present alternative means by which the problem can be better remedied.

Topic

The United States has one of the highest rates of murder in the world. Law enforcement agencies seem unable to cope with this problem. The only way to decrease the murder rate in the United States is to mandate the death penalty for murder.

How persuasive do you find this argument? Explain your point of view by analyzing the line of reasoning and the use of evidence in the argument. Discuss also what would make the argument more persuasive or would help you better evaluate its conclusion.

Step 1. **Read the topic to identify the premises and the conclusion.**

Remember that your job here is to find fault or demonstrate the weakness in both the premise and the argument.

Premises

(A) The United States has one of the highest murder rates in the world.
(B) Law enforcement agencies are unable to cope with the problem.

Conclusion: The only way to decrease the murder rate is to mandate the death penalty for murder.

Step 2. **Plan**

Paragraph 1—Introduction

Fault with the first premise—too general. How high is the rate? Is it increasing? Many countries' records are incomplete or nonexistent.

Paragraph 2—Fault with the second premise

Most countries do not have as efficient a record of tracking down murderers as the United States does, both because of technological sophistication and police training. This may partially explain the high statistics.

Paragraph 3—Fault with the conclusion

Very few murders are premeditated—most are committed in the heat of passion. (Cool, calculated murders are often committed for profit or by deranged minds; the first group of perpetrators considers the risk worth taking, and the second group is not even aware of the consequences.)

Paragraph 4—Fault with the conclusion

There are already several states where the death penalty is legal. None of them has demonstrated any appreciable decrease in murder when compared to states where it is not legal.

Paragraph 5—Conclusion

Thus, the death penalty is not a viable solution (restate why). Alternative—What might work better is to remove existing loopholes in the current penal system, such as parole from a life sentence. Life imprisonment should mean imprisonment for life.

Of course, you need to explain your points in greater depth than in the preceding outline. But the most important thing to remember is that in an argument, you must distinguish between the premise (or premises) and the conclusion and present evidence or reasoning to demonstrate the weaknesses in both. If you have time, you should indicate alternative solutions that you think may be better remedies.

Step 3. Now write!

Step 4. Proofread and edit

Good luck!

ADDITIONAL TOPICS FOR PRACTICE

ANALYSIS OF AN ISSUE

1. The juvenile crime rate in the United States has been steadily increasing in the past few years and shows no signs of abating. Some people place the blame for this situation on lack of parental involvement and on personal responsibility on the part of juveniles. Others believe that the government's lack of commitment to successful youth-oriented programs, such as Head Start, Job Corps, and drug treatment centers, is where the blame lies.

2. Recently, President Clinton signed a $265-billion defense authorization bill, one of the provisions of which requires the Pentagon to discharge troops who have HIV, the virus that causes AIDS. Those who support this provision believe that the combat readiness of the military is jeopardized by the presence of troops with HIV. Those who plan to have the ouster provision repealed claim that people who live with HIV are able to lead productive lives, provide for their families, and contribute to the country's security and well-being.

3. A new kind of war against cancer is being waged among the pharmaceutical companies, the Food and Drug Administration, and many physicians on one side; and patients, their families, and their physicians on the other. The first contends that chemotherapy is the only scientifically proven treatment to combat cancer, and no alternative treatments should be included. In opposition, patients and their families, as well as their physicians, maintain that patients have a right to control their own lives, which includes the right to choose companion therapies.

4. Although the Cold War era has ended, many people still believe that their causes are worth dying for. Some give their lives for their countries, others for their religions, and still others for their families or personal beliefs. Unless we can persuade these people that giving up their lives for their cause is useless, and even counterproductive, in the long run, the world will never be rid of war.

5. In recent years, one of the ongoing controversies in our society and in the courts is the issue of prayer in public schools. People on both sides of the issue base their arguments on the Constitution of the United States that guarantees freedom of religious expression. Since prayer is the essential common element in all religions, time should be set aside for prayer in all American public schools.

ANALYSIS OF AN ARGUMENT

1. Immigrants, both legal and illegal, have drained the nation's resources by stealing jobs from American citizens, overtaxing the public school system, and overburdening public assistance services, such as health and housing. The only solution to this deteriorating situation is to declare a moratorium on immigration for a few years and to deport illegal immigrants immediately.

2. In developed and developing nations, hunger, poverty, disease, and illiteracy ravage the lives of countless men, women, and children every day. At the same time, a large chunk of each nation's budget is devoted to increasing its arsenal of weapons and troops for use in real, imagined, or concocted hostility and war between tribes, ethnic groups, and neighboring nations. Unless this proclivity to war-making and warmongering is reversed, there will be nothing left worth fighting for since we will have destroyed humanity.

3. The landmark communications bill that President Clinton recently signed removes most prior restraints on companies in the communications industry in the spirit of free and open markets as a spur to competition. However, one of the provisions in the same bill places restrictions on the dissemination of pornographic material and other forms of indecent expression on the Internet. This is a blatant violation of one of the most dearly held freedoms of Americans, set forth in the First Amendment: the right of free speech and expression.

4. The cost of a college education is skyrocketting, as the availability of student loans and scholarships is shrinking. This situation is leading to many capable and deserving students being denied the right to a college education. These academically gifted students should be assisted by the federal government to attend the college of their choice.

5. The United States is a rich and colorful tapestry of ethnic groups—an intricate mosaic of cultures, religions, and social rituals. However, it is also a Tower of Babel of innumerable languages and dialects. If this country is to develop its unique identity through communication, understanding, and respect for its diversity, we must make English the official language of the nation.

Unit 6

MATHEMATICAL PROBLEM SOLVING AND REVIEW

The GMAT CAT Quantitative test contains a total of 37 questions—both Problem Solving and Data Sufficiency questions. You will have 75 minutes to complete this portion of the exam. Because Data Sufficiency questions are somewhat different from the standard multiple-choice questions you will encounter on the rest of the test, we have separated them into a separate review section—Unit 7.

The problem solving questions in this section are based on the math that is usually covered in high school mathmatics classes—arithmatic, algebra, and geometry.

There are two different types of arithmetic questions that will appear on the GMAT—one that asks you to perform a computation (add the fractions, multiply the decimals, manipulate the percents) and one that asks you to solve a word problem. Similarly, there will be algebraic computation problems (solve the equation, factor the expressions, manipulate the square roots) as well as word problems. As far as the geometry problems are concerned, you will only be asked to solve problems by working with geometric properties. You will not need to create proofs or state definitions.

In the following pages, you will find a thorough review of all of the mathematics covered on the GMAT. First, read the hints and strategies below, and remember them when you begin to practice problem solving.

HINTS AND STRATEGIES FOR MULTIPLE CHOICE MATH QUESTIONS

1. Do not waste any time doing computations that are not necessary. Remember that one of the five answers must be the correct one. Estimate as much as you possibly can as you try to determine which of the five answers must be correct.

2. You will not be given any scrap paper on which to work out problems. You must do all of your writing in the margin of the test booklet. Be sure to write as small as you can to conserve space.

3. Do not worry if there are questions that you cannot answer. Since you can not omit an answer, you should just guess.

4. Be careful (especially when solving geometry problems) to give your answer in the same units of measurement as the multiple-choice answers.

5. All fractions that appear as the answers to questions will be expressed in reduced form. Therefore, if you solve a problem and obtain a fraction as the answer, this fraction must be reduced before you will find it among the multiple-choice answers. Similarly, all square root answers must be expressed in reduced form. In geometrical problems involving π, look at the answer choices to determine if you are supposed to leave the answer in terms of π or use the approximate value, $\frac{22}{7}$.

6. Of course, you are not permitted to use a calculator to perform your computations. This means that you should brush up on the rules for multiplying and dividing numbers with decimals, etc. However, the problems are, in general, designed to not include messy computations. If you ever find yourself thinking, "I wish I had a calculator to help me with this problem," carefully look at the problem once again. There is quite possibly an easier way to do it that you may have missed.

7. If the answer you obtain does not match one of the choices given, it might still be right. Try to write it in a different form, and then see if it matches. For example, the answer $x^2 + 3x$ can also be written as $x(x + 3)$.

8. Make sure to answer the question that is being asked. People sometimes get a problem wrong because, after finding the value of x, they choose that value as the answer, when the problem was actually asking for the value, for example, of $x + 2$.

9. If you are stuck, try looking at the multiple-choice answers. Since one of them has to be right, the answers may give you some idea of how to proceed.

In the following section, all of the mathematics that you need to know for the GMAT is reviewed. Once you have studied it—and understood it—you can then take the mathematics portion of the exams that are included in this book with confidence.

ARITHMETIC

WHOLE NUMBERS

Definitions

The set of numbers {1, 2, 3, 4, . . .} is called the set of *counting numbers* and/or natural numbers, and/or sometimes the set *of positive integers*. (The notation { } means "set" or collection, and the three dots after the number 4 indicate that the list continues without end.) *Zero* is usually not considered one of the counting numbers. Together, the counting numbers and zero make up the set of *whole numbers.*

Place Value

Whole numbers are expressed in a system of tens, called the *decimal* system. Ten *digits*—0, 1, 2, 3, 4, 5, 6, 7, 8, and 9—are used. Each digit differs not only in *face* value but also in *place* value, depending on where it stands in the number.

Example 1

237 means

$$(2 \cdot 100) + (3 \cdot 10) + (7 \cdot 1)$$

The digit 2 has a face value of 2 but a place value of 200.

Example 2

35,412 can be written as:

$$(3 \cdot 10,000) + (5 \cdot 1,000) + (4 \cdot 100) + (1 \cdot 10) + (2 \cdot 1)$$

The digit in the last place on the right is said to be in the units or ones place, the digit to the left of that in the tens place, the next digit to the left of that in the hundreds place, and so on.

Odd and Even Numbers

A whole number is *even* if it is divisible by 2; it is *odd* if it is not divisible by 2. Zero is thus an even number.

Example

2, 4, 6, 8, and 320 are even numbers; 3, 7, 9, 21, and 45 are odd numbers.

Prime Numbers

The positive integer p is said to be a prime number (or simply, *a prime*) if $p \neq 1$ and the only positive divisors of p are itself and 1. The positive integer 1 is called a *unit*. The first ten primes are 2, 3, 5, 7, 11, 13, 17, 19, 23, and 29. All other positive integers that are neither 1 nor prime are *composite numbers*. Composite numbers can be *factored*, that is, expressed as products of their divisors or factors; for example, $56 = 7 \cdot 8 = 7 \cdot 4 \cdot 2$. In particular, composite numbers can be expressed as products of their *prime* factors in just one way (except for order).

To factor a composite number into its prime factors, proceed as follows. First, try to divide the number by the prime number 2. If this is successful, continue to divide by 2 until an odd number is obtained. Then, attempt to divide the last quotient by the prime number 3 and by 3 again, as many times as possible. Then, move on to dividing by the prime number 5 and other successive primes until a prime quotient is obtained. Express the original number as a product of all its prime divisors.

Example

Find the prime factors of 210.

$$2\,\overline{)210}$$
$$3\,\overline{)105}$$
$$5\,\overline{)\,35}$$
$$7$$

Therefore, $210 = 2 \cdot 3 \cdot 5 \cdot 7$ (written in any order), and 210 is an integer multiple of 2, of 3, of 5, and of 7.

Consecutive Whole Numbers

Numbers are consecutive if each number is the successor of the number that precedes it. In a consecutive series of whole numbers, an odd number is always followed by an even number and an even number by an odd. If three consecutive whole numbers are given, either two of them are odd and one is even or two are even and one is odd.

Example 1

7, 8, 9, 10, and 11 are consecutive whole numbers.

Example 2

8, 10, 12, and 14 are consecutive even numbers.

Example 3

21, 23, 25, and 27 are consecutive odd numbers.

Example 4

21, 23, and 27 are *not* consecutive odd numbers because 25 is missing.

THE NUMBER LINE

A useful method of representing numbers geometrically makes it easier to understand numbers. It is called the *number line*. Draw a horizontal line, considered to extend without end in both directions. Select some point on the line, and label it with the number 0. This point is called the *origin*. Choose some convenient distance as a unit of length. Take the point on the number line that lies one unit to the right of the origin, and label it with the number 1. The point on the number line that is one unit to the right of 1 is labeled 2, and so on. In this way, every whole number is associated with one point on the line, but it is not true that every point on the line represents a whole number.

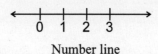

Number line

Ordering of Whole Numbers

On the number line, the point representing 8 lies to the right of the point representing 5, and we say 8 > 5 (read "8 is greater than 5"). One can also say 5 < 8 ("5 is less than 8"). For any two whole numbers a and b, there are always three possibilities:

$$a < b, \qquad a = b, \qquad \text{or} \qquad a > b.$$

If $a = b$, the points representing the numbers a and b coincide on the number line.

OPERATIONS WITH WHOLE NUMBERS

The basic operations on whole numbers are addition (+), subtraction (−), multiplication (· or ×), and division (÷). These are all *binary* operations—that is, one works with two numbers at a time in order to get a unique answer. The operations of addition and multiplication on whole numbers are said to be *closed* because the answer in each case is also a whole number. The operations of subtraction and division on whole numbers are not closed because the unique answer is not necessarily a member of the set of whole numbers.

Examples

$3 + 4 = 7$ a whole number

$4 \cdot 3 = 12$ a whole number

$2 - 5 = -3$ not a whole number

$3 \div 8 = \dfrac{3}{8}$ not a whole number

Addition

If addition is a binary operation, how are three numbers—say, 3, 4, and 8—added? One way is to write:

$$(3 + 4) + 8 = 7 + 8 = 15$$

Another way is to write:

$$3 + (4 + 8) = 3 + 12 = 15$$

The parentheses merely group the numbers together. The fact that the same answer, 15, is obtained either way illustrates the *associative property* of addition:

$$(r + s) + t = r + (s + t).$$

The order in which whole numbers are added is immaterial—that is, $3 + 4 = 4 + 3$. This principle is called the *commutative property* of addition. Most people use this property without realizing it when they add a column of numbers from the top down and then check their results by beginning over again from the bottom. (Even though there may be a long column of numbers, only two numbers are added at a time.)

If 0 is added to any whole number, the whole number is unchanged. Zero is called the *identity element* for addition.

Subtraction

Subtraction is the inverse of addition. The order in which the numbers are written is important; there is no commutative property for subtraction.

$$4 - 3 \neq 3 - 4$$

The $\neq$ is read "not equal."

Multiplication

Multiplication is a commutative operation:

$$43 \cdot 73 = 73 \cdot 43.$$

The result or answer in a multiplication problem is called the *product*.

If a number is multiplied by 1, the number is unchanged; the *identity element* for multiplication is 1.

Zero times any number is 0:

$$42 \cdot 0 = 0.$$

Multiplication can be expressed with several different symbols:

$$9 \cdot 7 \cdot 3 = 9 \times 7 \times 3 = 9(7)(3).$$

Besides being commutative, multiplication is *associative:*

$$(9 \cdot 7) \cdot 3 = 63 \cdot 3 = 189$$

and

$$9 \cdot (7 \cdot 3) = 9 \cdot 21 = 189.$$

A number can be quickly multiplied by 10 by adding a zero to the right of the number. Similarly, a number can be multiplied by 100 by adding two zeros to the right:

$$38 \cdot 10 = 380$$

and

$$100 \cdot 76 = 7,600.$$

Division

Division is the inverse of multiplication. It is not commutative:

$$8 \div 4 \neq 4 \div 8$$

The parts of a division example are named as follows:

$$\text{divisor} \overline{)\text{dividend}.}^{\text{quotient}}$$

If a number is divided by 1, the quotient is the original number.

Division by 0 is not defined (has no meaning). Zero divided by any number other than 0 is 0:

$$0 \div 56 = 0.$$

Divisors and Multiples

The whole number b *divides* the whole number a if there exists a whole number k such that $a = bk$. The whole number a is then said to be an integer *multiple* of b, and b is called a *divisor* (or *factor*) of a.

Example 1

3 divides 15 because $15 = 3 \cdot 5$. Thus, 3 is a divisor of 15 (and so is 5), and 15 is an integer multiple of 3 (and of 5).

Example 2

3 does not divide 8 because $8 \neq 3k$ for a whole number k.

Example 3

Divisors of 28 are 1, 2, 4, 7, 14, and 28.

Example 4

Multiples of 3 are 3, 6, 9, 12, 15, . . .

QUIZ

WHOLE NUMBER PROBLEMS

1. What is the prime factorization of 78?

2. What are the divisors of 56?

3. Which property is illustrated by the following statement?

    $(3 + 5) + 8 = 3 + (5 + 8)$

4. Which property is illustrated by the following statement?

    $(5 \cdot 7) \cdot 3 = 7 \cdot (5 \cdot 3)$

5. Find the first five multiples of 7.

SOLUTIONS

1. $78 = 2 \cdot 39 = 2 \cdot 3 \cdot 13$

2. The divisors of 56 are 1, 2, 4, 7, 8, 14, 28, 56.

3. The associative property of addition

4. The commutative property of multiplication

5. 7, 14, 21, 28, 35

FRACTIONS

Definitions

If a and b are whole numbers and $b \neq 0$, the symbol $\dfrac{a}{b}$ (or a/b) is called a fraction. The upper part, a, is called the *numerator*, and the lower part, b, is called the *denominator*. The denominator indicates into how many parts something is divided, and the numerator tells how many of these parts are taken. A fraction indicates division:

$$\frac{7}{8} = 8\overline{)7}.$$

If the numerator of a fraction is 0, the value of the fraction is 0. If the denominator of a fraction is 0, the fraction is not defined (has no meaning):

$$\frac{0}{17} = 0$$

$\dfrac{17}{0}$ not defined (has no meaning).

If the denominator of a fraction is 1, the value of the fraction is the same as the numerator:

$$\frac{18}{1} = 18.$$

If the numerator and denominator are the same number, the value of the fraction is 1:

$$\frac{7}{7} = 1.$$

Equivalent Fractions

Fractions that represent the same number are said to be *equivalent*. If m is a counting number and $\frac{a}{b}$ is a fraction, then: $\frac{m \times a}{m \times b} = \frac{a}{b}$ because $\frac{m}{m} = 1$ and $1 \times \frac{a}{b} = \frac{a}{b}$.

Example

$$\frac{2}{3} = \frac{4}{6} = \frac{6}{9} = \frac{8}{12}$$

These fractions are all equivalent.

Inequality of Fractions

If two fractions are not equivalent, one is smaller than the other. The ideas of "less than" and "greater than" were previously defined and used for whole numbers.

For the fractions $\frac{a}{b}$ and $\frac{c}{b}$:

$$\frac{a}{b} < \frac{c}{b} \text{ if } a < c \text{ and if } b > 0.$$

That is, if two fractions have the same denominator, the one with the smaller numerator has the smaller value.

If two fractions have different denominators, find a common denominator by multiplying one denominator by the other. Then use the common denominator to compare numerators.

Example

Which is smaller, $\dfrac{5}{8}$ or $\dfrac{4}{7}$?

$8 \cdot 7 = 56 =$ common denominator.

$$\dfrac{5}{8} \times \dfrac{7}{7} = \dfrac{35}{56} \qquad \dfrac{4}{7} \times \dfrac{8}{8} = \dfrac{32}{56}$$

Since $32 < 35$,

$$\dfrac{32}{56} < \dfrac{35}{56} \text{ and } \dfrac{4}{7} < \dfrac{5}{8}.$$

Reducing to Lowest Terms

The principle that

$$\dfrac{m \times a}{m \times b} = \dfrac{a}{b}$$

can be particularly useful in reducing fractions to lowest terms. Fractions are expressed in *lowest terms* when the numerator and denominator have no common factor except 1. To reduce a fraction to an equivalent fraction in lowest terms, express the numerator and denominator as products of their prime factors. Each time a prime appears in the numerator over the same prime in the denominator, $\dfrac{p}{p}$, substitute its equal value, 1.

Example

Reduce $\dfrac{30}{42}$ to an equivalent fraction in lowest terms:

$$\dfrac{30}{42} = \dfrac{2 \cdot 3 \cdot 5}{2 \cdot 3 \cdot 7} = 1 \cdot 1 \cdot \dfrac{5}{7} = \dfrac{5}{7}.$$

In practice, this can be done even more quickly by dividing the numerator and the denominator by any number, prime or not, which will divide both evenly. Repeat this process until there is no prime factor remaining that is common to both the numerator and the denominator:

$$\dfrac{30}{42} = \dfrac{15}{21} = \dfrac{5}{7}.$$

PROPER FRACTIONS, IMPROPER FRACTIONS, AND MIXED NUMBERS

Definitions

A *proper fraction* is a fraction whose numerator is smaller than its denominator. Proper fractions always have a value less than 1:

$$\frac{3}{4} \quad \frac{5}{8} \quad \frac{121}{132} \quad \frac{0}{1}.$$

An *improper fraction* is a fraction with a numerator equal to or greater than the denominator. Improper fractions always have a value equal to or greater than 1:

$$\frac{3}{2} \quad \frac{17}{17} \quad \frac{9}{1} \quad \frac{15}{14}.$$

A *mixed number* is a number composed of a whole number and a proper fraction. It is always greater than 1 in value:

$$3\frac{7}{8} \quad 5\frac{1}{4} \quad 11\frac{3}{14}.$$

The fraction $3\frac{7}{8}$ means $3 + \frac{7}{8}$ and is read "three and seven eighths."

To Change a Mixed Number into an Improper Fraction

Multiply the denominator by the whole number, and add this product to the numerator. Use the sum obtained as the new numerator, and keep the original denominator.

Example

Write $9\frac{4}{11}$ as an improper fraction:

$$9\frac{4}{11} = \frac{(11 \times 9) + 4}{11} = \frac{99 + 4}{11} = \frac{103}{11}.$$

Note: In any calculation with mixed numbers, first change the mixed numbers to improper fractions.

To Change an Improper Fraction into a Mixed Number

Divide the numerator by the denominator. The result is the whole-number part of the mixed number. If there is a remainder in the division process because the division does not come out evenly, put the remainder over the denominator (divisor). This gives the fractional part of the mixed number:

$$\frac{20}{3} = 3\overline{)20} = 6\frac{2}{3}.$$

MULTIPLICATION

Proper and Improper Fractions

Multiply the two numerators and then multiply the two denominators. If the numerator obtained is larger than the denominator, divide the numerator of the resulting fraction by its denominator:

$$\frac{3}{8} \times \frac{15}{11} = \frac{45}{88} \qquad \frac{3}{8} \times \frac{22}{7} = \frac{66}{56} = 1\frac{10}{56}$$

Multiplication of fractions is commutative. Three or more fractions are multiplied in the same way; two numerators are done at a time, and the result is multiplied by the next numerator.

The product in the multiplication of fractions is usually expressed in lowest terms.

Canceling

In multiplying fractions, if any of the numerators and denominators have a common divisor (factor), divide each of them by this common factor and the value of the fraction remains the same. This process is called *canceling* or *cancellation*.

Example

$$\frac{27}{18} \times \frac{90}{300} = \frac{27}{18} \times \frac{90}{300}$$

Divide second fraction by $\frac{10}{10}$

$$= \frac{27}{18} \times \frac{9}{30}$$

Cancel: 18 and 9 each divisible by 9; 27 and 30 each divisible by 3.

$$= \frac{\overset{9}{\cancel{27}}}{\underset{2}{\cancel{18}}} \times \frac{\overset{1}{\cancel{9}}}{\underset{10}{\cancel{30}}}$$

Multiply numerators; multiply denominators

$$= \frac{9 \times 1}{2 \times 10} = \frac{9}{20}.$$

Another method:

$$\frac{\overset{3}{\cancel{27}}}{\underset{2}{\cancel{18}}} \times \frac{\overset{3}{\cancel{9}}}{\underset{10}{\cancel{30}}} = \frac{3 \times 3}{2 \times 10} = \frac{9}{20}$$

Cancel: 27 and 18 have common factor 9; 9 and 30 have common factor 3.

Note: Canceling can take place only between a numerator and a denominator, in the same or a different fraction, never between two numerators or between two denominators.

Mixed Numbers

Mixed numbers should be changed to improper fractions before multiplying. Then multiply as described above.

Example

To multiply $\frac{4}{7} \times 3\frac{5}{8}$

change $3\frac{5}{8}$ to an improper fraction:

$$3\frac{5}{8} = \frac{(8 \times 3) + 5}{8} = \frac{24 + 5}{8} = \frac{29}{8}.$$

Multiply

$$\frac{\overset{1}{\cancel{4}}}{7} \times \frac{29}{\underset{2}{\cancel{8}}} = \frac{29}{14}$$

The answer can be left in this form or changed to a mixed number: $1\frac{1}{14}$.

Fractions with Whole Numbers

Write the whole number as a fraction with a denominator of 1 and then multiply:

$$\frac{3}{4} \times 7 = \frac{3}{4} \times \frac{7}{1} = \frac{21}{4} = 5\frac{1}{4}.$$

Note: When any fraction is multiplied by 1, its value remains unchanged. When any fraction is multiplied by 0, the product is 0.

Division

Reciprocals

Division of fractions involves reciprocals. One fraction is the *reciprocal* of another if the product of the fractions is 1.

Example 1

$\frac{3}{4}$ and $\frac{4}{3}$ are reciprocals since

$$\frac{\cancel{3}^1}{\cancel{4}_1} \times \frac{\cancel{4}^1}{\cancel{3}_1} = \frac{1 \times 1}{1 \times 1} = 1.$$

Example 2

$\frac{1}{3}$ and 3 are reciprocals since

$$\frac{1}{\cancel{3}_1} \times \frac{\cancel{3}^1}{1} = 1.$$

To find the reciprocal of a fraction, interchange the numerator and denominator—that is, invert the fraction, or turn it upside down.

Proper and Improper Fractions

Multiply the first fraction (dividend) by the reciprocal of the second fraction (divisor). Reduce by cancellation, if possible. If you wish to, change the answer to a mixed number when possible.

Example

$$\frac{9}{2} \div \frac{4}{7} = \frac{9}{2} \times \frac{7}{4}$$

The reciprocal of $\frac{4}{7}$ is $\frac{7}{4}$ because $\frac{4}{7} \times \frac{7}{4} = 1$

$$= \frac{63}{8}$$

$$= 7\frac{7}{8}$$

Mixed Numbers and/or Whole Numbers

Both mixed numbers and whole numbers must first be changed to equivalent improper fractions. Then proceed as described above.

Note: If a fraction or a mixed number is divided by 1, its value is unchanged. Division of a fraction or a mixed number by 0 is not defined. If a fraction is divided by itself or an equivalent fraction, the quotient is 1:

$$\frac{19}{7} \div \frac{19}{7} = \frac{19}{7} \times \frac{7}{19} \qquad \text{Reciprocal of } \frac{19}{7} \text{ is } \frac{7}{19}$$
$$= 1 \times 1 = 1$$

ADDITION

Fractions can be added only if their denominators are the same (called the *common denominator*). Add the numerators; the denominator remains the same. Reduce the sum to the lowest terms:

$$\frac{3}{8} + \frac{2}{8} + \frac{1}{8} = \frac{3 + 2 + 1}{8} = \frac{6}{8} = \frac{3}{4}.$$

When the fractions have different denominators, you must find a common denominator. One way of doing this is to find the product of the different denominators.

Example

$$\frac{5}{6} + \frac{1}{4} = ?$$

A common denominator is $6 \cdot 4 = 24$.

$$\frac{5}{6} \times \frac{4}{4} = \frac{20}{24} \quad \text{and} \quad \frac{1}{4} \times \frac{6}{6} = \frac{6}{24}$$

$$\frac{5}{6} + \frac{1}{4} = \frac{20}{24} + \frac{6}{24}$$

$$= \frac{20 + 6}{24}$$

$$= \frac{26}{24}$$

$$= \frac{13}{12}$$

$$= 1\frac{1}{12}$$

LEAST COMMON DENOMINATOR

A denominator that is smaller than the product of the different denominators can often be found. If the denominator of each fraction will divide into such a number evenly and it is the *smallest* such number, it is called the *least* (or *lowest*) *common denominator,* abbreviated as LCD. Finding a least common denominator may make it unnecessary to reduce the answer and enables one to work with smaller numbers. There are two common methods.

First Method

By Inspection

$$\frac{5}{6} + \frac{1}{4} = ?$$

LCD = 12 because 12 is the smallest number into which 6 and 4 divide evenly. Therefore:

$$12 \div 6 = 2 \qquad \text{multiply } \frac{5}{6} \times \frac{2}{2} = \frac{10}{12}$$

$$12 \div 4 = 3 \qquad \text{multiply } \frac{1}{4} \times \frac{3}{3} = \frac{3}{12}$$

Then:

$$\frac{5}{6} + \frac{1}{4} = \frac{10}{12} + \frac{3}{12}$$

$$= \frac{13}{12}$$

$$= 1\frac{1}{12}.$$

Second Method

By Factoring

This method can be used when the LCD is not recognized by inspection. Factor each denominator into its prime factors. The LCD is the product of the highest power of each separate factor, where *power* refers to the number of times a factor occurs.

Example

$$\frac{5}{6} + \frac{1}{4} = ?$$

Factoring denominators gives:

$$6 = 2 \cdot 3 \quad \text{and} \quad 4 = 2 \cdot 2$$

$$LCD = 2 \cdot 2 \cdot 3$$

$$= 12$$

Convert to LCD:

$$\frac{5}{6} \times \frac{2}{2} = \frac{10}{12} \qquad \frac{1}{4} \times \frac{3}{3} = \frac{3}{12}$$

$$\frac{5}{6} + \frac{1}{4} = \frac{10}{12} + \frac{3}{12}$$

$$= \frac{13}{12}$$

$$= 1\frac{1}{12}$$

The denominators 4 and 6 factor into $2 \cdot 2$ and $2 \cdot 3$, respectively. Although the factor 2 *appears* three times, its power is 2^2 from factoring 4. The factor 3 appears once, so its power is 3^1. Therefore, the LCD as a *product* of the *highest power of each separate factor* is $2 \times 2 \times 3$.

The factoring method of adding fractions can be extended to three or more fractions.

Example

$$\frac{1}{4} + \frac{3}{8} + \frac{1}{12} = ?$$

Factoring denominators gives:

$$4 = 2 \cdot 2 \qquad 8 = 2 \cdot 2 \cdot 2 \qquad 12 = 2 \cdot 2 \cdot 3$$

$$LCD = 2 \cdot 2 \cdot 2 \cdot 3$$

$$= 24$$

Convert to LCD:

$$\frac{1}{4} \times \frac{6}{6} = \frac{6}{24} \qquad \frac{3}{8} \times \frac{3}{3} = \frac{9}{24} \qquad \frac{1}{12} \times \frac{2}{2} = \frac{2}{24}$$

$$\frac{1}{4} + \frac{3}{8} + \frac{1}{12} = \frac{6}{24} + \frac{9}{24} + \frac{2}{24}$$

$$= \frac{6 + 9 + 2}{24}$$

$$= \frac{17}{24}$$

Addition of Mixed Numbers

Change any mixed numbers to improper fractions. If the fractions have the same denominator, add the numerators. If the fractions have different denominators, find the LCD of all the denominators and then add numerators. Reduce the answer if possible. Write the answer as a mixed number if you wish.

Example

$$2\frac{2}{3} + 5\frac{1}{2} + 1\frac{2}{9} = ?$$

Factoring denominators gives:

$$3 = 3 \qquad 2 = 2 \qquad 9 = 3 \cdot 3$$

$$LCD = 2 \cdot 3 \cdot 3$$
$$= 18$$

Convert to LCD:

$$\frac{8}{3} \times \frac{6}{6} = \frac{48}{18} \qquad \frac{11}{2} \times \frac{9}{9} = \frac{99}{18} \qquad \frac{11}{9} \times \frac{2}{2} = \frac{22}{18}$$

$$2\frac{2}{3} + 5\frac{1}{2} + 1\frac{2}{9} = \frac{8}{3} + \frac{11}{2} + \frac{11}{9}$$

$$= \frac{48}{18} + \frac{99}{18} + \frac{22}{18}$$

$$= \frac{48 + 99 + 22}{18}$$

$$= \frac{169}{18}$$

$$= 9\frac{7}{18}$$

SUBTRACTION

Fractions can be subtracted only if the denominators are the same. If the denominators are the same, find the difference between the numerators. The denominator remains unchanged.

Example 2

$$\frac{19}{3} - \frac{2}{3} = ?$$

$$= \frac{19 - 2}{3}$$

$$= \frac{17}{3}$$

$$= 5\frac{2}{3}$$

When fractions have different denominators, find equivalent fractions with a common denominator, and then subtract numerators.

Example 2

$$\frac{7}{8} - \frac{3}{4} = ?$$

Factoring denominators gives:

$$8 = 2 \cdot 2 \cdot 2 \qquad 4 = 2 \cdot 2$$

$$LCD = 2 \cdot 2 \cdot 2$$
$$= 8$$

Convert to LCD:

$$\frac{7}{8} = \frac{7}{8} \qquad \frac{3}{4} \times \frac{2}{2} = \frac{6}{8}$$

$$\frac{7}{8} - \frac{3}{4} = \frac{7}{8} - \frac{6}{8}$$

$$= \frac{7 - 6}{8}$$

$$= \frac{1}{8}$$

Mixed Numbers

To subtract mixed numbers, change each mixed number to an improper fraction. Find the LCD for the fractions. Write each fraction as an equivalent fraction whose denominator is the common denominator. Find the difference between the numerators.

Example

$$3\frac{3}{8} - 2\frac{5}{6} = ?$$

$$LCD = 24$$

$$3\frac{3}{8} - 2\frac{5}{6} = \frac{27}{8} - \frac{17}{6}$$

$$= \frac{81}{24} - \frac{68}{24}$$

$$= \frac{13}{24}$$

If zero is subtracted from a fraction, the result is the original fraction:

$$\frac{3}{4} - 0 = \frac{3}{4} - \frac{0}{4} = \frac{3}{4}.$$

QUIZ

FRACTION PROBLEMS

In the following problems, perform the indicated operations and reduce the answers to lowest terms.

1. $\dfrac{5}{12} \times \dfrac{4}{15}$

2. $\dfrac{1}{2} \div \dfrac{3}{8}$

3. $\dfrac{5}{12} + \dfrac{2}{3}$

4. $\dfrac{2}{3} - \dfrac{5}{11}$

5. $3\dfrac{1}{3} \times \dfrac{4}{5}$

6. $7\dfrac{4}{5} - 2\dfrac{1}{3}$

1. $\dfrac{5}{12} \times \dfrac{4}{15} = \dfrac{\overset{1}{\cancel{5}}}{\underset{3}{\cancel{12}}} \times \dfrac{\overset{1}{\cancel{4}}}{\underset{3}{\cancel{15}}} = \dfrac{1}{9}$

2. $\dfrac{1}{2} \div \dfrac{3}{8} = \dfrac{1}{2} \times \dfrac{8}{3} = \dfrac{1}{\underset{1}{\cancel{2}}} \times \dfrac{\overset{4}{\cancel{8}}}{3} = \dfrac{4}{3}$

3. $\dfrac{5}{12} + \dfrac{2}{3} = \dfrac{5}{12} + \dfrac{8}{12} = \dfrac{13}{12} = 1\dfrac{1}{12}$

4. $\dfrac{2}{3} - \dfrac{5}{11} = \dfrac{22}{33} - \dfrac{15}{33} = \dfrac{7}{33}$

5. $3\dfrac{1}{3} \times \dfrac{4}{5} = \dfrac{10}{3} \times \dfrac{4}{5} = \dfrac{\overset{2}{\cancel{10}}}{3} \times \dfrac{4}{\underset{1}{\cancel{5}}} = \dfrac{8}{3} = 2\dfrac{2}{3}$

6. $7\dfrac{4}{5} - 2\dfrac{1}{3} = \dfrac{39}{5} - \dfrac{7}{3} = \dfrac{117}{15} - \dfrac{35}{15} = \dfrac{82}{15} = 5\dfrac{7}{15}$

DECIMALS

Earlier, we stated that whole numbers are expressed in a system of tens, or the decimal system, using the digits from 0 to 9. This system can be extended to fractions by using a period called a *decimal point*. The digits after a decimal point form a *decimal fraction*. Decimal fractions are smaller than 1—for example, .3, .37, .372, and .105. The first position to the right of the decimal point is called the *tenths' place* since the digit in that position tells how many tenths there are. The second digit to the right of the decimal point is in the *hundredths' place*. The third digit to the right of the decimal point is in the *thousandths' place*, and so on.

Example 1
.3 is a decimal fraction that means

$$3 \times \dfrac{1}{10} = \dfrac{3}{10}$$

read "three-tenths."

Example 2
The decimal fraction of .37 means

$$3 \times \dfrac{1}{10} + 7 \times \dfrac{1}{100} = 3 \times \dfrac{10}{100} + 7 \times \dfrac{1}{100} = \dfrac{30}{100} + \dfrac{7}{100} = \dfrac{37}{100}$$

read "thirty-seven hundredths."

Example 3

The decimal fraction .372 means

$$\frac{300}{1,000} + \frac{70}{1,000} + \frac{2}{1,000} = \frac{372}{1,000}$$

read "three hundred seventy-two thousandths."

Whole numbers have an understood (unwritten) decimal point to the right of the last digit (e.g., 4 = 4.0). Decimal fractions can be combined with whole numbers to make *decimals*—for example, 3.246, 10.85, and 4.7.

Note: Adding zeros to the right of a decimal after the last digit does not change the value of the decimal.

Rounding Off

Sometimes, a decimal is expressed with more digits than desired. As the number of digits to the right of the decimal point increases, the number increases in accuracy, but a high degree of accuracy is not always needed. Then, the number can be rounded off to a certain decimal place.

To round off, identify the place to be rounded off. If the digit to the right of it is 0, 1, 2, 3, or 4, the round-off place digit remains the same. If the digit to the right is 5, 6, 7, 8, or 9, add 1 to the round-off place digit.

Example 1

Round off .6384 to the nearest thousandth.

The digit in the thousandths' place is 8.

The digit to the right in the ten-thousandths' place is 4, so the 8 stays the same.

The answer is .638.

Example 2

.6386 rounded to the nearest thousandth is

.639,

rounded to the nearest hundredth is

.64,

and rounded to the nearest tenth is

.6.

After a decimal fraction has been rounded off to a particular decimal place, all the digits to the right of that place will be 0.

Note: Rounding off whole numbers can be done by a similar method. It is less common but is sometimes used to quickly get approximate answers.

Example

Round 32,756 to the nearest *hundred*.

This means, to find the multiple of 100 that is nearest the given number.

The number in the hundreds' place is 7.

The number immediately to the right is 5,

so 32,756 rounds to 32,800.

DECIMALS AND FRACTIONS

Changing a Decimal to a Fraction

Place the digits to the right of the decimal point over the value of the place in which the last digit appears and reduce, if possible. The whole number remains the same.

Example

Change 2.14 to a fraction or mixed number. Observe that 4 is the last digit and is in the hundredths' place.

$$.14 = \frac{14}{100} = \frac{7}{50}$$

Therefore:

$$2.14 = 2\frac{7}{50}.$$

Changing a Fraction to a Decimal

Divide the numerator of the fraction by the denominator. First put a decimal point followed by zeros to the right of the number in the numerator. Subtract and divide until there is no remainder. The decimal point in the quotient is aligned directly above the decimal point in the dividend.

Example

Change $\frac{3}{8}$ to a decimal.

Divide

```
    .375
8)3.000
  24
  ‾‾
   60
   56
   ‾‾
    40
    40
    ‾‾
```

When the division does not terminate with a 0 remainder, two courses are possible.

First Method

Divide to three decimal places.

Example

Change $\frac{5}{6}$ to a decimal.

$$
\begin{array}{r}
.833 \\
6\overline{)5.000} \\
\underline{48} \\
20 \\
\underline{18} \\
20 \\
\underline{18} \\
2
\end{array}
$$

The 3 in the quotient will be repeated indefinitely. It is called an *infinite decimal* and is written .833. . . .

Second Method

Divide until there are two decimal places in the quotient, and then write the remainder over the divisor.

Example

Change $\frac{5}{6}$ to a decimal.

$$
\begin{array}{r}
.833 \\
6\overline{)5.000} = .83\frac{1}{3}\\
\underline{48} \\
20 \\
\underline{18} \\
20
\end{array}
$$

ADDITION

Addition of decimals is both commutative and associative. Decimals are simpler to add than fractions. Place the decimals in a column, with the decimal points aligned under each other. Add in the usual way. The decimal point of the answer is also aligned under the other decimal points.

Example

43 + 2.73 + .9 + 3.01 = ?

```
 43.
  2.73
   .9
  3.01
 49.64
```

SUBTRACTION

For subtraction, the decimal points must be aligned under each other. Add zeros to the right of the decimal point, if desired. Subtract as with whole numbers.

Examples

```
 21.567        21.567        39.00
 −9.4          −9.48        −17.48
 12.167        12.087        21.52
```

MULTIPLICATION

Multiplication of decimals is commutative and associative:

$$5.39 \times .04 = .04 \times 5.39$$
$$(.7 \times .02) \times .1 = .7 \cdot (.02 \times .1)$$

Multiply the decimals as if they were whole numbers. The total number of decimal places in the product is the sum of the number of places (to the right of the decimal point) in all of the numbers multiplied.

Example

8.64 × .003 = ?

```
 8.64          2          places to right of decimal point
 × .003       + 3         places to right of decimal point
 .02592        5          places to right of decimal point
```

A zero had to be added to the left of the product before writing the decimal point to ensure that there would be five decimal places in the product.

Note: To multiply a decimal by 10, simply move the decimal point one place to the right; to multiply by 100, move the decimal point two places to the right.

DIVISION

To divide one decimal (the dividend) by another (the divisor), move the decimal point in the divisor as many places as necessary to the right to make the divisor a whole number. Then move the decimal point in the dividend (expressed or understood) a corresponding number of places, adding zeros if necessary. Then divide as with whole numbers. The decimal point in the quotient is placed above the decimal point in the dividend after the decimal point has been moved.

Example
Divide 7.6 by .32.

$$.32\overline{)7.60} = 32\overline{)760.00}$$

$$
\begin{array}{r}
23.75 \\
\underline{64} \\
120 \\
\underline{96} \\
240 \\
\underline{224} \\
160 \\
\underline{160}
\end{array}
$$

Note: "Divide 7.6 by .32" can be written as $\dfrac{7.6}{.32}$. If this fraction is multiplied by $\dfrac{100}{100}$, an equivalent fraction is obtained with a whole number in the denominator:

$$\frac{7.6}{.32} \times \frac{100}{100} = \frac{760}{32}.$$

Moving the decimal point two places to the right in both the divisor and dividend is equivalent to multiplying each number by 100.

Special Cases

If the dividend has a decimal point and the divisor does not, divide as with whole numbers and place the decimal point of the quotient above the decimal point in the divisor.

If both dividend and divisor are whole numbers but the quotient is a decimal, place a decimal point after the last digit of the dividend and add zeros as necessary to get the required degree of accuracy.

Note: To divide any number by 10, simply move its decimal point (understood to be after the last digit for a whole number) one place to the left; to divide by 100, move the decimal point two places to the left; and so on.

PERCENTS

Percents, like fractions and decimals, are ways of expressing parts of whole numbers, as 93%, 50%, and 22.4%. Percents are expressions of hundredths—that is, of fractions whose denominator is 100.

Example

$$25\% = \text{twenty-five hundredths} = \frac{25}{100} = \frac{1}{4}$$

The word *percent* means *per hundred*. Its main use is in comparing fractions with equal denominators of 100.

RELATIONSHIP WITH FRACTIONS AND DECIMALS

Changing Percent into Decimal

Divide the percent by 100 and drop the symbol for percent. Add zeros to the left when necessary:

$$30\% = .30 \qquad 1\% = .01$$

Remember that the short method of dividing by 100 is to move the decimal point two places to the left.

Changing Decimal into Percent

Multiply the decimal by 100 by moving the decimal point two places to the right, and add the symbol for percent:

$$.375 = 37.5\% \qquad .001 = .1\%$$

QUIZ

DECIMAL PROBLEMS

1. Change the following decimals into fractions, and reduce.
   a. 1.16
   b. 15.05

2. Change the following fractions into decimals.

   a. $\dfrac{3}{8}$

   b. $\dfrac{2}{3}$

In the following problems, perform the indicated operations.

3. $3.762 + 23.43$

4. $1.368 - .559$

5. $8.7 \times .8$

6. $.045 \div .5$

SOLUTIONS

1.
   a. $1.16 = 1\frac{16}{100} = 1\frac{8}{50} = 1\frac{4}{25}$
   b. $15.05 = 15\frac{5}{100} = 15\frac{1}{20}$

2.
   a. $\frac{3}{8} = 8\overline{)3.000}$ → $.375$

   $\quad\quad 24$
   $\quad\quad \overline{60}$
   $\quad\quad -56$
   $\quad\quad \overline{40}$

   b. $\frac{2}{3} = 3\overline{)2.00}$ → $.666...$

   $\quad\quad 18$
   $\quad\quad \overline{20}$
   $\quad\quad -18$
   $\quad\quad \overline{20}$

3.
   $\quad 3.762$
   $+23.43$
   $\overline{27.192}$

4.
   $\quad 1.368$
   $\quad -.559$
   $\overline{\quad .809}$

5.
   $\quad 8.7$
   $\times .8$
   $\overline{6.96}$

6.
   $\quad 0.09$
   $.5\overline{)0.0.45}$

Changing Percent into Fraction

Drop the percent sign. Write the number as a numerator over a denominator of 100. If the numerator has a decimal point, move the decimal point to the right the necessary number of places to make the numerator a whole number. Add the same number of zeros to the right of the denominator as you moved places to the right in the numerator. Reduce where possible.

Examples

$$20\% = \frac{20}{100} = \frac{2}{10} = \frac{1}{5}$$

$$36.5\% = \frac{36.5}{100} = \frac{365}{1000} = \frac{73}{200}$$

Changing a Fraction into Percent

Use either of two methods.

First Method

Change the fraction into an equivalent fraction with a denominator of 100. Drop the denominator (equivalent to multiplying by 100) and add the % sign.

Example

Express $\frac{6}{20}$ as a percent.

$$\frac{6}{20} \times \frac{5}{5} = \frac{30}{100} = 30\%$$

Second Method

Divide the numerator by the denominator to get a decimal with two places (express the remainder as a fraction if necessary). Change the decimal to a percent.

Example

Express $\frac{6}{20}$ as a percent.

$$\frac{6}{20} = 20\overline{)6.00}^{.30} = 30\%$$
$$\underline{60}$$

QUIZ

PERCENT PROBLEMS

1. Change the following percents into decimals:

2. Change the following decimals into percents:

3. Change the following fractions into percents:

4. Change the following percents into fractions:

SOLUTIONS

1. a. 37.5% = 0.375

2. a. 0.625 = 62.5%

3. a. $\dfrac{7}{8} = 8\overline{)7.000}^{\,0.875} = 87.5\%$

4. a. $87.5\% = 0.875 = \dfrac{875}{1,000} = \dfrac{35}{40} = \dfrac{7}{8}$

Peterson's GMAT CAT Success

WORD PROBLEMS

When doing percent problems, it is usually easier to change the percent to a decimal or a fraction before computing. When we take a percent of a certain number, that number is called the *base*, the percent we take is called the *rate*, and the result is called the *percentage* or *part*. If we let B represent the base, R the rate, and P the part, the relationship between these quantities is expressed by the following formula:

$$P = R \cdot B$$

All percent problems can be done with the help of this formula.

Example 1

In a class of 24 students, 25% received an A. How many students received an A? The number of students (24) is the base, and 25% is the rate. Change the rate to a fraction for ease of handling and apply the formula.

$$25\% = \frac{25}{100} = \frac{1}{4}$$

$$P = R \times B$$

$$= \frac{1}{\cancel{4}} \times \frac{\overset{6}{\cancel{24}}}{1}$$
$$\phantom{= \frac{1}{4}} 1$$

$$= 6 \text{ students}$$

To choose between changing the percent (rate) to a decimal or a fraction, simply decide which would be easier to work with. In Example 1, the fraction was easier to work with because cancellation was possible. In Example 2, the situation is the same except for a different rate. This time, the decimal form is easier.

Example 2

In a class of 24 students, 29.17% received an A. How many students received an A?

Changing the rate to a fraction yields

$$\frac{29.17}{100} = \frac{2917}{10,000}$$

You can quickly see that the decimal is the better choice.

$$29.17\% = .2917$$

$$P = R \times B$$
$$= .2917 \times 24$$
$$= 7 \text{ students}$$

$$\begin{array}{r} .2917 \\ \times\ \ 24 \\ \hline 1.1668 \\ 5.834 \\ \hline 7.0008 \end{array}$$

Example 3

What percent of a 40-hour week is a 16-hour schedule?

40 hours is the base, and 16 hours is the part.

$$P = R \cdot B$$

$$16 = R \cdot 40$$

Divide each side of the equation by 40.

$$\frac{16}{40} = R$$

$$\frac{2}{5} = R$$

$$40\% = R$$

Example 4

A woman paid $15,000 as a down payment on a house. If this amount was 20% of the price, what did the house cost?

The part (or percentage) is $15,000, the rate is 20%, and we must find the base. Change the rate to a fraction.

$$20\% = \frac{1}{5}$$

$$P = R \times B$$

$$\$15,000 = \frac{1}{5} \times B$$

Multiply each side of the equation by 5.

$$\$75,000 = B = \text{cost of house}$$

Percent of Increase or Decrease

This kind of problem is not really new but follows immediately from the previous problems. First calculate the *amount* of increase or decrease. This amount is the *P* (percentage or part) from the formula $P = R \cdot B$. The base, *B*, is the original amount, regardless of whether there was a loss or gain.

Example

By what percent does Mary's salary increase if her present salary is $20,000 and she accepts a new job at a salary of $28,000?

Amount of increase is:

$$\$28,000 - \$20,000 = \$8000$$

$$P = R \cdot B$$

$$\$8000 = R \cdot \$20,000$$

Divide each side of the equation by $20,000. Then:

$$\frac{\overset{40}{\cancel{8,000}}}{\underset{100}{\cancel{20,000}}} = \frac{40}{100} = R = 40\% \text{ increase.}$$

Discount and Interest

These special kinds of percent problems require no new methods of attack.

Discount

The amount of discount is the difference between the original price and the sale, or discount, price. The rate of discount is usually given as a fraction or as a percent. Use the formula of the percent problems $P = R \cdot B$, but now *P* stands for the part or discount, *R* is the rate, and *B*, the base, is the original price.

Example 1

A table listed at $160 is marked 20% off. What is the sale price?

$$P = R \cdot B$$

$$= .20 \cdot \$160 = \$32$$

This is the amount of discount or how much must be subtracted from the original price. Then:

$$\$160 - \$32 = \$128 \text{ sale price}$$

Example 2

A car priced at $9,000 was sold for $7,200. What was the rate of discount?

$$\text{Amount of discount} = \$9000 - \$7200$$
$$= \$1800$$
$$\text{discount} = \text{rate} \cdot \text{original price}$$
$$\$1800 = R \cdot \$9000$$

Divide each side of the equation by $9000:

$$\frac{\overset{20}{\cancel{1800}}}{\underset{100}{\cancel{9000}}} = \frac{20}{100} = R = 20\%$$

Successive Discounting

When an item is discounted more than once, it is called successive discounting.

Example 1

In one store, a dress tagged at $40 was discounted 15%. When it did not sell at the lower price, it was discounted an additional 10%. What was the final selling price?

$$\text{discount} = R \cdot \text{original price}$$

$$\text{First discount} = .15 \cdot \$40 = \$6$$
$$\$40 - \$6 = \$34 \text{ selling price after first discount}$$

$$\text{Second discount} = .10 \cdot \$34 = \$3.40$$
$$\$34 - \$3.40 = \$30.60 \text{ final selling price}$$

Example 2

In another store, an identical dress was also tagged at $40. When it did not sell, it was discounted 25% all at once. Is the final selling price lower or higher than in Example 1?

$$\text{Discount} = R \cdot \text{original price}$$
$$= .25 \cdot \$40$$
$$= \$10$$
$$\$40 - \$10 = \$30 \text{ final selling price}$$

This is a lower selling price than in Example 1, where two successive discounts were taken. Although the two discounts from Example 1 add up to the discount of Example 2, the final selling price is not the same.

Interest

Interest problems are similar to discount and percent problems. If money is left in the bank for a year and the interest is calculated at the end of the year, the usual formula $P = R \cdot B$ can be used, where P is the *interest*, R is the *rate*, and B is the *principal* (original amount of money borrowed or loaned).

Example 1

A certain bank pays interest on savings accounts at the rate of 4% per year. If a man has $6,700 on deposit, find the interest earned after one year.

$$P = R \cdot B$$

interest = rate · principal

$$P = .04 \cdot \$6700 = \$268 \text{ interest}$$

Interest problems frequently involve more or less time than one year. Then the formula becomes

interest = rate · principal · time

Example 2

If the money is left in the bank for three years at simple interest (the kind we are discussing), the interest is

$$3 \cdot \$268 = \$804$$

Example 3

Suppose $6,700 is deposited in the bank at 4% interest for three months. How much interest is earned?

interest = rate · principal · time.

Here, the 4% rate is for one year. Since three months is $\dfrac{3}{12} = \dfrac{1}{4}$

$$\text{interest} = .04 \cdot \$6700 \cdot \frac{1}{4} = \$67.$$

QUIZ

PERCENT WORD PROBLEMS

1. Janet received a rent increase of 15%. If her rent was $785 monthly before the increase, what is her new rent?

2. School bus fares rose from $25 per month to $30 per month. Find the percent of increase.

3. A dress originally priced at $90 is marked down 35%, then discounted a further 10%. What is the new reduced price?

4. Dave delivers flowers for a salary of $45 a day, plus a 12% commission on all sales. One day his sales amounted to $220. How much money did he earn that day?

5. A certain bank pays interest on money market accounts at a rate of 6% a year. If Brett deposits $7,200, find the interest earned after one year.

SOLUTIONS

1. Amount of increase = $785 × 15% = $785 × .15 = $117.75

   New rent = $902.75

2. Amount of increase = $30 − $25 = $5

   Percent of increase = $\dfrac{5}{25} = \dfrac{1}{5} = 20\%$

3. Amount of first markdown = $90 × 35% = $90 × .35 = $31.50

   Reduced price = $90 − $31.50 = $58.50

   Amount of second markdown = $58.50 × 10% = $58.50 × .1 = $5.85

   Final price = $58.50 − $5.85 = $52.65

4. Commission = $220 × 12% = $220 × .12 = $26.40

   Money earned = $45 + $26.40 = $71.40

5. Interest = $7200 × 6% = $7200 × .06 = $432

SIGNED NUMBERS

In describing subtraction of whole numbers, we said that the operation was not closed—that is, 4 − 6 will yield a number that is not a member of the set of counting numbers and zero. The set of *integers* was developed to give meaning to such expressions as 4 − 6. The set of integers is the set of all *signed* whole numbers and zero. It is the set {..., −4, −3, −2, −1, 0, 1, 2, 3, 4, ...}

The first three dots symbolize the fact that the negative integers go on indefinitely, just as the positive integers do. Integers preceded by a minus sign (called *negative integers*) appear to the left of 0 on a number line.

Decimals, fractions, and mixed numbers can also have negative signs. Together with positive fractions and decimals, they appear on the number line in this fashion:

All numbers to the right of 0 are called *positive numbers*. They have the sign +, whether it is actually written or not. Business gains or losses, feet above or below sea level, and temperature above or below zero can all be expressed by means of signed numbers.

ADDITION

If the numbers to be added have the same sign, add the numbers (integers, fractions, decimals) as usual and use their common sign in the answer:

$$+9 + (+8) + (+2) = +19 \text{ or } 19$$
$$-4 + (-11) + (-7) + (-1) = -23.$$

If the numbers to be added have different signs, add the positive numbers and then the negative numbers. Ignore the signs, and subtract the smaller total from the larger total. If the larger total is positive, the answer will be positive; if the larger total is negative, the answer will be negative. The answer may be zero. Zero is neither positive nor negative and has no sign.

Example

$$+3 + (-5) + (-8) + (+2) = ?$$
$$+3 + (+2) = +5$$
$$-5 + (-8) = -13$$
$$13 - 5 = 8$$

Since the larger total (13) has a negative sign, the answer is −8.

SUBTRACTION

The second number in a subtraction problem is called the *subtrahend*. In order to subtract, change the sign of the subtrahend and then continue as if you were *adding* signed numbers. If there is no sign in front of the subtrahend, it is assumed to be positive.

Examples

Subtract the subtrahend (bottom number) from the top number.

$$
\begin{array}{rrrrr}
15 & 5 & -35 & -35 & 42 \\
\underline{5} & \underline{15} & \underline{-42} & \underline{42} & \underline{35} \\
10 & -10 & 7 & -77 & 7
\end{array}
$$

MULTIPLICATION

If two and only two signed numbers are to be multiplied, multiply the numbers as you would if they were not signed. Then, if the two numbers have the *same sign*, the product is *positive*. If the two numbers have *different signs*, the product is *negative*. If more than two numbers are being multiplied, proceed two at a time in the same way as before, finding the signed product of the first two numbers, then multiplying that product by the next number, and so on. The product has a positive sign if all the factors are positive or there is an even number of negative factors. The product has a negative sign if there is an odd number of negative factors.

Example 1

$$-3 \cdot (+5) \cdot (-11) \cdot (-2) = -330$$

The answer is negative because there is an odd number (three) of negative factors.

The product of a signed number and zero is zero. The product of a signed number and 1 is the original number. The product of a signed number and −1 is the original number with its sign changed.

Example 2

$$-5 \cdot 0 = 0$$
$$-5 \cdot 1 = -5$$
$$-5 \cdot (-1) = +5$$

DIVISION

If the divisor and the dividend have the same sign, the answer is positive. Divide the numbers as you normally would. If the divisor and the dividend have different signs, the answer is negative. Divide the numbers as you normally would.

Example 1

$$-3 \div (-2) = \frac{3}{2} = 1\frac{1}{2}$$
$$8 \div (-.2) = -40$$

If zero is divided by a signed number, the answer is zero. If a signed number is divided by zero, the answer does not exist. If a signed number is divided by 1, the number remains the same. If a signed number is divided by -1, the quotient is the original number with its sign changed.

Example 2

$$0 \div (-2) = 0$$
$$-\frac{4}{3} \div 0 \qquad \text{not defined}$$
$$\frac{2}{3} \div 1 = \frac{2}{3}$$
$$4 \div -1 = -4$$

QUIZ

SIGNED NUMBERS PROBLEMS

Perform the indicated operations:

1. $+ 6 + (-5) + (+2) + (-8) =$

2. $- 5 - (-4) + (-2) - (+6) =$

3. $-3 \cdot (+5) \cdot (-7) \cdot (-2) =$

4. $9 \div (-.3) =$

1. $+6 + (-5) = +1$
   $+1 + (+2) = +3$
   $+3 + (-8) = -5$

2. $-5 - (-4) = -5 + 4 = -1$
   $-1 + (-2) = -3$
   $-3 - (+6) = -9$

3. $-3 \cdot (+5) = -15$
   $-15 \cdot (-7) = +105$
   $+105 \cdot (-2) = -210$

4. $9 \div (-.3) = -30$

POWERS, EXPONENTS, AND ROOTS

EXPONENTS

The product $10 \cdot 10 \cdot 10$ can be written 10^3. We say 10 is raised to the *third power*. In general, $a \times a \times a \dots a$ n times is written a^n. The *base a* is raised to the nth power, and n is called the *exponent*.

Example 1

$3^2 = 3 \cdot 3$ read "3 squared"
$2^3 = 2 \cdot 2 \cdot 2$ read "2 cubed"
$5^4 = 5 \cdot 5 \cdot 5 \cdot 5$ read "5 to the fourth power"

If the exponent is 1, it is usually understood and not written; thus, $a^1 = a$.

Since

$$a^2 = a \times a \quad \text{and} \quad a^3 = a \times a \times a$$

then

$$a^2 \times a^3 = (a \times a)(a \times a \times a) = a^5.$$

There are three rules for exponents. In general, if k and m are any counting numbers or zero, and a is any number,

Rule 1: $a^k \times a^m = a^{k+m}$

Rule 2: $a^m \cdot b^m = (ab)^m$

Rule 3: $(a^k)^n = a^{kn}$

Example 2

Rule 1: $2^2 \cdot 2^3 = 4 \times 8 = 32$ and $2^2 \times 2^3 = 2^5 = 32$

Rule 2: $3^2 \times 4^2 = 9 \times 16 = 144$ and $3^2 \times 4^2 = (3 \times 4)^2 = 12^2 = 144$

Rule 3: $(3^2)^3 = 9^3 = 729$ and $(3^2)^3 = 3^6 = 729$

188

ROOTS

The definition of roots is based on exponents. If $a^n = c$, where a is the base and n the exponent, a is called the nth *root* of c. This is written $a = \sqrt[n]{c}$. The symbol $\sqrt{}$ is called a *radical sign*. Since $5^4 = 625$, $\sqrt[4]{625} = 5$ and 5 is the fourth root of 625. The most frequently used roots are the second (called the square) root and the third (called the cube) root. The square root is written $\sqrt{}$ and the cube root is written $\sqrt[3]{}$.

Square Roots

If c is a positive number, there are two values, one negative and one positive, that, when multiplied together, will produce c.

Example

$$+4 \cdot (+4) = 16 \quad \text{and} \quad -4 \cdot (-4) = 16$$

The positive square root of a positive number c is called the *principal* square root of c (briefly, the *square root* of c) and is denoted by $\sqrt{c}$:

$$\sqrt{144} = 12.$$

If $c = 0$, there is only one square root, 0. If c is a negative number, there is no real number that is the square root of c:

$$\sqrt{-4} \text{ is not a real number.}$$

Cube Roots

Both positive and negative numbers have real cube roots. The cube root of 0 is 0. The cube root of a positive number is positive; that of a negative number is negative.

Example 1

$$2 \cdot 2 \cdot 2 = 8$$

Therefore, $\sqrt[3]{8} = 2$.

$$-3 \cdot (-3) \cdot (-3) = -27$$

Therefore, $\sqrt[3]{-27} = -3$.

Each number has only one real cube root.

Example 2

Simplify $\sqrt{98}$

$$\sqrt{98} = \sqrt{2 \times 49}$$
$$= \sqrt{2} \times \sqrt{49} \quad \text{where 49 is a square number}$$
$$= \sqrt{2} \times 7$$

Therefore, $\sqrt{98} = 7\sqrt{2}$ and the process terminates because there is no whole number whose square is 2. $7\sqrt{2}$ is called a radical expression or simply a *radical*.

Example 3

Which is larger, $\left(\sqrt{96}\right)^2$ or $\sqrt{2^{14}}$?

$$\left(\sqrt{96}\right)^2 = \sqrt{96} \times \sqrt{96} = \sqrt{96 \times 96} = 96$$

$\sqrt{2^{14}} = 2^7 = 128$ because $2^{14} = 2^7 \times 2^7$ by Rule 1 or because $\sqrt{2^{14}} = (2^{14})^{1/2} = 2^7$ by Rule 3.

Since $128 > 96$,

$$\sqrt{2^{14}} > \left(\sqrt{96}\right)^2$$

Example 4

Which is larger, $2\sqrt{75}$ or $6\sqrt{12}$?

These numbers can be compared if the same number appears under the radical sign. Then the greater number is the one with the larger number in front of the radical sign.

$$\sqrt{75} = \sqrt{25 \times 3} = \sqrt{25} \times \sqrt{3} = 5\sqrt{3}$$

Therefore:

$$2\sqrt{75} = 2(5\sqrt{3}) = 10\sqrt{3}$$

$$\sqrt{12} = \sqrt{4 \times 3} = \sqrt{4} \times \sqrt{3} = 2\sqrt{3}$$

Therefore:

$$6\sqrt{12} = 6(2\sqrt{3}) = 12\sqrt{3}$$

Since $12\sqrt{3} > 10\sqrt{3}$,

$$6\sqrt{12} > 2\sqrt{75}$$

Note: Numbers such as $\sqrt{2}$ and $\sqrt{3}$ are called *irrational* numbers to distinguish them from *rational* numbers, which include the integers and the fractions. Irrational numbers also have places on the number line. They may have positive or negative signs. The combination of rational and irrational numbers, all the numbers we have used so far, make up the *real* numbers. Arithmetic, algebra, and geometry deal with real numbers. The number π, the ratio of the circumference of a circle to its diameter, is also a real number; it is irrational, although it is approximated by 3.14159. . . . Instructions for taking the GMAT say that the numbers used are real numbers. This means that answers may be expressed as fractions, decimals, radicals, or integers, whatever is required.

Radicals can be added and subtracted only if they have the same number under the radical sign. Otherwise, they must be reduced to expressions having the same number under the radical sign.

Example 5

Add

$$2\sqrt{18} + 4\sqrt{8} - \sqrt{2}.$$

$$\sqrt{18} = \sqrt{9 \times 2} = \sqrt{9} \times \sqrt{2} = 3\sqrt{2}$$

therefore,

$$2\sqrt{18} = 2(3\sqrt{2}) = 6\sqrt{2}$$

and

$$\sqrt{8} = \sqrt{4 \times 2} = \sqrt{4} \times \sqrt{2} = 2\sqrt{2}$$

therefore,

$$4\sqrt{8} = 4(2\sqrt{2}) = 8\sqrt{2}$$

giving

$$2\sqrt{18} + 4\sqrt{8} - \sqrt{2} = 6\sqrt{2} + 8\sqrt{2} - \sqrt{2} = 13\sqrt{2}$$

Radicals are multiplied using the rule that

$$\sqrt[k]{a \times b} = \sqrt[k]{a} \times \sqrt[k]{b}$$

Example 6

$$\sqrt{2}\left(\sqrt{2} - 5\sqrt{3}\right) = \sqrt{4} - 5\sqrt{6} = 2 - 5\sqrt{6}$$

A quotient rule for radicals similar to the product rule is

$$\sqrt[k]{\frac{a}{b}} = \frac{\sqrt[k]{a}}{\sqrt[k]{b}}$$

Example 7

$$\sqrt{\frac{9}{4}} = \frac{\sqrt{9}}{\sqrt{4}} = \frac{3}{2}$$

QUIZ

EXPONENTS, POWERS, AND ROOTS PROBLEMS

1. Simplify $\sqrt{162}$.

2. Find the sum of $\sqrt{75}$ and $\sqrt{12}$.

3. Combine $\sqrt{80} + \sqrt{45} - \sqrt{20}$.

4. Simplify $\sqrt{5}\left(2\sqrt{2} - 3\sqrt{5}\right)$.

5. Divide and simplify $\dfrac{15\sqrt{96}}{5\sqrt{2}}$.

6. Calculate $5^2 \times 2^3$.

SOLUTIONS

1. $\sqrt{162} = \sqrt{2 \cdot 81} = \sqrt{2} \cdot \sqrt{81} = 9\sqrt{2}$

2. $\sqrt{75} + \sqrt{12} = 5\sqrt{3} + 2\sqrt{3} = 7\sqrt{3}$

3. $\sqrt{80} + \sqrt{45} - \sqrt{20} = 4\sqrt{5} + 3\sqrt{5} - 2\sqrt{5} = 5\sqrt{5}$

4. $\sqrt{5}\left(2\sqrt{2} - 3\sqrt{5}\right) = 2\sqrt{10} - 3\sqrt{25} = 2\sqrt{10} - 3(5)$
$= 2\sqrt{10} - 15$

5. $\dfrac{15\sqrt{96}}{5\sqrt{2}} = \dfrac{15(4\sqrt{6})}{5\sqrt{2}} = \dfrac{60\sqrt{6}}{5\sqrt{2}} = 12\sqrt{3}$

6. $5^2 \times 2^3 = 25 \times 8 = 200$

ALGEBRA

Algebra is a generalization of arithmetic. It provides methods for solving problems that cannot be done by arithmetic alone or that can be done by arithmetic only after long computations. Algebra provides a shorthand way of reducing long verbal statements to brief formulas, expressions, or equations. After the verbal statements have been reduced, the resulting algebraic expressions can be simplified. Suppose that a room is 12 feet wide and 20 feet long. Its perimeter (measurement around the outside) can be expressed as

12 + 20 + 12 + 20 or 2(12 + 20).

If the width of the room remains 12 feet but the letter *l* is used to symbolize length, the perimeter is

12 + *l* + 12 + *l* or 2(12 + *l*).

Further, if *w* is used for width, the perimeter of *any* rectangular room can be written as 2(*w* + *l*). This same room has an area of 12 feet by 20 feet or 12 · 20. If *l* is substituted for 20, any room of width 12 has area equal to 12*l*. If *w* is substituted for the number 12, the area of any rectangular room is given by *wl* or *lw*. Expressions such as *wl* and 2(*w* + *l*) are called *algebraic expressions*. An *equation* is a statement that two algebraic expressions are equal. A *formula* is a special type of equation.

Evaluating Formulas

If we are given an expression and numerical values to be assigned to each letter, the expression can be evaluated.

Example 1

Evaluate $2x + 3y - 7$ if $x = 2$ and $y = -4$. Substitute given values

$$2(2) + 3(-4) - 7 = ?$$

Multiply numbers using rules for signed numbers

$$4 + -12 - 7 = ?$$

Collect numbers

$$4 - 19 = -15$$

We have already evaluated formulas in arithmetic when solving percent, discount, and interest problems.

Example

The formula for temperature conversion is

$$F = \frac{9}{5}C + 32,$$

where C stands for the temperature in degrees Celsius and F for degrees Fahrenheit. Find the Fahrenheit temperature that is equivalent to 20°C.

$$F = \frac{9}{5}(20°C) + 32 = 36 + 32 = 68°F$$

ALGEBRAIC EXPRESSIONS

Formulation

A more difficult problem than evaluating an expression or formula is to translate from a verbal expression to an algebraic one:

Verbal	Algebraic
Thirteen more than x	$x + 13$
Six less than twice x	$2x - 6$
The square of the sum of x and 5	$(x + 5)^2$
The sum of the square of x and the square of 5	$x^2 + 5^2$
The distance traveled by a car going 50 miles an hour for x hours	$50x$
The average of 70, 80, 85, and x	$\dfrac{70 + 80 + 85 + x}{4}$

Simplification

After algebraic expressions have been formulated, they can usually be simplified by means of the laws of exponents and the common operations of addition, subtraction, multiplication, and division. These techniques will be described in the next section. Algebraic expressions and equations frequently contain parentheses, which are removed in the process of simplifying. If an expression contains more than one set of parentheses, remove the inner set first and then the outer set. Brackets, [ ], which are often used instead of parentheses, are treated the same way. Parentheses are used to indicate multiplication. Thus $3(x + y)$ means that 3 is to be multiplied by the sum of x and y. The *distributive law* is used to accomplish this:

$$a(b + c) = ab + ac,$$

The expression in front of the parentheses is multiplied by each term inside. Rules for signed numbers apply.

Example 1
Simplify $3[4(2 - 8) - 5(4 + 2)]$.

This can be done in two ways.

Method 1
Combine the numbers inside the parentheses first:

$$3[4(2 - 8) - 5(4 + 2)] = 3[4(-6) - 5(6)]$$
$$= 3[-24 - 30]$$
$$= 3[-54] = -162.$$

Method 2

Use the distributive law:

$$3[4(2 - 8) - 5(4 + 2)] = 3[8 - 32 - 20 - 10]$$
$$= 3[8 - 62]$$
$$= 3[-54] = -162.$$

If there is a (+) before the parentheses, the signs of the terms inside the parentheses remain the same when the parentheses are removed. If there is a (−) before the parentheses, the sign of each term inside the parentheses changes when the parentheses are removed.

Once parentheses have been removed, the order of operations is multiplication and division, then addition and subtraction from left to right.

Example 1

$$(-15 + 17) \cdot 3 - [(4 \cdot 9) \div 6] = ?$$

Work inside the parentheses first:

$$(2) \cdot 3 - [36 \div 6] = ?$$

Then work inside the brackets:

$$2 \cdot 3 - [6] = ?$$

Multiply first, then subtract, proceeding from left to right:

$$6 - 6 = 0$$

The placement of parentheses and brackets is important. Using the same numbers as above with the parentheses and brackets placed in different positions can give many different answers.

Example 2

$$-15 + [(17 \cdot 3) - (4 \cdot 9)] \div 6 = ?$$

Work inside the parentheses first:

$$-15 + [(51) - (36)] \div 6 = ?$$

Then work inside the brackets:

$$-15 + [15] \div 6 = ?$$

Since there are no more parentheses or brackets, proceed from left to right, dividing before adding:

$$-15 + 2\frac{1}{2} = -12\frac{1}{2}.$$

OPERATIONS

When letter symbols and numbers are combined with the operations of arithmetic ($+$, $-$, $\cdot$, $\div$) and with certain other mathematical operations, we have an *algebraic expression*. Algebraic expressions are made up of several parts connected by a plus or a minus sign; each part is called a *term*. Terms with the same letter part are called *like terms*. Since algebraic expressions represent numbers, they can be added, subtracted, multiplied, and divided.

When we defined the commutative law of addition in arithmetic by writing $a + b = b + a$, we meant that a and b could represent any number. The expression $a + b = b + a$ is an *identity* because it is true for all numbers. The expression $n + 5 = 14$ is not an identity because it is not true for all numbers; it becomes true only when the number 9 is substituted for n. Letters used to represent numbers are called *variables*. If a number stands alone (the 5 or 14 in $n + 5 = 14$), it is called a *constant* because its value is constant or unchanging. If a number appears in front of a variable, it is called a *coefficient*. Because the letter x is frequently used to represent a variable, or *unknown*, the times sign $\times$, which can be confused with it in handwriting, is rarely used to express multiplication in algebra. Other expressions used for multiplication are a dot, parentheses, or simply writing a number and letter together:

$5 \cdot 4$ or $5(4)$ or $5a$.

Of course, 54 still means fifty-four.

Addition and Subtraction

Only like terms can be combined. Add or subtract the coefficients of like terms, using the rules for signed numbers.

Example 1
Add $x + 2y - 2x + 3y$.

$$x - 2x + 2y + 3y = -x + 5y$$

Example 2
Perform the subtraction:

$$-30a - 15b + 4c$$
$$- (- 5a + 3b - c + d)$$

Change the sign of each term in the subtrahend and then add, using the rules for signed numbers:

$$-30a - 15b + 4c$$
$$\underline{5a - 3b + c - d}$$
$$-25a - 18b + 5c - d$$

Multiplication

Multiplication is accomplished by using the *distributive property*. If the multiplier has only one term, then

$$a(b + c) = ab + bc.$$

Example 1

$$9x(5m + 9q) = (9x)(5m) + (9x)(9q)$$
$$= 45mx + 81qx$$

When the multiplier contains more than one term and you are multiplying two expressions, multiply each term of the first expression by each term of the second and then add like terms. Follow the rules for signed numbers and exponents at all times.

Example 2

$$(3x + 8)(4x^2 + 2x + 1) = 3x(4x^2 + 2x +1) + 8(4x^2 + 2x + 1)$$
$$= 12x^3 + 6x^2 + 3x + 32x^2 + 16x + 8$$
$$= 12x^3 + 38x^2 + 19x + 8$$

If more than two expressions are to be multiplied, multiply the first two, then multiply the product by the third factor, and so on, until all factors have been used.

Algebraic expressions can be multiplied by themselves (squared) or raised to any power.

Example 3

$$(a + b)^2 = (a +b)(a + b)$$
$$= a(a + b) + b(a + b)$$
$$= a^2 + ab + ba + b^2$$
$$= a^2 + 2ab + b^2$$

since $ab = ba$ by the commutative law.

Example 2

$$(a + b)(a - b) = a(a - b) +b(a - b)$$
$$= a^2 - ab + ba - b^2$$
$$= a^2 - b^2$$

Factoring

When two or more algebraic expressions are multiplied, each is called a factor, and the result is the *product*. The reverse process of finding the factors when given the product is called *factoring*. A product can often be factored in more than one way. Factoring is useful in multiplication, division, and solving equations.

One way to factor an expression is to remove any single-term factor that is common to each of the terms and write it outside the parentheses. It is the distributive law that permits this.

Example 1

$$3x^3 + 6x^2 + 9x = 3x(x^2 + 2x + 3)$$

The result can be checked by multiplication.

Expressions containing squares can sometimes be factored into expressions containing letters raised to the first power only, called *linear factors*. We have seen that

$$(a + b)(a - b) = a^2 - b^2$$

Therefore, if we have an expression in the form of a difference of two squares, it can be factored as:

$$a^2 - b^2 = (a + b)(a - b)$$

Example 2
Factor $4x^2 - 9$.

$$4x^2 - 9 = (2x)^2 - (3)^2 = (2x + 3)(2x - 3)$$

Again, the result can be checked by multiplication.

A third type of expression that can be factored is one containing three terms, such as $x^2 + 5x + 6$. Since

$$(x + a)(x + b) = x(x + b) + a(x + b)$$
$$= x^2 + xb + ax + ab$$
$$= x^2 + (a + b)x + ab$$

an expression in the form $x^2 + (a + b)x + ab$ can be factored into two factors of the form $(x + a)$ and $(x + b)$. We must find two numbers whose product is the constant in the given expression and whose sum is the coefficient of the term containing x.

Example 3

Find factors of $x^2 + 5x + 6$.

First find two numbers that, when multiplied, have +6 as a product. Possibilities are 2 and 3, −2 and −3, 1 and 6, −1 and −6. From these, select the one pair whose sum is 5. The pair 2 and 3 is the only possible selection, and so:

$$x^2 + 5x + 6 = (x + 2)(x + 3), \quad \text{written in either order.}$$

Example 4

Factor $x^2 - 5x - 6$.

Possible factors of −6 are −1 and 6, 1 and −6, 2 and −3, −2 and 3. We must select the pair whose sum is −5. The only pair whose sum is −5 is + 1 and −6, and so

$$x^2 - 5x - 6 = (x + 1)(x - 6).$$

In factoring expressions of this type, notice that if the last sign is a plus, both a and b have the same sign and it is the same as the sign of the middle term. If the last sign is a minus, the numbers have opposite signs.

Many expressions cannot be factored.

Division

Write the division example as a fraction. If numerator and denominator each contain one term, divide the numbers using laws of signed numbers and use the laws of exponents to simplify the letter part of the problem.

Example 1

Method 1

Law of Exponents

$$\frac{36mx^2}{9m^2x} = 4m^1x^2m^{-2}x^{-1} = 4m^{-1}x^1 = \frac{4x}{m}$$

Method 2

Cancellation

$$\frac{36mx^2}{9m^2x} = \frac{\overset{4}{\cancel{36}}m\cancel{x}x}{\underset{1}{\cancel{9}m\cancel{m}\cancel{x}}} = \frac{4x}{m}$$

This is acceptable because

$$\frac{ac}{bc} = \frac{a}{b}\left(\frac{c}{c}\right) \text{ and } \frac{c}{c} = 1$$

so that

$$\frac{ac}{bc} = \frac{a}{b}.$$

If the divisor contains only one term and the dividend is a sum, divide each term in the dividend by the divisor and simplify as you did in Method 2.

Example 2

$$\frac{9x^3 + 3x^2 + 6x}{3x} = \overset{3x^2}{\frac{\cancel{9x^3}}{\cancel{3x}}} + \overset{x}{\frac{\cancel{3x^2}}{\cancel{3x}}} + \overset{2}{\frac{\cancel{6x}}{\cancel{3x}}} = 3x^2 + x + 2$$

This method cannot be followed if there are two terms or more in the denominator since

$$\frac{a}{b+c} \neq \frac{a}{b} + \frac{a}{c}.$$

In this case, write the example as a fraction. Factor the numerator and denominator, if possible. Then use laws of exponents or cancel.

Example 3

Divide $x^3 - 9x$ by $x^3 + 6x^2 + 9x$.

Write as:

$$\frac{x^3 - 9x}{x^3 + 6x^2 + 9x}.$$

Both numerator and denominator can be factored to give:

$$\frac{x(x^2 - 9)}{x(x^2 + 6x + 9)} = \frac{\cancel{x}\cancel{(x+3)}(x-3)}{\cancel{x}\cancel{(x+3)}(x+3)} = \frac{x-3}{x+3}.$$

QUIZ

ALGEBRA PROBLEMS

1. Simplify $4[2(3-7) - 4(2+6)]$

2. Subtract
   $(-25x + 4y - 12z) - (4x - 8y - 13z)$

3. Multiply $(5x + 2)(3x^2 - 2x + 1)$

4. Factor completely $2x^3 + 8x^2 - 90x$

5. Factor completely $32x^2 - 98$

6. Divide $\dfrac{x^2 + 2x - 8}{x^2 - x - 20}$

SOLUTIONS

1. $4[2(3-7) - 4(2+6)] = 4[2(-4)-4(8)]$
    $$= 4[-8 - 32]$$
    $$= 4(-40)$$
    $$= -160$$

2. $(-25x + 4y - 12z) - (4x - 8y - 13z)$
    $$= -25x + 4y - 12z - 4x + 8y + 13z$$
    $$= -29x + 12y + z$$

3. $(5x + 2)(3x^2 - 2x + 1) = 5x\,(3x^2 - 2x + 1) + 2(3x^2 - 2x + 1)$
    $$= 15x^3 - 10x^2 + 5x + 6x^2 - 4x + 2$$
    $$= 15x^3 - 4x^2 + x + 2$$

4. $2x^3 + 8x^2 - 90x = 2x\,(x^2 + 4x - 45) = 2x\,(x + 9)(x - 5)$

5. $32x^2 - 98 = 2(16x^2 - 49) = 2(4x - 7)(4x + 7)$

6. $\dfrac{x^2 + 2x - 8}{x^2 - x - 20} = \dfrac{(x + 4)(x - 2)}{(x - 5)(x + 4)} = \dfrac{\overset{1}{\cancel{(x + 4)}}(x - 2)}{(x - 5)\underset{1}{\cancel{(x + 4)}}} = \dfrac{x - 2}{x - 5}$

EQUATIONS

Solving equations is one of the major objectives in algebra. If a variable x in an equation is replaced by a value or expression that makes the equation a true statement, the value or expression is called a *solution* of the equation. (Remember that an equation is a mathematical statement that one algebraic expression is equal to another.)

An equation may contain one or more variables. We begin with one variable. Certain rules apply to equations whether there are one or more variables. The following rules are applied to give equivalent equations that are simpler than the original:

> *Addition:* If $s = t$, then $s + c = t + c$.
>
> *Subtraction:* If $s + c = t + c$, then $s = t$.
>
> *Multiplication:* If $s = t$, then $cs = ct$.
>
> *Division:* If $cs = ct$ and $c \neq 0$, then $s = t$.

To solve for x in an equation in the form $ax = b$ with $a \neq 0$, divide each side of the equation by a:

$$\frac{ax}{a} = \frac{b}{a} \quad \text{yielding} \quad x = \frac{b}{a}$$

Then, $\dfrac{b}{a}$ is the solution to the equation.

Example 1

Solve $4x = 8$.

Write

$$\frac{4x}{4} = \frac{8}{4}$$

$$x = 2.$$

Example 2

Solve $2x - (x - 4) = 5(x + 2)$ for x.

$$2x - (x - 4) = 5(x + 2)$$

$2x - x + 4 = 5x + 10$ Remove parentheses by distributive law.

$x + 4 = 5x + 10$ Combine like terms.

$x = 5x + 6$ Subtract 4 from each side.

$-4x = 6$ Subtract $5x$ from each side.

$x = \dfrac{6}{-4}$ Divide each side by -4.

$= -\dfrac{3}{2}$ Reduce fraction to lowest terms.

The negative sign now applies to the entire fraction.

Check the solution for accuracy by substituting in the original equation:

$$2\left(-\frac{3}{2}\right) - \left(-\frac{3}{2} - 4\right) \stackrel{?}{=} 5\left(-\frac{3}{2} + 2\right)$$

$$-3 - \left(-\frac{11}{2}\right) \stackrel{?}{=} 5\left(\frac{1}{2}\right)$$

$$-3 + \frac{11}{2} \stackrel{?}{=} \frac{5}{2}$$

$$\frac{6}{2} + \frac{11}{2} \stackrel{?}{=} \frac{5}{2} \text{ check}$$

QUIZ

EQUATIONS PROBLEMS

Solve the following equations for x:

1. $3x - 5 = 3 + 2x$

2. $3(2x - 2) = 12$

3. $4(x - 2) = 2x + 10$

4. $7 - 4(2x - 1) = 3 + 4(4 - x)$

SOLUTIONS

1.
$$3x - 5 = 3 + 2x$$
$$\underline{-2x \qquad\qquad -2x}$$
$$x - 5 = 3$$
$$\underline{+5 \quad +5}$$
$$x = 8$$

2.
$$3(2x - 2) = 12$$
$$6x - 6 = 12$$
$$6x = 18$$
$$x = 3$$

3.
$$4(x - 2) = 2x + 10$$
$$4x - 8 = 2x + 10$$
$$4x = 2x + 18$$
$$2x = 18$$
$$x = 9$$

4.
$$7 - 4(2x - 1) = 3 + 4(4 - x)$$
$$7 - 8x + 4 = 3 + 16 - 4x$$
$$11 - 8x = 19 - 4x$$
$$11 = 19 + 4x$$
$$-8 = 4x$$
$$x = -2$$

WORD PROBLEMS INVOLVING ONE UNKNOWN

In many cases, if you read a word problem carefully, assign a letter to the quantity to be found, and understand the relationships between known and unknown quantities, you can formulate an equation in one unknown.

Number Problems and Age Problems

These two kinds of problems are similar to one another.

Example

One number is 3 times another, and their sum is 48. Find the two numbers.

Let x = second number. Then the first is $3x$. Since their sum is 48,

$$3x + x = 48$$
$$4x = 48$$
$$x = 12.$$

Therefore, the first number is $3x = 36$.

$$36 + 12 = 48 \text{ check}$$

Distance Problems

The basic concept is:

distance = rate · time.

Example

In a mileage test, a man drives a truck at a fixed rate of speed for 1 hour. Then he increases the speed by 20 miles per hour and drives at that rate for 2 hours. He then reduces that speed by 5 miles per hour and drives at that rate for 3 hours. If the distance traveled was 295 miles, what are the rates of speed over each part of the test?

Let x be the first speed, $x + 20$ the second, and $x + (20 - 5) = x + 15$ the third. Because distance = rate · time, multiply these rates by the time and formulate the equation by separating the two equal expressions for distance by an equal sign:

$$1x + 2(x + 20) + 3(x + 15) = 295$$
$$x + 2x + 3x + 40 + 45 = 295$$
$$6x = 210$$
$$x = 35.$$

The speeds are 35, 55, and 50 miles per hour.

CONSECUTIVE NUMBER PROBLEMS

This type usually involves only one unknown. Two numbers are consecutive if one is the successor of the other. Three consecutive numbers are of the form x, $x + 1$, and $x + 2$. Since an even number is divisible by 2, consecutive even numbers are of the form $2x$, $2x + 2$, and $2x + 4$. An odd number is of the form $2x + 1$.

Example

Find three consecutive whole numbers whose sum is 75.

Let the first number be x, the second $x + 1$, and the third $x + 2$. Then:

$$x + (x + 1) + (x + 2) = 75$$
$$3x + 3 = 75$$
$$3x = 72$$
$$x = 24.$$

The numbers whose sum is 75 are 24, 25, and 26. Many versions of this problem have no solution. For example, no three consecutive whole numbers have a sum of 74.

WORK PROBLEMS

These problems concern the speed with which work can be accomplished and the time necessary to perform a task if the size of the workforce is changed.

Example

If Joe alone can type a chapter in 6 days and Ann can type the same chapter in 8 days, how long will it take them to type the chapter if they both work on it?

We let x = number of days required if they work together, and then put our information into tabular form:

	Joe	Ann	Together
Days to type chapter	6	8	x
Part typed in 1 day	$\dfrac{1}{6}$	$\dfrac{1}{8}$	$\dfrac{1}{x}$

Since the part done by Joe in 1 day plus the part done by Ann in 1 day equals the part done by both in 1 day, we have

$$\frac{1}{6} + \frac{1}{8} = \frac{1}{x}.$$

Next we multiply each member by $48x$ to clear the fractions, giving:

$$8x + 6x = 48$$
$$14x = 48$$
$$x = 3\frac{3}{7} \text{ days.}$$

QUIZ

WORD PROBLEMS IN ONE UNKNOWN PROBLEMS

1. If 18 is subtracted from six times a certain number, the result is 96. Find the number.

2. A 63-foot rope is cut into two pieces. If one piece is twice as long as the other, how long is each piece?

3. Peter is now three times as old as Jillian. In six years, he will be twice as old as she will be then. How old is Peter now?

4. Lauren can clean the kitchen in 30 minutes. It takes Kathleen 20 minutes to complete the same job. How long would it take to clean the kitchen if they both worked together?

5. A train travels 120 miles at an average rate of 40 mph, and it returns along the same route at an average rate of 60 mph. What is the average rate of speed for the entire trip?

6. The sum of two consecutive odd integers is 68. Find the integers.

SOLUTIONS

1. Let x = the number.

    Then, $6x - 18 = 96$

    $$6x = 114$$
    $$x = 19.$$

    The number is 19.

2. Let x = the length of the short piece.

    Then, $2x$ = the length of the longer piece.

    And, $x + 2x = 63$

    $$3x = 63$$
    $$x = 21$$
    $$2x = 42.$$

    The pieces are 21 feet and 42 feet.

3. Let J = Jillian's age now;

$3J$ = Peter's age now;

$J + 6$ = Jillian's age in 6 years;

$3J + 6$ = Peter's age in 6 years.

Then,

$3J + 6 = 2(J + 6)$

$3J + 6 = 2J + 12$

$3J = 2J + 6$

$J = 6$

$3J = 18.$

Peter is currently 18 years old.

4. Let x = the number of minutes to do the job working together.

Lauren does $\dfrac{x}{30}$ of the job.

Kathleen does $\dfrac{x}{20}$ of the job.

$\dfrac{x}{30} + \dfrac{x}{20} = 1$ (Multiply by 60)

$2x + 3x = 60$

$5x = 60$

$x = 12$

It would take 12 minutes to do the job together.

5. The train takes $\dfrac{120}{40} = 3$ hours out, and the train takes $\dfrac{120}{60} = 2$ hours back. The total trip takes 5 hours. The total distance traveled is 240 miles. Then,

rate $= \dfrac{\text{distance}}{\text{time}} = \dfrac{240}{5} = 48$

The average rate is 48 mph.

6. Let x = the first odd integer.

Then, $x + 2$ = the second odd integer, and,

$x + x + 2 = 68$

$2x + 2 = 68$

$2x = 66$

$x = 33$

$x + 2 = 35.$

The numbers are 33 and 35.

LITERAL EQUATIONS

An equation may have other letters in it besides the variable (or variables). Such an equation is called a *literal equation*. An illustration is $x + b = a$, with x the variable. The solution of such an equation will not be a specific number but will involve letter symbols. Literal equations are solved by exactly the same methods as those involving numbers, but we must know which of the letters in the equation is to be considered the variable. Then the other letters are treated as constants.

Example 1

Solve $ax - 2bc = d$ for x.

$$ax = d + 2bc$$

$$x = \frac{d + 2bc}{a} \text{ if } a \neq 0$$

Example 2

Solve $ay - by = a^2 - b^2$ for y.

$$y(a - b) = a^2 - b^2 \qquad \text{Factor out common term.}$$

$$y(a - b) = (a + b)(a - b) \qquad \text{Factor expression on right side.}$$

$$y = a + b \qquad \text{Divide each side by } a - b \text{ if } a \neq b.$$

Example 3

Solve for S in the equation.

$$\frac{1}{R} = \frac{1}{S} + \frac{1}{T}$$

Multiply every term by RST, the LCD:

$$ST = RT + RS$$

$$ST - RS = RT$$

$$S(T - R) = RT$$

$$S = \frac{RT}{T - R} \qquad \text{If } T \neq R$$

QUADRATIC EQUATIONS

An equation containing the square of an unknown quantity is called a *quadratic* equation. One way to solve such an equation is by factoring. If the product of two expressions is zero, at least one of the expressions must be zero.

Example 1

Solve $y^2 + 2y = 0$.

$y(y + 2) = 0$ Remove common factor.

$y = 0$ or $y + 2 = 0$ Since product is 0, at least one of factors must be 0.

$y = 0$ or $y = -2$

Check by substituting both values in the original equation:

$(0)^2 + 2(0) = 0$

$(-2)^2 + 2(-2) = 4 - 4 = 0.$

In this case, there are two solutions.

Example 2

Solve $x^2 + 7x + 10 = 0$.

$x^2 + 7x + 10 = (x + 5)(x + 2) = 0$

$x + 5 = 0$ or $x + 2 = 0$

$x = -5$ or $x = -2$

Check:

$(-5)^2 + 7(-5) + 10 = 25 - 35 + 10 = 0$

$(-2)^2 + 7(-2) + 10 = 4 - 14 + 10 = 0.$

Not all quadratic equations can be factored using only integers, but solutions can usually be found by means of a formula. A quadratic equation may have two solutions, one solution, or occasionally no real solutions. If the quadratic equation is in the form $Ax^2 + Bx + C = 0$, x can be found from the following formula:

$$x = \frac{-B \pm \sqrt{B^2 - 4AC}}{2A}.$$

Example 3

Solve $2y^2 + 5y + 2 = 0$ by formula. Assume $A = 2$, $B = 5$, and $C = 2$.

$$x = \frac{-5 \pm \sqrt{5^2 - 4(2)(2)}}{2(2)}$$

$$= \frac{-5 \pm \sqrt{25 - 16}}{4}$$

$$= \frac{-5 \pm \sqrt{9}}{4}$$

$$= \frac{-5 \pm 3}{4}$$

This yields two solutions:

$$x = \frac{-5 + 3}{4} = \frac{-2}{4} = \frac{-1}{2} \text{ and}$$

$$x = \frac{-5 - 3}{4} = \frac{-8}{4} = -2.$$

So far, each quadratic that we have solved has had two distinct answers, but an equation may have a single answer (repeated), as in

$$x^2 + 4x + 4 = 0$$

$$(x + 2)(x + 2) = 0$$

$$x + 2 = 0 \text{ and } x + 2 = 0$$

$$x = -2 \text{ and } x = -2.$$

The only solution is -2.

It is also possible for a quadratic equation to have no real solution at all.

Example 4

If we attempt to solve $x^2 + x + 1 = 0$, by formula, we get:

$$x = \frac{-1 \pm \sqrt{1 - 4(1)(1)}}{2} = \frac{-1 \pm \sqrt{-3}}{2}.$$

Since $\sqrt{-3}$ is not defined, this quadratic has no real answer.

Rewriting Equations

Certain equations that are written with a variable in the denominator can be rewritten as quadratics.

Example 1

Solve $-\dfrac{4}{x} + 5 = x$.

$$-4 + 5x = x^2 \qquad \text{Multiply both sides by } x \neq 0.$$

$$-x^2 + 5x - 4 = 0 \qquad \text{Collect terms on one side of equals and}$$
$$\text{set sum equal to } 0.$$

$$x^2 - 5x + 4 = 0 \qquad \text{Multiply both sides by } -1.$$

$$(x - 4)(x - 1) = 0 \qquad \text{Factor}$$

$$x - 4 = 0 \quad \text{or} \quad x - 1 = 0$$

$$x = 4 \quad \text{or} \qquad x = 1$$

Check the result by substitution:

$$-\frac{4}{4} + 5 \overset{?}{=} 4 \text{ and } -\frac{4}{1} + 5 \overset{?}{=} 1$$
$$-1 + 5 = 4 \qquad -4 + 5 = 1$$

Some equations containing a radical sign can also be converted into a quadratic equation. The solution of this type of problem depends on the principle that

$$\text{If } A = B \quad \text{then} \quad A^2 = B^2$$

$$\text{and if } A^2 = B^2 \quad \text{then} \quad A = B \quad \text{or} \quad A = -B$$

Example 2

Solve $y = \sqrt{3y + 4}$

$$y = \sqrt{3y + 4}$$
$$y^2 = 3y + 4$$
$$y^2 - 3y - 4 = 0$$
$$(y - 4)(y + 1) = 0$$
$$y = 4 \text{ or } y = -1$$

Check by substituting values into the original equation:

$$4 \overset{?}{=} \sqrt{3(4) + 4} \text{ and } -1 = \sqrt{3(-1) + 4}$$
$$4 \overset{?}{=} \sqrt{16} \qquad -1 \overset{?}{=} \sqrt{1}$$
$$4 = 4 \qquad -1 \neq 1$$

The single solution is y = 4: the false root y = −1 was introduced when the original equation was squared.

QUIZ

EQUATION SOLVING PROBLEMS

Solve the following equations for the variable indicated:

1. Solve for W: $P = 2L + 2W$

2. Solve for x: $ax + b = cx + d$

3. Solve for x: $8x^2 - 4x = 0$

4. Solve for x: $x^2 - 4x = 21$

5. Solve for y: $\sqrt{y+1} - 3 = 7$

SOLUTIONS

1. $P = 2L + 2W$

   $2W = P - 2L$

   $W = \dfrac{P - 2L}{2}$

2. $ax + b = cx + d$

   $ax = cx + d - b$

   $ax - cx = d - b$

   $x(a - c) = d - b$

   $x = \dfrac{d - b}{a - c}$

3. $8x^2 - 4x = 0$

   $4x(x - 2) = 0$

   $x = 0, 2$

4. $x^2 - 4x = 21$

   $x^2 - 4x - 21 = 0$

   $(x - 7)(x + 3) = 0$

   $x = 7, -3$

5. $\sqrt{y + 1} - 3 = 7$

   $\sqrt{y + 1} = 10$

   $(\sqrt{y + 1})^2 = 10^2$

   $y + 1 = 100$

   $y = 99$

LINEAR INEQUALITIES

For each of the sets of numbers we have considered, we have established an ordering of the members of the set by defining what it means to say that one number is greater than the other. Every number we have considered can be represented by a point on a number line.

An *algebraic inequality* is a statement that one algebraic expression is greater than (or less than) another algebraic expression. If all the variables in the inequality are raised to the first power, the inequality is said to be a *linear inequality*. We solve the inequality by reducing it to a simpler inequality whose solution is apparent. The answer is not unique, as it is in an equation, since a great number of values may satisfy the inequality.

There are three rules for producing equivalent inequalities:

1. The same quantity can be added or subtracted from each side of an inequality.

2. Each side of an inequality can be multiplied or divided by the same *positive* quantity.

3. If each side of an inequality is multiplied or divided by the same *negative* quantity, the sign of the inequality must be reversed so that the new inequality is equivalent to the first.

Example 1

Solve $5x - 5 > -9 + 3x$.

$$5x > -4 + 3x \quad \text{Add 5 to each side.}$$
$$2x > -4 \quad \text{Subtract } 3x \text{ from each side.}$$
$$x > -2 \quad \text{Divide by +2.}$$

Any number greater than -2 is a solution to this inequality.

Example 2

Solve $2x - 12 < 5x - 3$.

$$2x < 5x + 9 \quad \text{Add 12 to each side.}$$
$$-3x < 9 \quad \text{Subtract } 5x \text{ from each side.}$$
$$x > -3 \quad \text{Divide each side by } -3,$$
$$\text{changing sign of inequality.}$$

Any number greater than -3—for example, $-2\frac{1}{2}$, 0, 1, or 4—is a solution to this inequality.

LINEAR EQUATIONS IN TWO UNKNOWNS

Graphing Equations

The number line is useful in picturing the values of one variable. When two variables are involved, a coordinate system is effective. The Cartesian coordinate system is constructed by placing a vertical number line and a horizontal number line on a plane so that the lines intersect at their zero points. This meeting place is called the *origin*. The horizontal number line is called the *x* axis, and the vertical number line (with positive numbers above the *x* axis) is called the *y* axis. Points in the plane correspond to ordered pairs of real numbers.

Example

The points in this example are:

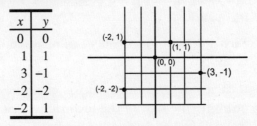

x	*y*
0	0
1	1
3	−1
−2	−2
−2	1

A first-degree equation in two variables is an equation that can be written in the form $ax + by = c$, where a, b, and c are constants. *First-degree* means that x and y appear to the first power. *Linear* refers to the graph of the solutions (x, y) of the equation, which is a straight line. We have already discussed linear equations of one variable.

Example

Graph the line $y = 2x - 4$.

First, make a table, and select small integral values of x. Find the value of each corresponding y, and write it in the table:

x	*y*
0	−4
1	−2
2	0
3	2

If $x = 1$, for example, $y = 2(1) - 4 = -2$. Then plot the four points on a coordinate system. It is not necessary to have four points; two would do since two points determine a line, but plotting three or more points reduces the possibility of error.

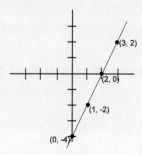

After the points have been plotted (placed on the graph), draw a line through the points and extend it in both directions. This line represents the equation $y = 2x - 4$.

Solving Simultaneous Linear Equations

Two linear equations can be solved together (simultaneously) to yield an answer (x, y), if it exists. On the coordinate system, this amounts to drawing the graphs of two lines and finding their point of intersection. If the lines are parallel and, therefore, never meet, no solution exists.

Simultaneous linear equations can be solved in the following manner without drawing graphs. From the first equation, find the value of one variable in terms of the other; substitute this value in the second equation. The second equation is now a linear equation in one variable and can be solved. After the numerical value of the one variable has been found, substitute that value into the first equation to find the value of the second variable. Check the results by putting both values into the second equation.

Example 1
Solve the system.

$$2x + y = 3$$
$$4x - y = 0$$

From the first equation, $y = 3 - 2x$. Substitute this value of y into the second equation to get

$$4x - (3 - 2x) = 0$$
$$4x - 3 + 2x = 0$$
$$6x = 3$$
$$x = \frac{1}{2}$$

Substitute $x = \dfrac{1}{2}$ in the first of the original equations:

$$2\left(\dfrac{1}{2}\right) + y = 3$$
$$1 + y = 3$$
$$y = 2$$

Check by substituting both x and y values into the second equation:

$$4\left(\dfrac{1}{2}\right) + -2 = 0$$
$$2 - 2 = 0$$

Example 2

A change-making machine contains \$30 in dimes and quarters. There are 150 coins in the machine. Find the number of each type of coin.

Let x = number of dimes and y = number of quarters. Then:

$$x + y = 150.$$

Since $.25y$ is the product of a quarter of a dollar and the number of quarters, and $.10x$ is the amount of money in dimes,

$$.10x + .25y = 30.$$

Multiply the last equation by 100 to eliminate the decimal points:

$$10x + 25y = 3,000.$$

From the first equation, $y = 150 - x$. Substitute this value in the equivalent form of the second equation.

$$10x + 25(150 - x) = 3,000$$
$$-15x = -750$$
$$x = 50$$

This is the number of dimes. Substitute this value in $x + y = 150$ to find the number of quarters, $y = 100$.

Check:

$$.10(50) + .25(100) = 30$$
$$\$5 + \$25 = \$30$$

QUIZ

LINEAR INEQUALITIES AND EQUATIONS PROBLEMS

1. Solve for x: $12x < 5(2x + 4)$

2. Solve for y: $6y + 2 < 8y + 14$

3. Find the common solution:

$x - 3y = 3$

$2x + 9y = 11$

4. A coin collection consisting of quarters and nickels has a value of $4.50. The total number of coins is 26. Find the number of quarters and the number of nickels in the collection.

5. Mr. Linnell bought 3 cans of corn and 5 cans of tomatoes for $3.75. The next week, he bought 4 cans of corn and 2 cans of tomatoes for $2.90. Find the cost of a can of corn.

SOLUTIONS

1. $12x < 5(2x + 4)$

$12x < 10x + 20$

$2x < 20$

$x < 10$

2. $6y + 2 < 8y + 14$

$6y < 8y + 12$

$-2y < 12$

$y > -6$

3. $x - 3y = 3$

$2x + 9y = 11$

Multiply the first equation by 3.

$3(x - 3y) = 3(3)$

$2x + 9y = 11$

$3x - 9y = 9$

$\underline{2x + 9y = 11}$

$5x \qquad = 20$

$x = 4$

Now substitute this answer for x in the second equation.

$$2(4) + 9y = 11$$
$$8 + 9y = 11$$
$$9y = 3$$
$$y = \frac{1}{3}$$

4. Let Q = the number of quarters in the collection. Let N = the number of nickels in the collection. Then, .25Q + .05N = 4.50.

Q + N = 26

Multiply the top equation by 100 to clear the decimals:

25Q + 5Nt= 450
Q + N = 26

Multiply the bottom equation by −5 and add:

$$
\begin{array}{r}
25Q + 5N = 450 \\
-5Q - 5N = -130 \\
\hline
20Q \qquad = 320 \\
Q = 16 \\
N = 10
\end{array}
$$

There are 16 quarters and 10 nickels.

5. Let c = the cost of a can of corn, and t = the cost of a can of tomatoes.

Then,

3c + 5t = 3.75
4c + 2t = 2.90

Multiply the top equation by 2, the bottom one by −5, and add:

$$
\begin{array}{r}
6c + 10t = 7.50 \\
-20c - 10t = -14.50 \\
\hline
-14c \qquad = -7.00 \\
c = .50
\end{array}
$$

A can of corn costs 50¢.

RATIO AND PROPORTION

Many problems in arithmetic and algebra can be solved using the concept of *ratio* to compare numbers. The ratio of a to b is the fraction $\frac{a}{b}$. If the two ratios $\frac{a}{b}$ and $\frac{c}{d}$ represent the same comparison, we write:

$$\frac{a}{b} = \frac{c}{d}.$$

This equation (statement of equality) is called a *proportion*. A proportion states the equivalence of two different expressions for the same ratio.

Example 1

In a class of 39 students, 17 are men. Find the ratio of men to women.

39 students − 17 men = 22 women.

Ratio of men to women is $\frac{17}{22}$, also written 17:22.

Example 2

A fertilizer contains 3 parts nitrogen, 2 parts potash, and 2 parts phosphate by weight. How many pounds of fertilizer will contain 60 pounds of nitrogen?

The ratio of pounds of nitrogen to pounds of fertilizer is 3 to $3 + 2 + 2 = \frac{3}{7}$. Let x be the number of pounds of mixture. Then:

$$\frac{3}{7} = \frac{60}{x}$$

Multiply both sides of the equation by $7x$ to get:

$$3x = 420$$
$$x = 140 \text{ pounds.}$$

COMPUTING AVERAGES

MEAN

Several statistical measures are used frequently. One of them is the *average* or *arithmetic mean*. To find the average of N numbers, add the numbers and divide their sum by N.

Example 1

Seven students attained test scores of 62, 80, 60, 30, 50, 90, and 20. What was the average test score for the group?

$$62 + 80 + 60 + 30 + 50 + 90 + 20 = 392$$

Since there are 7 scores, the average score was

$$\frac{392}{7} = 56.$$

Example 2

Joan allotted herself a budget of $50 a week, on the average, for expenses. One week, she spent $35, the next $60, and the third $40. How much can she spend in the fourth week without exceeding her budget?

Let x be the amount spent in the fourth week. Then:

$$\frac{35 + 60 + 40 + x}{4} = 50$$

$$35 + 60 + 40 + x = 200$$

$$135 + x = 200$$

$$x = 65.$$

She can spend $65 in the fourth week.

PLANE GEOMETRY

Plane geometry is the science of measurement. Certain assumptions are made about undefined quantities called points, lines, and planes, and then logical deductions about relationships between figures composed of lines, angles, and portions of planes are made based on these assumptions. The process of making the logical deduction is called a *proof*. In this summary we are not making any proofs but are giving the definitions frequently used in geometry and stating relationships that are the results of proofs.

ANGLES

A line in geometry is always a straight line. When two straight lines meet at a point, they form an *angle*. The lines are called *sides* or *rays* of the angle, and the point is called the *vertex*. The symbol for an angle is ∠. When no other angle shares the same vertex, the name of the angle is the name given to the vertex, as in angle *A:*

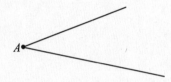

An angle may be named with three letters. Following, for example, *B* is a point on one side and *C* is a point on the other. In this case the name of the vertex must be the middle letter, and we have angle *BAC.*

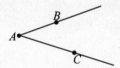

Occasionally, an angle is named by a number or small letter placed in the angle.

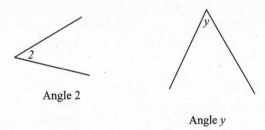

Angle 2   Angle *y*

Angles are usually measured in degrees. An angle of 30 degrees, written 30°, is an angle whose measure is 30 degrees. Degrees are divided into minutes; 60′ (read "minutes") = 1°. Minutes are further divided into seconds; 60″ (read "seconds") = 1′.

Vertical Angles

When two lines intersect, four angles are formed. The angles opposite each other are called *vertical angles* and are equal to each other.

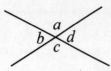

a and *c* are vertical angles. $\angle a = \angle c$

b and *d* are vertical angles. $\angle b = \angle d$

Straight Angle

A *straight angle* has its sides lying along a straight line. It is always equal to 180°.

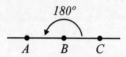

$\angle ABC = \angle B = 180°$

$\angle B$ is a straight angle.

Adjacent Angles

Two angles are *adjacent* if they share the same vertex and a common side, but no angle is inside another angle. $\angle ABC$ and $\angle CBD$ are adjacent angles. Even though they share a common vertex *B* and a common side *AB*, $\angle ABD$ and $\angle ABC$ are not adjacent angles because one angle is inside the other.

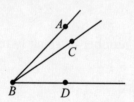

Peterson's GMAT CAT Success

Supplementary Angles

If the sum of two angles is a straight angle (180°), the two angles are *supplementary*, and each angle is the supplement of the other.

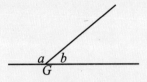

$\angle G$ is a straight angle = 180°.

$\angle a + \angle b = 180°$

$\angle a$ and $\angle b$ are supplementary angles.

Right Angles

If two supplementary angles are equal, they are both *right* angles. A *right* angle is one half a straight angle. Its measure is 90°. A right angle is symbolized by ∟.

$\angle G$ is a straight angle.

$\angle b + \angle a = \angle G$, and $\angle a = \angle b$. $\angle a$ and $\angle b$ are right angles.

Complementary Angles

Complementary angles are two angles whose sum is a right angle (90°).

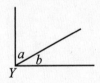

$\angle Y$ is a right angle.

$\angle a + \angle b = \angle Y = 90°$.

$\angle a$ and $\angle b$ are complementary angles.

Acute Angles

Acute angles are angles whose measure is less than 90°. No two acute angles can be supplementary angles. Two acute angles can be complementary angles.

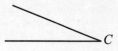

∠C is an acute angle.

Obtuse Angles

Obtuse angles are angles that are greater than 90° and less than 180°.

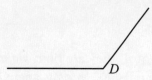

∠D is an obtuse angle.

Example 1

In the figure, what is the value of x?

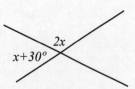

Since the two labeled angles are supplementary angles, their sum is 180°.

$$(x + 30°) + 2x = 180°$$
$$3x = 150°$$
$$x = 50°$$

Example 2

Find the value of x in the figure.

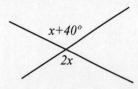

Since the two labeled angles are vertical angles, they are equal.

$$x + 40° = 2x$$
$$40° = x$$

Peterson's GMAT CAT Success

Example 3

If angle Y is a right angle and angle b measures $30°15'$, what does angle a measure?

Since angle Y is a right angle, angles a and b are complementary angles and their sum is $90°$.

$$\angle a + \angle b = 90°$$
$$\angle a + 30°15' = 90°$$
$$\angle a = 59°45'$$

LINES

A *line* in geometry is always assumed to be a straight line. It extends infinitely far in both directions. It is determined if two of its points are known. It can be expressed in terms of the two points, which are written as capital letters. The following line is called *AB*.

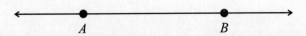

Or, a line may be given one name with a small letter. The following line is called line *k*.

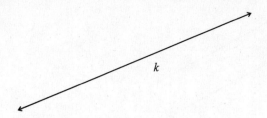

A *line segment* is a part of a line between two *endpoints*. It is named by its endpoints, for example, *A* and *B*.

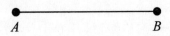

AB is a line segment. It has a definite length.

If point *P* is on the line and is the same distance from *A* as from *B*, then *P* is the *midpoint* of segment *AB*. When we say *AP* = *PB*, we mean that the two line segments have the same length.

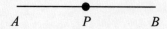

A part of a line with one endpoint is called a *ray*. *AC* is a ray with endpoint *A*. The ray extends infinitely far in the direction away from the endpoint.

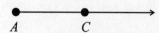

Parallel Lines

Two lines meet or intersect if there is one point that is on both lines. Two different lines may either intersect in one point or never meet, but they can never meet in more than one point.

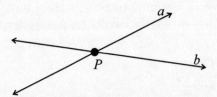

Two lines in the same plane that never meet no matter how far they are extended are said to be *parallel,* for which the symbol is ∥. In the following diagram, *a* ∥ *b*.

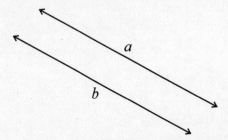

If two lines in the same plane are parallel to a third line, they are parallel to each other. Since *a* ∥ *b* and *b* ∥ *c*, we know that *a* ∥ *c*.

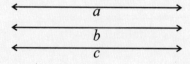

Peterson's GMAT CAT Success

Two lines that meet each other at right angles are said to be *perpendicular*, for which the symbol is ⊥. Line *a* is perpendicular to line *b*.

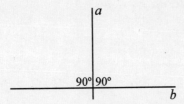

Two lines in the same plane that are perpendicular to the same line are parallel to each other.

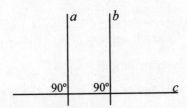

Line *a* ⊥ line *c* and line *b* ⊥ line *c*. Therefore, *a* ∥ *b*.

A line that intersects two other lines is called a *transversal*. Line *c* is a transversal that intersects lines *a* and *b*.

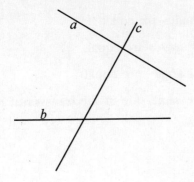

The transversal and the two given lines form eight angles. The four angles between the given lines are called *interior angles;* the four angles outside the given lines are called *exterior angles.* If two angles are on opposite sides of the transversal, they are called *alternate angles.*

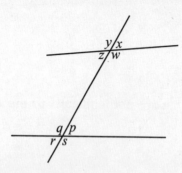

∠z, ∠w, ∠q, and ∠p are interior angles.

∠y, ∠x, ∠s, and ∠r are exterior angles.

∠z and ∠p are alternate interior angles; so are ∠w and ∠q.

∠y and ∠s are alternate exterior angles; so are ∠x and ∠r.

Pairs of *corresponding* angles are y and ∠q; ∠z and ∠r; ∠x and ∠p; and ∠w and ∠s. Corresponding angles are sometimes called exterior-interior angles.

When the two given lines cut by a transversal are parallel lines,

1. the corresponding angles are equal.

2. the alternate interior angles are equal.

3. the alternate exterior angles are equal.

4. interior angles on the same side of the transversal are supplementary.

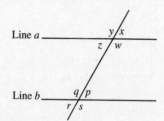

If line *a* is parallel to line *b:*

1. ∠y = ∠q, ∠z = ∠r, ∠x = ∠p, and ∠w = ∠s.

2. ∠z = ∠p and ∠w = ∠q.

3. ∠y = ∠s and ∠x = ∠r.

4. ∠z + ∠q = 180°, and ∠p + ∠w = 180°.

Because vertical angles are equal, $\angle p = \angle r$, $\angle q = \angle s$, $\angle y = \angle w$, and $\angle x = \angle z$. If any one of the four conditions for equality of angles holds true, the lines are parallel; that is, if two lines are cut by a transversal and one pair of the corresponding angles is equal, the lines are parallel. If a pair of alternate interior angles or a pair of alternate exterior angles is equal, the lines are parallel. If interior angles on the same side of the transversal are supplementary, the lines are parallel.

Example

In the figure, two parallel lines are cut by a transversal. Find the measure of angle y.

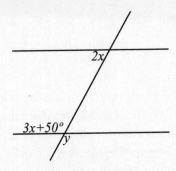

The two labeled angles are supplementary.

$$2x + (3x+50°) = 180°$$
$$5x = 130°$$
$$x = 26°$$

Since $\angle y$ is vertical to the angle whose measure is $3x + 50°$, it has the same measure.

$$y = 3x + 50° = 3(26°) + 50° = 128°$$

POLYGONS

A *polygon* is a closed plane figure that is composed of line segments joined together at points called *vertices* (singular, *vertex*). A polygon is usually named by giving its vertices in order.

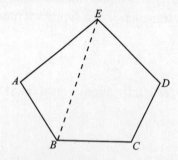

Polygon *ABCDE*

In the figure, points *A, B, C, D,* and *E* are the vertices, and the sides are *AB, BC, CD, DE,* and *EA. AB* and *BC* are *adjacent* sides, and *A* and *B* are adjacent vertices. A *diagonal* of a polygon is a line segment that joins any two nonadjacent vertices. *EB* is a diagonal.

Polygons are named according to the number of sides or angles. A *triangle* is a polygon with three sides, a *quadrilateral* a polygon with four sides, a *pentagon* a polygon with five sides, and a *hexagon* a polygon with six sides. The number of sides is always equal to the number of angles.

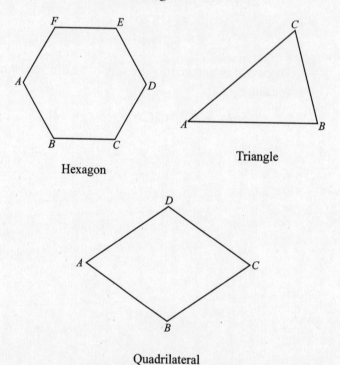

Hexagon

Triangle

Quadrilateral

The *perimeter* of a polygon is the sum of the lengths of its sides. If the polygon is regular (all sides equal and all angles equal), the perimeter is the product of the length of *one* side and the number of sides.

Congruent and Similar Polygons

If two polygons have equal corresponding angles and equal corresponding sides, they are said to be *congruent*. Congruent polygons have the same size and shape. They are the same in all respects, except possibly position. The symbol for congruence is ≅.

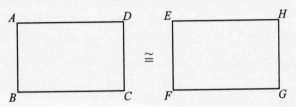

When two sides of congruent or different polygons are equal, we indicate the fact by drawing the same number of short lines through the equal sides.

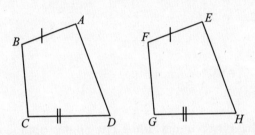

This indicates that *AB = EF* and *CD = GH*.

Two polygons with equal corresponding angles and corresponding sides in proportion are said to be *similar*. The symbol for similar is ∼.

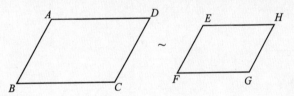

Similar figures have the same shape but not necessarily the same size.

A *regular polygon* is a polygon whose sides are equal and whose angles are equal.

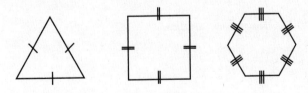

Triangles

A *triangle* is a polygon with three sides. Triangles are classified by measuring their sides and angles. The sum of the angles of a plane triangle is always 180°. The symbol for a triangle is Δ. The sum of any two sides of a triangle is always greater than the third side.

Equilateral

Equilateral triangles have equal sides and equal angles. Each angle measures 60° because $\frac{1}{3}(180°) = 60°$.

$AB = AC = BC$

$\angle A = \angle B = \angle C = 60°$

Isosceles

Isosceles triangles have two equal sides. The angles opposite the equal sides are equal. The two equal angles are sometimes called the *base* angles, and the third angle is called the *vertex* angle. Note that an equilateral triangle is isosceles.

$FG = FH$

$FG \neq GH$

$\angle G = \angle H$

$\angle F$ is the vertex angle.

$\angle G$ and $\angle H$ are base angles.

Peterson's GMAT CAT Success

Scalene

Scalene triangles have all three sides of different lengths and all angles of different measures. In scalene triangles, the shortest side is opposite the angle with the smallest measure, and the longest side is opposite the angle with the greatest measure.

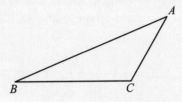

$AB > BC > CA$; therefore $\angle C > \angle A > \angle B$.

Right

Right triangles contain one right angle. Since the right angle is 90°, the other two angles are complementary. They may or may not be equal to each other. The side of a right triangle opposite the right angle is called the *hypotenuse*. The other two sides are called *legs*. The *Pythagorean theorem* states that the square of the length of the hypotenuse is equal to the sum of the squares of the lengths of the legs.

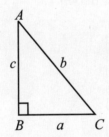

AC is the hypotenuse. AB and BC are legs.

$\angle B = 90°$

$\angle A + \angle C = 90°$

$a^2 + c^2 = b^2$

Example 1

If *ABC* is a right triangle with right angle at *B*, and if $AB = 6$ and $BC = 8$, what is the length of *AC*?

$$AB^2 + BC^2 = AC^2$$
$$6^2 + 8^2 = 36 + 64 = 100 = AC^2$$
$$AC = 10$$

If the measure of angle A is 30°, what is the measure of angle *C*?

Example 2

Since angles A and C are complementary:

$$30° + C = 90°$$
$$C = 60°.$$

If the lengths of the three sides of a triangle are a, b, and c and the relation $a^2 + b^2 = c^2$ holds, the triangle is a right triangle and side c is the hypotenuse.

Example 3

Show that a triangle of sides 5, 12, and 13 is a right triangle. The triangle will be a right triangle if $a^2 + b^2 = c^2$.

$$5^2 + 12^2 = 13^2$$
$$25 + 144 = 169$$

Therefore, the triangle is a right triangle, and 13 is the length of the hypotenuse.

Area of a Triangle

An *altitude* (or height) of a triangle is a line segment dropped as a perpendicular from any vertex to the opposite side. The area of a triangle is the product of one half the altitude and the base of the triangle. (The base is the side opposite the vertex from which the perpendicular was drawn.)

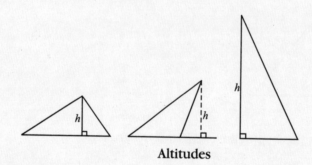

Altitudes

Example

Find the area, A, of the following isosceles triangle.

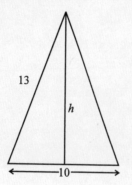

In an isosceles triangle, the altitude from the vertex angle bisects the base (cuts it in half).

The first step is to find the altitude. By the Pythagorean theorem, $a^2 + b^2 = c^2$; $c = 13$, $a = b$, and $b = \frac{1}{2}(10) = 5$.

$$b^2 + 5^2 = 13^2$$
$$b^2 + 25 = 169$$
$$b^2 = 144$$
$$b = 12$$
$$A = \frac{1}{2} \cdot \text{base} \cdot \text{height}$$
$$= \frac{1}{2} \cdot 10 \cdot 12$$
$$= 60$$

Similarity

Two triangles are *similar* if all three pairs of corresponding angles are equal. The sum of the three angles of a triangle is 180°; therefore, if two angles of triangle I equal two corresponding angles of triangle II, the third angle of triangle I must be equal to the third angle of triangle II, and the triangles are similar. The lengths of the sides of similar triangles are in proportion to each other. A line drawn parallel to one side of a triangle divides the triangle into two portions, one of which is a triangle. The new triangle is similar to the original triangle.

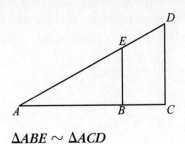

$\triangle ABE \sim \triangle ACD$

Example

In the following figure, if AC = 28 feet, AB = 35 feet, BC = 21 feet, and EC = 12 feet, find the length of DC if $DE \parallel AB$.

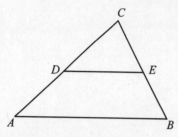

Because $DE \parallel AB$, $\triangle CDE \sim \triangle CAB$. Since the triangles are similar, their sides are in proportion:

$$\frac{DC}{AC} = \frac{EC}{BC}$$

$$\frac{DC}{28} = \frac{12}{21}$$

$$DC = \frac{12 \cdot 28}{21} = 16 \text{ feet.}$$

Quadrilaterals

A *quadrilateral* is a polygon that has four sides. The sum of the angles of a quadrilateral is 360°. If the opposite sides of a quadrilateral are parallel, the quadrilateral is a *parallelogram*. Opposite sides of a parallelogram are equal, and so are opposite angles. Any two consecutive angles of a parallelogram are supplementary. A diagonal of a parallelogram divides the parallelogram into congruent triangles. The diagonals of a parallelogram bisect each other.

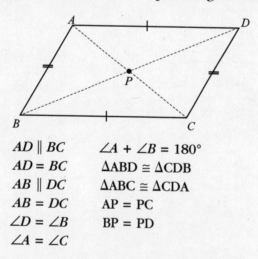

$AD \parallel BC$	$\angle A + \angle B = 180°$
$AD = BC$	$\triangle ABD \cong \triangle CDB$
$AB \parallel DC$	$\triangle ABC \cong \triangle CDA$
$AB = DC$	$AP = PC$
$\angle D = \angle B$	$BP = PD$
$\angle A = \angle C$	

Definitions

A *rhombus* is a parallelogram with four equal sides. The diagonals of a rhombus are perpendicular to each other.

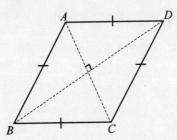

A *rectangle* is a parallelogram with four right angles. The diagonals of a rectangle are equal and can be found using the Pythagorean theorem, if the sides of the rectangle are known.

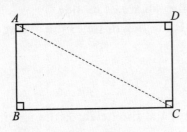

$$AB^2 + BC^2 = AC^2$$

A *square* is a rectangle with four equal sides.

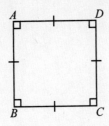

A *trapezoid* is a quadrilateral with only one pair of parallel sides, called *bases*. The nonparallel sides are called *legs*.

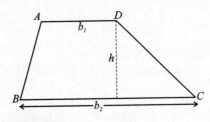

$AD \parallel BC$
AD and BC are bases.
AB and DC are legs.
h = altitude

237

Finding Areas

The area of any *parallelogram* is the product of the base and the height, where the height is the length of an altitude, a line segment drawn from a vertex perpendicular to the base.

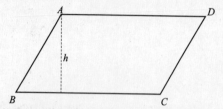

Since rectangles and squares are also parallelograms, their areas follow the same formula. For a *rectangle,* the altitude is one of the sides, and the formula is length times width. Since a *square* is a rectangle for which length and width are the same, the area of a square is the square of its side.

The area of a *trapezoid* is the height times the average of the two bases. The formula is:

$$A = b\,\frac{b_1 + b_2}{2}.$$

The bases are the parallel sides, and the height is the length of an altitude to one of the bases.

Example 1

Find the area of a square whose diagonal is 12 feet. Let s = side of square. By the Pythagorean theorem:

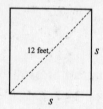

$$s^2 + s^2 = 12^2$$
$$2s^2 = 144$$
$$s^2 = 72$$
$$s = \sqrt{72}.$$

Use only positive value because this is the side of a square.

Since $A = s^2$

$A = 72$ square feet.

Example 2

Find the altitude of a rectangle if its area is 320 and its base is 5 times its altitude.

Let altitude = h. Then base = $5h$. Since $A = bh$,

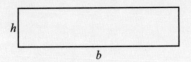

$$A = (5h)(h) = 320$$
$$5h^2 = 320$$
$$h^2 = 64$$
$$h = 8.$$

If a quadrilateral is not a parallelogram or trapezoid but is irregularly shaped, its area can be found by dividing it into triangles, attempting to find the area of each, and adding the results.

CIRCLES

Definitions

Circles are closed plane curves with all points on the curve equidistant from a fixed point called the *center*. The symbol ⊙ indicates a circle. A circle is usually named by its center. A line segment from the center to any point on the circle is called the *radius* (plural, radii). All radii of the same circle are equal.

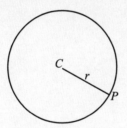

C = center
CP = radius = r

A *chord* is a line segment whose endpoints are on the circle. A *diameter* of a circle is a chord that passes through the center of the circle. A diameter, the longest distance between two points on the circle, is twice the length of the radius. A diameter that is perpendicular to a chord bisects that chord.

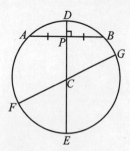

AB is a chord.
C is the center.
DCE is a diameter.
FCG is a diameter.
AB ⊥ DCE so AP = PB.

A *central angle* is an angle whose vertex is the center of a circle and whose sides are radii of the circle. An *inscribed angle* is an angle whose vertex is on the circle and whose sides are chords of the circle.

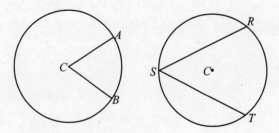

∠ACB is a central angle.
∠RST is an inscribed angle.

An *arc* is a portion of a circle. The symbol ∩ is used to indicate an arc. Arcs are usually measured in degrees. Since the entire circle is 360°, a semicircle (half a circle) is an arc of 180°, and a quarter of a circle is an arc of 90°.

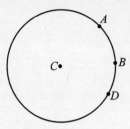

$\overset{\frown}{ABD}$ is an arc.

$\overset{\frown}{AB}$ is an arc.

$\overset{\frown}{BD}$ is an arc.

A central angle is equal in measure to its intercepted arc.

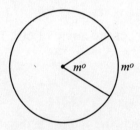

An inscribed angle is equal in measure to one-half its intercepted arc. An angle inscribed in a semicircle is a right angle because the semicircle has a measure of 180°, and the measure of the inscribed angle is one half of that.

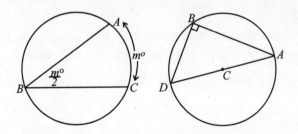

$\overset{\frown}{DA} = 180°$; therefore, $\angle DBA = 90°$.

Perimeter and Area

The perimeter of a circle is called the *circumference.* The length of the circumference is πd, where d is the diameter, or $2\pi r$, where r is the radius. The number π is irrational and can be approximated by $3.14159\ldots$, but in problems dealing with circles, it is best to leave π in the answer. There is no fraction that is exactly equal to π.

Example 1

If the circumference of a circle is 8π feet, what is the radius?

Since $C = 2\pi r = 8\pi$, $r = 4$ feet.

The length of an arc of a circle can be found if the central angle and radius are known. Then, the length of arc is $\dfrac{n°}{360°}(2\pi r)$, where the central angle of the arc is $n°$. This is true because of the proportion:

$$\frac{\text{arc}}{\text{circumference}} = \frac{\text{central angle}}{360°}.$$

Example 1

If a circle with radius of 3 feet has a central angle of $60°$, find the length of the arc intercepted by this central angle.

$$\text{Arc} = \frac{60°}{360°}(2\pi 3) = \pi \text{ feet.}$$

The area A of a circle is πr^2, where r is the radius. If the diameter is given instead of the radius,

$$A = \pi\left(\frac{d}{2}\right)^2 = \frac{\pi d^2}{4}.$$

Example 3

Find the area of a circular ring formed by two concentric circles of radii 6 and 8 inches, respectively. (Concentric circles are circles with the same center.)

The area of the ring will equal the area of the large circle minus the area of the small circle.

$$\begin{aligned}\text{Area of ring} &= \pi 8^2 - \pi 6^2 \\ &= \pi(64 - 36) \\ &= 28\pi \text{ square inches}\end{aligned}$$

Peterson's GMAT CAT Success

Example 4

A square is inscribed in a circle whose diameter is 10 inches. Find the difference between the area of the circle and that of the square.

If a square is inscribed in a circle, the diagonal of the square is the diameter of the circle. If the diagonal of the square is 10 inches, then, by the Pythagorean theorem,

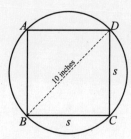

$$2s^2 = 100$$
$$s^2 = 50$$

The side of the square s is $\sqrt{50}$, and the area of the square is 50 square inches. If the diameter of the circle is 10, its radius is 5 and the area of the circle is $\pi 5^2 = 25\pi$ square inches. Then, the difference between the area of the circle and the area of the square is:

$$25\pi - 50 \text{ square inches} = 25\,(\pi - 2) \text{ square inches.}$$

Distance Formula

In the arithmetic section, we described the Cartesian coordinate system when explaining how to draw graphs representing linear equations. If two points are plotted in the Cartesian coordinate system, it is useful to know how to find the distance between them. If the two points have coordinates (a, b) and (p, q), the distance between them is:

$$d = \sqrt{(a-p)^2 + (b-q)^2}.$$

This formula makes use of the Pythagorean theorem.

Example

Find the distance between the two points (−3, 2) and (1, −1).

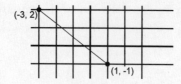

Let $(a, b) = (-3, 2)$ and $(p, q) = (1, -1)$. Then:

$$d = \sqrt{(-3-1)^2 + [2-(-1)]^2}$$
$$= \sqrt{(-4)^2 + (2+1)^2}$$
$$= \sqrt{(-4)^2 + 3^2}$$
$$= \sqrt{16+9} = \sqrt{25} = 5.$$

QUIZ

PLANE GEOMETRY PROBLEMS

1. In triangle QRS, ∠Q = ∠R and ∠S = 64°. Find the measures of ∠Q and ∠R.

2. In parallelogram ABCD, ∠A and ∠C are opposite angles. If ∠A = 12*x*° and ∠C = (10*x* + 12)°, find the measures of ∠A and ∠C.

3. What is the area of a trapezoid whose height is 5 feet and whose bases are 7 feet and 9 feet?

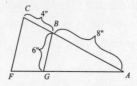

4. In the preceding figure, CF ∥ BG. Find the length of CF.

5. The hypotenuse of a right triangle is 25 feet. If one leg is 15 feet, find the length of the other leg.

6. Find the area of a circle whose diameter is 16 inches.

7. Find the distance between the points (−1, −2) and (5, 7).

SOLUTIONS

1. $\angle Q + \angle R + \angle S = 180°$

   $\angle Q + \angle R + 64° = 180°$

   $\angle Q + \angle R = 116°$

   Since $\angle Q = \angle R$, they must each have measures of 58°.

2. The opposite angles in a parallelogram are equal. Thus,

   $12x = 10x + 12$

   $2x = 12$

   $x = 6$

   Thus, $12x = 12(6) = 72$.

   $\angle A$ and $\angle C$ both measure 72°.

3. $A = h\left(\dfrac{b_1 + b_2}{2}\right) = 5\left(\dfrac{7 + 9}{2}\right) = 5\left(\dfrac{16}{2}\right) = 5(8) = 40$

   The area of the trapezoid is 40.

4. Since $CF \parallel BG$, $\triangle ACF \sim \triangle ABG$.

   Therefore, $\dfrac{6}{CF} = \dfrac{8}{12}$

   $8\,CF = 72$

   $CF = 9$ inches.

5. Using the Pythagorean theorem,

   $a^2 + 15^2 = 25^2$

   $a^2 + 225 = 625$

   $a^2 = 400$

   $a = \sqrt{400} = 20.$

   The length of the other leg is 20.

6. If $d = 16$, $r = 8$. $A = \pi r^2 = \pi(8)^2 = 64\pi$ The area of the triangle is 64π.

7. $d = \sqrt{(5 - (-1))^2 + (7 - (-2))^2}$

   $= \sqrt{6^2 + 9^2} = \sqrt{36 + 81} = \sqrt{117}$

   The distance between the points is equal to $\sqrt{117}$.

Unit 7

DATA SUFFICIENCY STRATEGIES AND REVIEW

A Data Sufficiency question is a particular type of math problem in which, instead of actually answering the question, you are simply asked to determine whether or not you have been given sufficient information to answer the question.

Data Sufficiency questions are the only problems on the GMAT for which you are not given five possible answers to the question being asked; instead, the five answer choices (A) through (E) represent a code to enable you to indicate whether the information you have been given is enough to answer the question.

Each Data Sufficiency question has the same format. First, you are asked a question for which there is not enough information to answer. Sample questions of this type are: "What is the value of x?" "Is Bob older than Paul?" etc. You are then given two additional statements, providing additional information about the question. Your job is to analyze these statements and decide if either or both of them gives you enough information to answer the question. Based upon what you decide, you then select one of the five answer choices.

These questions will be integrated with the Problem Solving questions in the Quantitative section, and you will have a total of 75 minutes in which to complete the entire section. There will be approximately 15 Data Sufficiency questions on the test.

The directions for the Data Sufficiency questions read as follows:

Directions: Each of the data sufficiency problems below consists of a question and two statements, labeled (1) and (2), in which certain data are given. You have to decide whether the data given in the statements are *sufficient* for answering the question. Using the data given in the statements *plus* your knowledge of mathematics and everyday facts (such as the number of days in July or the meaning of counterclockwise), you must indicate whether

- statement (1) ALONE is sufficient, but statement (2) alone is not sufficient to answer the question asked;
- statement (2) ALONE is sufficient, but statement (1) alone is not sufficient to answer the question asked;
- BOTH statements (1) and (2) TOGETHER are sufficient to answer the question asked, but NEITHER statement ALONE is sufficient;
- EACH statement ALONE is sufficient to answer the question asked;
- statements (1) and (2) TOGETHER are NOT sufficient to answer the question asked, and additional data specific to the problem are *needed*.

Numbers: All numbers are real numbers.

Figures: A figure accompanying a data sufficiency problem will conform to the information given in the question, but will not necessarily conform to the additional information given in statements (1) and (2).

Lines shown as straight can be assumed to be straight and lines that appear jagged can also be assumed to be straight.

You may assume that the position of points, angles, regions, etc., exists in the order shown and that angle measures are greater than zero.

All figures lie in a plane unless otherwise indicated.

Note: In data sufficiency problems that ask for the value of a quantity, the data given in the statements are sufficient only when it is possible to determine exactly one numerical value for the quantity.

Example

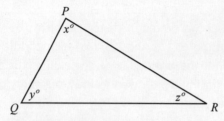

In $\triangle PQR$, what is the value of x?

(1) $PQ = PR$

(2) $y = 40$

Explanation

According to statement (1), $PQ = PR$; therefore, $\triangle PQR$ is isosceles and $y = z$. Since $x + y + z = 180$, it follows that $x + 2y = 180$. Since statement (1) does not give a value for y, you cannot answer the question using statement (1) alone. According to statement (2), $y = 40$; therefore, $x + z = 140$. Since statement (2) does not give a value for z, you cannot answer the question using statement (2) alone. Using both statements together, you can find y and z; therefore, you can find x, and the answer to the problem is choice (C).

The proper mode of working these questions is as follows:

1. Read statement (1). If statement (1) includes sufficient information to enable you to answer the question, write the letter "S" (for *Sufficient*) next to the (1). If (1) does not contain enough information to enable you to answer the question, write the letter "I" (for *Insufficient*) next to the (1).

2. Read statement (2). It is **crucial** at this time to treat statement (2) by itself—that is, to ignore the information statement (1) contained. If statement (2) includes sufficient information to enable you to answer the question, write the letter "S" (for *Sufficient*) next to the (2). If (2) does not contain enough information to enable you to answer the question, write the letter "I" (for *Insufficient*) next to the (2).

At this point in time, your paper will look like one of the four following possibilities:

| S (1) | I (1) | I (1) | S (1) |
| I (2) | S (2) | I (2) | S (2) |

In case number one (the first statement, by itself, is sufficient and the second is not), the answer is A. In case number two (the first statement by itself is insufficient, but the second is sufficient), the answer is B. In the *fourth* case (both statements, by themselves, are sufficient), the correct answer is choice (D).

In the third case (both statements, by themselves, are insufficient), you must go one step further. In this case, and in this case only, consider the two statements together. If, together, they enable you to answer the question, select choice (C). If, even with both statements together, you cannot answer the question, the correct answer is choice (E).

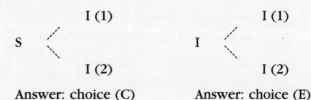

Answer: choice (C)   Answer: choice (E)

Note that, since the choices (A) through (E) are the same on every GMAT, you can save a lot of time by memorizing their meanings in advance and skipping the instructions when you actually take the GMAT.

So that you will better understand choices (A) through (E), five examples follow. Note that the answers have been designed so that the first question has choice (A), the second question has choice (B), and so on.

1. Pumps A and B, working together, can remove all the water from a tank in 30 minutes. How long will it take pump A to remove all the water in the tank?

    (1) Pump B alone can remove the water in 75 minutes.

    (2) Pump A's pipe is smaller than pump B's pipe.

The correct answer is (A). Statement (1) enables you to set up the equation as follows:

Pump B can remove $\dfrac{1}{75}$ in 1 minute.

Pump A can remove $\dfrac{1}{x}$ in 1 minute.

$$\frac{1}{75} + \frac{1}{x} = \frac{1}{30}$$

Pump A can remove the water in 50 minutes. (Of course, it is not necessary to solve the equation as long as you know that it can be solved.) Statement (2) is not relevant to the problem.

2. How far is it from point P to point Q?

    (1) Brian ran half the distance from P to Q in 12 minutes.

    (2) Janet ran in a straight line from P to Q in 20 minutes, at an average speed of 9 miles per hour.

The correct answer is (B). Without knowing Brian's speed, you cannot determine the distance that he ran. Therefore, statement (1) is insufficient. However, since Janet ran for 20 minutes at an average speed of 9 miles per hour, she ran a distance of 9 mph $\times \dfrac{1}{3}$ hour = 3 miles. Therefore, statement (2) is sufficient.

3.

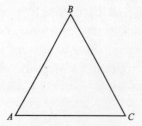

In triangle *ABC*, does angle *C* = 30°?

(1) *AB* = *BC*

(2) Angle *B* = 120°

The correct answer is (C). Both statements (1) and (2) are necessary. Statement (1) tells you that the triangle is isosceles; therefore, angle *A* = angle *C*. Because of information in statement (2), you know that angle *A* + angle *C* = 60°. (The sum of the angles in a triangle must equal 180°.) Therefore, angle *C* = 30°.

4. Pipe A and pipe B, working together, can fill a water tank in $1\frac{1}{3}$ hours. How long will it take for pipe A to fill the tank without pipe B?

(1) Pipe B could fill the tank in 4 hours without pipe A.

(2) Pipe A pumps in twice as much water as pipe B.

The correct answer is (D). According to statement (1), B could fill $\frac{1}{4}$ of the tank in one hour. Pipe A would fill $\frac{1}{x}$ of the tank in one hour. In $1\frac{1}{3}$ hours, they would fill $\frac{4}{3}\left(\frac{1}{4}+\frac{1}{x}\right) = 1$.

(1) gives us an answer for the length of time needed for A to fill the tank alone.

(2) tells us that if A can pump in $\frac{1}{x}$ in one hour, B would pump in $\frac{1}{2x}$ in one hour. In $1\frac{1}{3}$ hours, they would fill $\frac{4}{3}\left(\frac{1}{x}+\frac{1}{2x}\right) = 1$. Each statement alone answers the question.

5. Is *y* greater than *x*?

(1) 5*x* = 3*k*

(2) *k* = *y*²

The correct answer is (E). Statement (1) describes *x* and statement (2) describes *y* in terms of a common element, *k*, so that both statements (1) and (2) are needed.

Combining (1) and (2), we obtain $5x = 3y^2$, or $x = \frac{3}{5}y^2$. Then if, for example, *y* = 1, we have $x = \frac{3}{5}$, and *y* is bigger than *x*. Or, if *y* = 2, we have $x = \frac{12}{5}$, and *x* is bigger than *y*. And, of course, it could be possible that *x* = *y* = 0. Since we cannot determine the relative size, the correct answer is choice (E).

HINTS FOR ANSWERING DATA SUFFICIENCY QUESTIONS

THE "WHAT IS THE VALUE OF . . .?" QUESTION

More than half of the Data Sufficiency questions on the GMAT ask if you can determine the *value* of a certain quantity. Remember that for this type of question, a statement (or combination of statements) is sufficient only if it enables you to determine a single unique numerical value. Statements that determine two values or a range of values are always insufficient.

Example 1

What is the value of x?

(1) $4x = 12$

(2) $6x < 24$

The correct answer is (A). Statement (1) is sufficient since it tells us that x is 3. Statement (2) is insufficient since it tells us that x is any number less than 4.

Example 2

What is the value of x?

(1) $x = 2y$

(2) $x^2 = 16$

The correct answer is (E). Since x varies as y varies, x can be any number. Therefore, statement (1) is insufficient. Statement (2) is also insufficient since it tells us that x is either 4 or −4. Even together, we cannot determine the value of x.

Example 3

What is the value of x?

(1) $x + y = 6$

(2) $x - y = 4$

The correct answer is (C). Statement (1) is insufficient since, without knowing the value of y, it is impossible to determine a numerical value for x. Statement (2) is insufficient for the same reason. However, when you take statements (1) and (2) together, you obtain a system of simultaneous equations that can be solved for x.

Typically, when each statement either gives you or contains the information to write an equation with two unknowns, the answer will be choice (C), as above. However, look out for examples like those that follow.

Example 4

What is the value of x?

(1) $x + y = 6$

(2) $3x + 3y = 18$

The correct answer is (E). Statement (1) is insufficient since, without knowing the value of y, it is impossible to determine a numerical value for x. Statement (2) is insufficient for the same reason. When you take (1) and (2) together, you still cannot determine x, since (1) and (2), in fact, contain different forms of the same equation.

Example 5

What is the value of $3x - 5y$?

(1) $x + y = 6$

(2) $6x - 10y = 18$

The correct answer is (B). Statement (1) is insufficient since, without knowing the value of y, it is impossible to determine a numerical value for x. Statement (2), however, is sufficient, because if you divide both sides of the equation by 2, you obtain $3x - 5y = 9$.

THE "IS . . .?" QUESTION

The other type of Data Sufficiency question on the GMAT asks if a certain quantity has a certain value ("Is $x = 17$?") or if a certain geometric figure has a certain shape ("Is quadrilateral ABCD a parallelogram?"). Remember that in questions of this type, "Is . . .?" means "Does it absolutely have to be?" rather than, "Could it possibly be?"

The best way to approach these questions is to read one of the statements, then reread the question. If your answer to the question is, "Yes, it has to be," then the statement is sufficient. If, on the other hand, your answer is "Maybe it is, or maybe it isn't," then the statement is insufficient.

Example 1

Is $x = 0$?

(1) The sum of x and 4 is 4.

(2) The product of x and 0 is 0.

The correct answer is (A). Statement (1) tells us that $x + 4 = 4$. The only solution to this equation is $x = 0$, so statement (1) is sufficient. Statement (2) tells us that $x \cdot 0 = 0$. In this case, x could be 0, but it also might not be.

Example 2

Is triangle PQR a right triangle?

(1)   The measure of angle P is 35°.

(2)   The measure of angle Q is 55°.

The correct answer is (C). Neither statement (1) by itself nor statement (2) by itself, is sufficient since the knowledge of one of the angles of a triangle is not enough to tell us what the other angles are. If, however, we take the two statements together, we can determine if the triangle is a right triangle, since if we know two angles, we can determine the third.

GUESSING ON DATA SUFFICIENCY QUESTIONS

Often, when solving a Data Sufficiency question, you will find yourself in the situation of being unsure of whether one of the two given statements is sufficient or insufficient. Note that in any problem where you know the status of one of the statements but do not know the status of the other, you are, in fact, able to make an extremely educated guess, which will greatly improve your chances of coming up with the correct answer.

In the situation described below, you are able to eliminate all but two of the possible answers.

Situation 1

If you are certain that statement (1) is sufficient but are unsure about statement (2), then the only possible answers are choices (A) or (D).

S (1)

? (2)

Guess choice (A) or choice (D)

Situation 2

If you are certain that statement (2) is sufficient, but are unsure about statement (1), then the only possible choices are (B) or (D).

? (1)

S (2)

Guess choice (B) or choice (D)

Situation 3

If you are certain that each statement alone is insufficient, but are unsure about both statements together, then the only possible choices are (C) or (E).

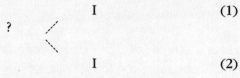

Guess choice (C) or choice (E)

In the situations described below, you are able to eliminate only two of the possible answers, but it is generally still to your benefit to guess.

Situation 4

If you are certain that statement (1) is insufficient but are unsure about statement (2), then the only possible choices are (B), (C), or (E).

I (1)

? (2)

Guess choices (B), (C), or (E).

Situation 5

If you are certain that statement (2) is insufficient but are unsure about statement (1), then the only possible choices are (A), (C), or (E).

? (1)

I (2)

Guess choices (A), (C), or (E).

DON'T DO MORE THAN NECESSARY

Remember that your job is only to determine whether you actually have enough information to find the answer. Do not waste your time trying to find the answer; stop once you have determined whether it is possible to find one or not.

BE CAREFUL TO ISOLATE STATEMENTS INITIALLY

Remember that both statements must be considered alone before you consider them together. When analyzing statement (1), be sure not to read statement (2). Similarly, when analyzing statement (2), be sure to forget the information in statement (1). Consider the statements together only after you have determined that they are both insufficient.

Following are several more solved examples to help you understand data sufficiency questions. Then, there is a practice test for you to try.

Peterson's GMAT CAT Success

ADDITIONAL SOLVED PROBLEMS

1. What is the value of x?

    (1) $x + y = 7$

    (2) $3x + 3y = 21$

The correct answer is (E). Both statements (1) and (2) are the same—multiply both sides of statement (1) by 3, and you will get statement (2). In general, when you have two unknowns, you need two equations to solve for the unknowns. Since we really only have one unique equation, the answer is choice (E).

2. A cylindrical tank holds 10,000 gallons. What is its height?

    (1)   A gallon of liquid equals 13 cubic feet.

    (2)   The diameter of the tank is 10 feet.

The correct answer is (C). Statement (1) will help you obtain the cubic volume of the tank in cubic feet but will not give you the dimensions. By giving you one dimension in statement (2), the necessary dimension (height) can be found. (In a cylinder, $V = \pi r^2 h$.)

3. An author is guaranteed minimum royalties of $1,856. How many copies of the book must be sold before additional royalties are earned?

    (1)   The author is to receive 5 percent of the net price that is received by the publisher.

    (2)   The list price of the book is $10.95.

The correct answer is (E). In order to determine how many copies of the book must be sold to reach the guaranteed minimum, you have to know the royalty rate and the net price received by the publisher.

   Statement (1) gives you the royalty rate, but statement (2) does not tell you what the publisher receives for the book. He certainly does not receive the list price, which is the price in the bookstore.

4. A train traveled for 5 hours and went from A to B. What is the distance between A and B?

    (1)   The train had to go through some hilly country and traveled at an average speed of only 50 miles an hour in that terrain.

    (2)   The train covered 150 miles through hilly country.

The correct answer is (E). Statements (1) and (2) together inform you that the train traveled through hilly country for 3 hours. However, neither statement gives you any information about the speed used in the remaining time. No solution is possible with this data.

DATA SUFFICIENCY REVIEW QUESTIONS

Directions: Each of the data sufficiency problems below consists of a question and two statements, labeled (1) and (2), in which certain data are given. You have to decide whether the data given in the statements are *sufficient* for answering the question. Using the data given in the statements *plus* your knowledge of mathematics and everyday facts (such as the number of days in July or the meaning of counterclockwise), you must indicate whether

- statement (1) ALONE is sufficient, but statement (2) alone is not sufficient to answer the question asked;
- statement (2) ALONE is sufficient, but statement (1) alone is not sufficient to answer the question asked;
- BOTH statements (1) and (2) TOGETHER are sufficient to answer the question asked, but NEITHER statement ALONE is sufficient;
- EACH statement ALONE is sufficient to answer the question asked;
- statements (1) and (2) TOGETHER are NOT sufficient to answer the question asked, and additional data specific to the problem are *needed*.

Numbers: All numbers are real numbers.

Figures: A figure accompanying a data sufficiency problem will conform to the information given in the question, but will not necessarily conform to the additional information given in statements (1) and (2).

Lines shown as straight can be assumed to be straight and lines that appear jagged can also be assumed to be straight.

You may assume that the position of points, angles, regions, etc., exists in the order shown and that angle measures are greater than zero.

All figures lie in a plane unless otherwise indicated.

Note: In data sufficiency problems that ask for the value of a quantity, the data given in the statements are sufficient only when it is possible to determine exactly one numerical value for the quantity.

Example

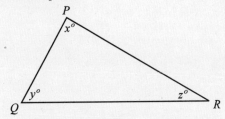

In $\triangle PQR$, what is the value of x?

    (1) $PQ = PR$

    (2) $y = 40$

Explanation

The correct answer is (C). According to statement (1), $PQ = PR$; therefore, $\triangle PQR$ is isosceles and $y = z$. Since $x + y + z = 180$, it follows that $x + 2y = 180$. Since statement (1) does not give a value for y, you cannot answer the question using statement (1) alone. According to statement (2), $y = 40$; therefore, $x + z = 140$. Since statement (2) does not give a value for z, you cannot answer the question using statement (2) alone. Using both statements together you can find y and z; therefore, you can find x.

1.   The number of eligible voters is 200,000. How many eligible voters voted?

    (1)   57 percent of the eligible men voted.

    (2)   91,200 men voted.

2.   Together, Joyce and Ellen weigh 300 pounds. How much does Ellen weight?

    (1)   Joyce weighs $1\frac{1}{2}$ times as much as Ellen.

    (2)   Ellen is 5 feet 3 inches tall.

3.   How much did it cost the Linnell Corporation for liability insurance in 1994?

    (1)   The company spent a total of $29,000 for liability insurance in 1993, 1994, and 1995.

    (2)   The company paid $7,000 for liability insurance in 1995.

4.

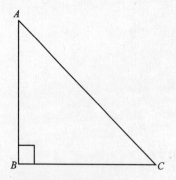

Does line AC = 5?

(1) $(AB)^2 + (BC)^2 = 25$

(2) $AB + BC = 7$

5. How many male business school graduates from a particular school will not work for state agencies?

(1) 60 out of the 300 business school graduates from the school were women.

(2) 30 percent of the male graduates will work for state agencies.

6. What are the dimensions of a box of 60 cubic feet of material?

(1) The length of the box is 6 feet.

(2) The depth of the box is $\dfrac{1}{3}$ of the length.

7. Is x larger than 4?

(1) x is larger than 0.

(2) $x^2 - 25 = 0$.

8. Did the MN Corporation have higher profits in 1993 or 1994?

(1) In 1995, the profits were two times that of 1994.

(2) In 1993, the profits were twice the average of the profits for 1993, 1994, and 1995.

9.

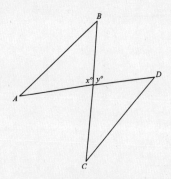

Is AD perpendicular to BC? AD and BC are intersecting straight lines.

(1) $x° = y°$

(2) $AB = CD$

10. How long will it take to empty a water tank if both faucet A and faucet B are used?

(1) The tank will empty in 36 minutes if only faucet A is used.

(2) The tank will empty in 45 minutes if only faucet B is used.

11. How much does each book on the bookshelf weigh?

(1) The books and the bookshelf weigh 43 pounds.

(2) The books are uniform in size.

12. K is an integer. Is K divisible by 14?

(1) K is divisible by 7.

(2) K is divisible by 2.

13.

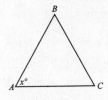 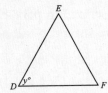

Is triangle ABC congruent to triangle DEF if AB = BC and DE = EF?

(1) Angle $x° = y°$

(2) AB = DE

14.

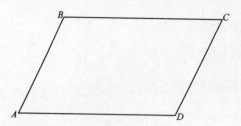

Is ABCD a parallelogram?

(1) Angle B = 100°

(2) AB = CD

15. Is n > p?

(1) $\dfrac{m}{n} = n + p$

(2) n > m

16. Do doctors make more than lawyers and accountants?

(1) An accountant's average salary is 20 percent higher than that of a lawyer.

(2) An accountant's average salary is 10 percent higher than that of a doctor.

17.

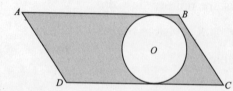

Circle O is inscribed in parallelogram ABCD, whose base is 12 inches. Find the area of the shaded portion.

(1) The radius of the circle is 4 inches.

(2) DC is twice as long as AD.

18. How many students registered for the Accounting I lecture?

(1) There are 80 girls registered for the lecture.

(2) 60 percent of the students in the lectures are boys.

19. Is x always less than y?

(1) $x < 3$

(2) $y > 3$

20. Ava, Doris, and Linda earn salaries totaling $120,000. What is Linda's salary?

(1) Doris's salary is 125 percent of Ava's salary.

(2) Linda's salary is 120 percent of Doris's salary.

21. An architect is planning a small rectangular entryway. The length of the hallway is to be $\frac{3}{4}$ of the width. What will the dimensions be?

    (1) The area is to be 108 square feet.

    (2) The ceiling will be $9\frac{1}{2}$ feet high.

22. How long would it take 12 men, each working at the same rate, to dig a trench?

    (1) Sewer pipes will be placed in the trench.

    (2) It would take 9 of the men $1\frac{1}{2}$ hours to dig a trench of the required size.

23. If it takes A and B 6 hours to paint a room, how long will it take A to do the room alone?

    (1) B alone can paint the room in 15 hours.

    (2) Both painters use latex paint and rollers.

24.

    What is the diameter of circle O?

    (1) The area of circle O = the circumference of the circle.

    (2) The circle has four central angles of 90° each.

25. One hundred eighty students are taking either accounting or law or both. How many attend each class?

    (1) 50 students are taking only law.

    (2) 130 students are taking accounting.

26. If n and k are even integers, is $\frac{n}{3} + \frac{k}{2}$ an integer?

    (1) n is a multiple of 3.

    (2) k is a multiple of 4.

27. The projected school tax rate is set at $11.25 per $1,000. What is X's house assessed for?

    (1) Mr. X will pay $202.50 in school taxes under the proposed new budget.

    (2) He paid $217.85 last year.

28. The area of circle A is 36% less than the radius of circle B. What is the radius of circle A?

    (1) The perimeter of circle B = 20π.

    (2) The diameter of circle B = 20 inches.

29. Is $x > y$?

    (1) $\dfrac{x + y}{2} > 0$

    (2) $y^2 - x^2$

30. What is the approximate distance between New York City and Montauk Point, Long Island?

    (1) Road map A shows that the distance from New York City to Hicksville is approximately 15 inches, when 1 inch = 1.3 miles.

    (2) Road map B shows that the distance from Hicksville to Montauk Point is approximately 36 inches when, 1 inch = 2.6 miles.

31. One hundred students are taking both law and accounting. How many students are taking only accounting?

    (1) 180 students are taking either law or accounting.

    (2) 50 students are taking law but not accounting.

32.

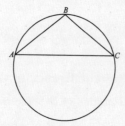

If AB = BC, how large is inscribed angle ABC?

    (1) A = 40°

    (2) AC is not a diameter.

33.

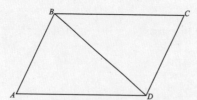

Find the area of ΔABD if BC = 8 inches.

    (1) A line dropped perpendicular to BC from AD = 5 inches.

    (2) ABCD is a parallelogram.

34. What is the length of the edge of a cube?

(1) The number of square inches in its total surface area is equal to 30 times the length of the edge.

(2) 25 times the length of the edge is equal to the number of cubic inches in the cube.

35. What is the value of y?

(1) $x + 2y = 7$

(2) $3x - y = 9$

36. Is x a positive number?

(1) $ax^2 = 16a$

(2) $x - a > 0$

37. What part of the distance from New York to Paris does the Concorde travel in $1\frac{1}{4}$ hours?

(1) The Concorde travels at 750 miles per hour.

(2) The Concorde travels from New York to Paris in $3\frac{1}{2}$ hours.

38.

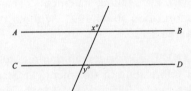

Does angle x = angle y?

(1) AB is not parallel to CD.

(2) $x = 70°$

39. Is it cheaper to drive to Boston from New York City than it is to fly the 250-mile distance?

(1) Round-trip airfare is $276 on shuttle flights.

(2) The average price per gallon of regular gas is $106\frac{9}{10}$¢.

40. A man walked around the outside of a field. How far did he walk?

(1) The field has an area of 900 square feet.

(2) The length of the field is $1\frac{1}{2}$ times its width.

Quick Score Answers

Data Sufficiency Review Questions

1. E	9. A	17. A	25. E	33. C
2. A	10. C	18. C	26. A	34. D
3. E	11. E	19. C	27. A	35. C
4. A	12. C	20. C	28. D	36. E
5. C	13. C	21. A	29. E	37. B
6. C	14. E	22. B	30. E	38. A
7. C	15. E	23. A	31. C	39. E
8. B	16. C	24. A	32. A	40. C

ANSWERS AND EXPLANATIONS

1. **The correct answer is (E).** Both statements (1) and (2) give us information about the men who voted. You have no information about the number or the percentage of eligible women who might have voted.

2. **The correct answer is (A).** Statement (1) gives you a relationship between Ellen's and Joyce's weight so that an algebraic solution can be found.

3. **The correct answer is (E).** Even taking statements (1) and (2) together, we cannot determine any specific information about 1994. Without this information the question cannot be answered.

4. **The correct answer is (A).** The Pythagorean theorem tells us that $AC^2 = 25$; therefore, $AC = 5$, as per information in statement (1). Statement (2) alone will not help us find AC. The sides can be 6 inches and 1 inch, as well as 2 inches and 5 inches. Therefore, statement (2) does not help you.

5. **The correct answer is (C).** You need both statements (1) and (2) to determine how many male graduates of the 300 will work for state agencies. Once you know that, you have enough information to determine how many will not.

6. **The correct answer is (C).** Statements (1) and (2) give us two of the dimensions of the box. The volume of the box = 60 cubic feet = length × width × depth (or height). $60 = 6 \times w \times 2$.

7. **The correct answer is (C).** Statement (1) tells you that x is a positive number, but it gives you no information about its size. Statement (2) becomes $x^2 = 25$. This does not answer the question by itself since x could be either +5 or −5. However, taking statements (1) and (2) together, we see that x must be 5.

8. **The correct answer is (B).** Statement (1) is insufficient since it does not relate profits to 1994 and 1993. Let x = average profit. As per (2), profits for 1993 were $2x$, and the combined profits for 1994 and 1995 had to equal x. Therefore, 1993 was larger than 1994.

9. **The correct answer is (A).** Statement (1), in effect, tells you that angle x and angle y are 90° each, or right angles ($x° + y° = 180°$). Therefore, line AD is perpendicular to BC. Statement (2) is of no use.

10. **The correct answer is (C).** Faucet A will drain $\frac{1}{36}$ of the tank in one minute. Faucet B will drain $\frac{1}{45}$ of the tank each minute. Therefore, faucets A and B will drain $\frac{1}{36} + \frac{1}{45}$ per minute, or $\frac{5}{180} + \frac{4}{180} = \frac{9}{180} = \frac{1}{20}$ of the tank will drain in one minute. The entire tank will drain in 20 minutes. Both statements (1) and (2) are necessary.

11. **The correct answer is (E).** Neither statement (1) nor statement (2) nor both together are sufficient. You must have information on the weight of the bookshelf and the number of books.

12. **The correct answer is (C).** In order for K to be divisible by 14, it would have to be divisible by both 7 and 2; therefore, both statements together are sufficient, but each statement alone is not.

13. **The correct answer is (C).** There are two isosceles triangles here. Statement (1) indicates that the triangles are similar, since angle $x° =$ angle $y°$, but it does not tell us anything about congruence. Statement (2) indicates that two sides of each triangle are equal to themselves and to each other. Statement (1) gives us the information that the similar angles are equal. Therefore, the triangles are congruent.

14. **The correct answer is (E).** Neither statement (1) nor statement (2) nor both together give you the information necessary. Statement (1) provides you with no relationship about the other angles. Statement (2) gives you no information, other than size, about the lines AB and CD.

15. **The correct answer is (E).** Since there is no restriction placed on n, except that it is larger than m, n can be a negative or a positive number. A quick check can be made:

Let $n = -1$; $m = -3$.

Then statement (1) becomes

$$\frac{m}{n} = n + p$$
$$\frac{m}{n} - n = p$$
$$\frac{-3}{-1} - (-1) = p$$

$+3 + 1$ or $4 = p$.

Therefore, p is larger than n in this case. However, if $n = 4$ and $m = 2$, p would equal $-\frac{3}{2}$.

16. **The correct answer is (C).** This can be determined by using statements (1) and (2), which together give a comparison for all three professions.

17. **The correct answer is (A).** In order to find the area of the shaded portion, it is necessary to find the area of the parallelogram and subtract the area of the circle. Statement (1) gives us the information to derive the area of the circle, which is πr^2, or 16π square inches. Since the circle is inscribed in the parallelogram, twice its radius is equal to the altitude of the figure. The area of the parallelogram is base × height, or 12 inches × 8 inches, or 96 square inches. Statement (2) is of no use.

18. **The correct answer is (C).** Statement (2) tells us that 40 percent of the students in the lecture are girls. If 40 percent of the total group equals 80, then $.4x = 80$, and $x = 200$ for a total. Both statements (1) and (2) are needed.

19. **The correct answer is (C).** Statement (1) tells us only that x is less than 3. Statement (2) gives us the information about y (greater than 3) that makes it possible to answer the question.

20. **The correct answer is (C).** Neither statement (1) nor statement (2) alone gives you enough of a relationship to answer the question. Both statement (1) and statement (2) are needed. If Ava's salary = x, then Doris's salary, as per statement (1), = $1.25x$. Then Linda's salary, as per (2), equals $1.20 (1.25x)$. The three salaries, then, are $x + 1.25x + 1.2 (1.25x) = \$120,000$.

21. **The correct answer is (A).** With the information in statement (1), the question can be answered because an algebraic relationship is established. The width = x; the length is $\left(\frac{3}{4}\right)x$. $x \times \left(\frac{3}{4}\right)x = 108$ square feet. The height of the ceiling is irrelevant.

22. **The correct answer is (B).** Statement (1) gives you no mathematical relationship, but statement (2) does. Each of the 9 men completed $\frac{1}{9}$ of the job in $1\frac{1}{2}$ hours. Therefore, in 1 hour, each would complete $\frac{1}{9} \div \frac{3}{2}$ or $\frac{1}{9} \times \frac{2}{3}$ or $\frac{2}{27}$ of the job. Twelve men would complete $\frac{24}{27} \times$ Time = 1 job.

$T = \frac{27}{24}$ or $\frac{9}{8}$ or $1\frac{1}{8}$ hours. (Solution is not necessary.)

23. **The correct answer is (A).** If B can paint a room in 15 hours, he paints $\frac{1}{15}$ in 1 hour; therefore, in 6 hours he paints $\frac{6}{15}$. A paints $\frac{1}{x}$ of the room in 1 hour, or $\frac{6}{x}$ in 6 hours.

$$\frac{6}{15} + \frac{6}{x} = 1 \text{ job}$$
$$\frac{2}{5} + \frac{6}{x} = 1$$
$$2x + 30 = 5x$$
$$30 = 3x$$
$$10 \text{ hours} = x$$

Only statement (1) helps us answer the question. Once again, note that it is not necessary to work the solution out in full.

24. **The correct answer is (A).** According to statement (1), the area, $\pi r^2 =$ the circumference, $2\pi r$. Therefore, $r = 2$ and the diameter is 4 inches. Any size circle would have four central angles of 90° each. Therefore, statement (2) does not help you.

25. **The correct answer is (E).** Since neither statement (1) nor statement (2) tells us how many students are taking both accounting and law, we cannot determine how many students are taking the law class.

Peterson's GMAT CAT Success

26. **The correct answer is (A).** If n is an even whole number, it would equal $2p$, where p is an odd or even integer.

    Statement (1) means that $n = 3 \times 2q$, or $6q$, where q is an integer, so that $\frac{n}{3}$ is always an integer. Since k is an even number, $\frac{k}{2}$ is an integer, so that statement (1) gives us the answer. Statement (2) adds nothing that we need to know.

27. **The correct answer is (A).** Statement (1) tells you what Mr. X will pay in taxes. Dividing $202.50 by .01125, the tax rate, will give you the assessed value of Mr. X's house. The information in statement (2) is irrelevant.

28. **The correct answer is (D).** Statement (1) means that the perimeter of the circle B is $2\pi r = 20\pi$. Therefore, the radius is 10. The area of the circle would be πr^2, or 100π. Therefore, the area of circle A would be 64 percent of 100π and the radius would be 8. Statement (2) tells you that the radius of circle B = 10 inches, and the calculation would be the same as for statement (1).

29. **The correct answer is (E).** The average shown in statement (1), $\frac{x+y}{2}$, would have to fall between x and y, but x could be a negative number and y a positive number; the average could still be greater than 0. In statement (2), if $x = 5$ and $y = 7$, the relationship would be $49 - 25 > 0$. Conversely, if $x = 5$ and $y = -7$, the relationship would still be $49 - 25 > 0$.

30. **The correct answer is (E).** Neither statement alone nor both together can help you. There is nothing in the given facts to indicate that Hicksville is on the direct line that leads from New York City to Montauk Point. It could be farther north or south.

31. **The correct answer is (C).** Statement (1) tells you that the entire population that exists equals 180 students. "Either . . . or" includes people taking both subjects or one (accounting) or the other (law). With statement (2), the entire population taking law is determined by the 100 students taking both law and accounting plus the 50 students who are taking only law, which totals 150. Total population minus the students taking law $(180 - 150) = 30$, the number of students who are only taking accounting.

32. **The correct answer is (A).** If AB = BC, line AB = line BC and angle A = angle C. Since statement (1) gives us a value for angle A and angle C, then inscribed angle ABC = 100°. All statement (2) tells us is that angle B is not a right angle.

33. **The correct answer is (C).** Since ABCD is a parallelogram, according to statement (2), $\triangle$ABD = $\triangle$BDC. The area of $\triangle$BDC = $\frac{1}{2} \times 5$ inches (the height) $\times$ 8 inches (base). Both statements are needed.

34. **The correct answer is (D).** There are 6 surfaces to a cube, and each surface has an area of x^2. The area of the 6 sides together = $6x^2 = 30x$. Therefore, $x = 5$. Statement (2) the volume of the cube is x^3. With statement (2) the relationship becomes $x^3 = 25x$ or $x^2 = 25$ with $x = 5$.

35. **The correct answer is (C).** Neither equation by itself enables you to find y, but, using both equations together, y can be determined.

36. **The correct answer is (E).** According to statement (1), $x^2 = 16$ or ± 4. If $x = -4$ and a is a negative number smaller than -4, then statement (2) would be true, but we have no information about a, so the question cannot be answered.

37. **The correct answer is (B).** The question does not ask how many miles, but what part of the distance; thus, statement (1) is of no help, since it gives you no information about the total distance. Statement (2) gives you a time relationship, so that $1\frac{1}{4}$ hours divided by $3\frac{1}{2}$ hours will tell you what part of the entire distance has been traveled.

38. **The correct answer is (A).** Since AB is not parallel to CD as stated in statement (1), angle x cannot = angle y. Statement (2) adds nothing to the problem.

39. **The correct answer is (E).** Statement (1) gives you the cost of the air flight. Statement (2) does not give you enough information to determine the amount of gallons of gas needed, nor does it give you the cost per mile to run the car.

40. **The correct answer is (C).** In order to know how far the man walks, you must know the perimeter of the field. Statement (1) is not sufficient because the area is composed of length × width, and many different combinations can equal 900 square feet. Statement (2) gives you a relationship that specifically expresses the length in terms of the width. Taking statements (1) and (2) together, you can write a single equation in one unknown, and solve it for the length. Therefore, the question can be answered by using both statements together. Neither statement alone helps.

Sentence Correction

PRACTICE TEST 1

Directions: In each of the following sentences, some part of the sentence or the entire sentence is underlined. Beneath each sentence, you will find five ways of phrasing the underlined part. The first of these repeats the original; the other four are different. If you think the original is better than any of the alternatives, select choice (A); otherwise, choose one of the others.

This is a test of correctness and effectiveness of expression. In choosing answers, follow the requirements of standard written English; that is, pay attention to grammar, choice of words, and sentence construction. Choose the answer that most effectively expresses what is presented in the original sentence; this answer should be clear and exact, without awkwardness, ambiguity, or redundancy.

1. The administrator stood up to say that, in his opinion, he thought the bill should be sent back to the chief.

   (A) stood up to say that, in his opinion, he thought the bill should be sent back
   (B) stood up to say that he thought the bill should be sent back
   (C) stood up to say that he thought the bill should be sent, in his opinion
   (D) stood up to say that, in his opinion, the bill should be sent
   (E) stood up to say that he thought the bill should be sent

2. The general let me know that he would be coming next week in his last e-mail.

   (A) that he would be coming next week in his last e-mail.
   (B) that he was coming next week in his last e-mail.
   (C) that he will come next week in his last e-mail.
   (D) in his last e-mail that he would be coming next week.
   (E) in his last e-mail that he was coming next week.

3. The main idea for our difficulties was quite obvious to those whom we had brought into the business.

   (A) to those whom we had brought
   (B) to them whom we had brought
   (C) to the ones whom we had brought
   (D) to those who we had brought
   (E) to those who we had brung

4. Ms. Deborah Carroll, head of the negotiating committee and <u>who is also a member of the advisory group</u>, will be taking care of the negotiations.

    (A) who is also a member of the advisory group
    (B) since she is a member of the advisory group
    (C) a member of the advisory group
    (D) also being a member of the advisory group
    (E) in addition, who is a member of the advisory group

5. <u>Having managed the team for eight years, he understood his athletes.</u>

    (A) Having managed the team for eight years, he understood his athletes.
    (B) After managing the team for eight years, his athletes were understood by him.
    (C) Having managed the team for eight years, his athletes were understood by him.
    (D) For eight years having managed the team, his athletes were understood by him.
    (E) Because he had managed the team for eight years, his athletes were understood by him.

6. <u>Since we are living</u> in Barcelona for twenty years, we are loath to move to Madrid.

    (A) Since we are living
    (B) Being that we are living
    (C) Being that we have been
    (D) Since we have been living
    (E) Since we were living

7. He said that, if <u>he were elected chairman and that if the monies were available, that</u> he would increase our expense accounts.

    (A) he were elected chairman and that if the monies were available, that
    (B) elected chairman, and monies were available, that
    (C) he were elected chairman and monies were available, that
    (D) he were elected chairman and monies were available,
    (E) elected chairman, and monies were available

8. <u>Due to the continual snow, a smaller number</u> of sports fans went to the Buffalo-Jets game.

    (A) Due to the continual snow, a smaller number
    (B) Due to the continuous snow, a smaller number
    (C) Due to the continual snow, a lesser number
    (D) Because of the snow that kept falling now and then, a smaller number
    (E) Because of the continual snow, a smaller number

9. <u>Whoever objects to me</u> going to the New Year's Eve party ought to speak up right now.

   (A) Whoever objects to me
   (B) Whomever objects to me
   (C) Whomever objects to my
   (D) Whoever objects to my
   (E) Whoever has an objection to me

10. The journalist, <u>who was a kind man, spoke to the interviewee and he</u> was very abrupt.

    (A) , who was a kind man, spoke to the interviewee and he
    (B) was a kind man and he spoke to the interviewee and he
    (C) spoke to the interviewee kindly and the interviewee
    (D) , a kind man, spoke to the interviewee
    (E) who was a kind man spoke to the interviewee and he

11. <u>As a child, my older brother took me to Milan to visit my aunt.</u>

    (A) As a child, my older brother took me to Milan to visit my aunt.
    (B) My older brother took me to Milan to visit my aunt as a child.
    (C) My older brother took me, as a child, to Milan to visit my aunt.
    (D) A child, my older brother took me to Milan to visit my aunt.
    (E) When I was a child, my older brother took me to Milan to visit my aunt.

12. I don't know <u>as I agree with your decision to try and</u> run for dogcatcher.

    (A) as I agree with your decision to try and
    (B) that I agree in your decision to try to
    (C) as I agree in your decision to try and
    (D) that I agree with your decision to try to
    (E) as I agree with your decision to try, to

13. It was <u>us who had left before Karen arrived.</u>

    (A) us who had left before Karen arrived.
    (B) we who had left before Karen arrived.
    (C) we who had went before Karen arrived.
    (D) us who had went before Karen arrived.
    (E) we who had left before the time Karen had arrived.

14. <u>Beside Susie, there were many students who were altogether irritated</u> by his behavior.

    (A) Beside Susie, there were many students who were altogether irritated
    (B) Beside Susie, there were many student who were altogether irritated
    (C) Besides Susie, there were many students who were altogether irritated
    (D) Besides Susie, there were many students who were altogether aggravated
    (E) Beside Susie, there were many students who were altogether aggravated

PRACTICE TEST 2

1. During the California experiment on lowering speeds on major freeways, the number of accidents on the freeways decreased markedly.

    (A) the number of accidents on the freeways decreased markedly.
    (B) the amount of accidents on the freeways decreased markedly.
    (C) there were less accidents on the freeways.
    (D) there were a fewer amount of accidents on the freeways.
    (E) they found there were many fewer accidents on the freeways.

2. Although the concept of unconscious motivational drives was not widely accepted until the mid-twentieth century, the basic concept had been described in the literary works of Dostoyevsky that were written well before Freud.

    (A) was not widely accepted until the mid-twentieth century, the basic concept had been
    (B) was not widely accepted until the mid-twentieth century, the basic concept was
    (C) was not widely accepted until the mid-twentieth century, the basic concept has been
    (D) had not been widely accepted until the mid-twentieth century, the basic concept has been
    (E) had not been widely accepted until the mid-twentieth century, the basic concept was

3. Ralph Nader correctly predicted that lives would be saved if speeding was to be limited to 55 miles per hour.

    (A) speeding was to be limited to
    (B) motorists limited their speed to
    (C) speeding did not exceed
    (D) a motorist was to limit his speed to
    (E) speeding by motorists was to be limited to

4. I have studied the works of Marcel Proust not only for the beauty of the language but also because they are very philosophical.

    (A) also because they are very philosophical.
    (B) because they are also very philosophical.
    (C) for their philosophy also.
    (D) because they are very philosophical also.
    (E) also for their philosophy.

5. The reason we are supporting Congressman Izzy White is because his extensive background in children's issues has made him uniquely qualified for a seat on this working committee.

    (A) because his extensive background in children's issues has made him uniquely qualified for
    (B) that his extensive background in children's issues have made him uniquely qualified for
    (C) that his extensive background in children's issues has made him uniquely qualified for
    (D) that his extensive background in children's issues has made him uniquely qualified to
    (E) because his extensive background in children's issues have made him uniquely qualified for

6. Writing a slam poem is as much an achievement as to finish a major work of the canon.

    (A) to finish
    (B) it is to finish
    (C) finishing
    (D) if you finished
    (E) to have finished

7. In his personal memoir, Mr. Gould discusses his early times, his wish to become a pianist and how he made his debut on the concert stage.

    (A) to become a pianist and how he made
    (B) that he become a pianist and how he made
    (C) to become a pianist and
    (D) that he become a pianist, and
    (E) that he become a pianist and that he make

8. The personal computer has changed work habits more than <u>any machine</u> of the last twenty years.

    (A) any machine
    (B) has any machine
    (C) any other machine
    (D) has any other machine
    (E) any other machine has

9. Anyone interested in Web design can find a job in the burgeoning Internet world <u>if you learn</u> basic programming, such as Adobe and Photoshop.

    (A) if you learn
    (B) if you will learn
    (C) if he would learn
    (D) by the study of
    (E) by studying

10. Leonardo is among the very few people <u>who critics regard as deeply meaningful in the history of both</u> art and science.

    (A) who critics regard as deeply meaningful in the history of both
    (B) whom critics regard as deeply meaningful in the history of both
    (C) whom critics regard as deeply meaningful both in the history of
    (D) who critics regard as deeply meaningful both in the history of
    (E) who is regarded by critics as deeply meaningful in the history of both

11. <u>Being that only 4 members of the board</u> agreed to the Mayor's demands, we can assume that he will not be happy.

    (A) Being that only 4 members of the board
    (B) Since 4 members of the board only
    (C) Being as only 4 members of the board
    (D) Seeing as how only 4 members of the board
    (E) Inasmuch as only 4 members of the board

12. The turnover rate in public school teaching has not <u>and, we hope, never will reach</u> a rate of 4 percent a year.

    (A) and, we hope, never will reach
    (B) reached and, we hope, never will
    (C) and hopefully never will reach
    (D) reached and, we hope, never will reach
    (E) reached and hopefully never will

13. Former New York City principals who believe they <u>may be affected</u> by the latest contract should call their chapter representative, the board suggested.

   (A) may be affected
   (B) may be effected
   (C) will have been affected
   (D) will be effected
   (E) will have been effected

14. That Buster Keaton's movies are meaningful in the history of the early years of film is undeniable, but Keaton <u>cannot scarcely be considered</u> the equal of such giants as Chaplin or Hitchcock.

   (A) cannot scarcely be considered
   (B) can scarcely be considered
   (C) cannot hardly be considered
   (D) cannot scarcely be considered to be
   (E) isn't hardly to be considered

PRACTICE TEST 3

Directions: In each of the following sentences, some part of the sentence or the entire sentence is underlined. Beneath each sentence, you will find five ways of phrasing the underlined part. The first of these parts repeats the original; the other four are different. If you think the original is better than any of the alternatives, select choice (A); otherwise, choose one of the others.

This is a test of correctness and effectiveness of expression. In choosing answers, follow the requirements of standard written English; that is, pay attention to grammar, choice of words, and sentence construction. Choose the answer that most effectively expresses what is presented in the original sentence; this answer should be clear and exact, without awkwardness, ambiguity, or redundancy.

1. The teacher's lecture was aimed toward whomever was in front of him.

   (A) was aimed toward whomever was in front of him.
   (B) was aimed toward whoever was in front of him.
   (C) was aimed at who was in front of him.
   (D) was aimed at whomever was in front of him.
   (E) was aimed towards whomever was in front of him.

2. Isaac, a boy with little talent for cooking, enjoys making oatmeal for breakfast.

   (A) Isaac, a boy with little talent for cooking, enjoys making
   (B) Isaac is a boy with little talent for cooking who enjoys to make
   (C) Isaac is a boy with little talent for cooking and who enjoys making
   (D) Isaac, who has little talent for cooking, enjoys to make
   (E) With little talent for cooking, Isaac is a boy who enjoys to make

3. The novel having been read carefully and many quotes having been taken, Jill felt wonderful about her proposed ten-page paper.

   (A) The novel having been read carefully and many quotes having been taken, Jill
   (B) Jill, who read the novel carefully and having taken many quotes
   (C) Reading the novel carefully and taking many quotes, Jill
   (D) Having read the novel carefully and many quotes having been taken, Jill
   (E) Because she had read the novel carefully and had taken many quotes, Jill

4. The tourists <u>enjoyed hiking on the trails, swimming in the pool, and, particularly, to jog</u> in the woods.

(A) enjoyed hiking on the trails, swimming in the pool, and, particularly, to jog

(B) enjoyed hiking on the trails, to swim in the pool, and, particularly, to jog

(C) enjoyed hiking on the trails, to swim in the pool, and particularly jogging

(D) enjoyed hiking on the trails, swimming in the pool, and, particularly jogging

(E) enjoyed to hike on the trails, to swim in the pool, and, particularly, to jog

5. <u>She is a true star, although she is badly behaved and wants acceptance.</u>

(A) She is a true star, although she is badly behaved and wants acceptance.

(B) Although she is badly behaved, she is a true star and wants acceptance.

(C) Although she is badly behaved, she is a true star although she wants acceptance.

(D) Hers is a true star although she is badly behaved and although she wants acceptance.

(E) Although she is badly behaved and wants acceptance, she is a true star.

6. The main idea of *The Great Gatsby* is how <u>success doesn't make you happy.</u>

(A) The main idea of *The Great Gatsby* is how success doesn't make you happy.

(B) The main idea of *The Great Gatsby* is that success doesn't make you happy.

(C) In *The Great Gatsby*, its main idea is how success doesn't make you happy.

(D) In *The Great Gatsby*, that success doesn't make you happy is the main idea.

(E) In *The Great Gatsby*, you are not made happy by success is the main idea.

7. After looking at both plays, <u>Alice assented that the first one was the best of the two.</u>

(A) Alice assented that the first one was the best of the two.

(B) Alice assented that the first was the best of the two.

(C) Alice assented that the first one was the better of the two.

(D) Alice assented that of the two the better one was the first .

(E) Alice assented that the best of the two was the first.

8. My uncle Clem is the most controversial person of all the persons I have ever met.

    (A) My uncle Clem is the most controversial person of all the persons I have ever met.

    (B) Of all the persons I have ever met, my uncle Clem is the most controversial person.

    (C) Of all the persons I have ever met, the most controversial person is my uncle Clem.

    (D) Of all the persons I have ever met, the most controversial is my uncle Clem.

    (E) My uncle Clem, of all the persons I have ever met, is the most controversial.

9. In the best of worlds, the pool table should be placed in a different room than one in which you want to dine.

    (A) the pool table should be placed in a different room than

    (B) the pool table ought to be placed in a different room from

    (C) the pool table should be placed in a different room from

    (D) the pool table ought to be placed in a different room than

    (E) you should place the pool table in a different room than

10. If we cooperate together by dividing up the assignment, we shall be able to go to lunch early.

    (A) If we cooperate together by dividing up the assignment

    (B) If we cooperate together by dividing the assignment

    (C) If we cooperate together by dividing the assignment

    (D) If we cooperate by dividing up the assignment together

    (E) If we cooperate by dividing the assignment

11. Inadequate quality assurance infuriates Ward, who wonders if it is part of a plan by the hospital administrators.

    (A) who wonders if it is part of a plan by the hospital administrators.

    (B) who wonders if the hospital administrators are part of the plan.

    (C) that wonder if it is part of a plan by hospital administrators.

    (D) wondering if this is part of a plan by hospital administrators.

    (E) who wonders if they are part of a plan by the hospital administrators.

12. Start the motor, and then you should engage the gears.

    (A) Start the motor, and then you should engage the gears.

    (B) Start the motor and then engage the gears.

    (C) Start the motor, then engaging the gears.

    (D) Start the motor, and then the gears should be engaged.

    (E) Starting the motor, the gears should then be engaged.

13. <u>Having lowered our eyes, the cantor led</u> us in song.

    (A) Having lowered our eyes, the cantor led

    (B) After we lowered our eyes, the cantor led

    (C) After we lowered our eyes, the cantor leads

    (D) After we had lowered our eyes, the cantor led

    (E) Having lowered our eyes, the cantor leads

14. <u>Crossing the street, a sport-utility vehicle almost killed me.</u>

    (A) Crossing the street, a sport-utility vehicle almost killed me.

    (B) A sport-utility vehicle almost killed me, crossing the street.

    (C) As I crossed the street, a sport-utility vehicle almost killed me.

    (D) A sport-utility vehicle, crossing the street, almost killed me.

    (E) Having crossed the street, a sport utility-vehicle almost killed me.

Quick Score Answers

Sentence Correction

Practice Test 1		Practice Test 2		Practice Test 3	
1. E	8. E	1. A	8. C	1. B	8. D
2. D	9. D	2. A	9. E	2. A	9. C
3. A	10. D	3. B	10. B	3. E	10. E
4. C	11. E	4. E	11. E	4. D	11. A
5. A	12. B	5. C	12. D	5. E	12. B
6. D	13. B	6. C	13. A	6. B	13. D
7. D	14. C	7. C	14. B	7. C	14. C

ANSWERS AND EXPLANATIONS

SENTENCE CORRECTION

Practice Test 1

1. **The correct answer is (E).** Unnecessary words are used very often. In this case, *in his opinion*, *up*, and *back* are not needed.

2. **The correct answer is (D).** Using *in his last e-mail* suggests that the general is coming inside the e-mail; the wizards of cyberspace are not capable of that yet. Choice (E) is incorrect because of the wrong tense.

3. **The correct answer is (A).** Remember that *whom* is required with the preposition *to*.

4. **The correct answer is (C).** Nouns in apposition must be parallel to one another: *the head* and *a member*.

5. **The correct answer is (A).** Remember in choice (C) to avoid the use of the passive voice.

6. **The correct answer is (D).** Which tense do you use for an action that was started in the past and that continues into the present? The present perfect tense. Avoid using *being that*.

7. **The correct answer is (D).** This sentence needs trimming. You can dispense with the overuse of the word *that* (two extra times) and the word *if*.

8. **The correct answer is (E).** In this case, *because of* is preferable to *due to* because it is used in an adverbial modifier.

9. **The correct answer is (D).** The possessive form of *me* (my) is used before a gerund that is used as a noun. *Whomever* is an object; *whoever* is used correctly as the subject.

10. **The correct answer is (D).** Use the words in apposition: *a kind man* is better than *who was a kind man*.

11. **The correct answer is (E).** To overcome the confusion of *as a child* and *my older brother*, you must specify the time frame with *When*.

12. **The correct answer is (B).** The use of the word *as* is slang and must be avoided in this context.

13. **The correct answer is (B).** *We* is right. Avoid using *had went* as a verb form.

14. **The correct answer is (C).** A human being can be irritated; a situation can be *aggravated. Beside* means standing next to you; you want the meaning of *in addition to,* which is *besides.*

Practice Test 2

1. **The correct answer is (A).** You should use the word *number* when you are counting a certain quantity. Choices (C) and (D) misuse *less* and *fewer,* and in choice (E), who is being referred to with the word *they*? There's no reference.

2. **The correct answer is (A).** In order to make the order of events clear, you have to use the past perfect tense *had been described* in this sentence.

3. **The correct answer is (B).** Choices (A), (C), and (E) suggest that driving a car at any speed is *speeding.*

4. **The correct answer is (E).** If you selected choice (A), (B), or (D), you went against the rules of parallel construction.

5. **The correct answer is (C).** You have to use the expression *the reason is that*—it's what's expected. The word *qualified* is connected to the word *for,* not *to.*

6. **The correct answer is (C).** You have to use parallel construction here once again, and *writing* is parallel to *finishing.*

7. **The correct answer is (C).** This is another example of parallel construction. You have to string a series of parallel nouns here: *years, desire,* and *debut.*

8. **The correct answer is (C).** Choices (A) and (B) are wrong because the personal computer is a contemporary machine, and, therefore, you have to use the word *other.* In choices (D) and (E), you do not need the word *has.* It's clumsy.

9. **The correct answer is (E).** Choice (D) has excessive verbiage. Choice (C) has the wrong tense, *would learn.* In choices (A) and (B) both, there's a problem with changing *anyone* to *you.*

10. **The correct answer is (B).** The pronoun *who* is the object of the verb *regard,* so you need *whom.* Choice (C) puts the word *both* in the wrong place.

11. **The correct answer is (E).** Choices (A) and (C) use *being that,* which is incorrect usage. In choice (B), *only* is not in the proper place.

12. **The correct answer is (D).** Choices (A), (B), and (E) leave out significant parts of the verb. *Hopefully* is wrong in choices (C) and (E).

13. **The correct answer is (A).** You have to use the word *affected,* which, in this case, means acted upon.

14. **The correct answer is (B).** *Isn't hardly, cannot hardly,* and *cannot scarcely* are called double negatives.

Practice Test 3

1. **The correct answer is (B).** The preposition *toward* has *whoever was in front of him* as its object. *Whoever* is the subject of *was.* So you can't use *whomever* here because it is in the objective case.

2. **The correct answer is (A).** This is a perfect example of the use of apposition.

3.   **The correct answer is (E).** One should always aim to use active verbs and expressions as opposed to passive ones. *Because*, in this case, links the two following subordinate notions.

4.   **The correct answer is (D).** This requires the use of parallel construction; in this case, all the verbs should end in *ing* to provide true congruence.

5.   **The correct answer is (E).** The truly important concept in this sentence is *she is a true star*. The best way to get real punch in this sentence is to put this phrase at the end.

6.   **The correct answer is (B).** In this sentence, *that success doesn't make you happy* is a clause that is the predicate nominative of the verb *is*.

7.   **The correct answer is (C).** When you compare two things, you have to use the word *better*. When you have more than two items, you must use the word *best*.

8.   **The correct answer is (D).** This follows the same notion as question 5. When you want to create an impact in a sentence, you can hold off the subject (in this case, *uncle Clem*) until the end.

9.   **The correct answer is (C).** Here, we are looking for the correct idiom; you have to use *different from*. Avoid a phrase like *had ought*.

10. **The correct answer is (E).** Avoid excessive wordiness. In this case, the word *cooperate* has the word *together* implied in it and the word *divide* contains the notion *up*.

11. **The correct answer is (A).** *Inadequate quality assurance* is singular, which requires a singular pronoun, *it*. Choice (B) is problematic because, without a pronoun, the meaning is indeterminate. The other choices are awkward.

12. **The correct answer is (B).** This sentence demands parallel use of verbs; *start* and *engage* are the proper choices.

13. **The correct answer is (D).** *Having lowered our eyes* is a dangling modifier.

14. **The correct answer is (C).** All the other choices misplace their modifiers.

Reading Comprehension

PRACTICE TEST 1

Directions: The questions in this group are based on the content of a passage. After reading the passage, choose the best answer to each question. Answer all questions following the passage on the basis of what is *stated* or *implied* in the passage.

Reading 1

The economic policies of the past six years have nurtured and sustained what is now the longest peacetime expansion on record. By December 1998, the 93rd month since the bottom of the last recession, 18.8 million jobs had been created (17.7 million of them since January 1993). More Americans are working than ever before, the unemployment rate is the lowest in a generation, and inflation remains tame. This record of achievement is especially noteworthy in light of the troubles experienced in the international economy in 1998. The United States has not entirely escaped the effects of this turmoil—and calm has not been restored completely abroad. But the fundamental soundness of the U.S. economy prevented it from foundering in the storms of 1998.

This Administration laid a strong policy foundation for growth in 1993 when the president put in place an economic strategy grounded in deficit reduction, targeted investments, and the opening of markets abroad. Since then, the federal budget deficit has come down steadily, and, in 1998, the budget was in the black for the first time since 1969. This policy of fiscal discipline, together with an appropriately accommodative monetary policy by the Federal Reserve, produced a favorable climate for business investment and a strong, investment-driven recovery from the recession and slow growth of the early 1990s. Even while reducing federal spending as a share of gross domestic product (GDP), the Administration has pushed for more spending in critical areas, such as education and training, helping families and children, the environment, health care, and research and development. Although international economic conditions have led to a dramatic widening of the trade deficit, the United States has succeeded in expanding exports in real (inflation-adjusted) terms by almost 8 percent per year since 1993.

Clearly, there is much for Americans to be proud of in the economic accomplishments of the past six years. But as recent events in the rest of the world have reminded us, our prosperity is threatened when the global economy does not function well. Our immediate challenge on the international front is to help ensure that the global economy rebounds and begins to regain strength. Our long-run challenge as we enter the twenty-first century will be to continue to build and refine the international economic arrangements so that countries can embrace opportunities to grow and develop through international trade and investment.

Challenges remain at home, as well. The restoration of fiscal discipline is one of the most important accomplishments of the past six years. But one very important challenge in the years ahead will be to maintain that discipline and to ensure that fiscal policy contributes to preparing the country for the demographic challenges it faces in the next century. That is why, in his 1998 State of the Union address, the president called for reserving the future budget surpluses until Social Security is reformed. In this year's State of the Union message, the president put forward his framework for saving Social Security while meeting the other pressing challenges of the twenty-first century.

A second major development of the past six years has been the reform of the nation's welfare system, which, together with the strong economy, has produced a dramatic reduction in welfare caseloads. Here, the challenge will be to continue to make work pay for all Americans who play by the rules and want to work, while preserving an adequate safety net. Finally, the strength of the American economy over the past six years should not blind us to the inevitability of change and the threat of disruption that is always present in a dynamic market economy. For example, difficult agricultural conditions in 1998 put stress on the new, market-oriented farm policy enacted in 1996. Similarly, the ongoing wave of mergers among large companies in the financial, telecommunications, and other industries has raised questions about the disruptions these reorganizations cause for communities and workers— questions that go beyond traditional antitrust concerns. Such questions may be better addressed by broader policies such as maintaining full employment and promoting education and training. The challenge here is to capture the long-run benefits from productivity—enhancing change without ignoring the short-run costs to those hurt by that change.

1. It can be inferred that the "longest peacetime expansion on record" occurred because of all of the following EXCEPT

   (A) millions of new jobs have been created.
   (B) the role the U.S. played in Eastern European turmoil.
   (C) unemployment is the lowest in twenty years.
   (D) inflation is under control.
   (E) the economy is, for the most part, sound.

2. The passage suggests that the budget was in the black for the first time since 1969 because of all of the following EXCEPT

    (A) overcoming demographic challenges.
    (B) deficit reduction.
    (C) appropriate monetary policy of the Federal Reserve.
    (D) reduced federal spending.
    (E) presidential economic strategy.

3. The attitude of the passage toward welfare recipients can best be described as

    (A) demanding.
    (B) cajoling.
    (C) dismissive.
    (D) indifferent.
    (E) patronizing.

4. We can infer that the safety net for older people mentioned in the passage

    (A) is connected to the vagaries of the employment rate.
    (B) is made strong by deficit reduction.
    (C) is dependent on Federal Reserve monetary policy.
    (D) is dependent on future budget surpluses.
    (E) is aimed at welfare recipients.

5. We can infer from the passage that the best way to deal with the disruptions caused by the ongoing wave of mergers is to

    (A) institute a program to help overseas workers.
    (B) raise the bar to receive welfare assistance.
    (C) promote education and training to provide full employment.
    (D) raise the minimum wage.
    (E) increase government controls.

6. It can be inferred that the best way to help foreign economies grow is

    (A) through corporate efforts and investments.
    (B) through government efforts and investments.
    (C) by making sure our domestic policy succeeds.
    (D) to allow the Federal Reserve to establish policy.
    (E) to save Social Security first.

Reading 2

In the early 1960s, the Council of Economic Advisers advocated activist macroeconomic policies based on the ideas of the British economist John Maynard Keynes. The Council diagnosed the economy at that time as suffering from "fiscal drag," arising from a large structural budget surplus. (The structural budget balance is the deficit or surplus that would arise from the prevailing fiscal stance if the economy were operating at full capacity.) The marginal tax rates then in effect, which were far higher than today's, were seen as causing tax revenues to rise rapidly as the economy approached full employment, draining purchasing power and slowing demand before full employment could be achieved. The problem was not the fact that Federal Government receipts and expenditures were sensitive to changes in economic activity—this sensitivity plays an important automatic stabilizing role, particularly when economic activity falters, as reduced tax payments and increased unemployment compensation help preserve consumers' purchasing power. The problem was that the automatic stabilizers kicked in too strongly on the upside, not only preventing the economy from reaching full employment but also, ironically, preventing the actual budget from balancing. Thus, President John F. Kennedy proposed a tax cut in 1962, which was enacted after his death in 1964.

This tax cut provided further stimulus to the economic recovery that had begun in 1961. The unemployment rate continued to fall, until early in 1966 it had dropped below the 4 percent rate that was considered full employment at the time. Inflation had been edging up as the unemployment rate came down, but it then began to rise sharply. Although the changed conditions appeared to call for fiscal restraint, President Lyndon B. Johnson was reluctant to raise taxes or scale back his Great Society spending initiatives. Meanwhile, Vietnam War spending continued to provide further stimulus.

At the time, policymakers believed that the rise in inflation could be unwound simply by moving the economy back to 4 percent unemployment, but when restraint was finally applied, it produced a rise in unemployment with little reduction in inflation. This so-called stagflation, together with a slowdown in productivity and a series of oil price shocks in the 1970s, dealt a serious setback to the prevailing view among economists that economic policy could be easily adjusted to achieve the goals of the Employment Act.

At the beginning of the administration of President Ronald Reagan in 1981, the economy was bouncing back from the short 1980 recession, but it was also experiencing very high inflation. President Reagan's program for economic recovery called for large tax cuts, increased defense spending, and reduced domestic spending. Although advocates of these policies invoked the 1964 tax cut as a precedent, the justification offered for this policy was not Keynesian demand stimulus. Rather it was the "supply-side" expectation that substantial cuts in marginal tax rates would call for so much new work effort and investment that the economy's potential output would grow rapidly, easing inflationary pressure and bringing in sufficient new revenue to keep the budget deficit from increasing. In the short run, however, this expansionary fiscal policy collided with an aggressive anti-inflationary monetary policy on the part of the Federal Reserve. The budget deficit ballooned in the deep recession of 1981–82, and it stayed large even after the Federal Reserve eased and the economy began to recover.

Compared with the 1961–69 expansion, the 1982–90 expansion was marked by higher levels of both inflation and unemployment. But the main distinguishing feature of this expansion was the large Federal budget deficits and their macroeconomic consequences. In the early 1980s, the combination of an expansionary fiscal policy and a tight monetary policy produced high real interest rates, an appreciating dollar, and a large current account deficit. (The current account, which includes investment income and unilateral transfers, is a broader measure of a country's international economic activity than the more familiar trade balance.) Although borrowing from abroad offset some of the drain on national saving that the budget deficit represented and prevented the sharp squeeze on domestic investment that would have taken place in an economy closed to trade and foreign capital flows, the effect of this policy choice was a decline in net national saving and investment after 1984. As in the 1961–69 expansion, inflation began to rise as the economy moved toward high employment. By this time, however, the prevailing view was that inflation could not be reversed simply by returning to the full-employment unemployment rate. Instead the economy would have to go through a period of subnormal growth in order to squeeze out inflation.

7. It can be inferred from this passage that

   (A) economic policy adjustment can easily control the economy.
   (B) Keynes' economic theory was proven correct.
   (C) stagflation can be controlled quickly through economic policy.
   (D) economic policy history illustrates the difficulty of controlling the economy.
   (E) Keynes' ideas have no effect on economic policy.

8. The problem that led to the development of Keynesian activism in the 1960s was

   (A) the budget deficit.
   (B) the budget surplus.
   (C) high unemployment.
   (D) the Vietnam War.
   (E) the oil price shocks.

9. We can infer that which of the following illustrates a Keynesian viewpoint?

   (A) Large tax cuts are good for the economy.
   (B) A tight monetary policy always succeeds.
   (C) High interest rates are usually necessary.
   (D) Budget deficits are good.
   (E) A budget surplus can cause fiscal drag.

10. We can infer from the passage that

  (A) a tax cut is always considered good.
  (B) a tax cut is always considered bad.
  (C) a tax cut can be helpful, depending on other factors.
  (D) one should never consider a tax cut.
  (E) a flat tax is best for the country.

11. Which of the following can help consumers' purchasing power?

  (A) the rise of tax revenues
  (B) an increase in unemployment compensation
  (C) allowing inflation to increase
  (D) government controls
  (E) a tight monetary policy

12. From the passage, we can infer that net national saving

  (A) was lower in the 60s than the 80s.
  (B) is not an important supply-side issue.
  (C) is unaffected by microeconomic policies.
  (D) was expected to fall in the 60s.
  (E) was higher in the 60s than the 80s.

Reading 3

It was over thirty years ago that Godzilla first walked the imaginary earth, along with all the others of that Japanese gang: Ordain, Mothra, Ghidra, and the rest. In virtually every one of these films, the city of Tokyo was featured as the movie monster's playground and was totally and repeatedly devastated in the process. The devastation continues to this day in Japanimation epics, where the destruction of Tokyo 2, 3, 4 proceeds in formulaic ritual. The psychic echoes of the carpet bombings and nuclear attacks in World War II are regenerated as manufactured images and exported all over the world.

The Japanese in World War II were the first to see their entire culture overcome and all but destroyed in the Black Rain of our technological future. The common wisdom is that we "won" the war against the foreign terror. Did we win the war? Did anyone? In the dark years of the war, following the economic devastation of the Great Depression, our economic models were rebuilt in the model of new machines for destruction and consumption. Men went to battle, women entered the military factories, and the countryside was emptied by a vast migration to the urban centers of industry. Rural communities were replaced by suburbs, rolling plains and hills by mazelike patterns resembling transistorized circuitry. The almost total replacement of nature and culture was accomplished with little resistance. Social relationships were replaced by statistical patterns of consumption, and the family and community were absorbed by a televised spectacle with little connection to either time or space.

As a child, my recurring nightmare was of being trapped alone in the darkness, locked outside of my house as the world was shaken by the thundering footfalls of an immense and unseen approaching giant. Thirty years later, Godzilla returns, amped by thirty years of progress in the spectacular replication of reality through special effects, and this time the monster arrives to destroy Manhattan, the generative center of the postindustrial apocalypse. Surveying the recent and upcoming lineup of Hollywood spectacles, one contemplates a landscape of almost total destruction. Last year, it was volcanoes and aliens. Next year, it will be monsters from the depths and comets from the heavens. The message coming through these collective dreams and nightmares is one of both memory and prophecy. Like the Japanese, we feel the delayed aftershocks of an event so destructive that our response has been a profound and numbing collective denial. For Americans, the devastation has been almost total. The illusion called "progress" largely masked our smooth descent into Armageddon. Although we never witnessed first-hand the havoc of nuclear wipeout, we've been like the victims of Chernobyl, wandering through the wreckage of a blasted culture while lost in gazing at our own reflection in a cloudy glass. As we go forward, the destruction inevitably escalates, while the technological world evolves through cycles of repetition and replication, eventually and inevitably leading to obsolescence. Driven by endless demand and mindless consumption, the consumer world can end only by being consumed.

Prophecy is really a function of memory. We look at the past and project the patterns we see into the future. In the age of the spectacle, we play out our prophecies and memories in a scenario born on sound stages and in special effects labs. Every year, we invest more of our resources toward a quest to achieve the perfect replication of reality. The image we perfect is that of our world being destroyed. Like children that have been violated, we are driven to express deep rage in orgies of projected violence. At the end of the millennium, the highest achievement of popular culture is the construction of the perfect disaster. *Titanic, Volcano, Independence Day, Terminator, Armageddon,* and *Godzilla* have become the true legacies of a culture on the brink of Judgment Day.

13.   It can be inferred that the passage is

(A) an attempt to criticize Hollywood's hold on films.
(B) a critique of the cinematic responses to nuclear weapons.
(C) a positive review of Japanese cinema.
(D) a sentimental view of films seen by the writer.
(E) a defense of consumerism.

14. We can infer that the phrase "Black Rain" refers to

    (A) meteorological conditions.
    (B) the result of the Great Depression.
    (C) cultural "fallout."
    (D) a film title.
    (E) a series of thriller films.

15. What relationship is suggested in this passage between WWII and Godzilla movies?

    (A) The movies hide the effects of war.
    (B) War and movies like Godzilla are completely separate.
    (C) Godzilla movies distract people from the effects of war.
    (D) Both war and Godzilla are examples of progress.
    (E) The movies replay the horrors of war by creating "monsters."

16. Which of the following attitudes toward "nature" can be inferred in the passage?

    (A) The world of nature is ideal and is counter to war and technology.
    (B) The natural world is a natural tool for technology.
    (C) Nature is reinvented in the world of Godzilla films.
    (D) Nature and technology can easily coexist.
    (E) Nature, especially volcanoes, can be destructive.

PRACTICE TEST 2

Reading 1

"The constitutional prohibition against 'double jeopardy' was designed to protect an individual from being subjected to the hazards of a trial and possible conviction more than once for an alleged offense. The underlying idea, one that is deeply ingrained in at least the Anglo-American system of jurisprudence, is that the State, with all its resources and power, should not be allowed to make repeated attempts to convict an individual for an alleged offense, thereby subjecting him to embarrassment, expense, and ordeal, compelling him to live in a continuing state of anxiety and insecurity as well as enhancing the possibility that even though innocent, he may be found guilty." The concept of double jeopardy goes far back in history, but its development has been uneven and its meaning has varied. The English development, under the influence of Coke and Blackstone, gradually came to mean that a defendant at trial could plead former conviction or former acquittal as a special plea in bar to defeat the prosecution. In this country, the common-law rule was, in some cases, limited to this rule and, in other cases, extended to bar a new trial, even though the former trial had not concluded in either an acquittal or a conviction. The rule's elevation to fundamental status by its inclusion in several state bills of rights following the Revolution continued the differing approaches. Madison's version of the guarantee, as introduced in the House of Representatives, read, "No person shall be subject, except in cases of impeachment, to more than one punishment or trial for the same offense." Opposition in the House proceeded on the proposition that the language could be construed to prohibit a second trial after a successful appeal by a defendant and would, therefore, either constitute a hazard to the public by freeing the guilty or, more likely, result in a detriment to defendants because appellate courts would be loath to reverse convictions if no new trial could follow. A motion to strike or "trial" from the clause failed. As approved by the Senate, however, and accepted by the House for referral to the States, the present language was inserted. The passage is often approvingly quoted by the Court.

The first bill of rights that expressly adopted a double jeopardy clause was the New Hampshire Constitution of 1784. "No subject shall be liable to be tried, after acquittal, for the same crime or offense."

A more comprehensive protection was included in the Pennsylvania Declaration of Rights of 1790, which had language that was almost identical to the present Fifth Amendment provision.

In *Crist* v. *Bretz* (1978) (dissenting), Justice Powell attributed to inadvertence the broadening the "rubric" of double jeopardy to incorporate the common-law rule against dismissal of the jury prior to verdict, a question the majority passed over as being "of academic interest only."

Throughout most of its history, this clause was binding only against the Federal Government. In *Palko* v. *Connecticut*, the Court rejected an argument that the Fourteenth Amendment incorporated all of the provisions of the first eight amendments as limitations on the States and enunciated the due process theory under which most of those amendments now apply to the States. Some guarantees in the Bill of Rights, Justice Cardozo wrote, were so fundamental that they are "of the very essence of the scheme of ordered liberty" and "neither liberty nor injustice would exist if they were sacrificed." But the double jeopardy clause, like so many other procedural rights of defendants, was not so fundamental; it could be absent, and fair trials could still be had. Of course, a defendant's due process rights, absent double jeopardy considerations per se, might be violated if the State "created a hardship so acute and shocking to be unendurable," but that was not the case in *Palko*. In *Benton* v. *Maryland*, however, the Court concluded "that the double jeopardy prohibition . . . represents a fundamental ideal in our constitutional heritage . . . Once it is decided that a particular Bill of Rights guarantee is 'fundamental to the American scheme of justice,' . . . the same constitutional standards apply against both the State and Federal Governments." Therefore, the double jeopardy limitation now applies to both federal and state rules on double jeopardy, with regard to such matters as when jeopardy attaches, and must be considered in the light of federal standards.

In a federal system, different units of government may have different interests to serve in the definition of crimes and the enforcement of their laws. Where different units have overlapping jurisdictions, a person may engage in conduct that will violate the laws of more than one unit. Although the Court had long accepted in dictum the principle that prosecution by two governments of the same defendant would not constitute double jeopardy, it was not until *United States* v. *Lanza* that the conviction in federal court of a person previously convicted in state court for performing the same acts was sustained. "We have here two sovereignties, deriving power from different sources, capable of dealing with the same subject-matter within the same territory. . . . Each government, in determining what shall be an offense against its peace and dignity, is exercising its own sovereignty, not that of the other." The "dual sovereignty" doctrine is not only tied into the existence of two sets of laws, often serving different federal-state purposes, and the now overruled principles that the double jeopardy clause restricts only the national government and not the States, but it also reflects practical considerations that undesirable consequences could follow an overruling of the doctrine. Thus, a State might preempt federal authority by first prosecuting and providing for a lenient sentence (as compared to the possible federal sentence) or acquitting defendants who had the sympathy of state authorities as against federal law enforcement. The application of the clause to the States has therefore worked no change in the "dual sovereign" doctrine. Of course, when, in fact, two different units of government are subject to the same sovereign, the double jeopardy clause does bar separate prosecutions by them for the same offense. The dual sovereignty doctrine has also been applied to permit successive prosecutions by two states for the same conduct.

1. Which case confirmed that a person convicted in a state court could not be convicted of the same offense in federal court?

   (A) *Coke* v. *Blackstone*
   (B) *United States* v. *Lanza*
   (C) *Crist* v. *Bretz*
   (D) *Palko* v. *Connecticut*
   (E) *Benton* v. *Maryland*

2. The first bill of rights to expressly adopt a double jeopardy clause was

   (A) the Pennsylvania Declaration of Rights.
   (B) in Maryland.
   (C) the New Hampshire Constitution.
   (D) in Connecticut.
   (E) developed by Justice Cardozo.

3. Which cause does not fall under the concept of double jeopardy?

   (A) anti-trust
   (B) war-crimes
   (C) capital offenses
   (D) international crimes
   (E) impeachment

4. What can we infer is the essence of Justice Cardozo's comments on double jeopardy?

   (A) Neither liberty nor justice would exist if it were sacrificed.
   (B) The double jeopardy clause is fundamental to American jurisprudence.
   (C) The Federal Government has the right to overrule the states.
   (D) We should ensure that double jeopardy should not create a hardship.
   (E) The double jeopardy clause is not necessary fundamental.

5. Which of the following best defines "dual sovereignty"?

(A) two separate but equal sources of power
(B) two sets of laws that obviate each other
(C) the English and American systems of law
(D) two sets of laws that derive power from the different sources
(E) two sets of laws derived from the same source

6. We can infer from this passage that

(A) the concept of double jeopardy is an attempt to limit government harassment.
(B) double jeopardy is only important in cases of impeachment.
(C) states have the upper hand in the conflict over double jeopardy.
(D) the federal government is more concerned with issues arising out of disputes over double jeopardy.
(E) double jeopardy is an overlooked part of American jurisprudence.

Reading 2

The challenge and task that you are undertaking is formidable. Changing the way campaigns are financed is a difficult job, particularly because it is something that will dramatically impact all of our lives. But clearly, something must be done. Too much time is spent raising money, and the current system is one that has been criticized regarding the way our democracy works.

I commend you for holding these hearings and hope you can arrive at a formula that is fair, nonpartisan, and nondiscriminatory and restores the American people's faith in our democracy.

In 1986, when I first decided to leave the Atlantic City Council and seek the open seat in Georgia's Fifth Congressional District, I was a grass-roots candidate. My background within the civil rights movement and my energies on the city council had been devoted to issues relating to low-income housing, neighborhood preservation, and homelessness. I didn't have a lot of supporters who were able to write my campaign checks for $1,000.

Faced with formidable opposition in the race, it was only with the support of labor union political action committees and a few others that I was able to mount a credible and ultimately successful bid for the Congress.

If not for the support of these special interests, this former civil rights worker, this fourth son of a sharecropper, would not have had a prayer to make it to the United States House of Representatives. Thus, I was surprised and dismayed in recent years to see political action committees under attack from so many different quarters, including many of my friends in the public interest communities.

Political action committees, especially those that are labor unions and ideological groups formed by those supporting or opposing abortion rights, gay rights, or gun control, give working people and people with little means the ability to participate in the political process. Many of these people who contribute with a "checkoff" or small deduction from their paycheck each week would effectively be denied participation in the process if not for their union or company political action committee.

Let there be no confusion. Minority women candidates from poor rural and urban districts are the beneficiaries of Political Action Committees. PACs take power and influence out of the hands of the "country club set" and put it in the hands of the people who cannot afford to write $500 or $1,000 checks.

This is one of the reasons PACs were established, and this is exactly why PACs should be protected in any campaign reform legislation. To do otherwise is to revert to a system controlled by wealthy individuals and millionaire candidates who bankroll their own campaigns.

I know there are those who believe that this was a position taken by Democrats who were the beneficiary of a majority of PACs at the time they controlled the House. Let me assure my colleagues that, even in light of my party's new Minority status in this House, even in light of the fact that a majority of SAC funds are now flowing into Republican coffers, I am still supportive of political action committees and their right to participate in the political process.

I know there are various proposals before this Committee not to reduce or lower PAC contribution, but to eliminate them altogether. Such a move should be resisted. Federal election law today permits candidates to accept a contribution of $5,000 in their primary and $5,000 in the general election. A reduction in the contribution limit will have a minimal impact on the contributions. It would have a disproportionate impact on minority candidates.

I believe that it has been noted before this Committee that the individual limit of $1,000 per person, per election, adopted in 1974, is worth only about $325 today when adjusted for inflation. Similarly, the $5,000 per election limit, when adjusted, is worth about $1,625. Inflation with no adjustment to compensate for it has had the effect of lowering individual and political action committee contribution limits year after year.

In 1994, a Common Cause study showed that lowering the PAC contribution limits would cost candidates in competitive races 3 percent of their PACWS contribution. Using the same numbers shows that a reduction in the limit will cost Members of the Congressional Black Caucus more than twice the amount. Minority candidates have worked too hard and too long to gain equal footing in the political system.

CBC and other minority candidates should not be discriminated against in any campaign finance formula. Indeed, Mr. Chairman, traditionally, one of the goals of reform has been to open the political process, not to throw up roadblocks to minority participation.

I believe that Congress should pass a strong campaign finance reform bill this year. But it cannot be considered true reform if it narrows the scope of who can participate and who can contribute in our political system.

Minorities and women have waited too long to have their voices heard in the Congress. We can not impede their gains by jeopardizing their future. To ensure that this is a fair process for all, this Committee should not lower the PAC limit by eliminating the PACs.

7. It can be inferred from the passage that the audience members of this speech are

   (A) members of the Bar Association.
   (B) representatives of political action committees.
   (C) members of Congress.
   (D) members of the press.
   (E) members of a New Jersey gardening club.

8. The attitude of the speaker can best be described as

   (A) reflecting the pernicious effects of PACs.
   (B) being supportive of ways that PACs help minority candidates.
   (C) sarcastic.
   (D) a vociferous attack on special interests.
   (E) thankful for the role of PACs in contemporary politics.

9. We can infer that the speaker's attitude toward PACs in response to his party's new minority status

   (A) is sense of relief.
   (B) is the same as when his party was the majority.
   (C) has changed to reflect his party's new status.
   (D) is a new sense of jealousy towards Republicans.
   (E) is in agreement with the majority of his party.

10. We can infer that one of the aims of the speaker of the passage is to

   (A) get contributions from large PACs.
   (B) make it difficult for PACs to influence races for office.
   (C) allow people of little means to participate in politics.
   (D) do away with PACs altogether.
   (E) have PACs give equally to both parties.

11. Limiting PACs will have what effect on minority candidates, according to the speaker of this passage?

   (A) There will be little or no effect on minority candidates.
   (B) The playing field will be even for all candidates, especially minorities.
   (C) The limitation will make it impossible for minority candidates to fund their races.
   (D) The limitation will make it more difficult for minority candidates to get funds for races.
   (E) Minority candidates will have more opportunities to enter political races.

12. Which one of the following is <u>not</u> revealed about the life of the speaker in the passage?

   (A) He is the son of a sharecropper.
   (B) He was devoted to issues pertaining to homelessness.
   (C) He was a grass-roots candidate.
   (D) He was a civil rights worker.
   (E) He supports gay rights.

Reading 3

"Congress shall make no law respecting an establishment of religion, or prohibiting the free exercise thereof; or abridging the freedom of speech, or of the press; or the right of the people peaceably to assemble, and to petition the Government for a redress of grievances."

Madison's original proposal for a bill of rights provision concerning religion read: "The civil rights of none shall be abridged on account of religious belief or worship, nor shall any national religion be established, nor shall the full and equal rights of conscience be in any manner, or on any pretense, infringed." The language was altered in the House to read: "Congress shall make no law establishing religion, or to prevent the free exercise thereof, or to infringe the rights of conscience." In the Senate, the section adopted read: "Congress shall make no law establishing articles of faith, or a mode of worship, or prohibiting the free exercise of religion . . ." It was in the conference committee of the two bodies, chaired by Madison, that the present language was written with its somewhat more indefinite "respecting" phraseology. Debate in Congress lends little assistance in interpreting the religion clauses; Madison's position, as well as that of Jefferson, who influenced him, is fairly clear, but the intent, insofar as there was one, of the others in Congress who voted for the language and those in the States who voted to ratify is subject to speculation.

The committee appointed to consider Madison's proposals, and on which Madison served, with Vining as chairman, had rewritten the religion section to read: "No religion shall be established by law, nor shall the equal rights of conscience be infringed." After some debate, during which Madison suggested that the word "national" might be inserted before the word "religion" as "pointing the amendment directly to the object it was intended to prevent," the House adopted a substitute reading. "Congress shall make no laws touching religion, or infringing the rights of conscience." On August 20, on motion of Fisher Ames, the language of the clause as quoted in the text was adopted. According to Madison's biographer, "There can be little doubt that this was written by Madison." It was at this point that the religion clauses were joined with the freedom of expression clauses. The Senate concurred the same day.

During House debate, Madison told his fellow Members that "he apprehended the meaning of the words to be, that Congress should not establish a religion, and enforce the legal observation of it by law, nor compel men to

Peterson's GMAT CAT Success

worship God in any Manner contrary to their conscience." That his conception of "establishment" was quite broad is revealed in his veto as president in 1811, of a bill which, in granting land, reserved a parcel for a Baptist Church in Salem, Mississippi; the action, explained President Madison, "comprises a principle and precedent for the appropriation of funds of the United States for the use and support of religious societies, contrary to the article of the Constitution which declares that 'Congress shall make no law respecting a religious establishment.'" Madison's views were no doubt influenced by the fight in the Virginia legislature in 1784–1785, in which he successfully led the opposition to a tax to support teachers of religion in Virginia and in the course of which he drafted his *Memorial and Remonstrance against Religious Assessments* setting forth his thoughts. Acting on the momentum of this effort, Madison secured passage of Jefferson's "Bill for Religious Liberty." The theme of the writings of both was that it was wrong to offer public support of any religion in particular or of religion in general.

The explication of the religion clauses by the scholars has followed a restrained sense of their meaning. Story, who thought that "the right of a society or government to interfere in matters of religion will hardly be contested by any persons who believe that piety, religion, and morality are intimately connected with the well being of the state, and indispensable to the administration of civil justice," looked upon the prohibition simply as an exclusion from the Federal Government of all power to act upon the subject. "The situation . . . of the different states equally proclaimed the policy, as well as the necessity of such an exclusion. In some of the states, Episcopalians constituted the predominant sect; in others Presbyterians; in others, Congregationalists; in others, Quakers; and in others again, there was a close numerical rivalry among contending sects. It was impossible, that there should not arise perpetual strife and perpetual jealousy on the subject of ecclesiastical ascendancy, if the national government were left free to create a religious establishment. The only security was in extirpating the power. But this alone would have been an imperfect security, if it had not been followed up by a declaration of the right of the free exercise of religion, and a prohibition (as we have seen) of all religious tests. Thus, the whole power over the subject of religion is left exclusively to the state governments, to be acted upon according to their own sense of justice, and the state constitutions; and the Catholic and the Protestant, the Calvinist and the Armenian, the Jew and the Infidel, may sit down at the common table of the national councils, without any inquisition into their faith, or mode of worship."

"Probably," Story also wrote, "at the time of the adoption of the constitution and of the amendment to it, now under consideration, the general, if not the universal, sentiment in America was, that Christianity ought to receive encouragement from the state, so far as was not incompatible with the private rights of conscience, and the freedom of religious worship. An attempt to level all religions, and to make it a matter of state policy to hold all in utter indifference, would have created universal disapprobation, if not universal indignation." The object, then, of the religion clause in this view was not to prevent general governmental encouragement of religion, of Christianity, but to prevent religious persecution and to prevent a national establishment.

This interpretation has long since been abandoned by the Court, beginning, at least, with *Everson* v. *Board of Education* in which the Court, without dissent on this point, declared that the Establishment Clause forbids not only practices that "aid one religion" or "prefer one religion over another," but as well, those that "aid all religions." Recently, relying on published scholarly research and original sources, Court dissenters have returned to the argument that, what the religion clauses, principally the Establishment Clause, prevent, is "preferential" governmental promotion of some religions, allowing general governmental promotion of all religion in general. The Court has not responded, though Justice Souter, in a major concurring opinion, did undertake to rebut the argument and to restate the Everson position.

13. Which of the following CANNOT be inferred from Madison's original proposal concerning religion?

   (A) There shall be no national religion.
   (B) A person's rights of conscience cannot be infringed.
   (C) A person's civil rights cannot be infringed on account of worship.
   (D) The States and the Federal Government are in complete accord concerning religion.
   (E) Congress shall not establish religion.

14. We can infer from this passage that Madison felt that

   (A) there were appropriate moments when the public should support religion.
   (B) there were some religious faiths that deserved federal dispensation.
   (C) land grants should provide for religious establishments.
   (D) there should be strict separation between education and religion.
   (E) there should be strict separation between public support and religion.

15. We can infer from Story's interpretation stated in this passage that

   (A) the States and the Federal Government are on the same page concerning religious freedom.
   (B) even though there can be no national religion, a state can choose to represent a religious belief.
   (C) states, rather than the federal government, should have power over the subject of religion.
   (D) one needs to be religious to "sit down at the common table of the national councils."
   (E) the national government should be "left free to create a religious establishment."

16. We can infer from the final paragraph of the passage that the Supreme Court is moving in which direction regarding religion?

(A) There should be more distance between government and promotion of all religion.

(B) The government should be more active in promoting religion.

(C) The government should move more towards Madison's position in his original proposal to Congress.

(D) The government should move toward the Everson position.

(E) Story's position is completely on the wrong track.

PRACTICE TEST 3

Reading 1

Abe Kobo stands out from his contemporaries in postwar Japanese literature in a number of ways. His work differs dramatically from the subjective, ultrarealistic, and "autobiographicalesque" style that characterizes a great deal of postwar literature in general and postwar Japanese literature in particular. Abe grew up in Manchuria, or Manchukuo, as the Japanese leasehold/puppet state was known at the time. As such, he presumably did not develop the deep ties to the concept of *furasato* (hometown) and the divine emperor that play large roles in the works of such contemporaries as Mishima Yukio and Nobel laureate Oe Kenzaburo. Furthermore, Abe did not undergo formal training in literature, as did so many of his contemporaries. Instead, he followed in his father's footsteps, studying medicine at Tokyo University. Unlike another famous medical doctor in Japanese literature, Mori Ogai, Abe did not excel in this field, nor did it seem that he had any particular enthusiasm for a life in medicine. It is said that he was allowed to graduate only on the condition that he promise never to practice medicine.

After the war, Abe began experimenting with various radical social and artistic theories. Abe joined a small literary/artistic/philosophical group called *Yoru no kai* (Night Association), and soon after his introduction to its leader, philosopher Hanada Kiyoteru, Abe joined the Japanese Communist Party (along with most of the rest of Japan's intelligentsia) and began experimenting with Marxism and surrealism in his literature. Unfortunately, very little from this period in Abe's career has been translated into English, but Abe's youth and idealism come through quite clearly in what are some of his most (blackly) humorous and outspoken works.

Abe's novels, however, are probably what he is known for in and out of Japan, despite his highly acclaimed short stories, his avant-garde plays, and his work as a photographer and sometimes composer. It was *Suna no onna* (*Woman in the Dunes*) that first brought Abe to the attention of the West. Or, rather, it was Teshigahara Hiroshi's film adaptation of the novel that, along with a prize at the Cannes Film Festival, brought Abe into the limelight. As such, this work is seen, rightly or wrongly, as Abe's masterpiece. Certainly, it marks somewhat of a transition in his career. Purged from the Japanese Communist Party only four months prior to its publication in June 1962, *Suna no onna*, while not a complete disavowal of Marxist ideology, clearly indicated a move away from the primacy of politics and ideology in his literature. The themes of alienation and homelessness, while not absent from his earlier works, come to the fore. It is in these novels that Abe captures the social impact of Japan's rapidly urbanizing, growth-centered corporate society on the individual. Nor is the relevance of these later novels limited only to Japan, but, rather, one could see these works as a discussion of the postmodern condition as a whole.

1. From this passage, we can infer that

   (A) Abe is the much copied icon of Japanese literature.
   (B) Mishima and Oe share his literary upbringing.
   (C) formal literary training is frowned upon in Japan.
   (D) Abe developed a unique literary point of view that stemmed from his childhood.
   (E) Abe maintained his Marxist views throughout his career.

2. We can infer that the speaker in the passage

   (A) thinks that *Woman in the Dunes* is Abe's masterpiece.
   (B) is indifferent to the values of *Woman in the Dunes*.
   (C) sees *Woman in the Dunes* as a Marxist diatribe.
   (D) considers *Woman in the Dunes* as a tale that explains the concept of *furasato*.
   (E) considers *Woman of the Dunes* important but not necessarily Abe's masterpiece.

3. From this passage, we can infer that Abe's works

   (A) reflect a subjective, autobiographical style.
   (B) explore his life as a doctor.
   (C) can be considered to be social commentary.
   (D) reflect an adherence to Marxist principles.
   (E) are borne out of his intensive study of his literary forebears.

4. Which of the following is NOT true of Abe Kobo?

   (A) He was born in China.
   (B) He joined the Japanese Communist Party.
   (C) *Furasato* does not play a major role in his works.
   (D) One can find traces of surrealism in his novels.
   (E) He is a noted filmmaker.

Reading 2

"WANTED—POSTMAN WITH BICYCLE." Only a temporary job, but almost tailor-made for Mario (Massimo Troisi), an introverted and uneducated yet sharply insightful young man, protagonist of Michael Radford's delightfully bittersweet, humane, humorous, moving—yet never sentimental—comedy, *Il Postino*. The job involves carrying the mail to just one illustrious addressee, the Chilean poet Pablo Neruda (Phillippe Noiret), who was exiled in the early 1950s to the Southern Italian island of Procida because of his communist views. Every day, Mario pedals up to the poet's new residence—a villa located on the top of a hill, surrounded by wild Mediterranean vegetation and overlooking the sea—carrying a leather bag full of correspondence: mostly, at least in his adolescent mind that is fueled by newsreel mythology, love letters from adoring women all over the world.

At first, of course, Mario and Neruda hardly talk. What is there to be said, anyway, between them? Intrigued by his own thoughts and feelings, the postman cannot find the words to express them, and he feels that the poet has better things to do than to listen to him. But, as the relationship develops, Mario finds an interlocutor and, with it, a voice: tentative at first, when he dares, after a farcical rehearsal in front of a mirror, to ask the poet for an autograph in the hope that this will impress his girlfriends in Naples—then progressively more secure. In Neruda-the-Man, he gradually discovers the parental figure to identify with and idealize; in Neruda-the-Poet, the language to make sense of his inner world. If Mario's real father is a silent, down-to-earth (or down-to-sea) fisherman with little understanding of his son's existential problems ("I am tired of being a man," Mario says, echoing Neruda's words), his dead mother is entirely absent—other than, that is, in the guises of Nature, both literally in the external world and literally in Neruda's, and then Mario's own, poetry: an all-embracing, all-containing, and nurturing sea that surrounds the beautiful, part-lush, part-desert island.

The film has the structure, familiar to fiction readers and cinema-goers alike, of a Bildungsroman. Witnessed by the poet himself, Mario's development into a mature man culminates in his achievement of potency, which finds its expression at three different but interconnected levels: (1) sexual, through his relationship, as passionate as it is clumsy, to maidenly, sensuous waitress Beatrice, whom he eventually marries, with Neruda's blessing and help; (2) literary, as Mario starts reading and producing verse himself and even suggesting to his own master an excellent adjective—*sad*—to describe what fishing nets look like. It is not a coincidence that he will unconsciously create his first metaphor when listening to Neruda's lyrical description of the sea: "I feel . . . weird and seasick," he says, "like a boat tossing around . . . words"; and finally (3) political, by tentatively opposing a local Mafioso boss and through an ill-fated involvement with a Communist demonstration, where he is invited to read one of his own Neruda-inspired poems to the crowd.

Part of the fascination of *Il Postino* consists in creatively immersing a real and contemporary character, the poet Pablo Neruda, here portrayed with much biographical accuracy, in an entirely fictional situation. But if the filmmaker's fantasy interplays with history, the external world also intrudes, and most tragically, into the artistic work: as soon as the shooting of *Il Postino* was over, Massimo Troisi, the actor in the title role, prematurely died. In the film, Mario is killed at a mass rally during an incident with the police: a conclusion perhaps ideological and aesthetically unnecessary but also providing the viewers who are aware of Troisi's death with a positively painful experience of life imitating art.

5. From the passage, we can infer that *Il Postino*

   (A) is a documentary of the poet Pablo Neruda.
   (B) is a tragedy that centers on the death of Mario.
   (C) mixes reality and fantasy to underline the power of poetry.
   (D) was banned because of its political position.
   (E) explores the sources of Neruda's poetry.

6. We can infer from the passage that the speaker is most interested in

   (A) psychology.
   (B) politics.
   (C) film theory.
   (D) the relationship between fiction and reality.
   (E) humor and its sources.

7. From the passage, which one of the following is stated as the most important gift given to Mario by Neruda?

   (A) a political viewpoint
   (B) a chance for a new job
   (C) a book of poetry
   (D) an introduction to a beautiful woman
   (E) a voice

8. Which of the following is NOT stated as an effect of Neruda on Mario?

   (A) sexual development
   (B) political change
   (C) Neruda helps Mario make sense of his emotions.
   (D) economically
   (E) literary development

9. From the passage, we can infer that the speaker's attitude toward the ending of the film is

   (A) that it is artistically wrong but emotionally powerful.
   (B) that it is the culmination of all the themes of the film.
   (C) that it is cheapened by the real-life death of the actor who plays Mario.
   (D) that it ignores Aristotle's theory concerning a proper ending.
   (E) laudatory.

10. Of the following roles that Neruda plays in the film, which does the speaker suggest is most important?

(A) political exile
(B) idealized father
(C) Communist firebrand
(D) go-between for Beatrice and Mario
(E) world-famous poet

Reading 3

Today, we have the longest peacetime expansion in our history. After years and years of deficits, we now have budget surpluses for years ahead. More people have a chance to realize the American dream than ever before. More children have the chance to realize their full potential than ever before. We've laid a foundation to preserve our prosperity for future generations.

Now, as the budget deadline rapidly approaches this year, we face many of the same tough choices again. And once again, I think the answer is clear: To build a strong nation in the new century, we must continue to invest in our future. That means we must strengthen Social Security, secure and modernize Medicare, and pay off the national debt in fifteen years, making America debt-free for the first time since 1835. And once again, it means we must invest in education, not sacrifice it.

Months ago, I sent Congress a responsible budget to maintain our fiscal discipline and honor our commitment to our children's education. So far, the Republicans in Congress haven't put forth a budget of their own. In fact, they're so busy trying to figure out how to pay for their irresponsible tax plan that they're in serious danger of not meeting their obligation to finish the budget by the end of the budget year. Even worse, they're preparing to pay for their own pet projects at the expense of our children's education.

We know now that the Republicans' risky tax cut would force us to slash vital funding for education by as much as 50 percent over the next ten years. But what many people don't know is that next year alone, the Republican plan would cut the bill that funds education by nearly 20 percent.

Now, if carried out, this plan would lead to some of the worst cuts in education in our history. More than 5,000 teachers, hired as part of my class size initiative, could be laid off. Fifty thousand students could be turned away from after-school and summer-school programs. More than 2 million of our poorest students in our poorest communities would have a smaller chance of success in school and in the workplaces of the future. These aren't just numbers on a balance sheet; they're vital investments in our children and our future.

In a time when education is our top priority, Republicans in Congress are making it their lowest priority. So let me be clear: If the Republicans send me a bill that doesn't live up to our national commitment to education, I won't hesitate to veto it. If it undermines our efforts to hire high-quality teachers to reduce class size or to increase accountability in our public schools, I will veto it. If it fails to strengthen Head Start, after-school, and summer-school programs, I'll veto it. If it underfunds mentoring or college scholarship programs, I will veto it. If it sends me a bill that turns its back on our children and their future, I'll send them back to the drawing board. I won't let Congress push through a budget that's paid for at the expense of our children and our future prosperity.

11. We can infer that the audience for the speaker in the passage is

   (A) Congress.
   (B) composed of common voters.
   (C) a group of public-school administrators.
   (D) a group of United Nations representatives.
   (E) a group of contributors to the Democratic Party.

12. Which of the following is NOT stated or implied in this passage?

   (A) Fifty-thousand students could be turned away from after-school programs.
   (B) Five-thousand teachers may be laid off.
   (C) Budget deficits will increase.
   (D) Education funding may be cut by 50 percent over a ten-year period.
   (E) The national debt may be paid off.

13. Which of the following is NOT stated or implied about education?

   (A) Higher education should be reserved for the elite.
   (B) The nation should view education as an investment.
   (C) Money for education should not exceed the parameters of fiscal discipline.
   (D) Education should be the primary goal for the congressional budget.
   (E) Education and national prosperity are deeply connected.

14. The use of words such as *irresponsible*, *risky*, and *pet projects* suggests which of the following about the speaker's attitude?

   (A) He is attempting to be conciliatory.
   (B) He is trying to convince Republicans to come to his side.
   (C) This is his attempt at humor.
   (D) He is appealing to the Republicans' sense of fiscal responsibility.
   (E) He is trying to bolster his position with the audience by attacking perceived adversaries.

Quick Score Answers					
Reading Comprehension					
Practice Test 1		Practice Test 2		Practice Test 3	
1. B	9. E	1. B	9. B	1. D	8. D
2. A	10. C	2. C	10. C	2. E	9. A
3. A	11. B	3. E	11. D	3. C	10. B
4. D	12. E	4. E	12. E	4. E	11. B
5. C	13. B	5. D	13. D	5. C	12. C
6. A	14. C	6. A	14. E	6. A	13. A
7. D	15. E	7. C	15. C	7. E	14. E
8. B	16. A	8. B	16. B		

ANSWERS AND EXPLANATIONS

READING COMPREHENSION

Practice Test 1

1. **The correct answer is (B).** This is the only detail not mentioned in the passage. Choices (A), (C), (D), and (E) are either directly mentioned in the passage or are paraphrases of details in the passage.

2. **The correct answer is (A).** Again, this is a question of detail and close reading. All but choice (A) are mentioned in the passage.

3. **The correct answer is (A).** The phrase "play by the rules and want to work" clearly demands what the welfare recipient has to do. The other words are all powerful and, in other contexts, have been hallmarks of attitudes toward welfare recipients.

4. **The correct answer is (D).** You have to figure out that the "safety net," rather than being connected to welfare, is connected to social security, which, in turn, will be affected by "future budget surpluses."

5. **The correct answer is (C).** The basis for this response is found in the last paragraph of the passage. Logic may dictate that choices (D) or (E) are sound solutions as well, but the thrust of the passage is to put the onus on the individual.

6. **The correct answer is (A).** Detail is provided in paragraph three, which states that foreign countries can see their economies grow through "international trade and investment."

7. **The correct answer is (D).** The thrust of the entire passage is to point out the difficulties of controlling the economy through the use of economic policy, which seems to change whenever an administration changes.

8. **The correct answer is (B).** This question requires a close reading of the first two paragraphs to get the right detail. Choices (D) and (E), for example, occurred in the next decade.

9. **The correct answer is (E).** This is also a question asking for the right detail that, in this case, is provided in the first paragraph, which discusses "fiscal drag."

10. **The correct answer is (C).** This can be determined when you compare the 60s to the 80s and find that in one case, the tax cut was beneficial, and in the other, it had a negative effect.

11. **The correct answer is (B).** The correct detail is provided in paragraph one. Questions like this can be difficult because the detail is sometimes provided in a sentence with many items listed; you have to be able to pick out the necessary detail to answer your question.

12. **The correct answer is (E).** The answer is provided in the sentence that reads, "there was a decline in net national saving and investment after 1984," and we have to assume that savings were higher in the 60s.

13. **The correct answer is (B).** The entire passage is a critique of nuclear weapons and films that have reflected a culture concerned with their own potential for destruction. There is an implicit criticism of Hollywood in the passage, but it is not the main thrust of the passage.

14. **The correct answer is (C).** The phrase "Black Rain" was originally meant to mean nuclear fallout, but it is cleverly used here to refer to problems of technology. The rest of the choices are far afield.

15. **The correct answer is (E).** This requires the reader to use inference and logic. The speaker in the passage suggests that movies play a psychological role for their audiences and exorcise fears very often at the same time as they are creating them.

16. **The correct answer is (A).** The speaker is setting up nature as a dialectical pole opposite of technology. The thrust of the passage is to romanticize nature and attack technology and the usage of its tools.

Practice Test 2

1. **The correct answer is (B).** This is correct by virtue of details presented in the passage. Choice (A) is not a court case and all the other choices refer to different concepts.

2. **The correct answer is (C).** Detail in the passage gives the date as 1784. Choice (A), Pennsylvania, was in 1790.

3. **The correct answer is (E).** Madison states clearly that *only* in cases of impeachment can someone be tried twice. The other cases, though perhaps grave, do not issue in the choice of going beyond double jeopardy.

4. **The correct answer is (E).** Though this defies common logic, the details are provided in the section dealing with Cardozo's commentary. Many of the other responses, choice (A) for example, sound correct but are wrong in this context.

5. **The correct answer is (D).** The concept refers to powers of the state and the federal government that allow each to work within its own jurisdiction and not cancel the power of the other.

6. **The correct answer is (A).** The main theme of the passage concerning double jeopardy is how to strike a balance between rightful use of the law and using law as a tool to harass or embarrass an individual

7. **The correct answer is (C).** The speaker is referring to issues directly related to himself and others as members of Congress. The other choices all imply a wrong sense of audience.

8. **The correct answer is (B).** Attitude is a synonym for tone. To pick out the correct tone one has to "listen" to the passage as you are reading it. In this case, the proper tone is "supportive," rather than the more negative tones of choices (A), (C), and (D), and the plain wrong tone of choice (E).

9. **The correct answer is (B).** This says something about the speaker's commitment to a concept rather than to expediency. He doesn't move with the prevailing winds. He tries to hold off choice (D), jealousy.

10. **The correct answer is (C).** The thrust of the passage is inclusionary; that is, to help women and other minority candidates obtain the money necessary to run for office. All the other choices refer to PACs (some in intelligent ways) but are not relevant to the question.

11. **The correct answer is (D).** The detail is provided clearly in the passage.

12. **The correct answer is (E).** Though in fact it may be true, this detail is the only one of the group that is not provided in the passage.

13. **The correct answer is (D).** Though the States and Federal Government ultimately came to agree on matters concerning religion, it had not yet happened the time in which the passage was written. All the other choices are clearly evident in the passage.

14. **The correct answer is (E).** Detail is provided in the fourth paragraph. Choice (D) is true in theory but is too narrow for the fullness of Madison's position. The rest of the choices confuse positions Madison took on respective issues.

15. **The correct answer is (C).** Story puts his trust in the States, not the Federal Government, to be fair and equitable in dealing with the demands of religion.

16. **The correct answer is (B).** We can infer that Judge Souter's need to restate the Everson position suggests that the court dissenters, even though not responding to the full Court, have been making their point clear.

Practice Test 3

1. **The correct answer is (D).** Abe's birth in China and his subsequent lack of study allowed him to develop his particular qualities. Choice (A) may be true, but we do not have enough information in this passage to know this information.

2. **The correct answer is (E).** The author of paragraph 3 considers the novel a "transition in his career"—certainly tepid words to describe a masterpiece. Choice (B) is closest of the other choices, but the speaker is not truly indifferent.

3. **The correct answer is (C).** A careful reading of the passage contradicts choices (A), (B), (D), and (E). Abe's works capture the social impact of rapid urbanization on the individual and, thus, can be considered social commentary.

4. **The correct answer is (E).** A major film was made based on Abe's novel, and he is a fine photographer, but details in the passage reveal that he is not a filmmaker.

5. **The correct answer is (C).** Once Mario learns about the power of words and poetry, he is able to change his life for the better. Choice (E) is the closest to the best answer of the other choices; nature, sexuality, politics, and language itself are seen as source material for Neruda, but this is not the thrust of the passage's intent.

6. **The correct answer is (A).** The main points of paragraphs 2 and 3 are psychoanalytic, underlining the hidden psychological ways the characters interact and the way an attentive viewer implicitly finds meaning. All of the other choices are mentioned in the passage, but psychology is the guiding light for the entire passage.

7. **The correct answer is (E).** In paragraph 2, Mario learns to "speak" in a new way, which gives him new confidence and self-esteem, enough to change his life forever. Mario may be influenced by Neruda's politics, but this is not the primary subject of their interaction.

8. **The correct answer is (D).** Though all the other changes may, in fact, lead to an economic change, it is not stated in the passage. All of the other choices are mentioned clearly in the passage.

9. **The correct answer is (A).** In the last paragraph the speaker states the conclusion is "aesthetically unnecessary," but the fact that Massimo Troisi died so soon after the film was made underscored the pathos of the film. Choice (C) is the exact opposite of the passage's intentions.

10. **The correct answer is (B).** The thrust of paragraphs 2 and 3 is the role of the psychological father; Neruda, as good father, gives Mario the tools to succeed in the world. The other roles are important but they do not come close to the importance of the father role.

11. **The correct answer is (B).** This is actually a presidential radio address and the audience is composed of people who can influence choices (A) and (E). As a reader, you have to hear the "voice" of the speaker of the passage and figure out who his "audience" is.

12. **The correct answer is (C).** The passage suggests there will be budget surpluses. All of the other choices are stated or implied in the passage.

13. **The correct answer is (A).** The passage is tilted toward the needs of those students who have not been included in the era of budget surpluses. All of the other choices are either clearly stated in the passage or can be seen to be implied by details in the passage.

14. **The correct answer is (E).** "Attitude" refers to the speaker's voice. In this case, the speaker is appealing to a broad constituency to put pressure on the Republicans to come to a budget agreement. Using this tone of attack suggests the speaker feels he has nothing to lose by being adversarial.

Critical Reasoning

PRACTICE TEST 1

Directions: For each question in this section, select the best of the answer choices given.

The following passage applies to **Questions 1 and 2.**

An analysis of recent stock market trends reveals that for the final quarter of 1999, every increase in the Japanese stock market was followed the very next day by an increase in the U.S. stock market. Analysts conclude from this data that American investors can greatly increase their profits by using these results to buy and sell their stocks on a daily basis by closely monitoring the Japanese stock market.

1. Which of the following facts, if true, best illustrates the flaw in the stock market analysts' conclusion?

   (A) The American and Japanese stock markets have been in operation for nearly a hundred years, and trends over short periods of time are not stable predictors of future activity.

   (B) The Japanese stock market has not been in operation for as long as the American stock market has been.

   (C) The kinds of businesses whose stocks are traded on the Japanese stock market are different from the kinds of businesses whose stocks are traded on the American stock market.

   (D) Japan and the U.S. do not use the same currency, and the currency exchange rate fluctuates even from day to day.

   (E) Trends in the European stock market have followed the Japanese stock market much more closely for a longer period of time than the American trends have done.

2. Which of the following examples illustrates reasoning that is the most similar to the reasoning used in the above passage?

(A) Gamblers who follow the progress of a particular racehorse increase their bets on that horse for races after the horse has won its previous race.

(B) College and university admissions officers select students for admission to their schools based solely on the grades that the students earn in classes taken in their final year of high school.

(C) Movie producers, seeing that a star's last two movies both performed very well financially, increase investments in that star's next movie.

(D) Scientists who monitor cell growth rates predict that the injection of a growth hormone stimulant into certain areas of a new cell will dramatically increase its growth rate.

(E) Newspaper publishers increase the amounts that they charge for advertising immediately after large increases in subscription levels.

3. Leonhard Euler, respected for hundreds of years as one of the world's greatest mathematicians, created a mathematical model in 1750 to predict the growth rate of the world's population. Although accurate for about fifty years following its creation, Euler's model has proven to be inaccurate as a way of calculating recent developments in population growth.

Which of the following statements can properly be concluded from the above information?

(A) Leonhard Euler prematurely received his reputation as a great mathematician because his predictions have not been accurate.

(B) Mathematical models cannot accurately predict future trends of world population growth.

(C) The data used by Leonhard Euler to create his mathematical model was faulty.

(D) Forces that affect population growth may intervene during time to alter the effectiveness of mathematical models.

(E) The growth rate of the world population in 1750 was much lower than the growth rate of the world population in 2000.

The following passage applies to **Questions 4 and 5.**

> In northern climates, leaving potted herbs outdoors during the winter is likely to kill them. As a result, the Agriculture Department of New England has recommended that anyone growing potted herbs outdoors should bring her plants indoors no later than October 1.

4. Which of the following is an assumption that is evident in the recommendation made by the Agriculture Department of New England?

   (A) People should grow potted herbs outdoors as much as possible.
   (B) The growth of potted herbs in New England is an important part of the local economy.
   (C) Winter weather can begin in New England as early as the beginning of October.
   (D) New England does not have a climate that is conducive to the successful growth of potted herbs.
   (E) Potted herbs that are exposed to winter weather earlier than October 1 will not be killed.

5. A person who hears the recommendation of the Agriculture Department of New England and brings indoors his flowering shrubs as well as his potted herbs is making which of the following assumptions?

   (A) A flowering shrub in New England is more valuable than a potted herb.
   (B) Flowering shrubs are affected by cold weather the same way that potted herbs are affected.
   (C) Flowering shrubs are as attractive indoors as potted herbs are.
   (D) Flowering shrubs can withstand changes in temperature much longer than any other type of flowering plant.
   (E) Flowering shrubs and potted herbs are both members of the same botanical class and order.

6. If Who is the name of the first baseman on a baseball team and What is the name of the second baseman, then Idontknow is the name of the third baseman.

Which of the following statements represents an accurate conclusion based on the above information?

(A) If Who is not the first baseman's name, then Idontknow is not the third baseman's name.

(B) If Idontknow is the third baseman's name, then Who must be the first baseman.

(C) If Idontknow is not the third baseman's name, then Who is not the first baseman.

(D) If Idontknow is not the third baseman's name, then What is not the second baseman.

(E) If Idontknow is not the third baseman's name, then Who is not the first baseman and What is not the second baseman.

7. In 1824, the Swedish chemist Jons Jakob Berzelius was the first scientist to isolate the element zirconium. In 1825, Berzelius isolated the element titanium. Finally, in 1828, Berzelius isolated the element thorium. Based on these discoveries, it is evident that the chemical structure of thorium is developed by combining zirconium and titanium.

Which of the following best states the flaw in the argument as stated above?

(A) Chemistry is not an exact science, so any conclusions reached by analyzing its results must be flawed.

(B) Scientific discoveries made in chronological order are not necessarily dependent upon each other.

(C) Reports of scientific discoveries in the early nineteenth century cannot be considered reliable because record-keeping was not as thorough as it is today.

(D) The argument above does not take into account the possibility that the chemical structure of thorium may be similar to other elements not mentioned in this argument.

(E) The argument does not mention whether Berzelius collaborated with any other scientists in making his discoveries.

8. At the beginning of the 1870s, political revolts were beginning in Cuba, led by revolutionaries who wanted political freedom from Spain. In 1873, the American schooner *Virginius* was seized by Spanish officials in Cuba, and 53 members of the crew were executed.

   Which of the following is the best illustration of an assumption made by the Spanish officials?

   (A) The Spanish officials believed that the crew members of the schooner *Virginius* were somehow involved in the political uprisings.

   (B) The Spanish officials were opposed to the political revolts and wanted Cuba to remain a colony of Spain.

   (C) The Spanish officials believed that executing American sailors would serve as an effective example to the political revolutionaries in Cuba.

   (D) The Spanish officials believed that America was attempting to exert political and military power over Cuba in the 1870s.

   (E) The Spanish officials believed that America wanted to take over Cuba as a colony for its own.

9. In 1566, members of a Jesuit religious order arrived in Florida and established a mission. The following year, typhoid fever killed two million Indians in South America.

   Concluding that the Jesuits were responsible for the typhoid among the South American Indians would require which of the following assumptions?

   (A) The Indians of South America were more susceptible to contracting the typhoid disease than other ethnic groups.

   (B) There were no Indian groups living in Florida at the time that the Jesuits arrived in 1566.

   (C) Typhoid did not exist in either North or South America before 1566.

   (D) Typhoid is an illness that is highly contagious and often fatal.

   (E) The Indian groups that lived in South America in the sixteenth century became extinct because of the typhoid epidemic.

The following passage applies to **Questions 10 and 11.**

A tax claim becomes secured on the date that it is recorded, if it is recorded after it is assessed. If a tax claim is assessed but never recorded, then it will not be secured. A tax claim that is recorded before it is assessed will become secured when it is assessed.

10. If a certain tax claim was recorded on February 1, 2000, which of the following can be concluded?

    (A) The tax claim has not been assessed until after February 1, 2000.

    (B) The tax claim was assessed sometime before February 1, 2000.

    (C) The tax claim could not be secured until after February 1, 2000, or later.

    (D) The tax claim becomes secured on February 1, 2000.

    (E) The tax claim will not be secured.

11. If a certain tax claim is secured, then which of the following must be true?

    (A) The claim has been assessed first and then recorded.

    (B) The claim has been recorded first and then assessed.

    (C) The claim has been either assessed or recorded, but not both.

    (D) The claim has been both assessed and recorded, in either order.

    (E) The claim has been recorded but not assessed.

12. During the past five years, student athletes at Union High School have consistently received higher grades than student athletes at any other school in the state. During the same time period, student athletes at Smith High School have consistently received lower grades than student athletes at any other school in the state. In order to achieve a level of academic equality throughout the state, the state school board should transfer the head coaches for all sports from Union High School to Smith High School next year.

Which of the following statements, if true, would most effectively weaken the above argument?

    (A) The grade point average for the entire student body of Smith High School has been higher than that of the entire student body of Union High School over the past five years.

    (B) The head coaches at all schools in the state do not teach any classes but are hired solely to perform their coaching duties.

    (C) The head coaches at Smith High School have been employed for an average of ten years longer than the head coaches at Union High School.

    (D) The athletic teams at Smith High School have higher winning percentages over the past five years than the teams at Union High School.

    (E) Union High School has twice as many students enrolled than Smith High School has.

13. One economic analyst, studying the levels of trade between England and China, has identified a trend toward increased importation into England of textiles and cloth made in China. Over the past ten years alone, the level of these materials made in China and sold in England has doubled. Therefore, the analyst predicts from this data that within the next ten years, the level of the textiles and cloth originating in China and sold in England will double again.

Which of the following statements, if true, most effectively supports the analyst's prediction?

(A) Chinese cloth products are generally recognized as being of a higher quality than the same products made in any other country.

(B) Economic trends in international trade generally remain stable over long periods of time.

(C) England and China have never been enemies in any international military conflict.

(D) The standard of living in China is much lower than in England, so that the cost of labor and, therefore, cost of the products coming from China will be much lower.

(E) The science of predicting trends in international trade has become much more accurate in recent years than when it began approximately 100 years ago.

PRACTICE TEST 2

Directions: For each question in this section, select the best of the answer choices given.

1. Acme Corporation just installed a system that will provide the company and its customers with access to a new Internet service that will increase Acme's computer speed by 100 times. For the past year, Acme's income was approximately $200,000. Acme now expects its income for the next year to increase by 100 times to approximately $20,000,000.

   Which of the following statements, if true, weakens Acme's conclusion about its future income?

   (A) Based on consumer questionnaires, most of Acme's customers now own computers and use the Internet to gain access to companies in order to buy products and services.

   (B) The system that increases Acme's computer speed is the most popular computer system sold to businesses in the past year and most of Acme's competitors now use the same system.

   (C) Three quarters of Acme's income is derived from sales that occur in the Acme showroom, from face-to-face meetings between customers and salesclerks.

   (D) In the past year, Acme has increased its use of the Internet as a sales tool and as a method of advertising products to its customers.

   (E) Internet use as a marketing tool has increased significantly worldwide in the past year.

2. A recent article in a leading medical journal reports that a statistical study has shown a connection between baldness in men and men suffering increased rates of heart disease. Specifically, because the rates of heart disease occurring in balding men are higher than in men not experiencing baldness, the editors of the medical journal recommend a course of action for balding men to lower their risk of heart disease.

    Which of the following, if true, indicates a flaw in the reasoning of the journal's editors?

    (A) The study that is the subject of the article was performed only on subjects from a single state.

    (B) Additional genetics studies have been unable to demonstrate conclusively that baldness in men is hereditary.

    (C) In the past ten years, heart disease and complications arising from it have killed more men than women.

    (D) The data for the study was collected only through questionnaires that the participating men completed by themselves, without involvement of doctors.

    (E) Heart disease in men has been shown to have a cause that is unrelated to the factors that cause baldness.

3. An invasion of alien attackers is attempting to take control of the world. If the attackers can take control of Asia, they will then also control Europe. If they can control Europe, they will control Africa. They will not get control of South America unless they first control both Asia and Africa. If they control Asia, Africa, and South America, they will control North America.

    According to the above argument, which of the following statements can be concluded if the attackers control both Asia and Africa?

    (A) The attackers also control South America.
    (B) The attackers also control North America.
    (C) The attackers also control Europe.
    (D) The attackers do not control North America.
    (E) The attackers do not control South America.

4. All students in public schools are guaranteed the right to a free and appropriate education. For children with various physical challenges or handicaps, determining what kind of education is "appropriate" can often lead to litigation between the parents of the child and the school district. Requiring parents to pay for these litigation costs would undermine the requirement that the appropriate education be provided for "free." There-fore, the public school district should be required to pay all litigation costs whenever parents of handicapped children challenge the education being provided.

Which of the following statements, if true, most seriously weakens the above argument?

(A) Parents of handicapped children often have many other additional expenses, including higher levels of health-care and medical equipment, that they need to pay.

(B) Over the past five years, 75 percent of all the challenges raised in courts by parents of handicapped children have been decided in favor of the school districts.

(C) Public school districts employ child psychologists whose job is to study and evaluate the children with special educational needs.

(D) School districts already spend at least one quarter of the annual budget to provide additional educational tools and equipment for handicapped children.

(E) School principals and other administrators are charged with the task of overseeing the progress of all of the students in their schools to help identify those with special educational needs.

5. Women should not serve in the military in active duty combat roles because women cannot perform all of the same physical tasks that men can. Because men are genetically larger and stronger, only men should be allowed to participate in active duty combat roles.

Which of the following statements, if true, provides the most support for the above argument?

(A) For the entire history of armed conflict in the world, only men have participated in active combat roles.
(B) Modern military conflict involves many more electronic, computerized tools, and weapons than ever before, so that coordination and skill are better indicators of an ability to succeed than sheer strength.
(C) Cultural biases and traditions support the limitations on placing women in active combat roles because women are traditionally pictured as more nurturing and caring individuals.
(D) Advances in electronic technology have resulted in additional equipment that soldiers in combat positions are required to carry, increasing the size and weight of handheld weapons and backpacks.
(E) Psychological tests have shown that women better demonstrate the characteristics that are recognized as essential for leadership positions.

6. The fat content of a company's brand of salted potato chips is equal to the fat content of the same company's unsalted potato chips. Because salt is a molecule that is a combination of sodium and chloride and the human body requires sodium for correct functioning of cell membranes, it is logical to conclude that people should select salted potato chips over unsalted potato chips.

Which of the following, if true, weakens the above argument?

(A) Sodium atoms undergo a chemical change when they join with chloride atoms, so that the sodium atoms in a salt molecule do not operate the same way as free sodium atoms do.
(B) Not everyone who eats potato chips has any medical requirements that limit their allowable levels of fat or sodium intake.
(C) Potato chips are not considered a "health food," according to a list published by the Food and Drug Administration.
(D) The cell membranes inside the human body function adequately with sodium levels with a range from 5 to 50 parts per million.
(E) The company in question has produced salted potato chips for many more years than it has produced unsalted potato chips.

7. Republican and democratic senators argued extensively over an increase in the national minimum wage salary. The democrats argued that the minimum wage needs to be increased by at least fifty cents each year for the next three years in order to keep up with the current rate of inflation. The republicans responded that no increase was necessary because the current level of the minimum wage salary is sufficient to keep a family of four, if both parents earned minimum wage for 40 hours per week, well above the federal poverty limit.

Which of the following statements, if true, would most strengthen the democrats' position on the issue of the minimum wage increase?

(A) The federal poverty limit is scaled so that the required income level increases for larger families.

(B) The last increase in the federal minimum wage salary level was more than five years ago.

(C) The president, who is a democrat, has stated that he will veto any additional spending proposals unless Congress first increases the minimum wage salary.

(D) The federal poverty limit is set well below the average standard of living and is not considered adequate for a family to live on.

(E) The size of the average family in America has been declining over the past decade, so that instead of four members it is down to three.

8. The concentration of a certain chemical in the bloodstream is increased during peak levels of physical exertion and is decreased when the body is at rest. To obtain accurate measurements of that chemical, therefore, doctors require patients to remain seated and motionless for at least 30 minutes before giving blood for the test.

The requirements of the doctors indicate that they are making which of the following assumptions?

(A) Measuring the level of this particular chemical in the bloodstream is an important part of a thorough physical examination.

(B) The amount of time required for the chemical's concentration to reach a resting level can vary widely in different people.

(C) The concentration of the chemical is best measured at low levels.

(D) Thirty minutes is the longest time necessary for a patient's heartbeat to reach a stable, resting level.

(E) The measurement of this chemical varies greatly among people with different levels of activity.

9. If Bill forgets his watch when he leaves the house to go to work, then he is late for all his meetings that day. If Bill is not late for his noon meeting, then he always goes out to the park at lunchtime. Today is Tuesday, and Bill forgot to take his watch with him to work.

Which of the following statements must be true, based on the above statements?

(A) Bill will be going to the park at lunchtime today.
(B) Bill will not be going to the park today.
(C) Bill will be late for his noon meeting.
(D) Bill was not late when he left the house.
(E) Bill was late when he left the house.

10. A particular construction project needs two operating loading machines in order to complete a job in one day. Today, Davis, one of the loading machine operators, is sick and cannot work. Therefore, the project will not be completed in one day.

Which of the following is an assumption that provides the basis for the above conclusion?

(A) The company will lose money if the project is not completed in one day.
(B) Davis is the best person to operate the loading machine.
(C) No other worker is available to operate the loading machine during Davis's absence.
(D) Davis's illness is very serious and his doctor ordered him to stay in bed.
(E) One loading machine working alone cannot complete the job in one day.

11. Channel 6 advertises that it has the most local news reporting in the city. Assuming that this claim is true, it is obvious that someone who wants to learn as much as possible about the day's news should watch Channel 6.

Which of the following statements would most effectively weaken the above argument?

(A) The city only has two stations that present any news broadcasts.
(B) Channel 6 broadcasts more sporting events and comedies than any other station in the city.
(C) Channel 6's claim is based only on the number of times the news is broadcast, including repeats of the same news reports.
(D) No other channel claims to broadcast as much news as Channel 6 does.
(E) Not everyone in the city cares about watching the news.

12. If one plus two equals three, then three plus two equals four. Three plus two does not equal four.

What can be concluded from the above statements?

(A) Three plus two equals five.
(B) One plus two equals three.
(C) One plus two does not equal three.
(D) Three plus two is greater than one plus two.
(E) Three is greater than one.

13. Since 1992, the ratings for conservative radio talk shows must have declined. In 1992, when the ratings for conservative radio talk shows reported their highest ratings as of that date, 67 percent of the population voted for a republican candidate in the national election. However, in the 1996 national election, only 39 percent of the population voted for a republican candidate.

Which of the following indicates an assumption made in the above argument?

(A) The policies proposed by the republican candidates in 1992 have not had their promised effects.
(B) The income level of the average household declined steadily between 1992 and 1996.
(C) Hosts of conservative radio talk shows encourage their listeners to vote for republican candidates.
(D) The total number of people listening to all radio talk shows in 1996 was lower than the number of people listening to all radio talk shows in 1992.
(E) The success of republican candidates in national elections is a direct indication of the listening audience for conservative radio talk shows.

PRACTICE TEST 3

1. Brand X disinfectant spray claims to be the best spray available because it kills germs faster than Brand Y and because it does not leave a soapy film the way Brand Y does.

   If Brand X's claim is true, then which of the following can properly be concluded?

   (A) Brand Y must be cheaper than Brand X.
   (B) Brand X must sell more bottles than Brand Y.
   (C) Brand Y is better than any of the other competing brands that were not mentioned in the argument.
   (D) Brand X and Brand Y combined sell more bottles than all other brands combined.
   (E) Killing germs is important to preventing colds and other illnesses.

2. David always wakes up before sunrise unless the sun rises before 6:00. Lisa does not wake up before David does if David wakes up before sunrise.

   On a day when the sun rises at 5:30, which of the following must be true?

   (A) David will wake up at 6:00.
   (B) Lisa will not wake up until 7:00.
   (C) Lisa will not wake up before David.
   (D) David will not wake up before sunrise.
   (E) David and Lisa will both wake up at the same time.

3. Any movie starring Clark Gable will win an Academy Award, but no movie starring Clark Gable will ever earn more than $5 million from ticket sales. Some movies that earn more than $5 million from ticket sales are directed by Alfred Hitchcock.

   Which of the following conclusions must be true, based on the above statements?

   (A) No movie directed by Alfred Hitchcock will win an Academy Award.
   (B) Some movies directed by Alfred Hitchcock may star Clark Gable.
   (C) Some movies earning more than $5 million in ticket sales may star Clark Gable.
   (D) No movie starring Clark Gable will win an Academy Award.
   (E) All movies directed by Alfred Hitchcock will win an Academy Award.

4. Harry's dog barks every time she hears the footsteps of a person walking toward his house. Therefore, Harry feels very secure at home because he knows his dog will warn him if an intruder approaches.

   This conclusion makes which of the following assumptions?

   (A) The dog would provide good protection after an intruder enters the house.
   (B) The dog will hear any intruder who approaches.
   (C) The dog has received special training as a guard dog.
   (D) Harry lives in a dangerous area.
   (E) Some intruders may not be people.

5. A review of a book on the origins of the science of geometry makes the assertion, "Seeing that so much of Greek is mathematics, it is arguable that, if one would understand the Greek genius fully, one must begin with understanding their geometry."

   Accepting this statement to be true, which of the following can be concluded?

   (A) Someone who understands Greek genius fully will be able to solve geometry problems.
   (B) The study of geometry began in the ancient Greek culture.
   (C) Geometry is the most historically important branch of mathematics.
   (D) Someone who does not understand geometry will not fully understand Greek genius.
   (E) Greek culture and Greek geometry are tightly interconnected.

6. In any year that Springfield Academy's boys soccer team wins at least ten games, the team will get to play in the championship tournament that year. If Springfield Academy's boys soccer team does not play in the championship tournament in any year, the school will lose alumni funding support the following year. In 1996, Springfield Academy received more alumni funding support than in any of the five previous years.

   Which of the following statements about Springfield Academy must be true?

   (A) The boys soccer team won at least ten games in 1996.
   (B) The boys soccer team played in the championship tournament in 1996.
   (C) The boys soccer team did not play in the championship tournament in 1995.
   (D) The boys soccer team won more than ten games in 1995.
   (E) The boys soccer team played in the championship tournament in 1995.

7. When Alice's husband gets home from work before she does, he has a habit of feeding their dog. Today, Alice had to work late, and her husband got home before she did. Therefore, Alice believes that her husband already fed their dog.

    Which of the following is an assumption that provides the basis for the above conclusion?

    (A) The dog needs to be fed every day.
    (B) Alice usually gets home before her husband does.
    (C) Alice's husband followed his usual habit today.
    (D) Alice had no opportunity to leave work earlier.
    (E) Alice's job is more important than her husband's job.

8. Students and alumni of England College have become tired of their school's bad reputation. To combat this problem, members of the board of trustees of England College have proposed changing the name of the school to American College.

    Which of the following statements, if true, points out the greatest flaw in the board's reasoning?

    (A) There already is a school in the same area named American College.
    (B) The name England College originated from David England, a hero of the American Revolutionary War and founder of the college.
    (C) England College has the highest rate of violent crime on campus among schools of its size.
    (D) Two other colleges have recently changed their names.
    (E) A poll of the school's students and alumni indicates that most of them would not vote in favor of changing the school's name.

9. The president of the Parent-Teacher Organization for Reasoner Elementary School has proposed a budget for the school that is balanced for the first time in three years. However, the president's budget eliminates some funding that the Parent-Teacher Organization used to provide to the Reasoner Elementary School to support school lunch programs for under-privileged students. It is clear, therefore, that the new budget will result in leaving many children without food.

Which of the following statements, if true, would weaken the above argument?

(A) The president's proposed budget also includes a decrease in tuition that parents of all students at the school had been required to pay into the school lunch program, regardless of whether their children took advantage of the lunch program.

(B) The president and the leaders of the PTO belong to different political parties.

(C) The president's budget is not likely to be accepted by the principal of the school or by the school board.

(D) The school lunch program began three years ago, the last time any PTO president proposed a balanced budget.

(E) The number of children using the school lunch program has declined for each of the past three years.

10. If National Financing does not agree to lend money to Enterprise, Inc., then Enterprise, Inc., will be forced to go out of business. Enterprise, Inc., cannot continue its operations without receiving temporary loans of at least $200,000 each month.

Which of the following statements, if true, would most strengthen the conclusion of the above argument?

(A) National Financing is the only company from which Enterprise, Inc., could receive any financial assistance.

(B) Enterprise, Inc., provides a service that is essential to many local businesses.

(C) While operating, Enterprise, Inc., can generate a monthly profit of more than $20,000.

(D) Enterprise, Inc., and National Financing are corporations from different states.

(E) The president of Enterprise, Inc., is also the president of National Financing.

11. In many large cities, dentists have been refusing to treat low-income or uninsured patients without receiving cash payment for services in advance. As a result, many people who need dental care are not receiving it. If this trend continues, society will be faced with a large portion of the population needing serious medical treatment. The legislature should pass a law to require dentists to treat patients whose annual income is below a certain minimum level, regardless of their immediate ability to pay.

    Which of the following statements, if true, would most effectively strengthen the above argument?

    (A) Many people in all parts of the country do not get dental insurance, whether or not they can afford it.
    (B) Dental care is not as essential as other forms of medical care.
    (C) The American Medical Society recently released the results of a study that links the infection that causes cavities with a form of blood disease.
    (D) Many dentists practicing in urban neighborhoods have begun instituting creative payment plans that allow their patients to work for the dentist to pay off their bills.
    (E) Every member of the legislature has an annual income that is well above the minimum level being proposed for the new legislation.

12. Only residents of Mountain City may be members of the City Zoning Board. Kevin is not a member of the City Zoning Board, so he must not be a resident of Mountain City.

    Which of the following statements is a hidden assumption in the above argument?

    (A) Kevin did not want to become a member of the City Zoning Board.
    (B) All residents of Mountain City automatically become members of the City Zoning Board.
    (C) The City Zoning Board requires a significant time commitment that many people cannot afford.
    (D) Kevin would like to be on the City Zoning Board.
    (E) Mountain City is considered a desirable place to live.

13. If the Silver Flyer, a train going to Chicago, leaves Philadelphia on time, then it will arrive in Chicago on time. If the train arrives in Chicago on time, then it always arrives in Los Angeles on time. Last Tuesday, the Silver Flyer arrived late in Chicago.

Which of the following is a valid conclusion based on the above statements?

(A) The Silver Flyer did not leave Philadelphia on time.
(B) The Silver Flyer was late leaving Chicago on its way to Los Angeles.
(C) The Silver Flyer arrived in Los Angeles on time.
(D) The Silver Flyer arrived late in Los Angeles.
(E) The Silver Flyer had mechanical problems during the trip from Philadelphia to Chicago.

Quick Score Answers

Critical Reasoning

Practice Test 1		Practice Test 2		Practice Test 3	
1. A	8. A	1. C	8. C	1. A	8. C
2. C	9. C	2. E	9. C	2. D	9. A
3. D	10. C	3. C	10. C	3. B	10. A
4. C	11. D	4. B	11. C	4. B	11. C
5. B	12. A	5. D	12. C	5. D	12. B
6. E	13. B	6. A	13. E	6. E	13. A
7. B		7. D		7. C	

ANSWERS AND EXPLANATIONS

CRITICAL REASONING

Practice Test 1

1. **The correct answer is (A).** The analysts' conclusion is based on the assumption that the U.S. stock market always follows the Japanese stock market, and that this trend will continue in the future. The first answer, choice (A), says that this assumption is incorrect, since trends over short periods of time are not suitable for predicting future activity. Each of the remaining choices, although statements that may be true, do not directly address this issue of future predictions.

2. **The correct answer is (C).** The initial argument suggests that by watching a recent trend, one can predict success in the future. This suggests that the answer could be either choice (A), (B), or (C). Choices (D) and (E) are incorrect because they are not predictions based on past performance but rather are predictions based on some other outside force. Of these three remaining choices, choice (C) is the best because it is the only one that considers the future performance of some new product, the new film, which presumably will have new writers, directors, cast, etc.; whereas the racehorse and student of choices (A) and (B) remain the same. Thus, choice (C) is the best analogy to the changing characteristics of the stock market, using past performance to try to predict a changing commodity in the future.

3. **The correct answer is (D).** Choice (A) is incorrect because one cannot conclude that Euler was not a great mathematician simply because one mathematical model has proven to be inaccurate. This choice does not account for all his other work. Choice (B) is incorrect because it is overly broad, lumping together all mathematical models; even though this one model has proven inaccurate, other models may work perfectly well. Choices (C) and (E) are incorrect because they are not supported by the argument, as nothing is said at all about the data or the actual growth rates. Therefore, by elimination, choice (D) remains as a statement of the "recent developments in population growth" that have made the model inaccurate.

ANSWERS AND EXPLANATIONS

4. **The correct answer is (C).** The recommendation links the phrase *winter weather* from choice (C), with the date at the beginning of October, showing an assumption that in New England, the winter weather can begin as early as the beginning of October. Thus, choice (C) is the best answer. Choices (A) and (B) are incorrect because they assume facts that are not part of the argument. Choice (D) goes beyond the scope of the argument, because nothing in the argument provides any information about growing potted herbs at other times of the year. Finally, choice (E) is incorrect because the argument does not give any information about the possibility of winter weather occurring before October first.

5. **The correct answer is (B).** A person who treats a flowering shrub the same way a potted herb is treated is assuming that the two plants are affected by the weather the same way. Thus, choice (B) is the best answer. Choices (A) and (C) make value judgments that are unsupported by the argument. Choice (D) not only adds facts that are not part of the argument, but also suggests that someone would NOT treat the two plants in the same way. Choice (E), although seeming to suggest that the two plants are similar, is incorrect because it adds facts that are not part of the argument and does not address the question as directly as choice (B) does.

6. **The correct answer is (E).** This argument presents two initial conditions, that Who and What be playing at first and second base, respectively; leading to one conclusion, that Idontknow will be playing at third base. If BOTH of the conditions are true, then the conclusion will follow. If the conclusion is not occurring, then BOTH of the initial conditions must not be true. In this particular argument, choices (A) and (B) are incorrect because the argument does not say that the only way for Idontknow to be at third base is for the initial conditions to be true. Choices (C) and (D) are similar to each other, but neither one is complete, because they only refer to one half of the initial condition. Choice (E) is correct, by connecting the conclusion to both of the initial conditions.

7. **The correct answer is (B).** The argument makes the common error that the timing of the three discoveries in chronological order—first one, then the second, then the third—implies that the third discovery was a result of or was caused by the earlier ones. While that may be true, such a conclusion, based solely on the chronological timing, is invalid. (Example: This morning, I took my umbrella to work, and at noon it began to rain. Therefore, I *incorrectly* conclude that taking my umbrella causes the rain.) Choice (B) is the best statement of this logical flaw.

8. **The correct answer is (A).** The officials who captured and killed the crew apparently connected the crew of that ship to the political uprisings. Thus, choice (A) is the best answer. All of the other statements may be true, but they do not directly explain the actions of the Spanish officials against the particular crew members of that ship.

9. **The correct answer is (C).** To conclude that the Jesuits are responsible for bringing and transferring the disease, one must eliminate any other possible source of the disease. Therefore, choice (C) is the best answer for a required assumption. If the disease had existed on the continents in question before the arrival of the Jesuits in 1566, then it may have been spread by means completely unrelated to the Jesuits. Choice (A) is incorrect because it assumes unnecessary facts, since nothing in the argument depends upon "other ethnic groups." Choice (B) is incorrect because the existence of other Indian groups is irrelevant to the argument. Choice (D) and (E) may both be true statements but do not directly link the Jesuits' arrival with this particular epidemic.

10. **The correct answer is (C).** The argument uses somewhat convoluted language but basically says that a claim has two requirements, recording and assessing, and that the claim will be secured after both of those have occurred, but not before. Therefore, knowing the date of recording, but not knowing about assessing, one can only conclude that the claim cannot be secured until on or after the recording date. This is a restatement of choice (C), which is the correct answer. Choices (A) and (B) cannot be concluded because the date of recording gives no information about the date of assessment. Choices (D) and (E) cannot be concluded because, without knowing both the assessment date and the recording date, one cannot make a particular conclusion about the secured tax claim. (Note that it does not matter if you understand the issues about tax claims, recording, etc. You just need to follow the logic of the words in the argument.)

11. **The correct answer is (D).** As noted in the previous answer, a claim must be both recorded and assessed in order to be secured. However, nothing in the argument requires that either one of these steps occur first. Therefore, choice (D) must be the answer.

12. **The correct answer is (A).** Transferring the coaches according to the proposal would require an assumption that the coaches are the ones responsible for the academic level of each school. Choice (A) is the best statement to weaken this assumption, by showing that the overall academic ability of the students at the two schools cannot be measured by the student-athletes alone; as a result, the coaching staff appears irrelevant. The remaining choices are all irrelevant because they do not directly address the academic performances of the students.

13. **The correct answer is (B).** The prediction assumes that the performance during the preceding ten years will be a good indication of the performance for the next ten years. Choice (B) best strengthens this conclusion by giving information to support the assumption. Choices (A) and (D) both provide an explanation for the past performance but do not support making a prediction that the performance will continue into the future. Choice (C) is entirely irrelevant to the argument. Choice (E) somewhat supports the prediction, but it is not as directly tied to the argument as choice (B) is.

Practice Test 2

1. **The correct answer is (C).** The argument rests on the assumption that the increase in computer speed will directly increase income by the same ratio. To weaken this argument, a statement must show that Acme's income does not depend directly on the computer. Choice (C) does this by showing that three quarters of Acme's income is not related to computer use. Choice (A) does not directly address Acme's income levels or methods of sale. Choice (B) says more about Acme's competitors than about Acme itself. Choice (D) does not link the increased use of the Internet to the amount of sales. In any event, choice (D) would strengthen, not weaken, the argument. Choice (E) supports the increase in income, but does not directly make any statement about Acme.

2. **The correct answer is (E).** The argument assumes that because baldness and heart disease appear to be statistically linked in the men participating in the study, then baldness and heart disease must be linked medically. To effectively weaken this argument, a statement must show that baldness and heart disease are not casually linked. Choice (E) accomplishes this by stating that heart disease has unrelated causes. Choices (A) and (D) attack the validity of the study, but not as directly as choice (E) does. Choice (B) makes a statement about baldness only, so it is not complete enough to weaken the argument about baldness and heart disease. Choice (C) is wrong for the same reason, except that it addresses only the heart disease issue.

3. **The correct answer is (C).** All of the statements *could* possibly be true under the right circumstances, but the only one that can logically be concluded using only the information that the attackers control Asia and Africa is choice (C), that the attackers control Europe. The second sentence of the argument says that if the attackers control Asia, they also control Europe. Therefore, choice (C) is correct. Choice (A) is possibly true but cannot be concluded. The word *unless* in the fourth sentence of the argument does not mean that controlling Asia and Africa will automatically lead to control of South America; it merely means that control of South America is possible, but there may be other requirements not given in this argument. Because control of South America cannot be assured, then control of North America cannot be assured either, so choice (B) is incorrect. Choices (D) and (E) are both incorrect because control of North America and South America could be possible but cannot be conclusively determined.

4. **The correct answer is (B).** The argument assumes that the parents' litigation costs are a necessary part of having a handicapped child. However, choice (B) suggests that the litigation costs may have been brought on by the parents themselves, as the challenges may be without merit since they are decided in favor of the schools. Choice (B) weakens the argument by showing that the school is not responsible, in most cases, for the parents' litigation costs. Choice (A) is incorrect because it does not focus on litigation costs or the school's involvement in the child's education. Choices (C) and (E) somewhat weaken the argument by showing that the school is already taking steps to identify special needs. However, these statements do not directly address the issue of litigation costs. Choice (D) is incorrect because it is irrelevant. The argument does not depend at all on other costs that the school may be incurring.

5. **The correct answer is (D).** The argument claims that women should be excluded from combat because men have greater physical size and strength. To strengthen this argument, therefore, the correct answer would have to show that size and strength are required elements. Choice (D) correctly makes this statement. Choices (A) and (C) are statements that suggest limiting women's roles, but not for reasons related to the argument given. So choice (D) is better. Choice (B) actually weakens the argument, suggesting that size and strength would not be important factors. Choice (E) is irrelevant because it does not relate to the positions in combat or the factors of size and strength.

6. **The correct answer is (A).** The argument makes the assumption that sodium is required for bodily functioning, so people should choose the salted potato chips to get the sodium from the salt. Choice (A) challenges this assumption and weakens the argument by showing that the sodium in salted potato chips is not useful for cell membrane functioning, so whether potato chips are salted or not is irrelevant to cell membrane function. Choices (B), (C), and (E) all are irrelevant to the argument because they do not address all of the issues involved in the argument. Choice (D) is close, but without knowing what the level of sodium is that comes from salted potato chips, the information in (D) is not helpful.

7. **The correct answer is (D).** The republican argument is that the poverty limit should be the measuring tool to decide if salaries are sufficient. Choice (D) challenges this argument and, therefore, strengthens the democrat argument by showing that the poverty limit is not a good measuring tool. Choices (A) and (B) are irrelevant without additional information about the actual amount of the income level. Choice (C) suggests that increasing the limit is necessary for the spending proposal to pass, but it does not attack the actual issue of the argument, which is the adequacy of the minimum wage. Choice (E), if true, actually supports the republican argument, since the minimum wage is said to support a family of four, but the average family size is actually smaller.

8. **The correct answer is (C).** The doctors know that the chemical level decreases when the body is at rest and they choose to take measurements after a resting period. This suggests that the doctors assume that the chemical is best measured at low levels, which is choice (C). Choice (A) is incorrect because the reason for the measurement is irrelevant to the argument. Choices (B) or (D) may be true statements, but no information is provided in the argument about the range of possible resting times, and therefore, neither answer is as good as choice (C). Choice (E) is incorrect because no information is provided about the actual amount of the measurement.

9. **The correct answer is (C).** The only logical conclusion is choice (C), that Bill will be late for his noon meeting, because the first sentence of the argument says that without his watch, Bill will be late for all his meetings. All of the other answer choices are statements that might or might not be true, but none of them can definitively be concluded from the information given.

10. **The correct answer is (C).** If the project cannot be completed because Davis cannot work, this suggests that Davis is irreplaceable. This suggests that choice (C) is the correct assumption. Choice (B) is very close to this answer, except it ignores the fact that some other worker may not be as good as Davis, but could still get the job done. Choices (A) and (D) are irrelevant to the problem and choice (E) merely repeats the first sentence of the problem.

11. **The correct answer is (C).** Channel 6's conclusion depends upon the interpretation of the phrase "the most local news." If choice (C) is correct, then someone watching Channel 6 news might just see the same news reports repeatedly and would not "learn as much as possible." Choice (A) is incorrect because, even though there is only one other station, that station may or may not broadcast more news than Channel 6. Choice (B) is incorrect because no relationship between sports, comedies, and movies is suggested. Choice (D) is incorrect because the claims of other stations are not discussed, only the actual news broadcasts. Finally, choice (E) is simply irrelevant to the amount of news that Channel 6 broadcasts.

12. **The correct answer is (C).** Because the second sentence says that the conclusion of the first sentence is false, then it can be concluded that the premise of the first sentence must also be false. Therefore, it can be concluded that one plus two does not equal three. This is choice (C). The other choices all seem to make "common sense" and seem to be true following the standard rules of mathematics, but they do not follow the rule given in this problem.

13. **The correct answer is (E).** The conclusion here is that a decline in votes for republicans can indicate a decline in ratings for conservative radio talk shows. This assumes that election results and radio ratings are directly related, as stated in choice (E). The other answer choices all make statements that are close to the topic but are not directly assumed.

Practice Test 3

1. **The correct answer is (A).** Because the Brand X claim only compares Brand X to Brand Y, and Brand X claims to be "the best" simply because it is better than Brand Y, then one can conclude that Brand Y must be the best of all of Brand X's competition. Therefore, choice (C) must be the correct answer. None of the statements about sales can be concluded since there is nothing in the argument that links quality of the product to actual sales levels. Finally, choice (E), although it may be correct, is irrelevant to this argument, which is strictly about the relative qualities of Brands X and Y.

2. **The correct answer is (D).** From the first sentence, if the sun rises before 6:00, then it can be concluded that David will not wake up before sunrise.

3. **The correct answer is (B).** Nothing in the two sentences of the problem directly links Gable and Hitchcock. Therefore, it is possible that the two could be linked, so choice (B) is correct. (Note that choice (B) does not say that *any* movies directed by Hitchcock *are* starring Gable; just that they could.) Choices (A) and (E) are incorrect because there is no link between Hitchcock and the Academy Awards. Choices (C) and (D) directly contradict the first sentence, so they are incorrect.

4. **The correct answer is (B).** Based on the first sentence, the dog will bark when she "hears" footsteps. The conclusion of the argument depends on the dog's hearing, suggesting choice (B). Choice (A) is incorrect because the problem only focuses on the situation of intruders as they approach the house, not after they enter. Choices (C), (D), and (E) are all irrelevant because they introduce facts that are not part of the problem.

5. **The correct answer is (D).** The argument establishes that understanding geometry is a requirement to understand Greek genius; without geometry, one cannot understand Greek genius. This is the statement contained in choice (D), which is the best answer. Choice (A) is very close, but presents the statement backward; instead of showing that an understanding of geometry is a requirement to understanding Greek genius, choice (A) shows it as a result. Choices (B), (C), and (E) all make unsupportable statements about connecting geometry or mathematics in general to Greek culture. These are incorrect because nothing in the argument makes this connection.

6. **The correct answer is (E).** Since the funding in 1996 was high, it can be concluded from the second sentence that the team must have been in the championship tournament in the preceding year, 1995. This is choice (E). Choices (A) and (B) are incorrect because they address the wrong year. Choice (C) directly contradicts the correct answer. Choice (D) is incorrect because the rule says the team must win "at least" ten games, not "more than ten."

7. **The correct answer is (C).** The key word to this problem is the word "habit" in the first sentence. Alice assumes that her husband follows his usual routine, so choice (C) is the best answer. None of the other answers is supported by anything in the problem.

8. **The correct answer is (C).** The people who are in favor of changing the name appear to assume that the name is the cause of the bad reputation. Choice (C), by suggesting another reason for the bad reputation, would weaken this conclusion. The other choices all may or may not be true, but do not directly address the assumption made in the problem.

9. **The correct answer is (A).** This problem assumes that if the PTO does not continue to put money into the school lunch program, then no money will be provided from any other source. Choice (A) would leave the families whose children attend the school with more money, presumably allowing them to put more money into the program, thereby weakening the conclusion of the argument. The other answer choices all make statements about topics that are not addressed in the problem so they are irrelevant.

10. **The correct answer is (A).** The conclusion assumes that National Financing is the only possible source of funding. Choice (A), by repeating this assumption, strengthens the argument. Choice (B) is incorrect because the survival of Enterprise, Inc., is not directly related to the importance of its services, at least as described in this problem. Choice (C) may appear to be relevant but does not address the problem of receiving monthly financing. Choices (D) and (E) may be true statements about the two corporations, but they do not mention the problem of financing.

11. **The correct answer is (C).** The argument claims that insufficient dental care will lead to more serious medical problems. Choice (C) provides one example of such a problem occurring, so it strengthens the argument. Choice (A) is incorrect because it is irrelevant; even if it is true that "many people" choose not to get insurance, this does not affect the argument that many people want insurance but cannot get it. Choice (B) is incorrect because it merely contradicts one of the statements of the argument. Choice (D) is incorrect because it actually weakens the argument by showing that there are other ways, besides new legislation, that could solve the problem. Choice (E) is incorrect because the income levels of the legislators is simply irrelevant to the argument.

12. **The correct answer is (B).** The conclusion here assumes that if Kevin were a member of the Zoning Board, then he would also be a resident of Mountain City. This suggests that all residents of Mountain City are members of the Zoning Board, which is choice (B). Choices (A), (C), and (D) are incorrect because the members' desires do not appear to be relevant. Choice (E) is not suggested at all by the problem.

13. **The correct answer is (A).** The argument sets up as a given statement that, if the Silver Flyer leaves Philadelphia on time, then it will always arrive in Chicago on time. Therefore, by arriving late, it is logical to conclude that it must have left Philadelphia late, so the answer is choice (A). All of the other answer choices are statements that may or may not be true, but they cannot be logically concluded from the information given in the argument.

Quantitative

PRACTICE TEST 1

PROBLEM SOLVING

> **Directions:** In this section solve each problem using any available space on the page for scratch work. Then indicate the best of all the answer choices given.
>
> **Numbers:** All numbers used are real numbers.
>
> **Figures:** Figures that accompany problems in the text are intended to provide information useful in solving the problems. They are drawn as accurately as possible EXCEPT when it is stated in a specific problem that its figure is not drawn to scale. All figures lie in a plane unless otherwise indicated.

1. If x and y are negative integers, which of the following must be true?

    I. $x < 0$
    II. $xy > 0$
    III. $x - y < 0$

    (A) I only
    (B) II only
    (C) I and II
    (D) I and III
    (E) I, II, and III

2. If each of the following fractions were written as a decimal, which would have the fewest number of nonzero digits to the right of the decimal point?

    (A) $\dfrac{1}{3}$

    (B) $\dfrac{1}{4}$

    (C) $\dfrac{1}{2}$

    (D) $\dfrac{1}{8}$

    (E) $\dfrac{2}{3}$

3. The price of a 19-inch computer monitor is reduced by $500 to a new price of $1,500. The percentage of change in the price of the monitor is

(A) 15%
(B) 25%
(C) $33\frac{1}{3}$%
(D) 50%
(E) $66\frac{2}{3}$%

4. What is the value of a if $25^{2a-2} = 125^{a+4}$?

(A) 6
(B) 2
(C) 16
(D) −6
(E) 8

5. Which of the following expressions cannot be equal to zero when $x^2 - 2x = 8$?

(A) $x^2 - 16$
(B) $x^2 + 3x - 4$
(C) $x^2 - 6x + 8$
(D) $x^2 - 8x + 16$
(E) $x^2 - 4$

6. John budgeted 50% of his take-home pay for household expenses, 20% for transportation, 15% for a retirement fund, and the remaining $240 for recreation. How much of his take-home pay did he budget for household expenses?

(A) $500
(B) $800
(C) $1,000
(D) $1,200
(E) $240

7. The average (arithmetic mean) of $5n + 2$ and another number is $3n$. What is the average of the other number and n?

(A) $4n + 1$
(B) $4n - 1$
(C) $n + 1$
(D) $n - 1$
(E) $8n$

8. A salesman makes a profit of 25% on all sales. How many fax machines will he have to sell for $375 each to make a total commission of at least $500?

(A) 4
(B) 5
(C) 6
(D) 15
(E) 20

9. If the radius of a circle is increased by 10%, by what percent does its area increase?

(A) 10%
(B) 20%
(C) 21%
(D) 25%
(E) 30%

10. Ron can type five forms of a test in 4 hours. Joan can type the same five forms in 6 hours. If they work together, how many hours would it take them to type ten forms of a test?

(A) $2\frac{2}{5}$

(B) $4\frac{4}{5}$

(C) 5

(D) 10

(E) $12\frac{2}{5}$

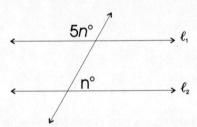

11. If l_1 is parallel to l_2 in the figure above, what is the value of n?

(A) 30
(B) 45
(C) 60
(D) 150
(E) 180

12. If $a * b = 3a - 4b + 1$, then $2 * 5 =$

    (A) -13

    (B) -10

    (C) 7

    (D) 10

    (E) 11

13. Cans of tennis balls were purchased for the tournament at a cost of $1.90 per can. Only $\frac{3}{4}$ of the cans were used for the tournament, so the 24 unused cans were returned for a refund. What was the cost of the cans of tennis balls used for the tournament?

    (A) $34.20

    (B) $45.60

    (C) $60.80

    (D) $124.20

    (E) $136.80

14. It takes 10 people 16 hours to complete a certain job. How many hours would it take 8 people, working at the same rate, to complete $\frac{3}{4}$ of the job?

    (A) 12

    (B) $12\frac{4}{5}$

    (C) 15

    (D) 16

    (E) 20

15. How many of the factors of 48 are divisible by 3?

    (A) 3

    (B) 5

    (C) 6

    (D) 7

    (E) 8

16. How many two-digit numbers can be written using digits 0 through 6 if no digit can be repeated and 0 cannot be the first digit?

    (A) 49

    (B) 42

    (C) 36

    (D) 30

    (E) 25

17. If $(x - 3)^2 = 81$, which of the following could be the value of $x + 3$?

(A) -15
(B) -9
(C) -3
(D) 6
(E) 12

18. Two cars left the same town traveling in the same directions. Car A traveled 40 miles per hour and left at 3:20. Car B traveled 50 miles per hour and left at 4:40. At what time will car B catch up with car A?

(A) 10:00
(B) 9:00
(C) 8:40
(D) 7:20
(E) 6:10

19. A team has wins, losses, and draws in a ratio of 5 to 4 to 1. If it played a total of 40 games, how many losses did it have?

(A) 4
(B) 10
(C) 16
(D) 20
(E) 24

20. The width of a rectangle is 6 cm less than the length. If the perimeter of the rectangle is 48 cm, what is the length of the rectangle in centimeters?

(A) 48
(B) 15
(C) 12
(D) 9
(E) 6

21. Ron wants to enclose a rectangular pasture that is adjacent to a river. If the side along the river is 50 feet long and does not require fencing, how many feet of fencing does he need to enclose 1,100 square feet?

(A) 22
(B) 94
(C) 100
(D) 144
(E) 150

22. Candy hearts were marked down to 30% to 50% on Valentine's Day. The following day, candy hearts were marked down an additional 25%. What was the lowest cost of a candy heart that originally sold for $28?

(A) $7
(B) $12.60
(C) $14
(D) $15.40
(E) $21

DATA SUFFICIENCY

Directions: Each of the data sufficiency problems below consists of a question and two statements, labeled (1) and (2), in which certain data are given. You have to decide whether the data given in the statements are *sufficient* for answering the question. Using the data given in the statements *plus* your knowledge of mathematics and everyday facts (such as the number of days in July or the meaning of counterclockwise), you must indicate whether

- statement (1) ALONE is sufficient, but statement (2) alone is not sufficient to answer the question asked;
- statement (2) ALONE is sufficient, but statement (1) alone is not sufficient to answer the question asked;
- BOTH statements (1) and (2) TOGETHER are sufficient to answer the question asked, but NEITHER statement ALONE is sufficient;
- EACH statement ALONE is sufficient to answer the question asked;
- statements (1) and (2) TOGETHER are NOT sufficient to answer the question asked, and additional data specific to the problem are *needed*.

Numbers: All numbers are real numbers.

Figures: A figure accompanying a data sufficiency problem will conform to the information given in the question, but will not necessarily conform to the additional information given in statements (1) and (2).

Lines shown as straight can be assumed to be straight and lines that appear jagged can also be assumed to be straight.

You may assume that the position of points, angles, regions, etc., exists in the order shown and that angle measures are greater than zero.

All figures lie in a plane unless otherwise indicated.

Note: In data sufficiency problems that ask for the value of a quantity, the data given in the statements are sufficient only when it is possible to determine exactly one numerical value for the quantity.

Example

In $\triangle PQR$, what is the value of x?

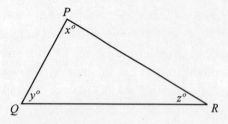

(1) $PQ = PR$

(2) $y = 40$

Explanation

According to statement (1), $PQ = PR$; therefore, $\triangle PQR$ is isosceles and $y = z$. Since $x + y + z = 180$, it follows that $x + 2y = 180$. Since statement (1) does not give a value for y, you cannot answer the question using statement (1) alone. According to statement (2), $y = 40$; therefore, $x + z = 140$. Since statement (2) does not give a value for z, you cannot answer the question using statement (2) alone. Using both statements together, since $x + 2y = 180$ and the value of y is given, you can find the value of x. Therefore, the answer is C.

1. If x is a prime number, what is the value of x?

    (1) $31 < x < 39$
    (2) $x - 2$ is a multiple of 5.

2. What is x?

    (1) $x^2 = 16$
    (2) $x = \sqrt{16}$

3. How much was the postage to mail a particular package?

    (1) The package weighed 12 ounces.
    (2) The first 8 ounces cost \$3.00, and each additional ounce costs \$1.50.

4. Joan had a total of \$16.50 in her coin bank. How many quarters does she have?

    (1) The bank contains only quarters and dimes.
    (2) There were 81 coins in the bank.

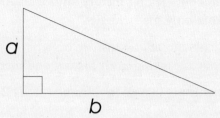

5. What is the area of the triangle shown above?

    (1) $b = 4a$

    (2) $a = \dfrac{12}{b}$

6. Adult and children's tickets are sold for the circus. If 100 adult tickets and 200 children's tickets were sold, how much money was collected for ticket sales?

    (1) Two adult tickets and four children's tickets cost $40.00

    (2) Adult tickets cost twice as much as children's tickets.

7. If $3^{2a-3} = 3^{b+3}$, what is $a + b$?

    (1) $3^{a-1} = 27$

    (2) $3^{a-b} = 9$

8. An urn contains only green and red balls. What is the ratio of green balls to red balls in the urn?

    (1) The number of red balls is twice the number of green balls.

    (2) The number of red balls is 5 more than the number of green balls.

9. What is the largest possible value of positive integer n?

    (1) n is a factor of $2^5 \times 6^2$ and $2^5 \times 3^4$.

    (2) n is a multiple of 6.

10. If $2x - y = 9$, what is the value of x?

    (1) $4x + 3y = 23$

    (2) $6x - 3y = 27$

11. What is the area of rectangle ABCD shown above?

    (1) AC = 25

    (2) BD = DC

12. There are 105 students taking history and/or mathematics. How many students are taking only mathematics?

    (1) Thirty students are taking history only.
    (2) Fifty students are taking both history and mathematics.

13. A rectangular picture is placed in a frame that is 2 inches wide. What is the area of the frame?

    (1) The area of the picture is 24 square inches.
    (2) The width of the picture is 4 inches.

14. Is it true that $a > b$?

    (1) $10a > 10b$
    (2) $ac > bc$

15. What is the ratio of x to y?

    (1) $2x = 3y$
    (2) $x + y = 10$

PRACTICE TEST 2

PROBLEM SOLVING

> **Directions:** In this section solve each problem using any available space on the page for scratch work. Then indicate the best of all the answer choices given.
>
> **Numbers:** All numbers used are real numbers.
>
> **Figures:** Figures that accompany problems in the text are intended to provide information useful in solving the problems. They are drawn as accurately as possible EXCEPT when it is stated in a specific problem that its figure is not drawn to scale. All figures lie in a plane unless otherwise indicated.

1. If x and y are both even integers, which of the following could be an odd integer?

   (A) $x + y$
   (B) $x - y$
   (C) xy
   (D) $x + y + 1$
   (E) $2(x + y)$

2. If each of the following fractions were written as a decimal, which would have the fewest number of nonzero digits to the right of the decimal point?

   (A) $\dfrac{7}{8}$

   (B) $\dfrac{1}{4}$

   (C) $\dfrac{2}{3}$

   (D) $\dfrac{5}{8}$

   (E) $\dfrac{1}{3}$

3. The price of a tennis racket decreased by 20% and then decreased by an additional 10%. This series of decreases is equivalent to a single decrease of

 (A) 30%
 (B) 25%
 (C) 28%
 (D) 35%
 (E) 40%

4. If $4^{2a + 3} = 8^{a - 1}$, then $a =$

 (A) -9
 (B) -4
 (C) -2
 (D) 4
 (E) 8

5. Which of the following expressions cannot be equal to zero when $x^2 - 3x = 4$?

 (A) $x^2 - 5x + 4$
 (B) $x^2 - 16$
 (C) $x^2 + 5x + 4$
 (D) $x^2 - 4x - 5$
 (E) $x^2 + 3x - 4$

6. John budgeted 50% of his take-home pay for household expenses, 20% for transportation, 15% for a retirement fund, and the remaining $240 for recreation. What was his take-home pay?

 (A) $2,000
 (B) $1,600
 (C) $1,200
 (D) $1,000
 (E) $850

7. A student had an average of 86 for three tests. If the student's highest test score was $2a$, what was the average of the student's two lowest scores?

 (A) $129 - 2a$
 (B) $258 - 2a$
 (C) $129 - a$
 (D) $258 + 2a$
 (E) $258 - a$

8. A salesman makes a profit of 20% on all sales. How many computers will he have to sell for $980 each to make a total commission of at least $1,000?

(A) 2
(B) 6
(C) 12
(D) 50
(E) 200

9. If one side of a square is increased by 4 inches and one side is decreased by 4 inches, a rectangle is formed whose area is 48 square inches. What is the area of the original square in square inches?

(A) 8
(B) 16
(C) 48
(D) 64
(E) 128

10. Printer A can complete a 50-page manuscript in 12 minutes. Printer B can complete the same manuscript in 30 minutes. How many minutes would it take both printers together to complete a 100-page manuscript?

(A) $17\dfrac{1}{7}$

(B) $20\dfrac{4}{7}$

(C) 24
(D) 42
(E) 84

11. The tennis pro shop sells only clothing, rackets, and accessories in the ratio of 6:4:3, respectively. If there are 60 rackets, how many accessories are in the shop?

(A) 10
(B) 20
(C) 30
(D) 45
(E) 50

12. If $*a* = -a^2$, then $*(-3)* =$

(A) −9
(B) −6
(C) 0
(D) 6
(E) 9

13. Mary purchased flowers for $2.50 per tray. She used only $\frac{3}{4}$ of the trays she purchased, so she returned 20 trays for a refund. What was the cost of the trays she used?

    (A) $37.50
    (B) $67.50
    (C) $120
    (D) $150
    (E) $200

14. It takes 8 people 12 hours to complete a certain job. How many hours would it take 6 people, working at the same rate, to complete $\frac{1}{2}$ of the same job?

    (A) 9
    (B) 8
    (C) 7
    (D) $6\frac{1}{2}$
    (E) $4\frac{1}{2}$

15. How many multiples of both 4 and 5 are there between 10 and 90 inclusive?

    (A) 4
    (B) 8
    (C) 10
    (D) 12
    (E) 16

16. How many two-digit numbers can be written using the digits 0 through 9 if no digit can be repeated?

    (A) 99
    (B) 90
    (C) 81
    (D) 72
    (E) 64

17. If $(x + 4)^2 = 64$, which of the following could be the value of $x - 4$?

    (A) −16
    (B) −12
    (C) −8
    (D) 8
    (E) 12

18. Two cars left Miami traveling in the same direction. Car A traveled 70 miles per hour and left at 2:40. Car B traveled at 60 miles per hour and left at 2:20. At what time will car A catch up to car B?

    (A) 4:20
    (B) 4:40
    (C) 5:10
    (D) 5:30
    (E) 6:00

19. A fruit salad has apples, bananas, and grapes in a ratio of 5 to 2 to 9. If a total of 128 pieces of fruit are in the salad, how many grapes were used?

    (A) 8
    (B) 10
    (C) 45
    (D) 56
    (E) 72

20. The width of a rectangle is 28 cm less than the length. If the perimeter of the rectangle is 252 cm, what is the length of the rectangle, in centimeters?

    (A) 128
    (B) 77
    (C) 64
    (D) 49
    (E) 28

21. Robert wants to enclose two rectangular pastures. If the width of the pasture is 30 feet and the total area enclosed is 1320 square feet, how many feet of fencing will Robert need?

    (A) 22
    (B) 44
    (C) 128
    (D) 178
    (E) 660

22. Shop clerks are given a discount of 10% to 20%. If an additional 10% were given to clerks on their birthday, what is the lowest price a clerk would pay on her birthday for an item that regularly sold for $24?

    (A) $.48
    (B) $4.80
    (C) $7.20
    (D) $16.80
    (E) $19.20

DATA SUFFICIENCY

Directions: Each of the data sufficiency problems below consists of a question and two statements, labeled (1) and (2), in which certain data are given. You have to decide whether the data given in the statements are *sufficient* for answering the question. Using the data given in the statements *plus* your knowledge of mathematics and everyday facts (such as the number of days in July or the meaning of counterclockwise), you must indicate whether

- statement (1) ALONE is sufficient, but statement (2) alone is not sufficient to answer the question asked;

- statement (2) ALONE is sufficient, but statement (1) alone is not sufficient to answer the question asked;

- BOTH statements (1) and (2) TOGETHER are sufficient to answer the question asked, but NEITHER statement ALONE is sufficient;

- EACH statement ALONE is sufficient to answer the question asked;

- statements (1) and (2) TOGETHER are NOT sufficient to answer the question asked, and additional data specific to the problem are *needed*.

Numbers: All numbers are real numbers.

Figures: A figure accompanying a data sufficiency problem will conform to the information given in the question, but will not necessarily conform to the additional information given in statements (1) and (2).

Lines shown as straight can be assumed to be straight and lines that appear jagged can also be assumed to be straight.

You may assume that the position of points, angles, regions, etc., exists in the order shown and that angle measures are greater than zero.

All figures lie in a plane unless otherwise indicated.

Note: In data sufficiency problems that ask for the value of a quantity, the data given in the statements are sufficient only when it is possible to determine exactly one numerical value for the quantity.

Example

In $\triangle PQR$, what is the value of x?

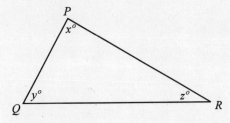

(1) $PQ = PR$

(2) $y = 40$

Explanation

According to statement (1), $PQ = PR$; therefore, $\triangle PQR$ is isosceles and $y = z$. Since $x + y + z = 180$, it follows that $x + 2y = 180$. Since statement (1) does not give a value for y, you cannot answer the question using statement (1) alone. According to statement (2), $y = 40$; therefore, $x + z = 140$. Since statement (2) does not give a value for z, you cannot answer the question using statement (2) alone. Using both statements together, since $x + 2y = 180$ **and the value of y is given**, you can find the value of x. Therefore, the answer is C.

1. What is the value of the integer x?

   (1) x is a prime factor of 45.
   (2) $3 \leq x \leq 9$

2. What is x?

   (1) $x = \sqrt{9}$
   (2) $x^2 - 9 = 0$

3. An investor bought shares of stock A and stock B. How many shares of each stock did he buy?

   (1) He bought twice as many shares of stock A as stock B.
   (2) Stock A costs twice as much as stock B.

4. Joan's coin bank contained \$16.50 in quarters and dimes. How many quarters did she have?

   (1) The number of quarters was 6 more than twice the number of dimes.
   (2) There were 81 coins in the bank.

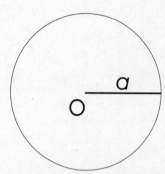

5. What is the circumference of the circle with center O?

    (1) The area of the circle is 64π.

    (2) The diameter of the circle is 16.

6. Movie tickets are available for adults and children. If 100 adult tickets and 300 children's tickets are sold, how much money is collected for ticket sales?

    (1) Two adult tickets and six children's tickets cost $36.

    (2) An adult ticket costs $2 more than a children's ticket.

7. If $5^{2a\ -\ 13} = 5^b$, what is $a + b$?

    (1) $5^{2a\ -\ 1} = 125$

    (2) $5^{a\ +\ 2b} = 25^4$

8. An urn contains only green and red balls. What is the ratio of green balls to red balls in the urn?

    (1) The number of red balls is $\dfrac{4}{5}$ the number of green balls.

    (2) The number of red balls is 8 less than the number of green balls.

9. What is the value of the sum of a sequence of three consecutive even integers?

    (1) The average of the three consecutive even integers is 14.

    (2) The product of the smallest and largest is 192.

10. Is it true that $a > b$?

    (1) $10 + a > b + 10$

    (2) $ac < bc$ and $c < 0$

11. If $8x - 3y = 28$, what is the value of x?

    (1) $6y = 16x - 56$

    (2) $2x - 5y = 24$

12. A garden is surrounded by a path that is 4 feet wide. What is the area of the path?

    (1)   The area of the path is $\frac{1}{4}$ of the area of the garden.

    (2)   The garden is circular with a 12-foot diameter.

13. One hundred cars on a particular lot were available with a compact disc player, a car phone, or both. How many cars had only a car phone?

    (1)   The number of cars with compact disc players was twice the number of cars with both a compact disc player and a car phone.

    (2)   Thirty cars had both, which was half the number of cars with compact disc players.

14.

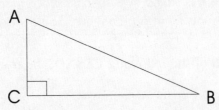

What is the area of the triangle shown above?

    (1)   AC = CB

    (2)   AB = 25

15. What is the ratio of men to women in an economics class?

    (1)   There are twice as many women enrolled as men.

    (2)   The ratio of men to the total number of students enrolled in the class is 1:3.

PRACTICE TEST 3

PROBLEM SOLVING

Directions: In this section solve each problem using any available space on the page for scratch work. Then indicate the best of all the answer choices given.

Numbers: All numbers used are real numbers.

Figures: Figures that accompany problems in the text are intended to provide information useful in solving the problems. They are drawn as accurately as possible EXCEPT when it is stated in a specific problem that its figure is not drawn to scale. All figures lie in a plane unless otherwise indicated.

1. If $xy < 0$, which of the following CANNOT be true?

    (A) $x < 0$
    (B) $y < 0$
    (C) $x + y > 0$
    (D) $\dfrac{x}{y} > 0$
    (E) $\dfrac{x}{y} < 0$

2. If each of the following fractions were written as a decimal, which would have the fewest number of nonzero digits to the right of the decimal point?

    (A) $\dfrac{1}{8}$

    (B) $\dfrac{1}{3}$

    (C) $\dfrac{2}{3}$

    (D) $\dfrac{3}{4}$

    (E) $\dfrac{5}{8}$

3. James was given a salary increase of 10% after his six months at a new job, followed by a 5% salary increase after the next six months. This series of raises is equivalent to a single raise of

 (A) 15%
 (B) 12.5%
 (C) 7.5%
 (D) 15.5%
 (E) 20%

4. If $\dfrac{0.64 \times 10^a}{1.6 \times 10^b} = 4 \times 10^2$, $a - b =$

 (A) 1
 (B) 2
 (C) 3
 (D) 4
 (E) 5

5. If $x^2 + 2x - 8 = 0$, which of the following could be x?

 (A) -8
 (B) -4
 (C) -2
 (D) 4
 (E) 8

6. John budgeted 50% of his take-home pay for household expenses, 20% for transportation, 15% for a retirement fund, and the remaining $240 for recreation. How much of his take-home pay did he budget for his retirement fund?

 (A) $240
 (B) $400
 (C) $1,200
 (D) $800
 (E) $1,600

7. The average (arithmetic mean) of 6 numbers is 4.5. When an additional number is included, the average of all 7 numbers is 5. What is the additional number?

 (A) 4.75
 (B) 6.0
 (C) 7.0
 (D) 8.0
 (E) 27.0

8. Band members sold candy bars for $.50 each to raise money for a band trip. One band member sold 75% of his candy bars and had 100 candy bars left. How much money did he collect?

   (A) $50
   (B) $75
   (C) $100
   (D) $150
   (E) $200

9. If the length of a rectangle is increased by 10% and its width decreased by 20%, by what percent does its area decrease?

   (A) 10%
   (B) 12%
   (C) 15%
   (D) 18%
   (E) 30%

10. One pipe fills a pool in 8 hours, and another pipe drains the pool in 12 hours. If both pipes are left open for 3 hours when the pool is empty, how much of the pool will be filled?

   (A) $\dfrac{5}{8}$

   (B) $\dfrac{1}{2}$

   (C) $\dfrac{3}{8}$

   (D) $\dfrac{1}{4}$

   (E) $\dfrac{1}{8}$

11. If the radius of a circle is doubled, by what percent does its area increase?

   (A) 2%
   (B) 50%
   (C) 200%
   (D) 300%
   (E) 400%

12. If $a\#b = a^2 + 2ab$, then $2\#4 =$

   (A) 6
   (B) 8
   (C) 16
   (D) 20
   (E) 24

13. Confetti was purchased in bags that cost $1.75 each. Only $\frac{1}{4}$ of the bags were needed for the party, so 60 bags were returned for a refund. What was the cost of the confetti for the party?

    (A) $75
    (B) $50
    (C) $35
    (D) $26.25
    (E) $25

14. It takes 6 people 10 hours to complete a certain job. How many hours would it take 10 people, working at the same rate, to complete $\frac{2}{3}$ of the same job?

    (A) $16\frac{2}{3}$

    (B) $13\frac{1}{3}$

    (C) $11\frac{1}{9}$

    (D) 6
    (E) 4

15. How many multiples of both 5 and 6 are there between 10 and 90 inclusive?

    (A) 17
    (B) 9
    (C) 6
    (D) 3
    (E) 2

16. How many different ways can the digits 0, 0, 2, and 5 be arranged so that there is always at least one 0 between 2 and 5?

    (A) 120
    (B) 60
    (C) 12
    (D) 6
    (E) 4

17. What is the smallest value of x for which

    $$\left(\frac{4}{x} + 16\right)(9 - x^2) = 0?$$

    (A) -4
    (B) -3
    (C) $-\frac{1}{4}$
    (D) $-\frac{1}{3}$
    (E) 3

18. Leslee types at an average rate of 60 words per minute. Joan types at an average rate of 100 words per minute. If Leslee begins typing a manuscript at 8:30, and Joan begins typing an identical copy of the same manuscript at 9:40, at what time will they be typing the same word?

    (A) 10:00
    (B) 11:15
    (C) 11:45
    (D) 12:00
    (E) 12:15

19. A coin bank has pennies, nickels, dimes, and quarters in a ratio of 8 to 4 to 6 to 2. If the total number of coins in the bank is 240, how many dimes are in the bank?

    (A) 24
    (B) 40
    (C) 48
    (D) 72
    (E) 96

20. The perimeter of a rectangle is 248 centimeters. If the length is 52 centimeters more than the width, what is the width of the rectangle in centimeters?

    (A) 196
    (B) 144
    (C) 88
    (D) 72
    (E) 36

21. Rhonda wants to enclose a rectangular horse pasture with the length of the pasture adjacent to a river. If the 100-foot side along the river does not require fencing, and she enclosed 4,200 square feet, how many feet of fencing will she need?

    (A) 283
    (B) 184
    (C) 142
    (D) 84
    (E) 42

22. A store manager receives a discount of 10% to 30%. If an additional 25% were given to managers for a holiday sale, what would be the lowest price of a glass vase with a price tag of $58?

    (A) $20.30
    (B) $26.10
    (C) $29
    (D) $31.90
    (E) $37.70

DATA SUFFICIENCY

Directions: Each of the data sufficiency problems below consists of a question and two statements, labeled (1) and (2), in which certain data are given. You have to decide whether the data given in the statements are *sufficient* for answering the question. Using the data given in the statements *plus* your knowledge of mathematics and everyday facts (such as the number of days in July or the meaning of counterclockwise), you must indicate whether

- statement (1) ALONE is sufficient, but statement (2) alone is not sufficient to answer the question asked;
- statement (2) ALONE is sufficient, but statement (1) alone is not sufficient to answer the question asked;
- BOTH statements (1) and (2) TOGETHER are sufficient to answer the question asked, but NEITHER statement ALONE is sufficient;
- EACH statement ALONE is sufficient to answer the question asked;
- statements (1) and (2) TOGETHER are NOT sufficient to answer the question asked, and additional data specific to the problem are *needed*.

<u>Numbers</u>: All numbers are real numbers.

<u>Figures</u>: A figure accompanying a data sufficiency problem will conform to the information given in the question, but will not necessarily conform to the additional information given in statements (1) and (2).

<u>Lines</u> shown as straight can be assumed to be straight and lines that appear jagged can also be assumed to be straight.

You may assume that the position of points, angles, regions, etc., exists in the order shown and that angle measures are greater than zero.

All figures lie in a plane unless otherwise indicated.

Note: In data sufficiency problems that ask for the value of a quantity, the data given in the statements are sufficient only when it is possible to determine exactly one numerical value for the quantity.

PRACTICE TEST 3

Example
In $\triangle PQR$, what is the value of x?

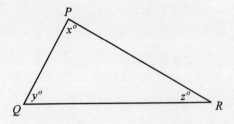

(1) $PQ = PR$

(2) $y = 40$

Explanation
According to statement (1), $PQ = PR$; therefore, $\triangle PQR$ is isosceles and $y = z$. Since $x + y + z = 180$, it follows that $x + 2y = 180$. Since statement (1) does not give a value for y, you cannot answer the question using statement (1) alone. According to statement (2), $y = 40$; therefore, $x + z = 140$. Since statement (2) does not give a value for z, you cannot answer the question using statement (2) alone. Using both statements together, since $x + 2y = 180$ and the value of y is given, you can find the value of x. Therefore, the answer is C.

1. If $a + b + c = 42$, what is the value of abc?

   (1) a, b, and c are consecutive even integers.
   (2) a, b, and c are positive integers.

2. What is the value of an even integer n?

   (1) $\sqrt{n}$ is an integer.
   (2) $0 < n < 20$

3. What is the cost of a 20-minute long-distance phone call?

   (1) Each minute costs 5 cents per minute.
   (2) The first 10 minutes cost 8 cents per minute, and each extra minute costs 12 cents.

4. Joan is 4 years younger than her brother Bill. How old is Bill?

   (1) Ten years ago, Bill was 4 years older than Joan.
   (2) Seventeen years ago, Bill was twice as old as Joan.

Peterson's: www.petersons.com

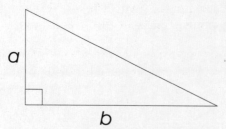

5. What is the perimeter of the triangle shown above?

    (1) $a = 3$ and $b = 4$
    (2) $a^2 + b^2 = 25$

6. A nutshop owner combines 6 pounds of peanuts with 4 pounds of cashews to sell as a nut mix. What is the cost of ten pounds of this mix?

    (1) The price of the cashews is twice the price of peanuts.
    (2) Three pounds of peanuts mixed with two pounds of cashews cost $9.80.

7. If $3^{a-2} = 3^{b+1}$, what is $a + b$?

    (1) $3^{2a-3} = 243$
    (2) $3^{3a} = 3^{3b+9}$

8. An urn contains only green and red balls. What is the ratio of green balls to red balls in the urn?

    (1) There are 20% more red balls than green balls.
    (2) The probability of drawing a green ball is $\dfrac{3}{4}$.

9. Is the positive integer n an odd integer?

    (1) n is a factor of $2^4 \times 3^2 \times 5$ and $6^2 \times 5^3$.
    (2) n is a multiple of 15.

10. If p is an integer, is p positive?

    (1) $pq > 0$
    (2) $q < 0$

11. What is the value of y?

    (1) $2x - y = -5$
    (2) $x = y - (3 - x)$

12. A survey of 600 computer owners revealed that they owned a modem and/or a scanner. How many of the people surveyed owned only a modem?

   (1) The number of people surveyed who owned only a modem was three times the number of people who owned only a scanner.

   (2) Four hundred people who were surveyed owned both a modem and a scanner, which was eight times the number of people surveyed who owned only a scanner.

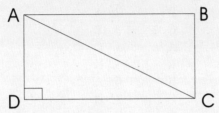

13. What is the area of rectangle ABCD?

   (1) $AD = \frac{1}{2}(DC)$
   (2) $(AC)^2 = (AD)^2 + (DC)^2$

14. What is the ratio of a to b?

   (1) $a = 5b + 1$
   (2) $a = \frac{b}{3}$

15. A rectangular parking lot is surrounded by a 3-foot-wide sidewalk. What is the area of the sidewalk?

   (1) The width of the parking lot is 25 feet less than the length.
   (2) The length of the parking lot is 52 feet.

Quick Score Answers

Quantitative

Practice Test 1		Practice Test 2		Practice Test 3	
Problem Solving	Data Sufficiency	Problem Solving	Data Sufficiency	Problem Solving	Data Sufficiency
1. C	1. D	1. D	1. E	1. D	1. A
2. C	2. B	2. B	2. A	2. D	2. E
3. B	3. C	3. C	3. E	3. D	3. D
4. C	4. C	4. A	4. D	4. C	4. B
5. B	5. B	5. E	5. D	5. B	5. A
6. B	6. A	6. B	6. A	6. A	6. B
7. D	7. D	7. C	7. D	7. D	7. A
8. C	8. A	8. B	8. A	8. D	8. D
9. C	9. A	9. D	9. D	9. B	9. E
10. B	10. A	10. A	10. D	10. E	10. C
11. A	11. C	11. D	11. B	11. D	11. B
12. A	12. C	12. A	12. B	12. D	12. B
13. E	13. C	13. D	13. B	13. C	13. E
14. C	14. A	14. B	14. C	14. E	14. B
15. B	15. A	15. A	15. C	15. D	15. C
16. C		16. B		16. D	
17. C		17. A		17. B	
18. A		18. B		18. B	
19. C		19. E		19. D	
20. B		20. B		20. E	
21. B		21. D		21. B	
22. A		22. D		22. B	

ANSWERS AND EXPLANATIONS

PRACTICE TEST 1

Problem Solving

1. **The correct answer is (C).** I is true since all negative integers are less than 0. II is true since the product of two negative integers is a positive integer. III may or may not be true. Let $x = -4$ and $y = -10$, then $-4 - (-10) = -4 + 10 = +6$, which is greater than 0.

2. **The correct answer is (C).** Convert each fraction to a decimal using long division (or from memory): $\frac{1}{3} = 0.033\ldots$, $\frac{1}{4} = 0.25$, $\frac{1}{2} = 0.5$, $\frac{1}{8} = 0.125$, $\frac{2}{3} = 0.66\ldots$

3. **The correct answer is (B).** The original price of the monitor is $500 + $1,500 = $2,000. The problem to solve is: $500 is what percent of $2,000? $500 = 2,000x$, where x is the percent. $\frac{500}{2,000} = x$, so $x = \frac{1}{4} = 25\%$.

4. **The correct answer is (C).** Convert each base to 5: $(5^2)^{2a-2} = (5^3)^{a+4}$, $5^{4a-4} = 5^{3a+12}$. Since the bases are equal, set the exponents equal and solve: $4a - 4 = 3a + 12$, $a = 16$.

5. **The correct answer is (B).** Solve $x^2 - 2x = 8$ by factoring $x^2 - 2x - 8 = 0$, $(x-4)(x+2) = 0$, $x = 4$, or $x = -2$. Replace x with 4 and -2 in each choice to find that choice (B) does not equal 0: $4^2 + 3(4) - 4 = 16 + 12 - 4 = 24$, $(-2)^2 + 3(-2) - 4 = 4 - 6 - 4 = -6$.

6. **The correct answer is (B).** First compute his take-home pay. Recreation accounts for 15% of his budget since $100\% - (50\% + 20\% + 15\%) = 15\%$. $240 is 15% of what amount? $240 = .15x$, where x represents the take-home pay. $\frac{240}{0.15} = x$, so $x = \$1,600$. Since 50% of the take-home pay is budgeted for household expenses, 50% of $1,600 = (.5)(1,600) = \$800$.

7. **The correct answer is (D).** Let x = the other number. $\frac{5n + 2 + x}{2} = 3n$. Solve for x: $5n + 2 + x = 6n$, $x = n - 2$. Then find the average of x and n: $\frac{n + n - 2}{2} = \frac{2n - 2}{2} = n - 1$.

8. **The correct answer is (C).** The salesman makes 25% of $375 for each fax machine sold or $.25(375) = \$93.75$. To make at least $500, he would have to sell at least 6 machines. Since you are not looking for an exact amount, round $93.75 to $100 and divide $500 by $100 to get 5, then reason that you must round this up to account for rounding $93.75 up to $100.

9. **The correct answer is (C).** Let r = radius so the original area is πr^2. The increased radius is then $1.1r$ for an area of $\pi(1.1r)^2 = \pi(1.21r^2) = 1.21\pi r^2$. The increase from πr^2 to $1.21\pi r^2$ is .21 or 21%.

10. **The correct answer is (B).** Let x equal the amount of time it would take to complete the job together. Ron would take 8 hours to complete the job alone, so he would complete $\frac{x}{8}$ of the job. Joan would take 12 hours to complete the job alone, so she would complete $\frac{x}{12}$ of the job. Then $\frac{x}{8} + \frac{x}{12} = 1$, $3x + 2x = 24$, $5x = 24$, and $x = \frac{24}{5} = 4\frac{4}{5}$.

11. **The correct answer is (A).** Since the lines are parallel, we know:

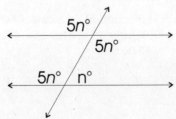

which means that $4n° + n° = 180°$, $6n = 180$, $n = 30$.

12. **The correct answer is (A).** Replace a with 2 and b with 5: $2 * 5 = 3(2) - 4(5) + 1 = 6 - 20 + 1 = -13$.

13. **The correct answer is (E).** Let $x =$ the total number of cans of tennis balls purchased. Twenty-four cans represent $\frac{1}{4}$ of the total, so $24 = \frac{1}{4}x$, $x = 96$ cans. Since 24 cans were returned, $96 - 24 = 72$ cans were used for a cost of $(\$1.90)(72) = \$136.80$.

14. **The correct answer is (C).** Note that with fewer people, the job will take longer to complete, so this can be set up as an indirect proportion: $p = \frac{k}{b}$, where p is the number of people needed to complete the job and b is the number of hours needed to complete the job. $10 = \frac{k}{16}$, $k = 10(16)$, $k = 160$. For 8 people, $8 = \frac{160}{x}$, $8x = 160$, $x = 20$ hours for the complete job. To complete $\frac{3}{4}$ of the job, it would take $\frac{3}{4}(20) = 15$ hours.

15. **The correct answer is (B).** List the factors of 48: 1, 2, 3, 4, 6, 8, 12, 16, 24, 48. Check the list for numbers that are divisible by 3: 3, 6, 12, 24, 48.

16. **The correct answer is (C).** There are 6 choices for the first digit since 0 cannot be used, and there are 6 choices for the second digit, for a total of $6 \times 6 = 36$.

17. **The correct answer is (C).** If $(x - 3)^2 = 81$, $x - 3 = \pm\sqrt{81}$, $x - 3 = \pm 9$. Either $x - 3 = 9$ so $x = 12$ or $x - 3 = -9$ so $x = -6$. Then $x + 2 = 15$ or -3.

18. **The correct answer is (A).** Using rate multiplied by time equals distance, and letting x represent the number of hours car A travels, car A travels $40x$ and car B travels $50\left(x - 1\frac{1}{3}\right)$. The cars have traveled the same distance when $40x = 50x - \frac{200}{3}$, $10x = \frac{200}{x}$, $x = \frac{20}{x} = 6\frac{2}{3}$ hours or 6 hours 40 minutes. Six hours 40 minutes after 3:20 is 10:00.

19. **The correct answer is (C).** The rates of 5 to 4 to 1 means $5x + 4x + x = 40$. Solve for x: $10x = 40$. $x = 4$. $4x$ represents the number of losses, so $4(4) = 16$ losses.

20. **The correct answer is (B).** Let x equal the length of the rectangle. Then the width is represented by $x - 6$. Since $P = 2l + 2w$, $48 = 2(x) + 2(x - 6)$. Solve for x: $48 = 2x + 2x - 12$, $48 = 4x - 12$, $60 = 4x$, $x = 15$.

21. **The correct answer is (B).** Let x equal the length of a side that is adjacent to the river. Then $50x = 1,100$, $x = 22$ feet. The amount of fencing needed is $2(22 \text{ feet}) + 50 \text{ feet} = 94 \text{ feet}$.

22. **The correct answer is (A).** The maximum discount is 50%. The additional 25% discount would make the total discount 75%. The candy heart would cost 25% of its original price, or $(0.25)(\$28) = \$7.00$.

Data Sufficiency

1. **The correct answer is (D).** The only prime number between 31 and 39 is 37, so statement (1) by itself is sufficient to answer the question. Checking primes, we see that $x = 7$ or $x = 17$. Both satisfy statement (2), so statement (2) alone is not sufficient to answer the question.

2. **The correct answer is (B).** If $x^2 = 16$, $x = -4$ or $+4$, so statement (1) alone is not sufficient to answer the question. If $x = \sqrt{16}$, $x = 4$, and statement (2) alone is sufficient to answer the question.

3. **The correct answer is (C).** Statement (1) alone does not provide information about the cost. Statement (2) alone gives a formula to compute the cost but no information on the weight. Therefore, both statements are needed to answer the question.

4. **The correct answer is (C).** Statement (1) is not sufficient to answer the question since many possibilities exist, such as 52 quarters and 35 dimes or 56 quarters and 25 dimes. Statement (2) alone is not sufficient since there are many combinations of coins that would total $16.50. Both statements together will provide a unique answer.

5. **The correct answer is (B).** The area of a triangle equals $\frac{1}{2}$ the base times the height. For the right triangle shown, $A = \frac{1}{2}ab$. Statement (1) can be used to write $A = \frac{1}{2}a(4a) = 2a^2$ but cannot give a numerical value for the area. Statement (2) can be solved for ab ($ab = 12$), which can be substituted for ab in the area formula.

6. **The correct answer is (A).** Let a equal the cost of an adult ticket and c equal the cost of a children's ticket. Statement (1) translates to $2a + 4c = \$40.00$. The total collected is $100a + 200c$. By multiplying the equation formed from statement (1) by 50, we can find the total collected. Statement (2) translates to $a = 2c$, which will not allow us to answer the question.

7. **The correct answer is (D).** From the data given in the problem, we know that $2a - 3 = b + 3$ or $2a - b = 6$. Using statement (1), $3^{a-1} = 3^3$, so $a - 1 = 3$, which can be solved for a. Knowing a, b can be found, and hence, $a + b$ can be found. From statement (2), $3^{a-b} = 3^2$ so $a - b = 2$. Combined with the equation given in the problem, this forms a system of two equations in two unknowns that can be solved.

8. **The correct answer is (A).** The problem asks you to find $\frac{g}{r}$, where g equals the number of green balls and r equals the number of red balls. Statement (1) translates to $r = 2g$, which can be solved for $\frac{g}{r}$ by dividing both sides of the equation by $2r$. Statement (2) translates to $r = 5 + g$, which cannot be solved for $\frac{g}{r}$.

9. **The correct answer is (A).** Statement (1) alone is sufficient to answer the question. Prime factor $2^5 \times 6^2$ as $2^5 \times 2^2 \times 3^2 = 2^7 \times 3^2$. The greatest common factor of $2^7 \times 3^2$ and $2^7 \times 3^2$ is $2^5 \times 3^2$. Statement (2) alone is not sufficient to answer the question since there are many multiples of 6.

10. **The correct answer is (A).** Using statement (1), you have two equations in two unknowns, which you can solve. Although statement (2) appears to have the same situation, notice that it is a multiple of the equation given in the problem statement since $2(2x - y = 9)$ is equivalent to $6x - 3y = 27$. Thus, statement (2) is not sufficient to answer the question.

11. **The correct answer is (C).** Statement (1) alone is not sufficient to answer the question. Statement (2) tells us that the rectangle is a square. Area equals $(AD)^2$. Using the Pythagorean theorem, $2(AD)^2 = (AC)^2 = 25$ [from statement (1)]. Thus, we can answer the question using both statements.

12. **The correct answer is (C).** Let h equal the number of students taking only history, m equal the number of students taking only mathematics, and b equal the number of students taking both courses. From the problem statement, $h + m + b = 105$. Statement (1) translates to $h = 30$, which is not sufficient to answer the question. Statement (2) translates to $b = 50$, which alone is not sufficient to answer the question. However, substituting both of these values into the equation from the problem statement, we can solve for m.

13. **The correct answer is (C).** Using statement (1), we cannot find the total area. If the picture was 4 inches by 6 inches, the total area would be $(6)(8) = 48$ square inches, but if it was 3 inches by 8 inches, the total area would be $(5)(10) = 50$ square inches. Thus, statement (1) alone is not sufficient to answer the question. Statement (2) alone is not sufficient to answer the question, but combined with statement (1), the area of the picture can be computed; then the total area, computed by adding 2 inches to the length and width, and finally subtracting the total minus the area of the picture to answer the question.

14. **The correct answer is (A).** Divide both sides of the inequality in statement (1) by 10: $a > b$. Statement (1) is sufficient to answer the question. Using the inequality in statement (2), we would have to divide both sides by c, but we don't know whether c is positive or negative. If $c < 0$, $\dfrac{ac}{c} < \dfrac{bc}{c}$, so $a < b$.

15. **The correct answer is (A).** Using (1): $2x = 3y$ can be written $\dfrac{x}{y} = \dfrac{3}{2}$, so the ratio of x to y is 3:2. Using statement (2), try substituting values for x and y. If $x = 1$, $y = 9$, and the ratio of x to y is 1:9. If $x = 2$, $y = 8$ and the ratio of x to y is 2:8 or 1:4. Statement (2) is not sufficient to answer the question.

PRACTICE TEST 2

Problem Solving

1. **The correct answer is (D).** The sum, difference, and product of two even integers is an even integer, so choices (A), (B), and (C) are eliminated. Multiplying the sum of an even (or odd) integer by 2 will result in an even integer, so choice (E) is eliminated. By elimination, this gives choice (D). Or, knowing that $x + y$ is even, adding 1 to an even integer results in an odd integer.

2. **The correct answer is (B).** Convert each fraction to a decimal using long division (or from memory) $\dfrac{7}{8} = 0.875$, $\dfrac{1}{4} = 0.25$, $\dfrac{2}{3} = 0.66\ldots$, $\dfrac{5}{8} = 0.625$, $\dfrac{1}{3} = 0.33\ldots$

3. **The correct answer is (C).** Choose a convenient starting price—$100. The 20% decrease in the price reduces the cost to $80. The following 10% decrease reduces the cost to $72 (0.1(80) = $8). The difference in price, $28, represents a 28% decrease in the original price. Algebraically, if p is the starting price, $.9(.8s) = .72s$, which represents a 28% decrease in price.

4. **The correct answer is (A).** Convert each base to 2: $(2^2)^{2a + 3} = (2^3)^{a - 1}$, $2^{4a + 6} = 2^{3a - 3}$. Since the bases are equal, set the exponents equal and solve: $4a + 6 = 3a - 3$, $a = -9$.

5. **The correct answer is (E).** Solve $x^2 - 3x = x$ by factoring: $x^2 - 3x - 4 = 0$, $(x - 4)(x + 1) = 0$, $x - 4 = 0$ or $x + 1 = 0$, $x = 4$ or $x = -1$. Replace x with 4 and -1 in each choice to find that choice (E) does not equal 0 for either value of x: $(4)^2 + 3(4) - 4 = 16 + 12 - 4 = 24$, $(-1)^2 + 3(-1) - 4 = 1 - 3 - 4 = -6$.

6. **The correct answer is (B).** Recreation accounts for 15% of his budget since $100\% - (50\% + 20\% + 15\%) = 15\%$. The question to answer is: 15% of what amount equals $240? $0.15x = 240$ where x is the take-home amount. Then, $x = \dfrac{240}{0.15} = \$1,600$.

7. **The correct answer is (C).** Let x and y represent the two lowest test scores. Then $\dfrac{2a + x + y}{3} = 86$. Solve for $x + y$: $2a + x + y = 3(80)$, so $x + y = 258 - 2a$. Now find the average of $x + y$: $\dfrac{x + y}{2} = \dfrac{258 - 2a}{2} = 129 - a$.

8. **The correct answer is (B).** The salesman makes 20% of $980 for each computer sold or $(.20)(\$980) = \$196$. To make at least $1,000, he would have to sell at least 6 computers. By approximating $196 with 200, dividing $1,000 by $200 gives 5 computers, which can be rounded up to account for the approximation.

9. **The correct answer is (D).** The area of the original square is x, $x = x^2$. The area of the rectangle is $(x + 4)(x - 4) = x^2 - 16 = 48$. Then, $x^2 = 64$.

10. **The correct answer is (A).** Let x equal the amount of time to complete the job with both printers working. Printer A would take 24 minutes to complete the job alone, so it would complete $\dfrac{x}{24}$ of the job. Printer B would take 60 minutes to complete the job alone, so it would complete $\dfrac{x}{60}$ of the job. Then $\dfrac{x}{24} + \dfrac{x}{60} = 1$, $5x + 2x = 120$, $7x = 120$, $x = \dfrac{120}{7} = 17\dfrac{1}{7}$ minutes.

11. **The correct answer is (D).** Since the ratio of rackets to accessories is 4:3, set up a proportion: $\dfrac{4}{60} = \dfrac{3}{x}$, where x is the number of accessories. Then, $4x = 180$, $x = 45$.

12. **The correct answer is (A).** $*(-3)* = (-3)^2 = 9$.

13. **The correct answer is (D).** Let x equal the total number of trays purchased. Twenty trays represent $\dfrac{1}{4}$ of the total, so $20 = \dfrac{1}{4}x$, $x = 80$. Thus, she used $80 - 20 = 60$ trays at a cost of $(\$2.50)(60) = \$150.00$.

14. **The correct answer is (B).** Note that with fewer people, the job will take longer to complete, so this can be set up as an indirect proportion: $p = \dfrac{k}{h}$, where p is the number of people needed to complete the job and h is the number of hours needed to complete the job. Then, $8 = \dfrac{k}{12}$, $k = 8(12) = 96$. For 6 people to complete the job, $6 = \dfrac{96}{x}$, $6x = 96$, $x = 16$ hours. To complete $\dfrac{1}{2}$ of the job, it would take $\dfrac{1}{2}(16) = 8$ hours.

15. **The correct answer is (A).** List multiples of 5 between 10 and 90: 10, 15, 20, 25, 30, 35, 40, 45, 50, 55, 60, 65, 70, 75, 80, 85, and 90. Check the list for numbers that are multiples of 4: 20, 40, 60, and 80.

16. **The correct answer is (B).** There are 10 choices for the first digit and 9 choices for the second digit, for a total of $10 \times 9 = 90$ numbers.

17. **The correct answer is (A).** If $(x + 4)^2 = 64$, $x + 4 = \pm\sqrt{64}$, $x + 4 = \pm 8$, $x = -4 \pm 8$. Then, $x - 4 = -4 \pm (8 - 4) = 0$ or -16.

18. **The correct answer is (B).** Using rate multiplied by time equals distance, and letting x represent the number of hours car A travels, car A travels $70x$ and car B travels $60\left(x + \dfrac{20}{60}\right)$, where $\dfrac{20}{60}$ represents the additional 20 minutes car B travels. Then, $70x = 60\left(x + \dfrac{20}{60}\right)$, $70x = 60x + 20$, $10x = 20$, $x = 2$. Car A left at 2:40 and traveled 2 hours, so it arrived at 4:40.

19. **The correct answer is (E).** The ratio of 5 to 2 to 9 means $5x + 2x + 9x = 128$. Solve for x: $16x = 128$, $x = 8$. Then, $9x$ represents the number of grapes so $9(8) = 72$ grapes.

20. **The correct answer is (B).** Let $x =$ the length of the rectangle. Thus, the width is represented by $x - 28$. Since $P = 2l + 2w$, $252 = 2(x) + 2(x - 28)$. Solve for x: $252 = 2x + 2x - 56$, $252 = 4x - 56$, $308 = 4x$, $x = 77$.

21. **The correct answer is (D).** $30(2x) = 1,320$, $60x = 1,320$, $x = 22$. Then, the total amount of fencing needed is $3(30 \text{ feet}) + 4(22 \text{ feet}) = 178$ feet.

22. **The correct answer is (D).** The maximum regular discount is 20%. The additional 10% discount would give the shop clerk a discount of 30%. The clerk would pay 70% of $24 = (0.70)(24) = \$16.80$.

Data Sufficiency

1. **The correct answer is (E).** The prime factors of 45 are 3 and 5. Since both 3 and 5 are included in the values given in statement (2), the answer cannot be determined from the given information.

2. **The correct answer is (A).** If $x = \sqrt{9}$, $x = 3$, so statement (1) alone is sufficient to answer the question. Solve $x^2 - 9 = 0$, factor: $(x - 3)(x + 3) = 0$ so $x = 3$ or $x = -3$. Therefore, statement (2) alone is not sufficient to answer the question, and the correct answer is (A).

3. **The correct answer is (E).** Statement (1) provides information to compare the number of each stock purchased, but not a specific number of stock purchased. Statement (2) contains information about the price of the stocks, but not the number purchased. More information is needed to answer the question.

4. **The correct answer is (D).** Using statement (1) and letting q be the number of quarters and d be the number of dimes, we have $q = 6 + 2d$ and $25q + 10d = 1,650$, a system of two equations with two unknowns which can be solved. Using statement (2), we have $q + d = 81$ and $25q + 10d = 1,650$, another system of two equations with two unknowns. So, either statement by itself is sufficient to answer the question.

5. **The correct answer is (D).** From statement (1), $A = \pi r^2$, which can be solved for r, the radius. Once the radius is known, circumference can be found using $C = 2\pi r$. Statement (1) alone is sufficient to answer the question. From statement (2), $d = 16$ which means $r = \frac{1}{2}d = \frac{1}{2}(16) = 8$, so the circumference can be found. Statement (2) is sufficient to answer the question.

6. **The correct answer is (A).** Let a = the cost of an adult ticket and c = the cost of a child's ticket. The problem wants total = $100a + 300c$. Statement (1) translates to $2a + 6c = \$36$. Multiply both sides of the equation by 50 to find the total. Statement (2) translates to $a = \$2 + c$, which is not sufficient to answer the question.

7. **The correct answer is (D).** From the data given in the problem we know $2a - 1 = b$ or $2a - b = 1$. Using statement (1), $5^{2a - 1} = 5^3$, so $2a - 1 = 3$. We can solve for a, find b using $2a - b = 1$, and answer the question. Statement (2) can be written as $5^{a + 2b} = (5^2)^4$ since $25 = 5^2$. Then, $5^{a + 2b} = 5^8$. Now that the bases are equal, set the exponents equal: $a + 2b = 8$. Combined with $2a - b = 1$, we have two equations in two unknowns that can be solved for a and b and used to answer the question.

8. **The correct answer is (A).** The problem asks you to find $\frac{g}{r}$, where g equals the number of green balls and r equals the number of red balls. Statement (1) translates to $r = \frac{4}{5}g$, which can be solved for $\frac{g}{r}$ by dividing both sides by r and multiplying both sides by $\frac{5}{4}$. Statement (2) translates to $r = g - 8$, which cannot be solved for $\frac{g}{r}$.

9. **The correct answer is (D).** Statement (1) can be used to write one equation in one unknown, which can be solved. Let x equal the smallest integer, then $\frac{x + (x + 2) + (x + 4)}{3} = 14$ can be solved. Statement (2) translates to $x(x + 4) = 192$, which can also be solved.

10. **The correct answer is (D).** Subtract 10 from both sides of the inequality in statement (1) to find that $a > b$. In statement (2), since $c < 0$, dividing both sides of the inequality by c will reverse the direction of the inequality, giving $a > b$.

11. **The correct answer is (B).** Rearrange the equation in statement (1) as $16x - 6y = 56$. Notice that this is double the equation given in the problem statement. Thus, the information is not sufficient to answer the question. Statement (2) provides a second unique equation, thus you have two equations in two unknowns and the question can be answered.

12. **The correct answer is (B).** Using (1): since the area of the garden is not known, you cannot compute $\frac{1}{4}$ of it. Thus, the area of the path cannot be determined. Using (2): since the diameter of the garden is 12 feet, the radius is half that amount, or 6 feet. Since the path is 4 feet wide, the total area of the garden and path can be computed. The area of the garden can be subtracted from this total, giving the area of the path. Note: Do not spend time computing the actual area of the path or the garden since you do not need this to determine whether the question can be answered.

13. **The correct answer is (B).** Let d equal the number of cars with compact disc players, p equal the number of cars with car phones, and b equal the number of cars with both. Then $d + p + b = 100$. Statement (1) translates to $d = 2b$, which is not sufficient to answer the question. Statement (2) translates to $I = 30$, $30 = \frac{1}{2}d$, so both b and d can be used in $d + p + b = 100$ to answer the question.

14. **The correct answer is (C).** The area of the right triangle shown equals $\frac{1}{2}(AC)(BC)$. Statement (1) is not sufficient to answer the question. Statement (2) alone provides information about the hypotenuse, not AC and BC. However, combining the information in statements (1) and (2) and using the Pythagorean theorem, $(AC)^2 + (AC)^2 = (AB)^2$, so $2(AC)^2 = 25$, $(AC)^2 = \frac{25}{2}$. Area equals $\frac{1}{2}(AC)^2$, so the question can be answered.

15. **The correct answer is (C).** Statement (1) translates to $w = 2m$, where w equals the number of women enrolled and m equals the number of men enrolled. Then, $\frac{m}{w} = \frac{1}{2}$, so the ratio of men to women is 1:2, and the question has been answered. Using statement (2), if the ratio of men to the total number of students is 1:3, then the ratio of women to the total is 2:3; so the ratio of men to women is 1:2, and the question has been answered.

Practice Test 3

Problem Solving

1. **The correct answer is (D).** Since $xy < 0$, either x or y could be less than 0 (but not both). This means that choice (D) is not true since $\frac{x}{y} < 0$.

2. **The correct answer is (D).** Convert each fraction to a decimal using long division (or from memory) $\frac{1}{8} = 0.125$, $\frac{1}{3} = 0.33...$, $\frac{2}{3} = 0.66...$, $\frac{3}{4} = 0.75$, $\frac{5}{8} = 0.625$.

3. **The correct answer is (D).** Choose a convenient starting salary: $100. The 10% increase in salary brings the salary up to $110. The following 5% increase brings the salary up to $115.50. The difference of $15.50 represents a 15.5% increase. Algebraically, if s is the starting salary, $1.05(1.10s) = 1.155s$ or 115.5% of the starting salary for an increase in salary of 15.5%.

4. **The correct answer is (C).** $\frac{0.64 \times 10^a}{1.6 \times 10^b} = 0.4 \times 10^{a-b} = 4 \times 10^{a-b-1}$. Now $4 \times 10^2 = 4 \times 10^{a-b-1}$ means $2 = a - b - 1$ and $3 = a - b$.

Peterson's GMAT CAT Success

5. **The correct answer is (B)**. Factor $x^2 + 2x - 8 = 0$, $(x + 4)(x - 2) = 0$. Set each factor equal to 0 and solve: $x + 4 = 0$, $x = -4$, $x - 2 = 0$, $x = 2$. Or replace x with each value to find that choice (B) is correct: $(-4)^2 + 2(-4) - 8 = 16 - 8 - 8 = 0$.

6. **The correct answer is (A)**. Recreation accounts for 15% of his budget since $100\% - (50\% + 20\% + 15\%) = 15\%$. Since $240 represents 15% of his take home pay for recreation, it also represents 15% for his retirement fund.

7. **The correct answer is (D)**. Let y = sum of the original 6 numbers and x = the additional number. Since $\frac{y}{6} = 4.5$, $y = 6(4.5) = 27$. $\frac{x+y}{7} = 5$, so $\frac{x + 27}{7} = 5$, $x + 27 = 7(5)$, $x + 27 = 35$, $x = 8$.

8. **The correct answer is (D)**. The remaining 100 candy bars represent 25% of the total. Thus, 100 is 25% of the total. $100 = .25x$, where x is the total number of candy bars. Then, $x = 400$. Thus, he sold $400 - 100 = 300$ for a total of $(.50)(300) = \$150$.

9. **The correct answer is (B)**. Let l be the original length and w be the original width. Then, $A = lw$. The new length is $1.1l$, and the new width is $0.8w$ for $A = (1.1l)(0.8w) = 0.88lw$ or a difference of $0.12 = 12\%$ from the original area.

10. **The correct answer is (E)**. In 3 hours, the pool is $\frac{3}{8}$ filled and $\frac{3}{12}$ emptied. Thus, $x = \frac{3}{8} - \frac{3}{12} = \frac{9}{24} - \frac{6}{24} = \frac{3}{24} = \frac{1}{8}$.

11. **The correct answer is (D)**. Try an example: if $r = 3$, $A = \pi r^2 = \pi(3^2) = 9\pi$. Doubling r gives 6, so the new area is $\pi(6r^2) = 36\pi$, an increase of $36\pi - 9\pi = 27\pi$. 27π is what percent of 9π? 300%. The correct choice is (D).

12. **The correct answer is (D)**. $2\#4 = (2)^2 + 2(2)(4) = 4 + 16 = 20$.

13. **The correct answer is (C)**. Let x equal the total number of bags of confetti purchased for the party. Sixty bags represent $\frac{3}{4}$ of the total, so $60 = \frac{3}{4}x$, $x = 80$ bags. Since 60 bags were returned, the cost for the party was $(\$1.75)(20) = \$35.00$.

14. **The correct answer is (E)**. Note that with more people, the job will take fewer hours to complete, so this can be set up as an indirect proportion: $p = \frac{k}{h}$, where p is the number of people needed to complete the job and h is the number of hours needed to complete the job. $6 = \frac{k}{10}$, $k = 6(10)$, $k = 60$. For 10 people, $10 = \frac{60}{x}$, $10x = 60$, $x = 6$ hours to complete the job. To complete $\frac{2}{3}$ of the job, it would take $\frac{2}{3}(6) = 4$ hours.

15. **The correct answer is (D)**. List multiples of 5 between 10 and 90 including 10 and 90: 10, 15, 20, 25, 30, 35, 40, 45, 50, 55, 60, 65, 70, 75, 80, 85, and 90. Check the list for numbers that are multiples of 6: 30, 60, and 90.

16. **The correct answer is (D).** There are three choices for the first digit. If 2 or 5 is the first digit, the next digit must be 0. Then, the third digit can be the other 0 or the nonzero digit not previously used. This accounts for four possibilities. If the first digit is 0, there are only two possibilities, 0205 or 0502, for a total of six possibilities.

17. **The correct answer is (B).** Set each factor equal to 0 and solve: $\frac{4}{x} + 16 = 0$, $\frac{4}{x} = -16$, $4 = -16x$, $-\frac{1}{4} = x$. $9 - x^2 = 0$, $9 = x^2$, $x = \pm 3$. The smallest value for x is -3.

18. **The correct answer is (B).** Rate multiplied by time equals the number of words. Let x equal the number of minutes Joan types, then $100x = 60(x + 70)$, where 70 represents the extra hour and 10 minutes Leslee types. Solve for x: $100x = 60x + 4,200$, $40x = 4,200$. $x = 105x$ or 1 hour and 45 minutes. An hour and 45 minutes after 9:40 is 11:50.

19. **The correct answer is (D).** The ratio of 8 to 4 to 6 to 2 means $8x + 4x + 6x + 2x = 240$. Solve for x: $20x = 240$, $x = 12$. $6x$ represents the number of dimes, so $6(12) = 72$ dimes.

20. **The correct answer is (E).** Let x equal the width of the rectangle. Then, the length is represented by $x + 52$, since $P = 2l + 2w$, $248 = 2(x + 52) + 2(x)$. Solve for x: $248 = 2x + 104 + 2x$, $248 = 4x + 104$, $144 = 4x$, $x = 36$.

21. **The correct answer is (B).** $100x = 4,200$, where x is the length of a side adjacent to the river. Then, $x = 42$ feet, and she needs $2(42) + 100 = 184$ feet of fencing.

22. **The correct answer is (B).** The maximum regular discount is 30%. The additional 25% discount would give the manager a discount of 55%. The manager would pay 45% of $58 = (0.45)(58) = \$26.10$.

Data Sufficiency

1. **The correct answer is (A).** By trial and error, $12 + 14 + 16 = 42$, which demonstrates that statement (1) alone is sufficient to answer the question. Since there are many combinations of positive integers that sum to 42 (for example, $1 + 2 + 39$ and $5 + 6 + 31$), statement (2) cannot be used to answer the question.

2. **The correct answer is (E).** Statement (1) has many answers such as 100 since $\sqrt{100} = 10$ and 36 since $\sqrt{36} = 6$. Statement (2) has many answers: 2, 4, 6 . . . even combining both statements, $\sqrt{16} = 4$ and $\sqrt{4} = 2$, it cannot be determined.

3. **The correct answer is (D).** Statement (1) alone can be used to compute the cost, and statement (2) alone can be used to compute the cost.

4. **The correct answer is (B).** Let J = Joan's age now and B = Bill's age now. From the problem we have $J = B - 4$. Statement (1) translates to $B - 10 = + 4(J - 10)$, which simplifies to $J = B - 4$, so it is not sufficient to answer the question. Statement (2) translates to $B - 17 = 2(J - 17)$, which simplifies to $B = 2J - 17$, giving two equations in two unknowns which is sufficient to answer the question.

5. **The correct answer is (A)**. Since the triangle is a right triangle, we can use the Pythagorean theorem to find the length of the hypotenuse, and using statement (1), we can then find the perimeter. Statement (2) would allow us to find the length of the hypotenuse, but we don't know the lengths of a and b.

6. **The correct answer is (B)**. Let p equal the cost per pound of peanuts and c equal the cost per pound of cashews. The problem asks for the total = $6p + 4c$. Statement (1) translates to $c + 2p$, which is not sufficient to answer the question. Statement (2) translates to $3p + 2c = \$9.80$. Multiply both sides of the equation by 2 to find the total.

7. **The correct answer is (A)**. From the data given in the problem, we know that $a - 2 = b + 1$ or $a - b = 3$. Using statement (1) and writing 243 as 3^5, $3^{3a-3} = 3^5$, so $2a - 3 = 5$. We can solve for a, find b using $a - b = 3$, and, hence, find $a + b$. Statement (2) implies that $3a + 3b + 9$, or $a - b = 3$, which is the same equation formed from the problem statement. Thus we have our equation in two unknowns, which is not sufficient to answer the question.

8. **The correct answer is (D)**. The problem asks you to find $\frac{g}{r}$, where g equals the number of green balls and r equals the number of red balls. Statement (1) translates to $g = r + 0.2r$ or $g = 1.2r$, which can be solved for $\frac{g}{r}$. Statement (2) means the ratio of green balls in the urn is 3 to 8, so for every 3 green balls, there must be $8 - 3 = 5$ red balls. This provides sufficient information to find $\frac{g}{r} = \frac{3}{5}$.

9. **The correct answer is (E)**. Statement (1) alone is not sufficient to answer the question since there are factors of $2^4 \times 3^2 \times 5$ and $6^2 \times 5^3$ that are even (e.g. 2, 6) and factors that are odd (e.g. 3, 9). Statement (2) alone is not sufficient to answer the question since some multiples of 15 are even (e.g. 30, 60) and some multiples are odd (e.g. 15, 45). The numbers 15 and 30 satisfy both statements, so even with both, the answer cannot be determined.

10. **The correct answer is (C)**. Statement (1) alone is not sufficient to answer the question since p and q could both be positive or p and q could both be negative. Statement (2) alone provides no information about p, but if q is negative and $pq > 0$, this implies that p must be negative. Note that although the answer to the question is no, the point here is that the question can be answered.

11. **The correct answer is (B)**. Statement (1) provides one equation in two unknowns, which does not provide sufficient information to find the value of y. Statement (2) appears to be one equation with two unknowns, but simplify it: $x = y - 3 + x$, $0 = y - 3$, $y = 3$, and the value of x can be found.

12. **The correct answer is (B)**. Let m equal the number of people surveyed who own only a modem, s equal the number of people surveyed who own only a scanner, and b equal the number of people surveyed who own both. Then $m + s + b = 600$. Statement (1) translates to $m - 3s$, which means that we have two equations with three unknowns, which is not sufficient to answer the question. Statement (2) translates to $b = 400$ and $b = 8s$. Combined with $m + s + b = 600$, the question can be answered.

13. **The correct answer is (E)**. Statement (1) provides data about the relationship between the lengths of two sides but is not sufficient to find the area. Statement (2) is the Pythagorean theorem and, while true, does not provide data to find the area of the rectangle.

14. **The correct answer is (B)**. Try substituting values for *a* and *b* in statement (1). If *b* = 4, *a* = 5(4) + 1 = 21. The ratio of *a* to *b* is 21:4. If *b* = 2, *a* = 5(2) + 1 = 11 and the ratio of *a* to *b* is 11:2. But these aren't equal ratios, so the question cannot be answered. Using statement (2), $a = \frac{b}{3}$, $3a = b$, $\frac{a}{b} = \frac{1}{3}$, so we can answer the question.

15. **The correct answer is (C)**. Statement (1) does not provide sufficient data to answer the question. The data can be translated to $w = l - 26$, where *w* equals the width of the parking lot and *l* equals the length of the parking lot. Statement (2) alone is not sufficient to answer the question. However, using both statements, the length and width of the parking lot are known (52 feet and 27 feet), the length and width of the total can be found (55 feet and 30 feet). Then, the total area minus the area of the lot would provide the area of the sidewalk.